JN
30
.M3
19

Mazzucelli, Cole+te.

rance and Germ y at
Maas icht.

FRANCE AND GERMANY AT MAASTRICHT

CONTEMPORARY ISSUES IN EUROPEAN POLITICS
VOLUME 3
GARLAND REFERENCE LIBRARY OF SOCIAL SCIENCE
VOLUME 1084

CONTEMPORARY ISSUES IN EUROPEAN POLITICS

CARL C. HODGE, *Series Editor*

FRANCE AND GERMANY AT MAASTRICHT
POLITICS AND NEGOTIATIONS TO CREATE THE EUROPEAN UNION

COLETTE MAZZUCELLI

GARLAND PUBLISHING, INC.
NEW YORK AND LONDON
1997

Copyright © 1997 by Colette Mazzucelli
All rights reserved

Library of Congress Cataloging-in-Publication Data

Mazzucelli, Colette.
    France and Germany at Maastricht : politics and negotiations to create
the European Union / Colette Mazzucelli.
        p.   cm. — (Garland reference library of social science ; vol. 1084.
Contemporary issues in European politics ; vol. 3)
    Includes bibliographical references and index.
    ISBN 0-8153-2195-3 (alk. paper)
    1. European Union.   2. France—Relations—Germany.   3. Germany—
Relations—France.   I. Title.   II. Series: Garland reference library of social
science ; v. 1084.   III. Series: Garland reference library of social
science.   Contemporary issues in European politics ; v. 3.
JN30.M355   1997
341.242'2—dc21   96–37688
                                                                                  CIP

Printed on acid-free, 250-year-life paper
Manufactured in the United States of America

To my family
in Naples and New York
and to V. Z. v. S.

THE MAASTRICHT EUROPEAN COUNCIL

Front Row (left to right): Prime Minister Wilfried Martens (Belgium), Prime Minister Aníbal Cavaco Silva (Portugal), President François Mitterrand (France), Her Royal Majesty Queen Beatrix (Netherlands), Prime Minister Ruud Lubbers (Netherlands), Prime Minister John Major (United Kingdom), Prime Minister Poul Schlüter (Denmark)

Middle Row (left to right): Foreign Minister Douglas Hurd (United Kingdom), Foreign Minister João de Deus Pinheiro (Portugal), Prime Minister Jacques Santer (Luxembourg), Prime Minister Charles J. Haughey (Ireland), Prime Minister Constantinos Mitsotakis (Greece), Federal Chancellor Helmut Kohl (Federal Republic of Germany), President Jacques Delors (European Commission), Prime Minister Felipe Gonzalez (Spain), Prime Minister Giulio Andreotti (Italy), Foreign Minister Hans van den Broek (Netherlands)

Top Row (left to right): Vice-President Frans Andriessen (European Commission), Foreign Minister Gianni de Michelis (Italy), Foreign Minister Roland Dumas (France), Foreign Minister Antonio Samaras (Greece), Foreign Minister Uffe Ellemann-Jensen (Denmark), Foreign Minister Mark Eyskens (Belgium), Foreign Minister Hans-Dietrich Genscher (Federal Republic of Germany), State Secretary for European affairs Carlos Westendorp (Spain), Foreign Minister Gerard Collins (Ireland), Foreign Minister Jacques Poos (Luxembourg), Secretary General Niels Ersbøll (Council Secretariat)

Photograph courtesy of the General Secretariat of the Council of the European Union

Contents

Series Editor's Preface

This is an important book. The relationship between France and Germany is at the very heart of the New Europe, both in the sense of the post-1945 diplomatic settlement, which from a Western perspective depended so much on Franco-German reconciliation, and in the more recent sense of the continent's reconstitution since the end of the Cold War. The joint leadership of France and Germany in the realization of the goals set by the Single European Act of 1986 represents the most recent and ambitious chapter in the story of what has been and remains the most critical bilateral partnership in contemporary Europe.

This is not only because of what reconciliation has meant to two historical foes as a diplomatic achievement in its own right, but also because of the implications for peace and prosperity for all Europe of the commitments made by France and Germany in the name of European economic and political integration. Their joint accomplishments over the past forty years give substantive cause for optimism in international relations. If Kant was right—that eternal peace is indeed possible for nations immersed in the positive calculations of commerce—Franco-German partnership is as close as we have come to proving the point. Like few other scholars of contemporary Europe, Colette Mazzucelli conveys here a sense of the mechanics and psychology of that partnership. This alone would merit its inclusion in the *Contemporary Issues* series.

However, Mazzucelli's contribution does not stop there. *France and Germany at Maastricht* is simply political science at its best. Its analytical narrative of Franco-German negotiations on monetary and political union is the most thorough and balanced account of *the* pivotal episode in the current project of European unity. It combines a comprehensive understanding of the national and sectoral interests at stake in the Maastricht negotiations with a firm grasp of the institutional and electoral environment in which negotiations proceeded. The depth and breadth of the research material required by a study of this variety alone is impressive, but Mazzucelli's lucid explanation of its meaning makes the book a valuable addition to the fields of European studies, comparative politics and international relations.

It has been a professional gratification to be able to bring her work to print with Garland Publishing.

Carl Cavanagh Hodge

Foreword

I am delighted that Dr. Mazzucelli has written a book devoted to the role of *France and Germany at Maastricht.*

The relationship between Paris and Bonn has been a major feature of the process of European construction practically since its very beginning in the very late 1940s. The negotiations that made possible the conclusion of the Treaty creating a European Union are an example—possibly the best up to now—of both the ambiguities and indispensable character of what has often been called—not without bitterness by some of the other partners of the European Community—the Franco-German "axis."

It is fortunate that, so soon after the signing (February 7, 1992) and the ratification (France, November 1, 1992—Germany, October 13, 1993) of the Maastricht Agreement, such a complete, well-documented, clear, and intelligent volume should be published on this most important but intricate subject. The fact that it comes out during the 1996 Revision Conference, convened to revise the European Treaties, with the goal of creating a closer and closer union among the peoples of Europe gives it an additional importance and dimension. The Presidency's Conclusions of the Turin European Council of March 24, 1996 describe the Revision Conference's agenda as follows:

> The European Council has defined in Madrid the agenda of the Union for the end of the century. The convening of the Intergovernmental Conference, which will today begin its examination of the revision of the Treaties with the purpose of creating an ever closer union among the peoples of Europe, constitutes the first step in this direction. We welcome it.
>
> In a Union firmly committed to the full implementation of the Treaties, including its provisions on economic and monetary union, the Conference will provide the opportunity for dealing more effectively with the internal and external challenges of the coming years.
>
> These challenges stem in particular from: changes in the international situation; globalization of the economy and its consequences for employment, competitiveness and job creation within the Union; terrorism, drug trafficking and international crime; migratory pressure; ecological imbalances.

Moreover, future enlargement, which represents a historic mission and a great opportunity for Europe, is also a challenge for the Union, in all its dimensions. In this perspective, institutions as well as their functioning and procedures have to be improved in order to preserve its capacity for action, while maintaining the *acquis communautaire* and developing it and also respecting the balance between the institutions. It is essential to sustain its features of democracy, efficiency, solidarity, cohesion, transparency and subsidiarity.

This is of course an enormous task for the European Union's fifteen member states and a very special challenge for Paris and Bonn.

The respective situation of both countries has undergone, of course, a total change since the fall of the Berlin Wall and German unification but especially since the beginning of the concretization and success of the sociological, economic and political aspects of this unification which, after seven somewhat agonizing years, is becoming a reality. This change has reinforced the ambiguities, not to say the contradictions, that have always been, since the beginning of the European construction's project, the essence of the Franco-German relationship. However, it has not fundamentally modified the leaders' political will in both Paris and Bonn, to remain, through a close cooperation, the engine of this construction.

The Franco-German "axis" can of course be a source of frustration for the other partners of the European Union, especially the most important ones. An indication, among others, of this frustration was the British veto of Belgian Prime Minister Dehaene's election to the European Commission's Presidency, which had been initiated, without real consultation with the United Kingdom, by Paris and Bonn.

At the same time, after two world conflicts which found their origin in the antagonism between Berlin and Paris, the new relationship which emerged in Franco-German relations in the 1950s in spite of all ambiguities and difficulties is a sort of miracle that is recognized and valued by Western European states, particularly among the small and medium-sized nations of the region.

The process of European construction has reached a critical stage. So has the relationship between Paris and Bonn. It is not the first time that this has occurred since the beginning of the efforts undertaken to build a somewhat coherent and, if possible, integrated European structure. Most of the preceding difficulties have been overcome, to be truthful, in a more or less satisfactory way.

But one of the main Founding Fathers of this European construction process, Jean Monnet, writes at the end of his *Mémoires:*

> Some people refuse to undertake anything if they have no guarantee that things will work out as they planned. Some people condemn themselves to immobility. Today, no one can say what form Europe will assume tomorrow, for the changes born of change are unpredictable.... Day-to-day effort is needed to make one's way forward: but what matters is to have an objective clear enough always to be kept in sight.

In the present context of the efforts to promote a European Union and Franco-German relations, Dr. Mazzucelli's book constitutes an extraordinarily useful contribution to the statesman's, diplomat's, scholar's and layman's reflections on these matters and provides extremely useful leads to all those who, in one way or another, are responsible for the destiny of the European Continent and its relations with other parts of the world, in particular its transatlantic allies.

Alfred Cahen
Ambassador of Belgium to Paris, France

Acknowledgments

For his patience and critical comments on this manuscript, the author owes a debt of gratitude to her mentor, Professor Emeritus Karl H. Cerny, and to his wife, Constance Cerny. She would also like to thank Professor Thomas Banchoff, Department of Government, Georgetown University and Professors Gregory Flynn and Lily Gardner Feldman, Center for Excellence in German and European Studies, Georgetown University.

In addition, numerous scholars in the United States and Europe have assisted the author during the course of her research. These individuals are: Professor Stanley Hoffmann, Center for European Studies, Harvard University; Professor Pierre-Henri Laurent, Department of History, Tufts University; Professor Alfred Grosser, Fondation Nationale des Sciences Politiques, Paris; Professor Joseph Rovan, Université de Paris; Professor Jean Klein, Institut Français des Relations Internationales (IFRI); Professor Christian Lequesne, Institut d'Etudes Politiques, Paris; Professor Wolfgang Wessels, Universität zu Köln; Professor Elfriede Regelsberger, Institut für Europäische Politik; Dr. Robert Picht, Deutsch-Französisches Institut, Ludwigsburg; Dr. Ingo Kolboom, Deutsche Gesellschaft für Auswärtige Politik (DGAP), Bonn; and Professor Roger Morgan, European University Institute, Florence.

Other individuals "working for Europe" were likewise generous with their time during my stays in Paris, Brussels and Bonn. Special appreciation is conveyed to Ambassador Alfred Cahen, Embassy of Belgium, Paris; Jean De Ruyt, Belgian Foreign Ministry, Brussels; Dr. Giuseppe Ciavarini Azzi and Dr. John Fitzmaurice, Secretariat General, European Commission, Brussels; and Dr. Thomas Grunert, Secretariat, European Parliament, Luxembourg.

Financial support from the Franco-American (Fulbright) Commission in Paris, the European Commission in Brussels, the Jean Monnet Council in Washington, D.C. and the Robert Bosch Foundation in Stuttgart made this book possible. Ambassador J. Robert Schaetzel and his wife, Imogen Schaetzel, of the Jean Monnet Council and Clifford P. Hackett provided valuable comments and criticisms during various stages of my research. Anneliese Eberle offered gracious assistance during my time at the Auswärtiges Amt. Tania von Uslar Gleichen, Rita Galambos, Julia Monar and

Bob Rosen carefully proofread the manuscript for biographical and linguistic accuracy. Carla di Mauro-Scarchilli provided assistance with the names and faces in the photo of the Maastricht European Council.

The author would also like to thank David Estrin and Phyllis Korper, Senior Editors, and Chuck Bartelt, Director of Computer Resources, Garland Publishing, Inc., for their assistance during the publication of this book. Carl Cavanagh Hodge, Series Editor, provided much encouragement along with his recommendation that the volume be included in the *Contemporary Issues* series.

During my first year lecturing with the Civic Education Project team in Hungary, colleagues at the Budapest Institute for Graduate International and Diplomatic Studies (BIGIS) and the Budapest University of Economic Sciences have provided a collegial and stimulating atmosphere in which to work. Warmest wishes are expressed to the faculty members at BIGIS and in the Departments of International Relations and European Studies at the University.

The support of family and friends on both continents during the past ten years enabled me to complete this book. Heartfelt appreciation is reserved for the Puliti family in Fiesole, Janet Feldman in Barrington, R.I., the Caussé family in Grenoble, Laura (Frisky) Thurston in Washington, D.C., the Le Bars family in Antony, the Pohlmann family in Cologne and the Öhlschläger family in Alfter.

Dr. Glenda Rosenthal, Director, Institute on Western Europe, Columbia University, offered friendly advice regarding this book during my time as a Visiting Scholar at the Institute in Summer 1996.

Last, but not least, for her sense of Europe and sense of humor, the author warmly thanks Sabine Ehmke-Gendron.

List of Abbreviations

AA	Auswärtiges Amt
BDA	Bundesvereinigung der Deutschen Arbeitgeberverbände
BDI	Bundesverband der Deutschen Industrie
BIGIS	Budapest Institute for Graduate International and Diplomatic Studies
BL	Basic Law
CAP	Common Agricultural Policy
CEP	Civic Education Project
CDA	Christen-Democratisch Appèl (Netherlands)
CDS	Centre des Démocrates Sociaux (France)
CDU	Christlich-Demokratische Union (Federal Republic of Germany)
CEU	Central European University
CFSP	Common Foreign and Security Policy
COREPER	Comité des Réprésentants Permanents (Committee of Permanent Representatives)
CSCE	Conference on Security and Cooperation in Europe
CSU	Christlich Soziale Union (Federal Republic of Germany)
DGAP	Deutsche Gesellschaft für Auswärtige Politik
DM	Deutsche Mark
EC	European Community
ECB	European Central Bank
ECJ	European Court of Justice
ECOFIN	Council of Economics and Finance Ministers
ECSC	European Coal and Steel Community
ECU	European Currency Unit
EDC	European Defense Community
EEC	European Economic Community
EFTA	European Free Trade Association
EMI	European Monetary Institute
EMS	European Monetary System
EMU	Economic and Monetary Union
ENA	École Nationale d'Administration
EP	European Parliament
EPC	European Political Cooperation
ERM	Exchange Rate Mechanism
ERT	European Round Table

ESCB	European System of Central Banks
ETUC	European Trade Union Confederation
EU	European Union
EURATOM	European Atomic Energy Community
EUREKA	European Programme for High Technology Research and Development
FAZ	Frankfurter Allgemeine Zeitung
FCC	Federal Constitutional Court (Karlsruhe, Federal Republic of Germany)
FDP	Freie Demokratische Partei
GDP	Gross Domestic Product
IFRI	Institut Français des Relations Internationales
IGC	Intergovernmental Conference
INF	Intermediate-range Nuclear Force
JHA	Justice and Home Affairs
MEP	Member of European Parliament
MRP	Mouvement Républicain Populaire
NATO	North Atlantic Treaty Organization
OECD	Organization for Economic Cooperation and Development
PCF	Parti Communiste Français
PDS	Partei des Demokratischen Sozialismus
PR	Parti Républicain (France)
PSF	Parti Socialiste Français
PvdA	Partij van de Arbeid (Netherlands)
QMV	Qualified Majority Voting
RPR	Rassemblement pour la République
SEA	Single European Act
SGCI	Secrétariat général du comité interministériel pour les questions de coopération économique européenne
SPD	Sozialdemokratische Partei Deutschlands
TEU	Treaty on European Union
TGV	Train à Grande Vitesse
TREVI	Terrorisme, Radicalisme, Extrémisme, et Violence Internationale
TUC	Trades Union Congress
UDF	Union pour la Démocratie Française
UNICE	Union of Industrial and Employers' Confederations of Europe
UK	United Kingdom
UN	United Nations
WEU	Western European Union

We have a few hours to rest, and a few months to succeed. Then...
—Then, we will encounter great obstacles which will enable us to move forward again. That's the point, isn't it? ... That is exactly the point. You have understood everything about Europe.

The events which strike me and which occupy all of my thoughts lead me to general conclusions about what must be done. Then, circumstances determine the opportunity, suggesting or bringing to me the means. I know how to wait a long time for favorable circumstances. In Cognac, we know how to wait. It's the only way to make a good product.

Jean Monnet, *Mémoires*[1]

[1] Throughout this book, the quotes at the beginning of each chapter are taken from Jean Monnet, *Clefs pour l'Action* (Paris: Association des Amis de Jean Monnet, 1988). The translations are the author's.

France and Germany at Maastricht

CHAPTER I

Introduction

The rulers of our countries, taken separately, are responsible today, as yesterday, to defend a certain conception of the national interest resulting from numerous influences among which the most conservative have the greatest weight. However clear-sighted they may be, it is difficult, almost impossible, for them to change those things which exist and which they are responsible to administer. They can wish to do so in their innermost convictions, but they must be accountable to their Parliament, to public opinion, and they are often slowed down by their own departments which want to keep everything in order. This is all quite natural. If governments and administrations were ready at any moment to change the existing order of things, this would be a state of incessant disorder. I know from experience that change can only come from external forces under the influence of necessity, but inevitably not from violence.

Jean Monnet, *Mémoires*

This volume analyzes French and German diplomacy during the intergovernmental conferences (IGCs) on economic and monetary union (EMU) and political union and the subsequent national treaty ratification process in each country. It uses various approaches to explore the domestic-international interactions predominant during internal bargaining in Paris and Bonn and external negotiations at different levels among working groups, personal representatives, ministers and political leaders in Brussels.

Why is this topic important? There are at least two reasons. The historic importance of Franco-German relations in the European Community (EC) is an essential starting point.[1] For over thirty years, the "privileged partnership" has launched initiatives in European construction. The European Monetary

---

[1] F. Roy Willis, *France, Germany and the New Europe* (London: Stanford University Press, 1968); Haig Simonian, *The Privileged Partnership* (Oxford: Clarendon, 1985); Julius W. Friend, *The Linchpin: French-German Relations, 1950–1990* (New York: Praeger with CSIS, 1991); Robert Picht (Hg.), *Das Bündnis im Bündnis* (Berlin: Severin und Siedler, 1982); Ernst Weisenfeld, *Quelle Allemagne pour la France?* (Paris: Armand Colin, 1989); Patrick McCarthy, ed., *France—Germany 1983–1993* (New York: Macmillan,1993).

System (EMS) is one example. In the aftermath of German unification, the significance of the Franco-German tandem for European integration is even greater as both states adjust to the new Europe. A second point of departure is that the major initiatives on EMU came during the German and French Presidencies of the Council of Ministers in 1988 and 1989, respectively. Chancellor Helmut Kohl and President François Mitterrand sustained the momentum toward political union in a series of three Franco-German letters to the Irish, Italian and Dutch Presidencies during 1990–1991.[2] In short, the IGCs were the culmination of an active period of development in the European Community. Franco-German initiatives were the driving force at the time.

During the two intergovernmental conferences other member states situated, and at times adjusted, their positions according to the emerging Franco-German consensus or compromise on a particular issue. It is no surprise, therefore, that because of successive enlargements Franco-German relations "increasingly find expression as part of a multilateral negotiating dynamic (among states and institutions) within the European Community."[3] Ambassador Philippe de Schoutheete defines the Franco-German relationship as a Community "subsystem" based on its intensity, duration, formalization, effectiveness and acceptability.[4] In light of changes in Europe since 1989, however, it remains to be seen whether the Franco-German duo will continue to play the same pivotal role in an enlarged European Union (EU).[5]

A FRAMEWORK FOR AN ANALYSIS OF THE MAASTRICHT PROCESS: INTEGRATING THREE APPROACHES

The decisions taken to amend the original Treaties of Paris and Rome, which founded the European Coal and Steel Community (ECSC), the European Economic Community (EEC) and EURATOM in the 1950s, resulted

---

[2] The three Franco-German letters are reproduced in Finn Laursen and Sophie Vanhoonacker, eds., *The Intergovernmental Conference on Political Union* (Maastricht: European Institute of Public Administration, 1992), 276; 313–314; 415–418.

[3] Christian Lequesne, "Formulation des politiques communautaires de consultation avec la RFA en France," in *Motor für Europa?*, Hrsg. Robert Picht and Wolfgang Wessels (Bonn: Europa Union Verlag, 1990), 144. The additional words in parentheses are the author's.

[4] Philippe de Schoutheete, "The European Community and its sub-systems," in *The Dynamics of European Integration,* ed. William Wallace (London: Royal Institute of International Affairs, 1990), 106–111.

[5] Hugh Miall, *Shaping a New European Order* (London: RIIA, 1994).

in a series of intergovernmental conferences and national ratification processes by which the member states sought to shape the course of European integration well into the next millennium. Andrew Moravcsik's analysis of the Single European Act (SEA) negotiations in light of neo-functionalist and intergovernmentalist approaches revived the theoretical debate about European integration.[6] Yet, within this general debate it is necessary to make a distinction between the role of the European Commission in Community decision-making procedures and negotiations and its role in the IGC process. Intergovernmentalism stresses the lack of influence by the Community institutions in negotiations among the member states. This study argues that the Single European Act and the Treaty on European Union were the results of IGC processes which cannot be subsumed under intergovernmentalism. It posits that the IGC processes which created the ECSC, EEC and EURATOM, or the twenty-year period in the history of integration after the Luxembourg Compromise of 1966, are adequately explained by the intergovernmentalist framework. This is not true in the context of the "1992" process to complete the internal market or the negotiations and ratifications to amend the original Treaties which occurred after 1985. Therefore, this study introduces a conceptual framework which departs from a purely intergovernmentalist perspective. This framework aims to illustrate the ways in which the IGC process is *sui generis*.

In her analysis of the role that the European Round Table (ERT) played during the SEA negotiations, Maria Green Cowles argues that neither neo-functionalism nor intergovernmentalism is adequate to explain the mobilization and activities of the ERT.[7] In her view, these analytical frameworks are more successful in their explanations of developments in the European Economic Community during the 1960s. Cowles concludes that "new conceptualizations of European integration are necessary." This is certainly true. However, unlike integration, the IGC process includes prenegotiations, intergovernmental conference negotiations and subsequent treaty ratifications involving member states and Community institutions. To analyze the entire process, several existing approaches can, and should, be combined to explain the level of analysis, the actors involved and the sub-processes which link domestic bargaining and European negotiations.

---

[6]Andrew Moravcsik, "Negotiating the Single European Act: National Interests and Conventional Statecraft in the European Community," *International Organization* 45 (1991): 651–688.

[7]Maria Green Cowles, "Setting the Agenda for a New Europe: The ERT and EC 1992," *Journal of Common Market Studies* 33 (December 1995): 501–526.

The results of the two intergovernmental conferences were inextricably linked in the minds of the political leaders, ministers, civil servants and bankers from the participating member states and Community institutions. Many of these same actors were subsequently involved in the domestic ratification processes that had to be completed in order for the Treaty to come into effect. Thus, this book not only analyzes the IGCs but also considers the actors and bargaining which shaped the domestic ratification debates in France and Germany. These debates brought out in the popular consciousness many of the most crucial issues during the IGCs. In this sense, the debates illustrate the impact of Maastricht as a learning experience on those political leaders and civil servants involved throughout the entire IGC process.

Moreover, the use of the three approaches in a framework to analyze the links among the intergovernmental conference prenegotiations, negotiations and national ratifications allows the reader to consider the role of a new actor which emerged during the Maastricht process: the politico-administrative hybrid. This actor provided a linchpin between the domestic (administrative and political) and European (elite and popular) levels during the different sub-processes of internal bargaining and external negotiations which defined Maastricht as a learning experience. Prior to outlining a framework which incorporates Putnam's two-level games, Aberbach, Putnam and Rockman's four images of civil servants and Monnet's integrative bargaining, it is necessary to discuss why other approaches were not chosen.

Functionalism/Neo-Functionalism
In the 1940s and 1950s, functionalists, led by David Mitrany, asserted and defended the proposition that the development of international economic and social cooperation is a major prerequisite for the ultimate solution of political conflicts and the elimination of war. Functionalism is a horizontal approach, shifting attention away from the vertical divisions of human society which are symbolized by the sovereignty of states, toward the various layers of social need that cut across national dividing lines. It stresses the question of what contributions are essential to the creative work of solving common problems rather than that of which sacrifices are required for the negative task of reconciling conflicting interests.[8] Functionalism relies on an administrative network of officials, working in specialized agencies of an economic and social nature, who are responsive to the needs of the international community. However, the functionalists' tenet that the promotion of human welfare could be separated from politics is one of its major weaknesses.

---

[8] Inis L. Claude, Jr., *Swords into Plowshares* (New York: Random House, 1984), 379–380.

Jean Monnet, a functionalist himself, held a view of the European Coal and Steel Community which focused on a gradual expansion of technical activities across sectors. Yet, his view of integration was intrinsically political as well as psychological. In this sense, Monnet was not a systematic functionalist. Functionalism's primary concern with problems which may be tentatively described as nonpolitical, i.e., welfare and social justice, is the main reason why this approach is not used in this volume. The inherently political nature of the Maastricht process, and the weight of national civil servants throughout the prenegotiations, negotiations and subsequent ratifications, call for other approaches.

The recognition of the "pervasiveness and priority of politics" stimulated the elaboration of a variant of functionalism, known as neo-functionalism. This approach, evident in the works of Ernst B. Haas and Leon N. Lindberg, makes primary reference to the integrative endeavors of the original six member states of the European Coal and Steel Community, the European Economic Community and EURATOM. Whereas classical functionalism relies upon the "cooperative pursuit of common interests in nonpolitical fields to generate political changes conducive to peace," neo-functionalism stresses the utility of such enterprises as "elements in a program of political engineering, as contributors to the realization of political designs."[9]

Neo-functionalists believe that a prerequisite to "effective problem-solving" was a supranational agency which "slowly extends its authority so as to progressively undermine the independence of the nation-state." Political actors would "shift their loyalties, expectations and political activities toward a new center, whose institutions possess or demand jurisdiction over the pre-existing national states." Starting with a key sector, such as coal and steel, a process of spillover would expand the scope of the supranational agency to encompass all important functions. Neo-functionalists thought that a supranational agency, such as the European Commission, would lead the integration process, coopting national civil servants and representatives of interest groups for that purpose.[10] On the other hand, critics of this approach did not believe that a body such as the Commission, without an electoral or parliamentary base, could offer the leadership required to overcome resistance to the integration process, particularly from the member states. In their view, the neo-functionalists underestimated the state, in particular its ability "to stop or slow down the building of a central political system" and the resolve of

---

[9] Ibid., 405.

[10] John Pinder, "European Community and Nation-state: A Case for a Neo-federalism?," *International Affairs* 62 (Winter 1985–1986): 43.

national bureaucracies "to resist the transfer of power" to a new central authority.[11]

During the initial phase to set the agenda for the EMU process, the European Commission was an active initiator. Commission President Jacques Delors worked in tandem with leaders in the European Council, particularly Kohl and Mitterrand, and with central bankers in the Delors Committee to clarify and define the issues on the table for the upcoming intergovernmental conference. Pinder argues that neo-functionalism did not foresee the extension of Community competencies to include EMU. Yet, the linkage Delors made between the completion of the internal market, as envisaged in the Single European Act, and the liberalization of capital on the road to EMU does fit within a neo-functionalist framework.

This book posits that one of Delors' main contributions as European Commission President was the fact that he altered the nature of bargaining relations within the European Council. This is why Monnet's approach to integrative bargaining is fleshed out as one of three complementary approaches to analyze the Maastricht process instead of relying solely on the notion of "upgrading the common interest" advocated by neo-functionalists. At this point though it is necessary to evaluate the relevance to the Maastricht process of another approach in which the exclusive focus is on the relative power among states and their role in the bargaining process, otherwise defined as intergovernmentalism.

Intergovernmental Institutionalism/Liberal Intergovernmentalism/ Regime Theory

The early research of Andrew Moravcsik defines an "intergovernmental institutionalist" approach in order to analyze the IGC negotiations leading up to the Single European Act. Since his early writings, Moravcsik has refined his theoretical framework, which he terms a "liberal intergovernmentalist" approach, to explain the evolution of the European Union. His argument is that "the EC can be analyzed as a successful intergovernmental regime designed to manage economic interdependence through negotiated policy coordination."[12] However, whereas Moravcsik's initial analysis dealt with the SEA negotiations, his later writings focus on Community policy making. In these writings, he differentiates between two distinct and separate types of negotiation processes; however, given this distinction, no assessment is made

---

[11] Stanley Hoffmann, "Reflections on the Nation-state in Western Europe Today," *Journal of Common Market Studies* (September–December 1982): 30.

[12] Andrew Moravcsik, "Preferences and Power in the European Community: A Liberal Intergovernmentalist Approach," *Journal of Common Market Studies* (December 1993): 474.

to determine if and how the two processes may interact. Since Moravcsik is interested in the elaboration of a general theory of integration, the distinction between Community decision making and the IGC process to reform the Treaties of Paris and Rome is an essential one. This distinction is a building block to our theoretical and practical understanding of the types of interaction between states and institutions which define integration in the European Community.

This distinction is particularly noteworthy because, as a result of the Maastricht process, the scope of interaction between states and institutions has expanded to include policy matters relating to the common foreign and security policy and justice and home affairs within the European Union. Thus, the daily negotiation processes in the Union have become even more complex. This is due, in part, to the fact that policies in the second and third pillars, which for the most part are still in the realm of intergovernmental cooperation, now interact with policies in the European Community pillar, subject to the influence of supranational decision making.[13] All of these policies must be negotiated within the institutional framework of the European Union, which, contrary to Moravcsik's assertion is much more than "a passive structure, providing a contractual environment conducive to efficient intergovernmental bargaining."[14]

Although Moravcsik is concerned primarily with the elaboration of a liberal theory of domestic preferences, to complement his intergovernmental bargaining analysis, he overlooks the ways in which national civil servants and leaders learn the lessons taken from those negotiations which (1) define the normal integration process and (2) occur as part of the intergovernmental conference process. Instead, Moravcsik develops an elaborate framework which (1) stresses the autonomy of national leaders and (2) leaves the role of national civil servants, in relation to the domestic economic interests he emphasizes, in the shadows. His lack of attention with respect to the role of civil servants does not enable Moravcsik to distinguish among levels of negotiation. This is a curious omission given his goal to explain and understand integration and Treaty reform as policy processes.

---

[13]The pillar structure of the Treaty on European Union incorporates the European Community policies, including EMU, within the first pillar. These exist alongside the common foreign and security policy (CFSP), or second pillar, and cooperation in justice and home affairs, otherwise known as the third pillar. This pillar includes policies such as asylum, immigration, police cooperation across borders, cooperation against drug trafficking and the fight against terrorism.

[14]Moravcsik, "Preferences and Power in the European Community," 508.

In terms of the definition of national preferences and strategy formulation, it can be argued that during a specific type of negotiation, like the IGC process, trade-offs are essential at the domestic and European levels. As the EMU process illustrated, the relative power of the states in question is a crucial factor in the overall equation, but not the only one. The fact that France and Germany could come to any bilateral agreement at all, within the larger multilateral framework, attests to a willingness on both sides to move beyond purely national interests in the definition of a "community" approach. Here liberal theory, with its emphasis on "non-power incentives and variations in the capacity to communicate and cooperate," can provide a point of departure for our understanding of how states adapt preferences and use tactics to advance both their own, and the more general, interest.

One thing which studies in the liberal tradition have in common is an emphasis on the ways in which "increased transactions and contacts changed attitudes and transnational coalition opportunities, and the ways in which institutions helped to foster such interaction." As Nye explains, "...In short, (these studies) emphasized the political process of learning and of redefining national interests, as encouraged by institutional frameworks and regimes."[15] A key question in the liberalist tradition which Moravcsik does not ask is: How can increased elite contacts across state borders, among central banker governors in the Delors Committee, national civil servants in the Monetary Committee and European Commission representatives, affect the capacity of these individuals to communicate in a common language?

Moravcsik acknowledges that critics may challenge his "liberal understanding of state preferences...which draws on contemporary theories of economic interdependence to explain national preferences" in favor of "alternative conceptions based on ideology or geopolitics." The Maastricht experience clearly illustrates that economic interdependence was not the sole motivation on the part of the member states to conclude a Treaty; ideology and geopolitics played significant roles. First, the idea to create a European Union had a strong resonance among leaders in the European Council, particularly Mitterrand and Kohl, whose personal and political experiences were closely associated with the integration movement from its inception. Second, the change in the geopolitical situation on the Continent after 1989–90 led most European leaders to search for an alternative to the traditional balance of power or hegemonial politics which has characterized the evolution of the European state system. It is necessary to view the Maastricht experience in this light to understand the motivations of the political leaders and officials during the entire IGC process. These motivations cannot be understood solely

---

[15]Joseph S. Nye, Jr., "Neorealism and Neoliberalism," *World Politics* 40 (1988): 239.

by considering negotiation strategies and tactics; reference must also be made to the tremendous efforts of all parties concerned to achieve national ratifications by deadlines set down in the Treaty. Here it is important to distinguish Maastricht as process from Maastricht as Treaty. The Treaty became a reality only after the IGC process was completed with the final national ratification in Germany on 12 October 1993.

Moravcsik does assert that critics may question his use of an intergovernmental theory of bargaining "with its stress on bargaining power rooted in unilateral alternatives, competing coalitions, the possibilities for linkage, and the controlled delegation of power to supranational institutions under conditions specified by functional theories of regimes and 'two-level' games views of domestic polities."[16] One of the criticisms made here is that while Moravcsik does draw attention to the relevance of two-level games, he does not make any distinction as to the specific case in which the approach could be most appropriately used. This book employs two-level games to explain certain aspects of the IGC process. It also acknowledges, however, that the two-level games approach is inadequate as an explanation of daily negotiations involving Community policies like structural funds. Here Gary Marks' multilevel governance provides an important contribution to the literature by highlighting the influence and role of sub-national governments and interests during the Community negotiation process.[17] In terms of the IGC process, the role of the Länder at the sub-national level was clearly decisive regarding the principle of subsidiarity.

Moravcsik's references to two-level games are made in support of a general thesis that (1) integration strengthens the autonomy of national leaders; and (2) "the EC's 'democratic deficit' may be a fundamental source of its success." In light of the Maastricht experience, these views are questionable at best. This experience revealed the tremendous weight of politico-administrative hybrids and civil servants throughout the IGC process and the reliance of national leaders on these individuals to accomplish detailed work in daily negotiations. In the German case, their influence was evident at both the national and sub-national levels. The Maastricht Treaty also introduced the idea of greater independence and weight for national central bankers and finance ministers in EMU policy making. And as the national ratification processes of the Treaty revealed, the democratic deficit threatens the future of integration considerably more than it contributes to the Community's success.

---

[16]Moravcsik, "Preferences and Power in the European Community," 518.

[17]Gary Marks, "Structural Policy and 1992," in *Europolitics,* ed. Alberta Sbragia (Washington, DC: The Brookings Institution, 1992), 191–224.

Finally, liberal intergovernmentalism does not address in a convincing way questions about the role of the state or government as a rational actor. Indeed the rational and unitary nature of governments has been questioned by scholar-practitioners like Ulrich Everling who see governments as "prisoners of both domestic and international circumstances." The emphasis on multiple levels, with a gradually increasing interaction of competencies and responsibilities shared among sub-national, national and Community authorities, is yet another way of viewing integration.

Federalism/Neo-Federalism/ Cooperative Federalism

Advocates of a federal approach to explain the Community experience argue that neo-functionalists took too facile a view of the possibilities for a transfer of national competencies to federal institutions, without a clear sense about the conditions under which integrative steps would be possible and without appreciating the strength of the nation-state. On the other hand, federalists criticize realists and proponents of regime theory for being too reductionist about the possibilities of movement in the direction of federal institutions with substantial competencies.

Federalists also argue that neo-functionalists appeared strangely uninterested in evaluating how far any particular functions needed to be performed by supranational institutions. The assumption that such institutions would come to assume all important functions "begged the critical question of the circumstances in which states would establish institutions with federal characteristics, or transfer competencies to them," as they did when they launched the European Communities in the 1950s. Nor did the neo-functionalists seem much concerned about the form of democratic control by European institutions that can be seen as a corollary of the more far-reaching transfers of competence. The classic federalists were clearer about this, proposing democratic federal institutions to accompany the transfer of the more basic competencies such as money, taxation or armed forces. But because they did not "consider any process of establishing federations other than through a single act transferring to them coercive and security powers, their thinking was not directly applicable to the transfer of less fundamental competencies."[18]

Federalists assert that however favorable the conditions may be for steps toward federal institutions and competencies, such steps are not likely to be taken without adequate political leadership. In their view, neo-functionalists were "justifiably criticized for concentrating on the Commission

---

[18]Pinder, "European Community and Nation-state: A Case for a Neo-federalism?," 51.

as the political motor for integration." Proponents of federalism acknowledge that the European Parliament (EP) has the electoral base that the Commission lacks. Yet, the political leadership which Parliament has shown with such initiatives as the Draft Treaty establishing the European Union could not secure major reforms, as distinct from public support for such reforms, without corresponding leadership from the member states. In this sense, federalists argue that approaches which understate the need for national leadership will, like neo-functionalism, separate themselves to that extent from political reality.[19]

In his more recent work, Pinder has defined a variant of federalism, which he terms a neo-federalist approach, as a way to consider multilateral negotiations between states and institutions within the overall integration process to build the European Union. Pinder has long argued that the tendency "to identify federalism with a great leap to a federation with military and coercive power inhibits practical thought about the prospects for taking further steps in a federal direction, whether in the form of a system of majority voting to complete the internal market, developing the EMS in the direction of monetary union, an increase in the powers of the European Parliament, or a package of such reforms that could deserve to be called European Union." Neo-federalism is an attempt to synthesize the federalist and neo-functional approaches. Specifically, it offers a way to supplement federalist theory, which has tended to focus on the design of a constitution by a constituent assembly without considering the process of steps which may make that feasible; and it fills the gaps in neo-functionalism caused by the neglect of some essential political and economic forces, including the federalist motive, and of constitutional questions.[20]

The neo-federalist approach attributes key importance to the role of political vision and of a supportive and convincing economic doctrine. The significance of economic growth and interdependence and the increased strength of internal linkages as elements of the integration process are also highlighted. The emphasis of this approach, however, is on the momentum imparted to EMU by Community and national elites who have a federalist orientation and who seek mutual benefits from further integration. Of crucial importance is the role of political leadership in pursuing a long-term view of the integration process and in maintaining a constitutional perspective on how to deal with the fundamental problems in integration. Neo-federalists argue that the integration process has been consistently pushed forward by policy actors whose outlook is shaped by a critique of the nation-state as the most appropriate unit to deal with economic and security problems that transcend borders.

---

[19]Ibid., 53.

[20]John Pinder, *European Community* (Oxford: Oxford University Press, 1991), 217.

Another variant of federalism aims to explain the EMU policy process as a transition to a system in which national governments and supranational institutions engage to an advanced degree in joint problem solving exercises with a shift to majority voting in most cases. This approach, known as cooperative federalism, describes a mode of decision making characteristic of a high level of integration. As opposed to lowest common denominator or splitting the difference decision making, characteristic of intergovernmentalism, upgrading the common interest is emphasized. Majority voting is the rule with unanimity as the exception. In cooperative federalism, states remain the vehicle of integration but engage to a considerable extent in the sharing of competencies with Community institutions. The degree to which joint action is carried out stresses problem solving instead of mere coordination or cooperation.

Clearly the process of monetary integration in Europe has been influenced by federalist-minded officials and leaders dating back to Jean Monnet in the 1950s. In recent decades, German leaders including Helmut Schmidt, Hans-Dietrich Genscher and Helmut Kohl worked to make the idea of monetary union a concrete goal in the face of reservations and reluctance on the part of the Bundesbank. German ambitions for European integration, in tandem with the political vision and momentum imparted by Jacques Delors as Commission President, fueled the debate about a federal future for the proposed union.

It can also be argued, however, that each of the variants of federalism presented here underestimates the complex and contradictory nature of the relationship between the process of integration and the structure of the nation-state. It is true that there is a strong commitment in favor of a federalist approach to integration among a core group of Christian Democratic leaders represented in the European Council. As this volume illustrates, the results obtained at the Maastricht European Council are not readily explained unless reference is made to the ideological and political beliefs of Chancellor Helmut Kohl. However, his beliefs are rooted in the notion of decentralized federalism as practiced in the Federal Republic of Germany. It is clear that an increase in the sharing of competencies between states and Community institutions, or cooperative federalism, leads to a centralization of power within the various layers of the Council structure, thus aggravating the democratic deficit. Countries like Great Britain and France remain unwilling to give increased powers to the European Parliament precisely because of the loss of national sovereignty this implies. Significant political forces in both countries, the Tories and the Gaullists, respectively, are not in favor of a federalist vocation for the European Union. This is because federalism limits the independence of states vis-à-vis the institutions with which competencies are shared even though this approach envisages a system based on the state as the basic political unit. The results of the referendums in Denmark and France in 1992 attest to this fact.

Neo-federalism also rests on a premise that federal ideas best define the nature of interest politics at the European level. This may be true, but ideas and interests interact in a more complex way in practice. The nature and scope of the EMU process was a reflection above all of the interests and power of national central bankers. Monetary integration depended on key bargains struck between Community institutions, particularly the Council, and central bankers throughout the IGC process. EMU was legitimized as much by political leaders as it was by reference to the interests and expertise of central bank governors. Some central bankers remained uncommitted to a federal economic and monetary union. But all were committed to price stability and central bank independence in the use of monetary policy instruments. EMU was viewed as a means to secure these ends. The self-interest of national central bankers may well be substantially altered but only after a long process of learning through the various stages of EMU. An important issue to consider in this context is the structure of institutions like the European Monetary Institute (EMI) in Stage Two, and the European Central Bank (ECB) in Stage Three, and whether or not these institutions are constituted in such a way as to promote the sharing of competencies characteristic of cooperative federalism.[21] For the time being, this remains an open question.

Highlighting the Relevance of Three Approaches

Instead of contrasting variants of functionalism with intergovernmentalism or federalism, this book brings together three approaches to analyze the IGC process: Putnam's two-level games; Aberbach, Putnam and Rockman's four images of civil servants; and Jean Monnet's practical and purposeful way of doing things. Here an approach is "a predisposition to adopt a particular conceptual framework and to explore certain types of hypotheses toward the generation of theory."[22] Each approach can offer the reader part of an overall understanding of the IGC process by highlighting the levels of analysis (Putnam's two-level games), the actors (four images of civil servants and politico-administrative interactions), and the different aspects of the negotiating process (Monnet's integrative bargaining, distributive bargaining, attitudinal structuring, intraorganizational bargaining).

---

[21]Kenneth Dyson, *Elusive Union* (London and New York: Longman Group Limited, 1994, 311.

[22]James A. Bill and Robert L. Hardgrave, Jr., *Comparative Politics: The Quest for Theory* (Lanham, MD: University Press of America, 1981), 24.

Putnam's Two-Level Games

Robert D. Putnam's two-level games approach is useful due to his focus on both internal bargaining at the domestic level and external negotiations at the international level. In the European and IGC contexts, Putnam's approach is essential owing to the fact that decision making in the Council on treaty reform is fundamentally a matter of multilateral negotiations and parliamentary ratification in which political leaders and domestic civil servants play a dominant role. An exclusive focus on the systemic level, characteristic of regime theory, does not explain the reasons why Community member states adopted their respective negotiating positions nor why these positions converged at specific points during the IGCs.[23] As most negotiators acknowledge, bargaining among domestic constituents is key to the eventual conclusion of an international negotiation. Moreover, the support of domestic actors is essential to assure subsequent parliamentary ratification of any treaty. Putnam argues that any approach to international negotiation must be rooted in an understanding of domestic politics or the power and preferences of the major actors at the national level.[24]

The crucial element of Putnam's approach is the "win-set," defined for a given domestic constituency as the set of all possible international agreements that would "win"—that is, gain the necessary majority among the constituents when simply voted up or down.[25] Putnam argues that three sets of factors decide win-set size: Level II or domestic preferences and coalitions; Level II institutions; and Level I or international negotiators' strategies.[26]

Putnam's two-level games also explain an "integrative approach" in that state leaders are forced to balance domestic and international concerns during the negotiating process. The approach is "state-centric," not in "the realist sense of emphasizing nation-states as units" but in that chief executives and state bureaucracies are viewed as "actors whose aims cannot be

---

[23] Andrew Moravcsik, "Negotiating the Single European Act," in *The New European Community,* eds. Robert O. Keohane and Stanley Hoffmann (Boulder & Oxford: Westview Press, 1991), 75 points out the need to focus on the international implications of domestic politics in future research on the European Community.

[24] Robert D. Putnam, "Diplomacy and Domestic Politics: The Logic of Two-level Games," *International Organization* 42 (1988): 427–460; Peter B. Evans, Harold K. Jacobson and Robert D. Putnam, eds., *Double-Edged Diplomacy: International Politics and Domestic Bargaining* (Berkeley: University of California Press, 1993); Helen Milner, "International Theories of Cooperation Among Nations: Strengths and Weaknesses," *World Politics* 44 (1992): 466–496.

[25] Putnam, "Diplomacy and Domestic Politics," 437.

[26] Ibid., 442.

reduced to reflections of domestic constituent pressure." [27] This approach is useful to analyze the EMU and political union IGCs for several reasons. First, it helps to explain how domestic constraints can define the essential issues that emerge on each IGC agenda. Second, it reveals how the contours of a state's bargaining position are shaped by international, and national, constraints. Third, the approach also serves the purpose of highlighting the role of the leader at the nexus between domestic and international affairs. It suggests specific reasons, other than domestic pressures, which explain his choice of a negotiating strategy.

The last point makes Putnam's approach particularly relevant to any explanation of Mitterrand and Kohl's individual strategies as well as their joint strategy during the IGCs—although for quite different reasons in each case. In the French case, it was the absence of domestic constraints which allowed Mitterrand a free hand in strategy formulation. In the German case, Kohl's hands were tied owing to the leverage exercised by domestic institutions and party interests. In their development of a joint strategy both leaders were committed to a federal vocation for Europe. Yet, paradoxically, Kohl's domestic constraints reinforced his position on this issue while Mitterrand's concern for the French domestic political situation made his position somewhat more nuanced. Any analysis of Kohl's strategy, and to a lesser degree Mitterrand's, requires, however, an understanding of the explicit link in each leader's mind between both intergovernmental conferences and the domestic constraints this link implied. Writings that seek to apply Putnam's approach exclusively to the EMU conference, leaving out the political union negotiations, cannot take into account the essential nature of the leaders' European strategies, which were influenced to a degree by steps already taken in the integration process. Nor can these writings consider the full range of political constraints involved in the domestic bargaining and ratification processes.[28] The usefulness of Putnam's approach is that it alerts the reader to the fact that leaders often formulate strategy in the face of domestic constraints which sometimes work to their advantage. On the other hand, Putnam's approach illustrates that leaders can use strategies decided on at the European level in order to force domestic policy change on an unwilling

---

[27]Peter B. Evans, "Building an Integrative Approach to International and Domestic Politics," in *Double-Edged Diplomacy*, 401–402.

[28]Examples of writings that apply Putnam's approach to EMU are Kenneth Dyson, Kevin Featherstone and George Michalopoulos, "The Politics of EMU: The Maastricht Treaty and the Relevance of Bargaining Models" and Dorothee Heisenberg, "German Financial Hegemony or Simply Smaller Win-Sets? An Examination of the Bundesbank's Role in EMS and EMU Negotiations," Papers for delivery at the 1994 Annual Meeting of the American Political Science Association, New York, September 1–4, 1994.

political establishment. The phenomenon most distinctive of the two-level games approach is defined by Putnam as synergy, in which international actions are employed to alter outcomes otherwise expected in the domestic arena.[29] Specifically, by setting the EMU and political union agendas and linking issues between the two IGCs, Kohl and Mitterrand responded to national and transnational pressures to develop the European polity. In so doing, both leaders shaped the way in which issues were decided domestically. In the German case, the weakening of the link between the IGCs, otherwise known as *Parallelität,* complicated the domestic ratification process.

Putnam says that the only formal link between Level I and Level II is the chief negotiator. He also considers the possibility that the chief negotiator's preferences may diverge from those of his constituents. Putnam cites three motives of the chief negotiator: enhancing his standing in the Level II game by increasing his political resources or by reducing potential losses; shifting the balance of power at Level II in favor of domestic policies that he prefers for exogenous reasons; and, finally, pursuing his own conception of the national interest in the international context.[30] In terms of the IGC process, the three domestic factors which Putnam's approach illustrates are: the structure of domestic preferences; state institutions involved in the Treaty ratification processes; and government strategies to obtain internal support. Each factor is essential in any consideration of the levels of negotiation and the subsequent relations among civil servants, ministers and political leaders which define the IGC process. Moreover, these domestic factors also explain the actions and roles of civil servants involved in the national Treaty ratification processes. This is particularly true in the German case where no popular referendum took place.

Andrews argues that "once attention shifts from the origins of the Treaty to the process of its ratification by the various EC member states, the analytical focus does properly shift from an intergovernmental institutionalist framework to include a greater emphasis on subnational politics."[31] Using Putnam's approach as a point of departure, in combination with other approaches, this volume makes the case that it is not possible to divorce the analytical framework of IGC negotiations from the political developments

---

[29]Moravcsik, "Integrating International and Domestic Theories of International Bargaining," in *Double-Edged Diplomacy*, 26.

[30]Evans, "Building an Integrative Approach to International and Domestic Politics," 457.

[31]David M. Andrews, "The Global Origins of the Maastricht Treaty on EMU: Closing the Window of Opportunity," in *The State of the European Community*, Volume 2, eds. Alan W. Cafruny and Glenda G. Rosenthal (Boulder & London: Lynne Rienner, 1993), 119.

or constraints at the domestic level.[32] The two must be considered together.

Aberbach, Putnam and Rockman's Four Images of Civil Servants

At the domestic level, this book focuses on the attitudes and responsibilities of civil servants and their relationships with political leaders. The approach of Aberbach, Putnam and Rockman uses four images to explore the relationships between bureaucrats and politicians in Western democracies.[33] In their book, the scholars argue that the development of politico-administrative hybrids, described as Image IV, characterizes the policy process in recent decades. In the modern state, the "pure hybrid" stands in marked contrast to his Image I counterpart, the classical administrator defined by Max Weber. Image IV only vaguely resembles Image II, in which the distinction is made between the "facts and knowledge" which civil servants bring to their work and the "interests and values" emphasized by politicians.[34] Image III comes closest to the "pure hybrid" with one crucial difference: "whereas politicians articulate broad, diffuse interests of unorganized individuals, bureaucrats mediate narrow, focused interests of organized clienteles." In other words, "politicians seek publicity, raise innovative issues, and are energizing to the policy system, whereas bureaucrats prefer the back room, manage incremental adjustments, and provide policy equilibrium according to Webster, 'a state of balance between opposing forces and actions.'"[35]

Aberbach, Putnam and Rockman's Image IV is a useful tool to analyze the Maastricht process in terms of the levels of bargaining which took place during the IGCs: working group, civil servant, ministerial and head of state and government as well as the subsequent roles that politico-administrative hybrids and other civil servants played during the national ratifications in France and Germany.[36] This study explains the relationship between bureaucrats and politicians in the Maastricht context by considering

---

[32]Andrews makes the argument that this analytical shift is possible.

[33]Joel D. Aberbach, Robert D. Putnam and Bert A. Rockman, eds., *Bureaucrats and Politicians in Western Democracies* (Cambridge: Harvard University Press, 1981).

[34]Ibid., 6.

[35]Ibid., 9.

[36]In the last phase of the EMU conference, the working group was added as a fourth level of negotiations. The national civil servants and European Commission representatives which comprised the working group were responsible for discussions on highly technical issues of EMU necessary to achieve accord on a treaty among the member states. There was no parallel working group for the IGC on political union.

Image IV as its authors intended: as a speculation on the possible disappearance of the Weberian distinction between the roles of bureaucrat and politician in the final decades of the century. Thus, beyond an examination of the increasing politicization of bureaucrats, the focus of this approach is on the possible bureaucratization of politicians during the IGC process.

This approach is also important for our understanding of the role of civil servants in democratic government. In a general context, it is necessary to explore the contribution of civil servants to public policy in an era in which many individuals look disapprovingly on the increased role of bureaucracy in modern government.[37] In the IGC context, it is essential to consider the negative press that the European Community attracts owing to the democratic deficit because of the prominent role of Image IV hybrids and civil servants during the Maastricht process. Specifically, what might the emergence of politico-administrative hybrids mean for the viability of democratic government in the transnational European polity?

The Community decision-making context is characterized by a diffusion of power among institutions, member states and interests within the emerging European polity. However, the entire IGC process has resulted in a concentration of power within the Council structure. This leads us to question whether the blurred distinction between civil servants and politicians in the IGC context is a threat to democratic control given the disproportionate influence on the IGC process of a small number of individuals operating in the tightly knit environment of the Council. Although the decisions agreed to in Maastricht were made by elected political leaders, the agenda preparation for a Treaty reform that influences the lives of millions of Europeans, was carried out by a small, non-elected politico-administrative elite with limited input from national parliaments, regional governments or societal interests. This "behind closed doors" phenomenon was typified by the French experience of Maastricht and its consequences were strikingly evident during the national ratification debate.

In their analysis of Image IV, Aberbach, Putnam and Rockman cite the findings of Campbell and Szablowski. The latter team's focus on civil servants in central agencies relied on extensive data material gleaned from interviews.[38] In other books, Campbell refers to the approach of Aberbach,

---

[37]Francis E. Rourke, "The 1993 John Gaus Lecture: Whose Bureaucracy Is This Anyway? Congress, the President and Public Administration," *Political Science and Politics* XXVI (1993): 691; "Who Really Runs Japan? Stay Tuned," *New York Times*, December 24, 1993; "Japan's Bureaucracy: No Sign It's Losing Any Power," *New York Times*, February 27, 1994.

[38]Colin Campbell and George J. Szablowski, *The Superbureaucrats: Structure and Behavior in Central Agencies* (Toronto: Macmillan Press, 1979).

Putnam and Rockman in his research on the way in which civil servants function in the public policy process.[39] Campbell also cites other writings on French and German civil servants used for this study. These include Suleiman's books on the French bureaucracy, a journal article by Putnam analyzing senior civil servants in Britain, Germany and Italy and an edited volume on the political role of top civil servants in Western Europe.[40] In addition the more recent literature by Quermonne on the bureaucratic apparatus of the state and Ziller on French and German civil servants[41] is used to analyze bureaucratic preferences during the Maastricht process based on Aberbach, Putnam and Rockman's approach. Each of these sources illustrates that administrative elites are inherently political in so far as they participate in decision-making processes of a political nature, which is clearly the case for civil servants involved in the European Community. Their importance as a political elite is also highlighted by their crucial position in IGC decision making. Aberbach, Putnam and Rockman's approach is useful precisely because of the light it sheds on both civil servants and their masters. The focus of most writings on European integration has been less on the administrative, technocratic elites involved and more on the input of political leaders.

Politico-administrative hybrids and national civil servants were present in all phases of the negotiation and ratification processes. Moreover, they form a crucial linkage between the national and European arenas of decision making. Aberbach, Putnam and Rockman's approach adds to and complements that of Putnam's two-level games because these actors often have a crucial impact on IGC decision making. This is due to one important advantage they have over their political masters: continuous day-to-day involvement in the negotiation and ratification processes. The focus on the role of national administrative elites negotiating in the Council machinery emphasizes the intergovernmental nature of the IGC process. National officials are expected to act as an extension of their member state and rigidly follow national instructions when negotiating in Brussels. In this sense, they serve as "infantry" in that their

---

[39]Colin Campbell, *Managing the Presidency* (Pittsburgh: University of Pittsburgh Press, 1986), 206–208.

[40]Ezra N. Suleiman, *Les hauts fonctionnaires et la politique* (Paris: Seuil, 1976); Ezra N. Suleiman, *Les élites en France* (Paris: Seuil, 1979); Robert D. Putnam, "The Political Attitudes of Senior Civil Servants in Western Europe: A Preliminary Report," *British Journal of Political Science* 3 (July 1973): 257–290; Mattei Dogan, ed., *The Mandarins of Western Europe* (New York: Sage, 1975).

[41]Jean-Louis Quermonne, *L'appareil administratif de l'Etat* (Paris: Collection Points, 1991); Jacques Ziller, "Hauts fonctionnaires et politique en République Fédérale d'Allemagne," *Revue Internationale des Sciences Administratives* 1 (1981): 31–41; Jacques Ziller, *Administrations comparées* (Paris: Montchrestien, 1993).

politico-administrative role is that of simply carrying out the instructions from their political masters.

On the other hand, the focus on Image IV hybrids and national civil servants can also be seen in light of a bureaucratic *engrenage* or "interpenetration" in which administrative elites are the two-faced gatekeepers of European policy, looking towards their national as well as the European arena and conducting negotiations between the two. They still operate as an extension of their member state but in a less strictly coordinated way. In other words, these officials aim more at achieving progress during negotiations at the European level than at rigidly defending national interests. Since they must work with a redefined national interest, they can operate more independently and be more flexible than in the intergovernmental model. These officials also take the input of the supranational Commission quite seriously as more like a thirteenth party in the negotiations. Instead of intergovernmentalizing or supranationalizing the IGC process, the role of national officials in this scenario can be characterized as "joint problem solvers."[42] In such a capacity, they can use agenda preparation as a tool to facilitate the integrative bargaining and attitudinal structuring characteristic of Monnet's approach.

On EMU, for instance, *engrenage* involved "the inclusion of relevant national civil servants (and central bankers) to gain additional information and insights and to establish a solid network of influence" via a socialization process. This socialization process occurred at the European and domestic levels throughout the negotiations and national ratifications. In this sense, *engrenage* is "a two-way process for establishing a set of mutually rewarding interactions."[43] However, it also involves tensions between different levels: political (European Council) and technical (ECOFIN Council); European (Delors Commission) and national (Monetary Committee).[44] The important issue to assess in terms of Aberbach, Putnam and Rockman's approach

---

[42]Sandra Pellegrom, "National Civil Servants in EC Environment Policy: A New Elite and Its Role in European Integration," Paper presented at the workshop National Political Elites and European Integration, ECPR Joint Sessions of Workshops, Madrid, 17–22 April 1994 (mimeo), 4–5.

[43]Dietrich Rometsch and Wolfgang Wessels, "The Commission and the Council of Ministers," in *The European Commission*, eds. Geoffrey Edwards and David Spence (Essex: Longman Group Limited, 1994), 213.

[44]The ECOFIN Council is comprised of the economics and finance ministers of the member states. The Monetary Committee is made up of senior officials from the ministries of finance and the central banks of the member states. Its task is to prepare the agenda of discussions for the ECOFIN Council. In the Maastricht context, the personal representatives of the finance ministers also sat on the Monetary Committee. This assured the continuity of the negotiation process.

is whether the role of national civil servants as "joint problem solvers" corresponds more closely to Image IV than the other images described and the implications of this evolution for democratic, as opposed to technocratic, government.

Monnet's Approach

Jean Monnet was aware of how dependent political leaders are on intense bureaucratic preparation. In his eyes, to influence that preparation was to shape, even to make, their decisions.[45] Emile Noël explains that the need to make proposals, to negotiate, to act solely in the European interest, and to enshrine that interest in permanent institutions, was one of Monnet's guiding principles.[46] In this book Monnet's approach is defined as the way in which he assembled people around a table to negotiate a treaty.[47] In 1950, when Monnet chaired the meetings for the formation of the European Coal and Steel Community, he wanted the participants to focus on the common interest, rather than on trades between conflicting interests, and to maximize the advantages of their joint undertaking, rather than to exchange separate gains and losses with each other. He discouraged compromises in which a party would barter a concession on one issue against some advantage on an entirely different issue. Monnet felt logrolling or heterogeneous package deals would not be conducive to a constructive, joint effort on behalf of common objectives.[48]

In the words of Monnet's longtime associate, Pierre Uri, his approach involves the use of creative imagination "to find solutions which are not simply compromises where you take 30% of what one side wants and 40% of what the other side wants and forget the rest. Synthesis, in the chemical sense of the term, where the product is different from its components, is quite another matter," he writes.[49] The focus of Monnet's approach is on those "variable-sum" games during which negotiators are engaged in joint problem-solving, trying to maximize their joint gains. Monnet had this type

---

[45]François Duchêne, "Jean Monnet's Methods," in *Jean Monnet: The Path to European Unity*, eds. Douglas Brinkley and Clifford Hackett (New York: St. Martin's, 1991), 189–190.

[46]"Address by Emile Noël," in *Jean Monnet, Proceedings of Centenary Symposium organized by the Commission of the European Communities*, Brussels, 10 November 1988 (Luxembourg: Office for Official Publications of the European Communities, 1989), 48.

[47]Pierre Uri, *Penser pour l'Action* (Paris: Editions Odile Jacob, 1991), 314; Jean Monnet, *Mémoires* (Paris: Fayard, 1976), 377–382.

[48]Fred Charles Iklé, *How Nations Negotiate* (Millwood, N.Y.: Kraus Reprint, 1987), 118–121.

[49]"Address by Pierre Uri," in *Jean Monnet: Proceedings of Centenary Symposium*, 54.

of activity in mind when he spoke of lining up all the negotiators on one side of the table and their problems on the other. [50]

In this sense, Monnet's approach resembles integrative bargaining, which has been defined as a sub-phase of the negotiating process.[51] Integrative bargaining was originally identified in the writings of an American pioneer in business management, Mary Parker Follett.[52] There are several tactical matters involved in integrative bargaining including agenda setting, the search for alternate solutions and reporting of respective preferences or utility functions.[53] Certain conditions must also prevail before the integrative bargaining process will function. These conditions have been explained in terms of motivation, information, language, and trust.[54]

In addition to integrative bargaining, three other sub-processes are inherent in most negotiations: distributive bargaining; attitudinal structuring; and intraorganizational bargaining.[55] These sub-processes occur in negotiations even if integrative bargaining does not. Some form of distributive bargaining is found in all negotiations. It involves the compromise tactics that Monnet sought to transcend. Monnet also sought to break the spirit of domination among states. Unlike de Gaulle, he did not reason in terms of the balance of power.[56] Thus, attitudinal structuring was for Monnet an inherent part of the bargaining process to create an atmosphere of mutual trust and understanding among conference participants. Intraorganizational bargaining, in which a negotiator at the table has to deal with actors "behind his chair" in the national capital, is an important element in Putnam's two-level games. It is also a facet of bargaining which Monnet dealt with in the Community context.

The Monnet approach is particularly useful to analyze the EMU conference because it brings out the dynamics of one sub-process of

---

[50]Robert D. Putnam, "The Western Economic Summits: A Political Interpretation," in *Economic Summits and Western Decision-Making*, ed. Cesare Merlini (London: Croom Helm, 1984), 46.

[51]Ibid., 45–43.

[52]An insightful volume on the philosophy of Mary Parker Follett is E. M. Fox and L. Urwick, eds., *Dynamic Administration* (New York: Hippocrene, 1982). The resemblance between the ideas of Follett and Monnet on integration is striking. Compare Mary Parker Follett, *Creative Experience* (New York: Longmans, Green, 1924) and Jean Monnet, *Mémoires* (Paris: Fayard, 1976).

[53]Richard E. Walton and Robert B. McKersie, *A Behavioral Theory of Labor Negotiations* (Ithaca: ILR, 1991), 145–155.

[54]Ibid., 155–159.

[55]Ibid., 380–420.

[56]Edward Vose Gulick, *Europe's Classical Balance of Power* (New York: W.W. Norton, 1967).

negotiations, integrative bargaining. This sub-process involves more than the search for compromise characteristic of classical IGC diplomacy. The creation of a new institution, or context, is emphasized as a part of a common solution to a problem. In this sense, Monnet's approach is in the tradition of neoliberal institutionalism because of its emphasis on "patterns of cooperation and discord that can be understood only in the context of the institutions that help define the meaning and importance of state action." [57]

The Monnet approach requires an idea and a timetable. The aim of the Schuman Plan Conference, namely, Franco-German reconciliation by pooling coal and steel under the authority of a supranational institution, is perhaps the best example of this approach. In Monnet's view, European unity would occur by creating institutions and fixing timetables for the practical implementation of ideas driving integration. In the Maastricht context, Commission President Jacques Delors' contributions to the IGC process reveal a great deal about the Monnet legacy to European integration.

In Monnet's approach, dramatic initiatives, at the point of greatest resistance, provide an essential, but risky, leap into the unknown. Berndt von Staden writes that operating at the right level, that is, above the lowest common denominator, at the point where consensus is still just possible, is a high art of which Monnet was an unbeatable master.[58] Duchêne explains that Monnet's view of the way the Community worked was essentially psychological and political. It was not really constitutional, still less abstract. It did not depend on precedents and not very much on books either. Monnet was suspicious of precedents and books. Instead, he had a sharp nose for real information and influence, irrespective of where they were located, high or low. His operations must be seen in terms of this pervasive and purposeful informality.[59]

---

[57]Robert O. Keohane , *International Institutions and State Power* (Boulder & London: Westview Press, 1989), 2. Keohane and Hoffmann offer three propositions about the nature of the Community institutions: "The EC is best characterized as neither an international regime nor an emerging state but as a network involving the pooling of sovereignty; the political process of the EC is well described by the term supranationality as used by Ernst Haas in the 1960s; however, the EC has always rested on a set of intergovernmental bargains, and the Single European Act is no exception to this generalization." Robert O. Keohane and Stanley Hoffmann, "Institutional Change in Europe in the 1980s," in *The New European Community*, 10.

[58]Berndt von Staden, Seminar on European Integration, Georgetown University, Spring 1990, (mimeo). State Secretary von Staden was West German Ambassador to the United States and a friend of Monnet.

[59]François Duchêne, "Jean Monnet's Methods," in *Jean Monnet: The Path to European Unity*, 189–190.

Scholars have commented on the contribution of Monnet's approach to the democratic deficit.[60] Paradoxically, although Monnet worked with elites his entire life to promote unity, his was a civilian approach. As Duchêne states, this approach was much closer to the outlook of the citizen than that of the bureaucrat. Monnet worked on the assumption that all parties would benefit from European unity. He used the language of business, of community and of civil politics to make his case for closer integration among the Six.[61] Monnet's emphasis on persuading elites had much to do with the closed way in which foreign policy was made in an earlier era. He was sincere in his belief that "We are uniting people, not forming a coalition of states." However, Community policy was, and remains to the present day, highly technical and therefore incomprehensible to the average citizen.

As a result of events beyond Monnet's control, the evolution of Community policy making throughout the 1970s and 1980s was in the direction of increased bureaucratization. The centralization of decision making among political leaders in the European Council and the distance from national parliaments and publics became even greater. Also absent were talented personalities like Pierre Uri who could draft treaty language that was presentable to national publics. The Community became more distant and diverse. The resulting democratic deficit was striking and the search for the general interest became even more difficult. If Monnet were alive today, would he recognize the need to modify the emphasis on elites and persuade the people that the European Union is relevant to their daily lives? This is a rhetorical question, but it is one worth asking given the role that Delors or a revised Action Committee for Europe[62] might play in the present context.

Monnet's approach uses *engrenage* in a type of open-ended functionalism. *Engrenage* connotes the enmeshment of member units and the "locking-in" of whatever integrative steps are achieved. It is likely to be limited in scope. *Engrenage* may somewhat reduce the alternatives for

---

[60]George Ross, *Jacques Delors and European Integration* (New York: Oxford University Press, 1995), 98–101.

[61]François Duchêne, *Jean Monnet: The First Statesman of Interdependence* (New York and London: W.W. Norton & Company, 1994), 363.

[62]The Action Committee for Europe is the successor to Jean Monnet's original Action Committee for the United States of Europe, founded in 1955. Monnet's original Action Committee was a transnational network of elite personalities in industry, trade unions and national parliaments who promoted European integration. Its successor organization was relaunched in the early 1980s by some of Monnet's close associates notably Max Kohnstamm. References to the Action Committee for Europe's activities in the Maastricht context appear throughout the book.

member units making the costs of opting out of joint policies higher than those of continued involvement. As a process, *engrenage* clearly lacks the dynamism sometimes implied in the functional and geographic expansionist logic of spillover.[63] Integrationists and statists both acknowledge though that neither process is automatic. Early integration theorists, like Ernst Haas, believed that spillover was dependent on the continued division of Germany and "the tacit recognition of that status in the minds of West German leaders."[64] It is less clear that Monnet believed *engrenage*, or integration, to be dependent on a divided Germany.

Unlike Walter Hallstein, Commission President in the 1960s, Monnet was never a systemic functionalist. As Ludlow explains, the functionalist approach, "often quite mistakenly identified with a crude, mechanistic spillover thesis, was based on a fundamentally different insight into the integration process and the role of the member states in it." Monnet's approach was essentially a long-term calculation that the EC institutions would gain in authority vis-à-vis the member states, "not by confrontation but by the education of the political classes in the reality of their common interests, through involvement in the integration process itself." The key was "a tight link between the supranational institutions and a series of commitments in specific policy areas that those who acceded to the Treaties agreed were best administered in common." [65]

Monnet made strategic choices to get others involved in European integration; he directed the initiatives even if others, including national leaders and officials, carried out his ideas. By using *engrenage*, Monnet involved committed participants in the integration process; in spillover national leaders and officials also take their own initiatives to direct the course of integration. Thus, a crucial difference between *engrenage* and spillover can be stated as follows. Spillover is a more pluralistic process in which national actors can also drive integration; in *engrenage* Monnet himself was the force behind the scenes who had a decisive impact on integration.

In the Maastricht context, it is important to assess the extent to which Delors used *engrenage* as a means to enable the Commission to play a strategic role on EMU. This role has been defined as that of a "policy entrepreneur" in which the Commission took advantage of existing

---

[63]Ernst Haas, *The Uniting of Europe* (Stanford: Stanford University Press, 1958), 283–317.

[64]Keohane and Hoffmann, "Institutional Change in Europe in the 1980s," 18–19.

[65]Peter Ludlow, "The European Commission, " in *The New European Community*, 110.

opportunities to define EMU as a priority on the EC agenda.[66] An exclusively intergovernmental institutionalist framework applied to the EMU conference "underestimates the extent to which domestic constraints are in turn influenced by the operation of transgovernmental networks of elites;"[67] within this transnational environment, the Delors Commission seized an opportunity to promote the European interest as a policy entrepreneur. Specifically, it exploited existing opportunities brought about as a result of the dynamics of integration embodied in the SEA and aimed to increase the level of integration among the member states by placing other integrative measures on the agenda for EMU.

INTEGRATING LEVELS, IMAGES AND BARGAINS IN A FRAMEWORK OF ANALYSIS

Each of the three approaches used in this study has a social-psychological orientation. This orientation reflects an emphasis on the role of the individual in relations among nations, also known as the first image.[68] Two- level games emphasize the strategic aims of the "chief of government." As the key negotiator for each state, this leader is trying to reconcile interests at the European and domestic levels. The four images of civil servants make a distinction between ordinary civil servants and those officials who use their influence close to the source of political power to shape policy making below the level of their political masters. Monnet's approach focuses on the capacity of political leaders and higher civil servants to link internal bargaining with European negotiations throughout the entire IGC process. Specifically, the actors involved attempt to find solutions to common problems via bargains that reflect the European, as well as the national, interest.

Raymond Aron's description of two individuals symbolic of inter-state relations, the diplomat and the soldier, is relevant to a consideration of the actions of individuals at the crossroads between European negotiations

---

[66]Stephen George, "The European Commission: Opportunities Seized, Problems Unresolved," Paper presented to the Fourth Biennial International Conference of the European Community Studies Association, Charleston, South Carolina, May 11–14, 1995. The reference to the European Commission as a policy entrepreneur on EMU was made during a panel session by Jonathan Davidson.

[67]Ibid., 1.

[68]Kenneth N. Waltz, *Man, the State and War* (New York: Columbia University Press, 1959), 16–41. The second and third images are the internal structure of states and the international system of states, respectively.

and domestic bargaining during the Maastricht process.[69] Specifically, Maastricht represented an attempt by political leaders, civil servants and bankers to replace the soldier by the diplomat as the dominant figure in the emerging European system. In the words of one French ambassador, François Scheer, the Community is a "school of diplomacy" in which negotiation is "one of man's best inventions to replace war." After centuries as a "field of battle," the Community has emerged as a "field of diplomacy," on which the virtues of will, patience, reason and courage count.[70]

Clearly during the French and German ratification processes of the Maastricht Treaty, the role of citizens, Image IV hybrids and civil servants shaped the course of integration. In the French case, the popular referendum decided the Treaty's fate. Although the decision to call the referendum was taken by the French President, the result was less state driven than originally expected by the political establishment. In fact, the referendum result was rooted in the ambiguities of societal expectations, fears and ignorance about the integration process. In the German case, ministers, Image IV hybrids and civil servants in the *Auswärtiges Amt* (Ministry of Foreign Affairs) and Ministry of Finance were closely involved in the ratification process; yet, it was their interactions with politicians and civil servants in the Bundesrat and Bundestag that enabled the parliamentary ratification of the Treaty to be completed by the December 1992 deadline.

The three approaches used in this study were chosen with the goal of explaining an entire learning process consisting of prenegotiations, the two intergovernmental conferences and national ratifications of the Maastricht Treaty in two states. The approaches complement each other and are interdependent: no one approach alone offers the insights or explanation which all three together can provide. While there is some similarity between Putnam's two-level games and intergovernmentalism or Monnet's approach and neo-functionalism, these comparisons only go so far. The aim of including three approaches is two-fold: to elaborate a new framework to explain a process which has previously not been identified or analyzed in the literature in this way; and to get beyond the confines of the intergovernmental-supranational debate which limits us to explanations more relevant during the era following the Luxembourg Compromise and preceding the Single European Act.

---

[69]Raymond Aron, *Peace and War* (New York: Anchor Books, 1973), 6.

[70]François Scheer, "Europe et Diplomatie," Conférence prononcée à l'occasion de la remise des diplômes aux étudiants de l'Institut d'Etudes Politiques de Strasbourg, samedi, 21 novembre 1992, 10.

Putnam's two-level games illustrate the extent to which states still matter in European integration while acknowledging that states are not always unitary or rational actors able to implement a precisely defined strategy. Where two-level games part company with the intergovernmentalist approach is in its emphasis on direct communications among transnational actors at the domestic level which can influence a state's strategy at the international one. Here Putnam's approach must take into account that, in the case of the European Community, "the frequency and scope of bargaining enhanced the potential for 'cross-table' alliances between domestic interests to put pressure on their respective governments to adopt mutually supportive policies": not just between central bankers but between foreign ministers like Roland Dumas and Hans-Dietrich Genscher. Interactions were multifaceted and intense, influencing at times the extent to which domestic leaders could control access to the European level.[71] Putnam's approach should also emphasize to a greater extent multiple levels, particularly the role of sub-national actors like the Länder. This is because these actors influenced both the definition of German goals at the bargaining table and how the national ratification process obtained the consent of the Länder to Maastricht.

The use of the four images of civil servants enables us to consider the role of those actors who had perhaps the greatest weight in the overall process as it unfolded from day to day. This approach ties in an analysis of actors at Level II discussed in two-level games and enables us to take a liberal approach at the domestic level by considering the extent to which national civil servants acted in a way so as to facilitate joint problem solving among the Twelve and the Community institutions at the European level. The difficulty with this approach is that while it allows us to assess the relations between civil servants and their political masters, it does not provide us with the means to get inside the heads of the actors defined as politico-administrative hybrids. Specifically, it does not answer the question: What makes individuals who operate between national and European capitals tick? How they work at the level under the political leadership is important. Specifically, the four images bring out the lack of a single approach which can give us an idea of how civil servants' actions were influenced by the learning curve the IGC process represents. Aberbach, Putnam and Rockman's approach does allow, however, for a focus on different levels of negotiation and analysis at which the existence of "turf-fighting" among officials representing distinct policy areas, i.e., EMU or political union was apparent. Turf-fighting represents "another dimension of Community bargaining, reflecting the operation of corporate self-interests at the European level." Throughout the EMU process, this difference of interests was apparent between the ECOFIN Council and the Monetary Committee, on the one hand, and the General Affairs

---

[71]Dyson, Featherstone and Michalopoulos, "The Politics of EMU: The Maastricht Treaty and the Relevance of Bargaining Models," 11.

Council and the European Council, on the other. Dyson, Featherstone and Michalopoulos argue that it is an "oversimplification" to refer to "Council bargaining" as if it occurred in a single institution.[72] This book instead emphasizes the importance of understanding the nature of the Council's institutional structure which involves levels of responsibility across functional sectors.

At the level of negotiation, it is fair to say that "turf-fighting" at the European level within the Council structure was mirrored at the domestic level. For example, the Elysée and Quai d'Orsay (Ministry of Foreign Affairs) had different interests concerning decision making on EMU than the Trésor. It is more questionable to assert that President Mitterrand colluded with Dumas to neutralize the power of the Trésor by insisting that officials from the Quai d'Orsay be in attendance during the EMU negotiations.[73] In fact, the organization of the two IGCs was structured from the start with the personal representatives of the foreign ministers assigned to take part in both conferences. Moreover, it is not clear that there was always greater institutional capacity for policy coordination at the national level than at the European one, as Dyson, Featherstone and Michalopoulos suggest. The German case illustrates that the policy coordination carried out by national civil servants proved difficult at times. This was due to the diverse personnel involved: the Chancellor's Office, the numerous ministries involved in EMU and political union, the Bundesrat, Bundestag and Bundesbank and the German Permanent Representation in Brussels.

At the level of analysis, different civil servants, ministers and heads of state and government within France and Germany held competing views concerning various issues on the table which cut across both IGCs, like the voting procedures to enter into Stage Three of EMU or increased powers for the European Parliament. This in turn influenced diplomacy at the state level among the numerous actors within the Community system. The attempt to include within a single text issue areas as diverse as EMU, CFSP and the third pillar led to difficulties in the organization and coordination of bureaucratic personnel throughout the IGC process. This impacted on the conclusion of the negotiations during the Maastricht European Council and resulted in numerous difficulties which citizens later had in understanding the language in which the Treaty was drafted.

Although Monnet's approach employs elites to drive the integration process, it also provides insight into the need for good organization of a limited number of persons in an IGC process and the clear drafting of a Treaty text so as to make the result comprehensible to the average person. The inclusion of Monnet's approach in the framework of this study is less

---

[72]Ibid., 10.
[73]Ibid., 11.

an attempt to assess the relevance of neo-functionalism to the IGC process as to consider the nature of, and relations between, domestic bargains and European negotiations. Monnet's approach to integration sheds light on the roles of civil servants, Image IV hybrids and political leaders throughout the Maastricht process by enabling the reader to distinguish more clearly among the different sub-processes present during internal bargaining (in strategy formulation during the IGCs and tactics to ratify the Treaty) and external negotiations at the European level.

The problematic aspect of Monnet's approach in the IGC context relates to the increasing expansion of the Community along functional, geographic and linguistic lines. When his approach was first used in 1950, the actors around the table were representatives of a rather homogeneous Community of Six. Monnet's influence at the center of the Schuman Plan Conference was also unprecedented in French diplomatic history and in international relations. Within a Community of Twelve, Delors' influence, particularly on EMU, was significant. Yet, his influence must be seen in the dual context of time and space: the quick tempo of German unification and the perception most Europeans had of the shifting balance of power to the East. The existence of transnational forces as a result of integration was seen by most, if not all, participants involved in the Maastricht process in relation to the changing nature and size of certain nation-states, particularly Germany and the former Soviet Union.

The challenge of the Maastricht process was how to use the tension between national goals and European interest, which has existed throughout the Community's history, to create an entity within which the evolving system of geopolitical and socio-economic relations would find constructive definition well into the next century. The increased number of issues to negotiate, member states at the table and working languages used each impacted on the use of Monnet's approach. The greater complexity of the Maastricht negotiations and national ratifications, as compared to those of the Single European Act or those leading up to the Treaties of Paris and Rome, made the presence of politico-administrative hybrids an intrinsic part of the IGC process.

In this volume, the use of Monnet's approach is meant to bring out the capacity of these Image IV hybrids to operate as transelite networks which foster the integration process. It ties in with the attempt of the Aberbach, Putnam and Rockman approach to consider the role of national officials as "joint problem solvers" who consider the European Commission as a serious participant in the IGC process. Finally, a look at the nature of integrative bargaining enables us to focus on a sub-process of negotiations which also has relevance in the domestic context. The use of Monnet's approach at the European level influenced the decisions agreed to at Maastricht. These decisions then impacted on the ways in which the national ratification processes were carried out in the member states. For example, throughout the internal debate which characterized the German ratification, attempts at distributive and integrative bargaining, and attitudinal structuring, were present as the representatives of the federal government had to strike deals with the Bundesrat and Bundestag to ratify the Treaty. Thus, it would be unwise not to consider the relevance of Monnet's approach to the IGC process. Integrative bargaining is important in and of itself to shed light on the evolution of integration.

PLAN OF THE BOOK

Fellowships from the Franco-American (Fulbright) Commission, the Jean Monnet Council, the European Commission and the Robert Bosch Foundation enabled the author to undertake research on the IGCs and national ratification processes in Paris, Brussels and Bonn. The author's understanding of the subtler points of the IGC negotiations is a direct result of her internship experience in the Institutional Affairs Division of the Secretariat General at the European Commission. Her practical knowledge of the Treaty ratification by the Bundestag and Bundesrat is a result of her involvement in the process as a Bosch Fellow in the *Auswärtiges Amt*. Information gleaned from over one hundred interviews with bureaucrats and politicians in France, Belgium and Germany made this study possible. Those institutions represented include the European Commission, Council of Ministers and Parliament, the French and German Permanent Representations to the European Communities, the German Chancellery, *Auswärtiges Amt*, Federal Ministries of Finance, Economics and the Interior, the Representation of the State of Bavaria to the European Communities, the Elysée, the Quai d'Orsay and French Ministry of Economics and Finance and the local government institutions in the region of Nord-Pas-de-Calais. As requested, the author respects the anonymity of some of her sources. To organize and write this book, the author relied on detailed information in *Agence Europe* and daily clippings from newspapers in Europe and the United States.

Chapter I presents the analytic framework the book uses to explain the Maastricht process. Chapter II places the IGCs in historical context by highlighting the major developments during two distinct phases that preceded French and German diplomacy at Maastricht. A consideration of several important actors during these phases follows. Chapter III analyzes the prenegotiation of the IGCs by presenting the preferences and views of the French and German civil servants. It assesses the influence of institutional structures and party systems and the strategies of French and German leaders on IGC diplomacy using the approaches presented here. Chapter IV explains French and German diplomacy vis-à-vis the other member states and the European institutions during the EMU conference. Chapter V assesses French and German diplomacy vis-à-vis the other member states and the European institutions during the IGC on political union. Chapter VI focuses on the decisions of Mitterrand and Kohl, and the contributions of Delors, in terms of each leader's strategy at the Maastricht European Council. Chapters VII and VIII analyze the Maastricht debates and ratifications in France and Germany, respectively. The Conclusion presents the extent of, and limits to, Franco-German cooperation during the Maastricht process. It also assesses the strengths and weaknesses of the competing approaches used in this study. Finally, the significance of the overall results of the IGC process for the future of European integration is explained.

CHAPTER II

The Historical Prelude to Maastricht

The art of persuasion has its limits. One often attributed to me a capacity in this field which I do not possess. Norman Montaigu apparently said about me "He's not a banker, he's a conjurer," the latter term refers to an extremely clever man capable of magic. Certainly, he knew banking affairs better than myself and anyone else, but he did not understand the strength of simple ideas.

There are no premature ideas, there are timely moments for which one must know how to wait.

Jean Monnet, *Mémoires*

From early 1983 until mid–1990, two phases can be distinguished which describe the important developments in French, German and European diplomacy that culminated in the successful conclusion of the Maastricht negotiations. The initial phase, from 1983 to 1987, saw the consolidation of the Exchange Rate Mechanism (ERM) of the European Monetary System, the launching of the single market process, the enlargement of the Community to include Spain and Portugal, and the negotiations which led to the Single European Act under the Luxembourg Presidency.[1] The early years of the second phase, from 1987–1990, included the Brussels European Council on 11–12 February 1988, followed by the re-election of Mitterrand to the Elysée in May and the successive months of dramatic change on the Continent which took place under the French Presidency of the Council. After a brief overview of the major developments during these two phases, this chapter highlights the roles of four individuals who influenced events up until the Strasbourg European Council in December 1989. These persons were François Mitterrand, Helmut Kohl, Hans-Dietrich Genscher, and Jacques Delors.

---

[1] Michael Sutton, "France and the Maastricht Design," *The World Today* (January 1993): 4.

PHASE I: STEPS TO LUXEMBOURG

On 21 March 1983, a key decision to keep the French franc in the Exchange Rate Mechanism of the European Monetary System set the course for Mitterrand's European policy.[2] The President's decision was accompanied by an economic policy of rigor. It also illustrated that regardless of the influence exercised by various counselors at the Elysée or outside experts, the power to resolve the issue was Mitterrand's alone.[3] This episode constituted a critical learning experience for the French political establishment. The lesson was clear: German policy makers would respect the French government only if it had a strong currency. The policy of the *franc fort* had begun, to be pursued with an impressive bipartisan continuity. As economics and finance minister in the Socialist government (1981–1984), Delors learned first hand the powerful constraints and costs imposed on national economic policy making by the asymmetry of the EMS.[4]

Mitterrand's decision to give a new priority to European Community affairs would translate into a remarkable personal engagement during the French Presidency of the Council of Ministers in the first semester of 1984.[5] During the French Presidency, Mitterrand's obstinate resolve to bring the Community out of crisis led him to conduct thirty bilateral meetings with the other nine heads of government during his six-month tenure. Mitterrand was also determined to chart a new course in the form of a political project for the Community. On an official visit to the Hague on 7 February 1984, the President indicated his readiness to consider reforms to improve coherence in the working methods of the Council of Ministers. He also welcomed Chancellor Kohl's proposition, elaborated at the Stuttgart European Council in June 1983, to establish a permanent secretariat for European Political Cooperation (EPC).[6]

---

[2]Christian Lequesne, *Paris-Bruxelles* (Paris: Presses de la Fondation Nationale des Sciences Politiques, 1993), 142.

[3]Ibid., 144.

[4]Dyson, *Elusive Union*, 115.

[5]Philippe Moreau Defarges, "'J'ai fait un rêve...' Le président François Mitterrand, artisan de l'union européenne," *Politique Etrangère* (2/85): 359.

[6]"Le réveil de l'espérance européenne," (7 février 1984) in François Mitterrand, *Refléxions sur la politique extérieure de la France* (Paris: Fayard, 1986), 267–279.

In an address Mitterrand gave to the European Parliament on 24 May 1984,[7] he underlined the need to strengthen the Community as the central part of the European edifice. However, the President was not adverse to adding areas of cooperation, like the technological collaboration featured in the EUREKA proposal, in order to attack the structural fragmentation of the Continent.[8] This type of activity, defined as Europe *à geometrie variable*[9] keeps the core of Community legislation, or the *acquis communautaire*, constant while grafting on to that core selective collaboration for particular kinds of policy areas. Yet, the fact that these policies occur outside traditional Community competencies led some countries, notably BENELUX and Italy, to question France's commitment to European integration.[10] In Mitterrand's eyes, however, Europe *à geometrie variable* corresponded to an evolving economic and political reality in the late twentieth century derived from the international pressures on nation-states.[11]

In his address before the European Parliament, the French President illustrated his vision of Europe with decisions to support both the Mediterranean enlargement and the establishment of an Ad Hoc Committee on Institutional Reform—subsequently known as the Dooge Committee after the name of its chairman. The second decision was a direct response by Mitterrand to the European Parliament's initiative for wide-reaching Community reform, the Draft Treaty establishing the European Union. Mitterrand's choice of Maurice Faure as French representative on the Dooge Committee was a propitious one, given Faure's considerable role in negotiating the Treaty of Rome and in persuading the National Assembly to ratify it.[12]

Mitterrand also suggested using the Draft Treaty establishing the European Union and the Solemn Declaration on European Union as the basic working documents in preparatory discussions leading to an intergovernmental conference to amend the Treaties of Paris and Rome including areas not in the original Treaties. The Draft Treaty establishing the European Union, an initiative of Altiero Spinelli and those members of the

---

[7]"Une victoire de la Communauté sur elle-même," (24 mai 1984) in Mitterrand, *Refléxions sur la politique extérieure de la France*, 280–297.

[8]Pierre-Henri Laurent, "Eureka, or the Technological Renaissance of Europe," *The Washington Quarterly* (Winter 1987): 59.

[9]Helen Wallace with Adam Ridley, *Europe: The Challenge of Diversity*, Chatham House Papers 29 (London: The Royal Institute of International Affairs, 1985), 36–38.

[10]Jean de Ruyt, *L'Acte unique européen* (Bruxelles: Université Libre de Bruxelles, 1991), 61.

[11]Pinder, "European Community and Nation-state: A Case for a Neo-federalism?," 49.

[12]Sutton, "France and the Maastricht Design," 4.

European Parliament known as the "Crocodile Club," had its origins in 1980. Following a year of discussion, Parliament voted on 9 July 1981 to agree to the drawing up of a draft treaty containing an outline of the Community's new tasks and the corresponding reforms. In January 1982 the EP's Committee on Institutional Affairs was set up. Two years of work in committee was required before the draft treaty was accepted by a vote of 237 to 31 with 43 abstentions on 14 February 1984.[13]

The Solemn Declaration on European Union was a watered-down version of the Genscher-Colombo Plan, an attempt in 1981 by foreign minister Hans-Dietrich Genscher and his Italian counterpart, Emilio Colombo, to relaunch the integration process and quicken the pace toward European Union. Its aims stressed a strategic role for the European Council, a single Council of Ministers for Community affairs and policy issues in the field of European Political Cooperation, a return to majority voting in the Council of Ministers and greater powers for the European Parliament. A strengthened role for the Presidency and the creation of a small secretariat for EPC were also proposed. Unfortunately, the initiative was ill-timed due to other items on the Community agenda, including struggles over the budget and the British rebate. Moreover, the plan suggested the transformation of political cooperation into a real common foreign and security policy. This posed problems for France and Denmark, which considered a step of this kind to be premature. The fact that the initiative never received the support of France effectively sealed its fate. The German Presidency under the strong leadership of Chancellor Kohl brought the initiative to a conclusion in the form of the Solemn Declaration at the Stuttgart European Council on 17–19 June 1983.[14]

Despite France's resistance to the Genscher-Colombo Plan, one of Mitterrand's most significant contributions to the integration process was his decision to name Jacques Delors as candidate for the Presidency of the European Commission in the summer of 1984. Delors spearheaded the Commission's presentation of a program to complete the internal market in July 1985, a project which marked the beginning of the *rélance européenne* of the 1980s. In the words of Pascal Lamy, Delors' *chef de cabinet*,[15] both internal and external pressures created by the gradual decline of Europe during the 1970s required a new approach. Instead of choosing one area, such as defense, monetary integration or institutional development, a three-stage

---

[13]European Parliament, *Battling for the Union: Altiero Spinelli* (Luxembourg: Office for Official Publications of the European Communities, 1988).

[14]Gianni Bonvicini, "The Genscher-Colombo Plan and the 'Solemn Declaration on European Union,'" in *The Dynamics of European Union*, ed. Roy Pryce (London: Croom Helm, 1987), 174–187.

[15]"Die Drahtzieher," *Manager Magazin* (5/92): 173.

approach based on the fundamental purpose of the Community—the creation of a genuinely common market—was chosen by the Commission.[16] Its overall program for "1992" was set out in the Cockfield White Paper, drafted by Lord Cockfield, then a Vice-President of the Commission of the European Communities.[17] In the internal market project, Stage One marked the revival of Jean Monnet's approach. Stage Two involved institutional development. Stage Three required the negotiation and implementation of the Delors Package.

The Delors Commission's initiative to launch the "1992" process used a Monnet trademark: namely, a direct appeal to individual economic agents, the businessmen and consumers of the new Europe[18] who gradually recognized their power to make governments act. Each measure to complete the internal market, approximately 279 directives[19] required confidence reciprocally shared, cooperation implicitly understood and compromise among member states. In the Monnet tradition, the internal market process sets up a dynamic disequilibrium which must be addressed. Disequilibrium can lead to forward momentum given a dynamic conjunction of opportune moments in time and visionary political leadership.

Even though the political leadership in Europe did seize the moment in the mid–1980s, the revival of the Monnet approach faced formidable obstacles. This was due in large part to the fact that the completion of the internal market had to address problems at two very different levels.[20] At the elite level, the decision to use qualified majority voting in the Council on matters relating to the internal market and to provide the Community with sufficient resources to implement its programs was essential. At the societal level, innovative measures were necessary to inform ordinary citizens about

---

[16]Pascal Lamy, "The Brussels European Council of February 1988," Boston, 1 March 1988 (mimeo).

[17]Paolo Cecchini, *The European Challenge 1992* (Aldershot: Wildwood House, 1988).

[18]Axel Krause, *Inside The New Europe* (New York: HarperCollins, 1992).

[19]The Council and the Commission of the EEC exercise their powers through "legal acts" the form and effect of which are defined in Article 189: "A directive shall be binding, as to the result achieved, upon each Member State to which it is addressed, but shall leave to the national authorities the choice of form and methods." Eric Stein, Peter Hay and Michael Waelbroeck, *European Community Law and Institutions in Perspective* (Charlottesville, VA: The Michie Company, 1976), 32–33.

[20]Interview, Klaus-Peter Nanz, German Permanent Representation to the European Communities, 26 August 1992.

the unique nature of the "1992" program and the effects of Community law on their daily lives.

As Delors explained, the revival of the Monnet approach involved an idea and a timetable—the creation of a genuinely common market by 1992. During Stage Two of the approach to create the common market, the negotiation and implementation of the Single European Act promoted institutional development in the European Communities.[21] At the Milan European Council on 28–29 June 1985, the heads of state and government unanimously approved the White Paper. Genscher proposed an ambitious agreement on decision making which aimed to move away from invoking the Luxembourg Compromise and instead to increase the use of majority voting and refrain from the use of the veto.[22] Several states, including Great Britain found this unacceptable and the text was rejected. However, foreign minister Andreotti called for a majority vote on whether to convene an intergovernmental conference under Article 236 EEC. On procedural grounds, Britain opposed the use of a majority vote, but Thatcher's protests were rejected. The conference was scheduled to take place under the Luxembourg Presidency in Fall 1985.

The results of the intergovernmental conference, in the form of amendments to the Treaties of Paris and Rome known as the Single European Act, led to an increased use of majority voting in the Council of Ministers in certain areas of internal market policy. The institutional changes strengthening the rights of the European Parliament, most notably the introduction of the cooperation procedure, involved Parliament early in the process of shaping Community legislation. The executive powers of the Commission were also widened, although its administrative reform as a European institution remained necessary and urgent.[23] The Single European Act's new decision-making procedure started on 1 July 1987. This breakthrough was followed eight months later by the achievement of Stage Three—the Delors Package.[24]

---

[21]Claus-Dieter Ehlermann, "The Institutional Development of the EC under the Single European Act," *Aussenpolitik* II (1990): 135–146; Christian Engel and Wolfgang Wessels, eds., *From Luxembourg to Maastricht: Institutional Change in the European Community after the Single European Act* (Bonn: Europa Union, 1992).

[22]Moravcsik, "Negotiating the Single European Act," 60–64.

[23]Ludlow, "The European Commission," in *The New European Community*, 126–129.

[24]Frans Andriessen, "In the Wake of the Brussels Summit," *European Affairs* 2 (Summer 1988): 14–26.

PHASE II: JOURNEY TO A KNOWN DESTINATION

When Delors launched the goal to complete the internal market, he was aware that this would put in place the conditions for an EMU initiative. He astutely linked internal market reform and EMU by introducing the directive on capital liberalization. The Single European Act, which enabled the "1992" program to move ahead, was also "to shift the center of gravity in the EMS and EMU policy process." This shift was from a reliance on intergovernmental bargaining in the Council to a more supranational style of integrative bargaining. Common interests and momentum, established in agreeing on the Act, facilitated a new cohesion while promoting a major advance in European monetary integration.[25]

The integration dynamic that pushed the internal market process forward prompted the German foreign minister to issue the Genscher Memorandum. This document responded to Delors' strategy on EMU and to French plans for economic and monetary union in Europe advocated by the Conservative economics and finance minister Edouard Balladur.[26] In Genscher the European Commission and the French had found an ally within the German domestic bargaining arena: one who was sufficiently powerful to broker German support.[27] At the Brussels European Council, agreement was reached on a financial reform package which enabled the Community to carry out the plans outlined in the Single European Act. In the words of one seasoned Community diplomat, Chancellor Kohl provided the leadership of a strong member state to resolve what was essentially the same set of issues before the Danish Presidency only a few weeks before.[28]

During a meeting of the ECOFIN Council, on 15 March, the German finance minister, Gerhard Stoltenberg, submitted a paper which stated that the German government would be willing to consider reforms leading to EMU, if the capital liberalization directive was adopted. EMS reform, and subsequent change at the European level, could only come about if there was domestic acceptance by France and Italy of full liberalization of capital. Delors' proposed linkage made EMU a serious proposition among Community member states.[29] In early June agreement on the adoption of the directive was reached. This set the background for the European Council later in the month.

---

[25]Dyson, *Elusive Union*, 116.

[26]Elke Thiel, "From the Internal Market to an Economic and Monetary Union," *Aussenpolitik* I (1989): 68.

[27]Dyson, Featherstone and Michalopoulos, "The Politics of EMU: The Maastricht Treaty and the Relevance of Bargaining Models," 4.

[28]Interview, French Permanent Representation to the European Communities, 25 November 1992.

[29]Dyson, Featherstone and Michalopoulos, "The Politics of EMU," 4.

On 27–28 June 1988, the heads of state and government, meeting in Hannover, asked a committee under the chairmanship of Jacques Delors to prepare a report on economic and monetary union. It is highly significant that the committee, composed mainly of the central bank governors (acting in a personal capacity), was asked to draw up a report indicating how an objective already agreed might be implemented. The European Council was both asserting its authority over monetary policy, while also drawing cautious central bankers into the policy process.[30] The momentum which emerged as a result of this decision illustrates the manner in which *engrenage* can establish a solid network of influence in support of integration among national officials, whether central bankers or civil servants.

This book makes the case that the Delors Commission's strategy on EMU was to include the central bankers early in the process, both to get their input and to assure them that there would be no unpleasant surprises as the process gained momentum. Nonetheless, *engrenage* involved tensions at different levels, i.e., European Council (political), ECOFIN (ministerial) and central bankers (technical) as well as a set of mutually rewarding interactions. The EMU process allowed the Commission, under Delors' leadership, to play the role of a policy entrepreneur. In this sense, it played a strategic role, seizing the right political moment to drive the integration process via EMU. The Commission's use of *engrenage* as part of its overall strategy meant involving both national civil servants and interest groups in the EMU process. The key point to underline is that the Delors Commission took the leadership initiative, along with France and Germany, to get other member states involved in the negotiation process.

The German Presidency of the Council of Ministers coincided with the re-election of François Mitterrand to the Elysée on 8 May 1988. During his second term, the primary focus of French diplomacy was the "German question."[31] As Gorbachev's dramatic changes in central and eastern European policy increased the prospects of German unity, French European policy sought to anchor the Federal Republic to the West. At the time of Mitterrand's re-election, West Germany was nervous about the withdrawal of US missiles from Europe under the Intermediate-range Nuclear Force (INF)

---

[30]Ibid., 4–5.

[31]Renata Fritsch-Bournazel, "German Unification: Views from Germany's Neighbors," in *German Unification in European Perspective*, ed. Wolfgang Heisenberg (London: Brassey's, 1991), 70–87; Wolfgang Asholt and Ingo Kolboom, "Frankreich und das vereinte Deutschland," *Europa- Archiv* 7 (1992): 179–186. French reactions to German unification are described in Horst Teltschik, *329 Tage* (Berlin: Siedler, 1991) and Stephen F. Szabo, *The Diplomacy of German Unification* (New York: St. Martin's, 1992).

Treaty agreed between the Soviet Union and the United States. France, which could extend its nuclear umbrella to West Germany, urgently wanted changes in West German monetary policy. Roy Jenkins argued that Paris was still looking for a partner to steer a course in Community affairs during Mitterrand's second term at the Elysée.[32] Garret Fitzgerald suggests that defense and monetary policies were "ultimately the keys" to unity and that the basis for a deal already existed between France and West Germany shortly after Mitterrand's re-election.[33]

The plan for EMU was the one which would most obviously influence the lives of millions of Europeans. The Spanish Presidency, under the chairmanship of Prime Minister Felipe Gonzalez, set a high priority on clear decisions on monetary union and social policy at the Madrid European Council on 26–27 June 1989.[34] In retrospect, the most significant achievement of the meetings of the heads of state and government in Madrid was that it dealt with the "British problem."[35] In her memoirs, Lady Thatcher writes that for her EMU went to "the very heart not just of the debate about Europe's future but about Britain's future as a democratic, sovereign state." She was not prepared to compromise.[36] Prime Minister Gonzalez shrewdly acknowledged the existence of a solid coalition of members in the Council who felt that even modest concessions from Thatcher on monetary union were worth obtaining.[37] As part of a compromise decision, achieved in the belief that the Delors Committee had carried out the mandate given in Hannover, the heads of state and government agreed that the first stage of EMU should start on 1 July 1990. An intergovernmental conference to map out its later stages should be called after that date.[38] Significantly, 1 July 1990 also marked the coming into force of the capital liberalization directive. This was a necessary prerequisite to achieve EMU. Lady Thatcher explains that her conditions regarding EMU were met at Madrid in that the outcome of an intergovernmental conference on

---

[32]Roy Jenkins, "Who Will Lead Europe?," *Financial Times*, April 29, 1988.

[33]"Paris-Bonn Deal 'Key to European Unity'," *Financial Times*, May 11, 1988.

[34]"L'avenir de l'Espagne dépend de son intégration à l'Europe," *Le Figaro*, 8 juin 1989.

[35]Peter Ludlow, "The Broad Lines of Policy in 1989," in *The Annual Review of European Community Affairs 1990*, ed. Peter Ludlow (London: Brassey's, 1990), XLIV.

[36]Margaret Thatcher, *The Downing Street Years* (New York: HarperCollins, 1993), 719.

[37]Ludlow, "The Broad Lines of Policy in 1989," XLIII.

[38]"The History of the Maastricht Summit," *The Economist*, November 30, 1991.

EMU had been left open and its timing unclear.[39] An obvious eleven-to-one split on the European Social Charter, with Thatcher alone in opposing it, was adroitly sidestepped. It carried over to the French Presidency which began on 1 July 1989.

France aimed to make EMU and social policy the essential dossiers of its Council Presidency.[40] Accordingly, ECOFIN Council President, economics and finance minister Bérégovoy, devoted an informal meeting at Cap d'Antibes in southern France on 9–10 September to the preparation of the first stage of EMU and the intergovernmental conference on the second and third stages.[41] A few days earlier the High Level Group for economic and monetary union, presided over by Elisabeth Guigou, held its first meeting. Each country sent one representative from the ministry of foreign affairs and the ministry of finance, with the Federal Republic of Germany also adding a representative from the federal ministry of economics. Thus, coordination to prepare the IGC between the work of the General Affairs Council and the work of the ECOFIN Council was achieved.[42] The "Guigou Group" attempted to clarify the issues raised by the request for respecting at the same time (1) parallelism between economic and monetary integration, (2) the principle of subsidiarity and (3) the diversity of specific (national) situations. The response of the Group was to formulate a long list of questions with respect to the single market, economic and social cohesion, macroeconomic policies, institutional developments and the functioning of the European System of Central Banks. The Group did not propose replies to these questions but instead pointed out that on several key points fundamental disagreements prevailed between Great Britain and her Community partners.[43]

The process of German unification, coupled with the fall of Communism in eastern Europe, gathered momentum in November and December 1989. France, caught off guard by the rhythm of events on the other side of the Rhine, made EMU the cornerstone of its European policy. Mitterrand's European policy at this time has been described as "confused." Two factors though helped Mitterrand and his colleagues to recover their balance in the face of a solid Bonn-Brussels connection. Primo, France was in the chair of the rotating Council Presidency. This responsibility demanded an active role in developing a Community response to changes in Germany. Secondly, the French Euro-reflex was highly developed: after all, the Community venture

---

[39]Thatcher, *The Downing Street Years*, 752.

[40]Christian Lequesne, "Frankreich," in *Jahrbuch der europäischen Integration 1989/90* Hrsg. Werner Weidenfeld and Wolfgang Wessels (Bonn: Institut für Europäische Politik, 1990), 323–324.

[41]Agence Europe, 9 septembre 1989.

[42]Ibid., 7 septembre 1989.

[43]Jørgen Mortensen, "Managing the Community's Economy," in *The Annual Review of European Community Affairs 1990*, 32.

had its origins in making war between France and Germany impossible.[44] On EMU French logic was clear and simple. Increased integration was necessary in order to anchor Germany firmly in the West and to avoid dominance in the monetary field by the Bundesbank. A pooling of sovereignty would increase French leverage by giving it a seat on the Board of Directors of the future European Central Bank.[45]

An extraordinary meeting of the European Council was called in Paris on 18 November to discuss the rapidly evolving situation in central and eastern Europe. The challenges of upheaval on the Continent prompted a far-sighted and timely response from Commission President Delors who acted quickly to consolidate political relations with Bonn. The Strasbourg European Council on 8–9 December 1989 was also mainly about the evolution in central and eastern Europe, leaving little time for the preparation of EMU. President Mitterrand had hoped to end his six-month Presidency of the Council with a decision to convene the intergovernmental conference charged with preparing the necessary reform of the Treaties by early 1990. However, on Chancellor Kohl's insistence the conference was postponed until after the German elections in November. Here Delors played a key role as mediator between Mitterrand and Kohl to facilitate the emergence of a Franco-German negotiating line on the date to begin the intergovernmental conference.[46] In accordance with the Franco-German line, the IGC was planned for December 1990 by a majority of eleven states in favor.[47] The British government, which dissented, had preferred to await the results of the first stage of EMU before moving any further ahead in the field of institutional changes.[48]

The origins of the IGC on political union can be traced back to this period as well. This is because the internal dynamics of the Community, with a progressive extension of competencies at the European level, fostered a reflection on further institutional developments. The European Parliament, in a resolution adopted late in 1989, established an explicit link between EMU and general Treaty reform. The Parliament asked that the IGC "have a mandate to revise the Paris and Rome Treaties in order to reinforce the

[44]Ludlow, "The Broad Lines of Policy in 1989," XLVIII.

[45]Claire Tréan, "Genèse d'un traité," *Le Monde*, 30 avril 1992.

[46]Charles Grant, *Delors: Inside the House That Jacques Built* (London: Nicholas Brealey Publishing, 1994), 141.

[47]Wilhelm Schönfelder/Elke Thiel, "The Shaping of the Framework for a Single Currency in the Course of the EMU Negotiations," Presentation for the Robert Bosch Foundation Spring Speaker Series on the Evolution of Europe in the 1990s, The Cosmos Club, March 16, 1995.

[48]Mortensen, "Managing the Community's Economy," 33.

efficiency and the democratic character of decision making within the Community."[49]

An external factor, namely, the collapse of the Soviet empire in central and eastern Europe, also contributed to the evolution of thinking on political union. This change served as a catalyst for the establishment of a common foreign and security policy, one of the key issues in the entire negotiation on political union. A third factor, closely linked to the collapse of Communism in the eastern part of the Continent, was German unification. This was after all one of two themes that precipitated the first Kohl-Mitterrand initiative on political union and the calling of Dublin I. In a testimony to the vision of Konrad Adenauer, Chancellor Kohl aimed to make European integration the privileged framework of action for a unified Germany.[50]

The prospect of future Community enlargements in 1989–1990 did not really play a crucial role in the decision to convene a conference on political union. With the passage of time, however, and as the number of applicant countries increased, two schools of thought emerged on the issue of institutional reform in the IGC context. One the one hand, there were those who believed that the institutional reforms proposed during the negotiations were insufficient to accommodate the number of member states asking for Community membership. On the other, there were those who felt that the negotiators' ideas on institutional reform were too ambitious and would create a wall between the Community and the newly emerging democracies in central and eastern Europe.[51] The tension between these two schools remained throughout the Maastricht process.

Dramatis Personae on the European Stage
This section explores the roles of several key actors who helped write the historical prelude to Maastricht. The focus on individuals here complements the conceptual framework of the three approaches developed in subsequent chapters. The emphasis in Putnam's two-level games is clearly on the chief of government and his strategy. Thus, the actions of Mitterrand, Kohl and Genscher concretize and relativize some of the ideas presented in Putnam's approach. The four images of civil servants consider interactions between politicians and bureaucrats. The role of Delors as a politico-administrative hybrid in the Image IV mold and his use of Monnet's approach make a consideration of his actions in this earlier period equally relevant.

---

[49]J. Cloos, G. Reinesch, D. Vignes et J. Weyland, *Le Traité de Maastricht* (Bruxelles: Bruylant, 1994), 45.

[50]Ibid., 46–47.

[51]Ibid., 47–48.

President François Mitterrand

Three factors have been identified as influencing Mitterrand's commitment to integration: his historical perspectives including his experiences of the war years; his ideals which stressed a belief in the need for a European political authority and a central role for France; and, most importantly, national self-interest and party advantage to which he applied political acumen to bargain his way to leadership of the French Left.[52]

Although Mitterrand was sympathetic to the European idea from its inception, he adopted a pragmatic attitude which enabled him to unite various factions of the French Socialist party (PSF) during the 1970s. The differences, particularly over economic policy and the European Community, were major ones. The various factions, as well as the French Communist party (PCF), often held contradictory views. In his attempt to unite the Left, Mitterrand sacrificed clarity to ambiguity. Mitterrand forged links with both the anti-integration Socialist factions, notably CERES, and the anti-EC French Communists in order to develop a common platform which would win him the French Presidency.[53]

As Mitterrand's own position became secure, and the Socialists were forced to acknowledge the need for integration policies, his commitment to integration came to the fore, albeit with rather painful consequences. The party *volte face* on the European Monetary System in 1983 has been alluded to previously. Mitterrand's decision on EMS was aided by the decline of the French Communists which left CERES without a strong anti-EMS ally. The Communists' decline enabled Mitterrand to align himself with a moderate wing of the Socialist party, including Michel Rocard.[54] He also astutely used the 1983 crisis to force CERES to reshape its Euro-policy in order to survive.[55]

In addition to economic and monetary policy, Mitterrand's European ambitions clearly focused on social affairs and a European political union which has security and defense at its core. Mitterrand realized that political union and Franco-German relations are inextricably intertwined. Therefore, the French President cultivated a good working relationship with Kohl early on. He also sought the advice and used the talents of a fellow Socialist, Jacques Delors, in European affairs.

The success of Mitterrand's personal diplomacy during the French Presidency and the subsequent breakthrough at the Fontainebleau European Council in 1984 imparted a momentum to the idea of a package deal that would incorporate liberalization of the single market and decision-making

---

[52]Elizabeth Hayward, "The European Policy of François Mitterrand," *Journal of Common Market Studies* 31 (June 1993): 270.

[53]Ibid., 272.

[54]Dyson, *Elusive Union*, 115.

[55]Hayward, "The European Policy of François Mitterrand," 73.

reform in the Community. This momentum was sustained until the conclusion of the Maastricht negotiations. One book that compares De Gaulle and Mitterrand depicts the latter as an "architect" in European affairs who "knows how to reconcile French interests with European progress." Its author, a noted French journalist, observes that while lacking a certain Gaullist prestige, the trio Mitterrand-Kohl-Delors avoided the psychological dramas in Brussels which marked the General's era.[56] After his re-election to the Elysée in 1988, however, Mitterrand's commitment to European unity faced an unexpected test: the disintegration of the postwar order.

The evolution of events after the fall of the Berlin Wall in late 1989 revealed a French leadership style in disarray. Mitterrand's leadership, or the apparent lack of it, allowed Helmut Kohl to dominate the scene.[57] As Stanley Hoffmann observed, Mitterrand's own policies remained somewhat inconsistent: "the embrace of further European integration and of NATO on the international stage did not always work well with the remnants of a highly Gaullist defense policy at home."[58] Undoubtedly, his first term success enabled Mitterrand to acquire both admiration and prestige on the European scene. However, his personality, which made it extremely difficult for even those close to him to read his innermost thoughts, allowed Mitterrand to monopolize French foreign and defense policy even more than de Gaulle.[59] The institutional structure of the Vth Republic cloaked his absolute power in constitutional authority. This is one of the reasons why after 1989 the extent to which Mitterrand had any proactive policy of his own, any "grand design," was not as clear as his reactions to German initiatives on national unity and European Union.

The President, an intellectual steeped in European history and literature, emerged as a head of state trapped in a vision of nineteenth-century Europe with its nationalistic rivalries and balance of power politics. His talks with Gorbachev in Kiev and his visit to a clearly collapsing East Germany in December 1990, while affirming Mitterrand's autonomous will, undoubtedly risked "some measure of the trust that had been built up in the German-French EC relationship."[60] These actions also revealed the extent to which the "image of Rapallo," or an alliance between Germany and the Soviet Union, influenced

---

[56]Alain Duhamel, *De Gaulle-Mitterrand. La Marque et la Trace* (Paris: Flammarion, 1991), 91–115.

[57]Stanley Hoffmann, "The Case for Leadership," *Foreign Policy* 81 (Winter 1990–1991): 24.

[58]Ibid.

[59]Jolyon Howorth, "The President's Special Role in Foreign and Defense Policy," in *De Gaulle to Mitterrand. Presidential Power in France* ed. Jack Hayward (New York: New York University Press, 1993), 166.

[60]Ronald Tiersky, "France in the New Europe," *Foreign Affairs* 71 (Spring 1992): 132.

the French national psyche.[61] Mitterrand still believed in European construction with Franco-German relations at its core. However, the weight of history and the French institutional structure strongly influenced his attempts to formulate a European strategy. This structure maintained the illusion that a Europe so far removed from the French people could make policies in a manner uncontested by the public.[62] The implications of this misjudgment profoundly influenced the course of integration as later chapters underscore.

Chancellor Helmut Kohl / Foreign Minister Hans-Dietrich Genscher
Although he came to power already committed to European integration, Helmut Kohl established his reputation early as a local politician not a world statesman. In contrast to his French counterpart, Kohl is noted for a decentralized leadership style. As party leader, the German Chancellor is also markedly concerned with the CDU. Kohl is not a charismatic leader, but he remains close to public thinking. This fact explains most of his success.[63] One of Kohl's major assets, aside from his political intuition, is his ability to identify the key issues on which to compromise. His genuine belief in the European idea and his natural sense of optimism enabled Kohl to forge an excellent working relationship with the new Commission President, Jacques Delors, after 1985. His constant support of European initiatives, in tandem with France, led to the highly successful German Presidency in 1988.

Throughout his career in Bonn, Kohl had often been accused of lacking vision, of being a skillful politician rather than a statesman. He was not viewed as an initiator but instead as a somewhat reluctant follower of Hans-Dietrich Genscher, whose support was crucial to Kohl's political survival. International events revealed Kohl to be as much a champion of West European integration as a German patriot, keen on restoring as much German sovereignty as the circumstances allowed. His view of the FRG was "as an actor and not an object."[64]

As Kohl's coalition partner, Genscher had his own policy agenda at both the domestic and European levels. His actions in the Maastricht context illustrate the need to consider levels below the chief of government in two-level games. The role of Genscher is strikingly illustrated by the memorandum

---

[61]Renata Fritsch-Bournazel, "Rapallo et son image en France," *Documents: Revue des questions allemandes* (2/82): 3–12.

[62]Alain Genestar, *Les péchés du prince* (Paris: Grasset, 1992), 169- 185.

[63]Ferdinand Müller-Rommel, "Federal Republic of Germany: A System of Chancellor Government," in *Cabinets in Western Europe*, eds. Jean Blondel and Ferdinand Müller-Rommel (London: Macmillan, 1988), 164–165.

[64]Hoffmann, "The Case for Leadership," 23.

on EMU which he issued to the General Affairs Council, comprising the foreign ministers of the Community member states, in February 1988. The Genscher Memorandum suggested that the European Currency Unit (ECU) could serve initially as a parallel currency and later, after a transition period of several years, as the single currency for the proposed European Union. The rationale for the proposal was two-fold: a single currency and a European Central Bank were "economically necessary" for the completion of the internal market; and Europe's dependence on the dollar would be reduced. Genscher's initiative created a background to policy, a disposition to respond to opportunities in a particular way.[65] This is important to emphasize in terms of Putnam's approach because the key agenda-setting role was played by the foreign minister rather than the Chancellor. This process reflected both the strength of the principle of departmentalism within Level II institutions and the nature of Kohl's more relaxed leadership style, which influenced Level I strategy in terms of EMU policy.[66] Genscher's role also supports the idea of transnational issue linkage within two-level games.[67] Only by advocating EMU at the European level, did Genscher receive French and Italian support for the capital liberalization directive which proved to be in the German domestic interest.

Until the German Revolution of 1989, Genscher ran foreign policy and left defense policy to Kohl's CDU and the CSU. This frustrated many Christian Democrats who were denied any substantive role in foreign policy. It also produced a politically uneven division of labor. The Revolution of 1989 suddenly merged foreign and domestic policy and brought Kohl into an arena that previously had been largely Genscher's. Although Kohl and Genscher were a study in contrasts both in personality and in style, they were similar in their tactical skills and political instincts.[68]

The German Chancellor was especially adept at outmaneuvering more attractive and highly regarded rivals within his own party and emerging as the winner. His opponents tended to underestimate him, yet he combined an exhaustive knowledge of Christian Democratic Party politics with what one

---

[65]Dyson, *Elusive Union*, 127.

[66]It is important to underline that Genscher had an unusual amount of power and scope for initiative as foreign minister because of his position as junior coalition partner in Kohl's government and his extraordinary ministerial experience during an 18-year period. It is also true that the ultimate political decision to set a fixed date for the transition to the final stage of EMU was taken by Kohl. The ministerial and technical levels, represented by the ministry of finance and the Bundesbank, respectively, were bound by this decision.

[67]Putnam, "Diplomacy and Domestic Politics" in *Double-Edged Diplomacy*, 448.

[68]Szabo, *The Diplomacy of German Unification*, 19–20.

observer has described as "a phenomenal instinct for the latent majority."[69] Kohl was slow to realize that the opening of the Berlin Wall on 9 November 1989 meant rapid unification, however. As a politician, he was faced with the growing problem of massive emigration, which only accelerated after the Wall's breach, and the consequent need to stabilize the situation. This led the Chancellor to seek a European Community solution to this problem by including asylum and visa policy issues on the IGC prenegotiation agenda.[70] He was pushed as well by the East German Communist leader, Hans Modrow, who spoke early on of confederative arrangements. Kohl only came to see unification as both inevitable and a winning issue after he began to travel in East Germany in December 1989.[71]

It was Kohl's consistent reaffirmation of the Federal Republic's Western European identity during the various stages of unification which smoothed the European Community's adaptation to the reality of one Germany. Kohl articulated the dominant view in both the governing coalition and the opposition when he stated the following before the first all-German Bundestag: "Germany is our fatherland, Europe our future. The nucleus and basis for Europe's integration are to us the European Community, which we aim to develop into a European Union."[72] Kohl acknowledged from the outset that the starting point for Germany's partnership in the EC revolves around its relationship to France. In a policy statement to the Bundestag in 1987, Kohl described the Franco-German friendship as "the dynamic force in the process of European unification."[73]

One astute observer of Germany and the Community asserts that all of the Federal Republic's goals in the decade before unification contained "elements of realism and responsibility, of individualistic national interest, and of collective European interest."[74] The Federal Republic's "active pursuit of EPC

---

[69]Ibid., 20.

[70]Colette Mazzucelli, *A Decision in Dublin, An Agenda in Rome: Convening Parallel Conferences on European Union*, Monnet Case Studies in European Affairs (New York: The Jean Monnet Council, 1995), 3.

[71]Szabo, *The Diplomacy of German Unification*, 20–21.

[72]"Policy Statement by Helmut Kohl, Federal Chancellor to the Bundestag," 18 March 1987 in *European Political Cooperation* (Bonn: Press and Information Office, 1988), 379.

[73]"Policy Statement by Helmut Kohl, Federal Chancellor to the Bundestag," 18 March 1987 in European Political Cooperation (Bonn: Press and Information Office, 1988), 379.

[74]Lily Gardner Feldman, "Germany and the EC: Realism and Responsibility," *The Annals* 531 (January 1994): 27.

and political union reflected the dual goals of national political and economic interests, satisfied through an internally coherent and externally assertive EC, and an idealistic conviction, based on German history, that the EC represented an antidote to excessive nationalism."[75]

President Jacques Delors

As Commission President, Delors' first initiative to complete the internal market illustrated both vision and pragmatism, qualities considered by many to be intrinsic to Monnet's approach.[76] It is an approach which requires a high degree of flexibility, political intuition, creative intellectual power and the ability to recognize the futility of insisting on a solution which is absolutely unacceptable for one member state.[77] Delors' use of Monnet's approach was brilliantly illustrated by his work on the Delors Committee. The initiatives he took to create this committee and to chair its proceedings illustrate his use of *engrenage* to promote the Commission's role as a policy entrepreneur.

On EMU Delors says: "When I saw the movement accelerating, I said to myself, we need—following the method which has always worked so well—a committee which would provide the intellectual and technical framework for subsequent political decisions."[78] Delors also knew that several central bank governors resented his presence as chair of the committee and set about winning their confidence. In the early meetings, he limited the agenda to a discussion of basic principles and of what had gone wrong with previous attempts at EMU. The central bank governors began to realize that the chairman was not trying to force their hands by pushing acceptance of his set blueprint for change. Delors says it made a difference when "we decided to speak only in English, so they did not have to wear headphones. This speeded up the discussion and put them at ease."[79] This point illustrates the importance of the use of a common language in Monnet's approach to integrative bargaining—both in linguistic terms and in the sense of being certain that all parties around the table share the same definition of terms used in discussions.

As chair of the Delors Committee, the Commission President helped in other ways to create a good atmosphere. Pöhl remarked: "Delors was more flexible than I expected and my concerns did not fully materialize. The

---

[75]Ibid., 30.

[76]Clifford P. Hackett, "Jean Monnet, Europe and the United States," in *Jean Monnet et l'Europe d'aujourd'hui*, eds. Giandomenico Majone, Emile Noël and Peter Van den Bosche (Baden-Baden: Nomos, 1989), 163–170.

[77]Hanns Jürgen Küsters, "Jean Monnet and the European Union," in *Jean Monnet et l'Europe d'aujourd'hui*, 56.

[78]Grant, *Delors: Inside the House That Jacques Built*, 119.

[79]Ibid., 122.

substance of the report came from the governors, not Delors. His contribution was small, but we made him famous." To which Delors replied, very much in the spirit of Monnet, "I'm delighted that Pöhl says that, because if he'd said: "It's a scandal, Delors wanted to impose his own project,' we wouldn't have got the report.... One of the great ways to make progress when your own authority is not unquestioned is to get others to promote your ideas."[80]

The Delors Report laid the foundation for the step-by-step approach of Monnet that would infuse the entire EMU conference: "the creation of an economic and monetary union must be viewed as a single process. Although this process is set out in stages which guide the progressive movement to the final objective, the decision to enter upon the first stage should be a decision to embark on the entire process."[81] Here the leadership role of the Commission as spokesperson for the European interest was indispensable. Without Delors' input, it is doubtful that EMU would have materialized solely on the basis of Franco-German cooperation. His mediation skills with Mitterrand and Kohl were decisive to the EMU process.

In her memoirs, Margaret Thatcher's criticism of Delors was that he had "altogether slipped his leash as a *fonctionnaire* and become a fully fledged political spokesman for federalism." Lady Thatcher was also quick to point out that the consequent "blurring of the roles of civil servants and elected representatives was more in the continental tradition" than in the British one.[82] Thatcher was lashing out against the momentum building toward EMU, as a result of Delors' initiatives, a momentum which she recognized as forward movement toward political union as well. Two speeches that Delors made, one before the European Parliament in July 1988 and the other in September at a conference of the Trades Union Congress (TUC) in Bournemouth, infuriated the British Prime Minister. The source of Thatcher's anger and frustration was her concern that British democracy was in danger of being subordinated to the demands of a remote European bureaucracy, determined to extend its competencies as far as possible to advance the "1992" single market process.

The success of the Brussels European Council in early 1988 allowed Delors to shift the Community's agenda from the internal market to the social dimension and economic and monetary union.[83] This shift to policy areas which Thatcher clearly opposed, and one of Delors' remarks before the

---

[80]Ibid., 123.

[81]Ibid., 124. This statement is taken from Paragraph 39 of The Delors Report. The Delors Committee, *Report on Economic and Monetary Union in the European Community* (Luxembourg: Office for Official Publications of the European Communities, 1989).

[82]Thatcher, *The Downing Street Years*, 742.

[83]Grant, *Delors: Inside the House That Jacques Built*, 88.

European Parliament during his July speech, led Thatcher to believe that he had exceeded the bounds of his competence. Delors had stated, "In 10 years, 80 per cent of economic legislation, perhaps even tax and social, will come from the EC." By making these statements, Delors saw his job as trying to provoke a debate on where the EC was heading.[84] Thatcher was determined to move the Community in an entirely different direction as she pointed out in her famous Bruges speech on 22 September 1988. In her view, "We have not successfully rolled back the frontiers of the state in Britain only to see them reimposed at a European level with a European superstate exercising a new dominance from Brussels."

Delors' emphasis on the "joint exercise of sovereignty" in the Community clearly countered Thatcher's views on sovereignty. Here Delors departed from Monnet's approach by taking on a member state in a direct confrontation. In a key speech in 1989, also made at the College of Europe, Delors underlined the need to reconcile "necessity and the ideal" in the service of European unity. In his description of the Community as "a concept full of meaning," he emphasized the strength of the European institutions in a Community based on law. The "joint exercise of sovereignty" by member states, Delors explained, is for the profit of all in a type of "positive sum game."

In this speech, Delors explained why he was inclined to move away from Monnet's step-by-step approach: "time is short," he said.[85] The speed of change on the Continent gave Delors reason for concern that the Community could never fulfill its obligations in the East and on the world stage with its present decision-making procedures. This was the reason for a new political initiative. As Delors stated: "The Commission is ready for it and will play its full part in pointing the way. It will propose answers to the questions raised by another quantum leap: who takes the decisions; how do the various levels of decision making intermesh (subsidiarity always); who puts decisions into practice; what resources will be available; what will it mean in terms of democracy?"[86]

As Commission President, Delors had to reconcile the political requirements of his job—mediation between national interests—with the more technical and technocratic aspects—the formulation and implementation of policies designed to serve the common, European interest. There is a tension here which is at times apparent. For example, at a conference celebrating the centenary of Monnet's birth, President Delors addressed the issue of Community openness vis-à-vis citizens. His remarks illustrate a sensitivity to

---

[84]Ibid.

[85]"Address by Jacques Delors, President of the Commission of the European Communities at the College d'Europe," Bruges, Belgium, October 17, 1989 (Brussels: Commission of the European Communities, 1989), 13.

[86]Ibid., 14.

the common man and a concern for integration, not by balancing different national interests, but on the basis of a common will:

> If the proposals considered by the Community and the decisions it takes are not part and parcel of public life and do not concern national parliaments as much as they should, we are bound to fail. This is where the first democratic deficit lies.... My guess would be that not more than 7% of Europeans know what we are talking about in the Community today. The conclusion is obvious. We must arouse public interest by being open and by getting people talking about European problems. This is even more important than producing a treaty tomorrow giving new powers to the European Parliament. I am being straight with you when I say that this is the real issue. When a Head of Government or a Minister goes back home flexing his muscles like Rambo and says, "I won at the Council last night," things have come to a pretty pass, because the fact is that the Twelve, even the strongest, will win together or lose together. Politics must be given a European dimension. [87]

Delors' attempts to give politics "a European dimension" were at the very heart of the Commission's leadership style as a policy entrepreneur. Delors emphasized the role of the Commission as a lean institution, not a "bloated bureaucracy," whose limited size helped it to maintain a strategic focus. The Delors Commission wanted to maintain a certain "critical mass," not just balance off its powers with those of other EC institutions. Its goal was to drive the pace of integration as a conceptualizer, not only manage daily Community affairs as a technocratic administration. In this sense, the Commission's role in the IGC process was a critical test of its ability to exploit existing circumstances and shape the course of Community affairs for decades to come. The EMU process offered the Commission the chance to show that it is uniquely placed as an institution geared toward strategic policy development.

---

[87]"Closure of Symposium by Jacques Delors," in *Jean Monnet, Proceedings of the Centenary Symposium*, 119–120.

CHAPTER III

The Maastricht Prenegotiation: French and German Domestic Contexts

> In the course of my successive duties, I never had the feeling to follow a career or to belong to a hierarchy, whether it was French, English, American or European. If I acted, however, in the context of official mandates, I always carefully watched over their drafting. And if I had at my disposal administrative machinery, I limited its size or I only managed that part which was useful to a direct course of action.
>
> It is a lot to ask most minds only to imagine something never seen and to accept the risk for it.
>
> Jean Monnet, *Mémoires*

Prenegotiation is "the span of time and activity in which the parties move from conflicting unilateral solutions for a mutual problem to a joint search for cooperative multilateral or joint solutions."[1] Clearly the EMU preparatory work, dating back to the Delors Committee, was in a more advanced state than that of political union. Nevertheless, the Dublin European Council's decision in June to call a second IGC, to run parallel to the first, indicated that discussions would commence in earnest that summer to "clarify ideas" and to make decisions on the organization of the two IGCs prior to the start of negotiations on 14 December 1990.[2]

---

[1] I. William Zartman, "Prenegotiation: Phases and Functions," in *Getting to the Table*, ed. Janice Gross Stein (Baltimore and London: The Johns Hopkins University Press, 1989), 4.

[2] The two intergovernmental conferences actually opened on 15 December in Rome.

This chapter considers the working methods of the prenegotiation and Franco-German inputs into its agenda. An overview of the dominant issues which emerged on EMU and political union follows. The three approaches in this volume are then used to analyze the prenegotiation.

ORGANIZATION AND WORKING METHODS
This section gives an outline of the organization and working methods of each IGC prenegotiation under the Irish (January-June 1990) and Italian (July-December 1990) Presidencies.

EMU
Throughout 1990 the finance ministers' personal representatives usually met two times a month to discuss issues related to EMU. These representatives also sat on the Monetary Committee. This helped to assure the continuity of the prenegotiation process at the official level because the Committee submitted key analytical documents to the IGC. The finance ministers met about once a month at the margins of the ECOFIN Council to consider the outstanding issues not resolved at the official level. The heads of state and government met four times as the European Council in 1990 to set the overall guidelines for the prenegotiation: Dublin I (28 April 1990); Dublin II (25–26 June 1990); Rome I (27–28 October 1990); Rome II (14–15 December 1990).

One distinctive feature shaped external negotiations on EMU.[3] Negotiations were essentially structured by the tabling of two main sets of papers during the prenegotiation: the Communication of the Commission of 21 August 1990 and, incorporating the conclusions of the Rome I European Council in October, its "Draft treaty amending the Treaty establishing the European Economic Community with a view to achieving economic and monetary union" of December; and the draft statute for the European System of Central Banks, presented by the Committee of Central Bank Governors.[4]

---

[3] External negotiations are defined as the discussions at different levels in the Council. These negotiations are always viewed in relation to internal , or domestic, bargaining to build a consensus in the formulation of national positions on key issues. Roger Fisher, "Negotiating Inside Out: What are the Best Ways to Relate Internal Negotiations with External Ones?," in *Negotiation Theory and Practice*, eds. J. William Breslin and Jeffrey Z. Rubin (Cambridge: The Program on Negotiation at Harvard Law School, 1991), 71–79.

[4] Dyson, *Elusive Union*, 146; Commission of the European Communities, *Intergovernmental Conferences: Contributions by the Commission* (Luxembourg: Office for Official Publications of the European Communities, 1991), 5–62; Committee of Governors of the Central Banks of the Member States of the European Economic Community, *Draft Statute of the European System of Central Banks and of the European Central Bank* (Basel, 27 November 1990).

During the Irish Presidency, the finance ministers' personal representatives were already at work shaping an agenda that brought domestic forces on board. Discussions were as much "a process of finding a solution that is supportable as of finding support for an ideal solution."[5] Under the Italian Presidency, in the second half of 1990, the momentum of the EMU prenegotiation grew as the member states considered contributions by the Commission and the Monetary Committee. In terms of the organization of the work on the two IGCs, Rome I adopted a pragmatic approach. The national governments chose the members of their delegations to the IGCs and the European Commission was invited to participate and to name its own representative. The necessary coherence between the two conferences would be assured by the foreign ministers assisted by their personal representatives. These representatives also participated in the work of the EMU conference. The coherence and the parallelism of the two conferences were also assured by the European Commission President and by the successive Presidencies of the Council. The European Parliament was associated with the IGCs' work through a series of interinstitutional meetings throughout 1991.[6]

Political Union
In early 1990, the rapid pace of changes in East and West Germany, and in the eastern part of the Continent, focused public attention and diplomatic and political discussions at the highest levels on political union.[7] The main task of the Irish Presidency during the first half of 1990 was to facilitate and organize

---

[5] Zartman, "Prenegotiation: Phases and Functions," 11.

[6] The coherence of the work on the two IGCs was not totally satisfactory with regard to parallelism between EMU and political union. The finance ministers would show some reluctance to allow the foreign ministers to deal with changes regarding issues particularly difficult to negotiate. Yves Doutriaux, *Le Traité sur l'Union Européenne* (Paris: Armand Colin, 1992), 37. On institutional matters, however, there would be a good debate, linking the two conferences, on the powers of the European Parliament in both EMU and political union. This would occur later in the negotiations under the Dutch Presidency. Interview, Dutch Permanent Representation to the European Communities, 23 November 1992.

[7] Peter Ludlow, "The First Phase: January-April 1990," in *The Annual Review of European Community Affairs 1991*, eds. Peter Ludlow, Jørgen Mortensen and Jacques Pelkmans (London: Brassey's, 1992), 396.

discussions on political union as the agenda for a second IGC took shape. Prior to calling a second IGC, Thatcher suggested that the foreign affairs ministers clarify the issues to be dealt with in the context of political union. The decision of Dublin I to involve the foreign ministers in the preparations for political union strengthened the tendency toward an incrementalist strategy. The Action Committee for Europe had suggested the creation of a special group of "wise men" to prepare the agenda for the second IGC. The European Council decided, however, that both preparations and negotiations were to be kept firmly in the hands of the General Affairs Council, assisted by COREPER and the Political Committee, and serviced by the Council Secretariat.[8]

On the basis of work done at the official level, the foreign ministers were responsible to decide on the general orientation of further discussions. This was the task of an informal meeting of the General Affairs Council in Parknasilla, Ireland, on 18–19 May. This meeting illustrated the need for an incremental approach to treaty reform in part to stick as closely as possible to the rule of consensus among the Twelve.[9] It was also important because the foreign ministers introduced their personal representatives who would henceforth be responsible for discussions on treaty reform. Most of the personal representatives were also the member states' permanent representatives to the Community institutions, known as the ambassadors in COREPER. A significant exception was Pierre de Boissieu, who headed the economic affairs division in the Quai d'Orsay. As Dumas' personal representative, de Boissieu would emerge as a dominant figure at the official level.[10]

Immediately after the foreign ministers' meeting the Presidency carefully worked out a note to serve as the basis of their contribution to the debate during Dublin II. This note, which was pragmatic, aimed to achieve consensus positions. Thus, it represented the least common denominator among the Twelve. In contrast, the personal representatives, who met for the first time on 6 June, envisaged a different approach to discussions on political union. Their work represented an exercise in taking stock of ideas, or a presentation of positions that was not based on consensus.[11]

By mid-June, the personal representatives and their foreign ministers agreed on a more elaborate version of their paper which was submitted to the European Council during its meeting on 25–26 June. Its four-part structure set the general framework for the prenegotiation under the Italian Presidency: the overall objectives of political union (scope, institutions, general principles);

---

[8] Ibid., 406.

[9] Ludlow, "Political Union and the Future of NATO: May-July 1990," in *The Annual Review of European Community Affairs 1991*, 413–414.

[10] Ibid., 414.

[11] Cloos, Reinesch, Vignes et Weyland, *Le Traité de Maastricht*, 56.

democratic legitimacy; efficiency and effectiveness of the Community and its institutions; and the unity and coherence of the Community's international action.[12]

The different national delegations, plus the European Commission and Parliament, used the time until Rome I in October to clarify and present their ideas on political union.[13] The personal representatives organized their work around the four themes of their June paper for Dublin II.[14] The Italian Presidency, aided by the Council Secretariat, used the "coloratura principle" to assemble various contributions by national governments in a creative manner to promote consensus.[15]

It was primarily on the basis of the report drawn up by the personal representatives, reviewed by the foreign ministers during their meeting on 22 October, that Rome I evaluated progress made on political union. Thatcher insisted on a series of footnotes which the Italian Presidency inserted in its "Conclusions." These footnotes stated that the British delegation preferred not "to judge in advance the debate to occur during the intergovernmental conference" in several areas: legislative powers for the European Parliament; European citizenship; and the common foreign and security policy (CFSP). British opposition served as a point of crystallization for the Eleven to advance the prenegotiation.[16]

After Rome I the personal representatives intensified their work on a number of precise questions. The Council Secretariat assisted in this effort by its circulation of "questionnaires," in which national delegations were asked to outline their positions on issues relevant to the prenegotiation. In addition, a group of advisers, working at the various national permanent representations of the member states to the Communities, had recently begun their work as the "Friends of the Presidency." The input of this group was helpful as the personal representatives and the European Commission President began to

---

[12]Ludlow, "Political Union and the Future of NATO," 414.

[13]This section draws in part on Cloos, Reinesch, Vignes et Weyland, *Le Traité de Maastricht*, 59–69.

[14]Ludlow, "Launching the IGCs: July–December 1990," in *The Annual Review of European Community Affairs 1991*, 430–431.

[15]The "coloratura principle" refers to a genius for improvisation and creative ingenuity to promote consensus.

[16]Cloos, Reinesch, Vignes et Weyland, *Le Traité de Maastricht*, 63. In Rome the United Kingdom played the role of a "footnote state." In 1985, during negotiations on the Single European Act, Denmark, Greece and Ireland played a similar role. Each state objected to many of the provisions in the treaty text by asking the Luxembourg Presidency to insert footnotes at the bottom of its pages.

sketch the contours of a future draft treaty.[17]

On 30 November, the Presidency's summary of "the outcome of the proceedings of the personal representatives and the ministers of foreign affairs" was completed. This document was the work of the Council Secretariat under the direction of its Secretary General, Niels Ersbøll. It was adopted without amendment by the ministers of foreign affairs and was taken as the basic text on the IGC agenda by Rome II.[18] In its work, the Italian Presidency sought not only to emphasize key issues but to orient the future negotiations by identifying the positions of minority delegations.[19]

FRANCO-GERMAN INPUTS

This section highlights the influence of bilateral cooperation between France and Germany into multilateral talks on EMU and political union during the prenegotiation.

EMU

One instance of Franco-German cooperation during the prenegotiation involved the stages of transition. This issue illustrates that France and Germany took joint positions on EMU while considering the requirements of their respective domestic interests. During an informal meeting of the ECOFIN Council on 7–8 September in Rome, the transition to Stage Two of EMU emerged as the dominant issue. France, Italy, Belgium, Luxembourg and Denmark supported the Commission's proposal to begin Stage Two on 1 January 1993. Spain advocated 1 January 1994 as the starting date and argued for a Stage Two of longer duration. Germany, the Netherlands, Great Britain, Greece, Ireland and Portugal did not want to set a date to start Stage Two.[20]

The resolution of this difference of views began to emerge soon after the ECOFIN Council meeting. At the 56th Franco-German summit in Munich ten days later the German Foreign Minister released the text of a letter to his French colleague. Genscher assured Dumas that the Chancellor and the Bonn government favored beginning Stage Two on 1 January 1993.[21] This date was favored by both Mitterrand and Kohl. In their initial joint letter to the Irish Presidency of the Council, dated 18 April 1990, both leaders affirmed their belief that Maastricht should enter into force by this same date of 1 January 1993. Their goal was to keep the momentum of the integration process going by fixing a date to begin the implementation of the Maastricht Treaty and Stage Two of EMU.

---

[17]Interview, Jim Cloos, Permanent Representation of Luxembourg to the European Communities, 23 November 1992.

[18]Ludlow, "Launching the IGCs: July-December 1990," 441.

[19]Doutriaux, *Le Traité sur l'Union Européenn*, 47.

[20]Wilhelm Schönfelder/Elke Thiel, *Ein Markt—eine Währung* (Baden-Baden: Nomos, 1994), 101.

[21]Ludlow, Launching the IGCs: July-December 1990," 425.

Within the German government, however, there was a divergence of viewpoints. Genscher and the State Minister for European affairs in the *Auswärtiges Amt*, Irmgard Adam-Schwaetzer, had spoken out publicly for a starting date of 1 January 1993 for Stage Two. The federal ministries of finance and economics did not rule out 1 January 1994 provided certain convergence criteria were met. In some respects, this was a German fallback position in the event that a date had to be set. The Bundesbank wanted no set date to be fixed.[22] In response to domestic pressure, Chancellor Kohl adopted, in the weeks prior to Rome I, a compromise proposal of 1 January 1994.[23] This proposal was put forward by Spain with the backing of France and Germany. Kohl emphasized the importance of a political deadline in the matter as in so many other significant issues in Community affairs.

Throughout the prenegotiation, France and Germany strove to establish joint positions on other crucial issues like the requirement to make national central banks independent prior to Stage Three, no financing of budget deficits by member governments and the need for real progress on convergence in order for member states to enter into Stage Two. These points were all emphasized in the Conclusions of the Rome I European Council.

Political Union

The idea to convene an IGC on political union gathered momentum in early 1990 owing to the support of the European Parliament and the Belgian delegation, which issued a memorandum to its Community partners on 20 March. The Belgian Memorandum left open the question of whether a second IGC should be convened, or if issues of political union should be treated, with those on EMU, in one conference. Its major contribution was to structure, in a clearer fashion, most of the basic ideas about political union. This initiative left the door open for the Franco-German tandem to play once again its role as the "motor for Europe."[24]

Kohl and Mitterrand met four times between January and May.[25] The prospect of German unification, and the changes this would introduce in

---

[22]Schönfelder/Thiel, *Ein Markt—eine Währung*, 104.

[23]In one account of the EMU negotiations, written by a participant working for the Commission, the Dutch Finance Minister, Wim Kok, is credited for tabling the compromise proposal of 1 January 1994. Alexander Italianer, "Mastering Maastricht: EMU Issues and How They Were Settled," in *Economic and Monetary Union: Implications for National Policy Makers*, ed. Klaus Gretschman (Maastricht: European Institute of Public Administration, 1993), 64.

[24]Cloos, Reinesch, Vignes et Weyland, *Le Traité de Maastricht*, 52.

[25]Ludlow, "The First Phase: January–April 1990," 402.

economic and political relations among states on the Continent, called for a solid bilateral initiative in favor of strengthening the multilateral context of Community action. The first Kohl-Mitterrand letter, dated 19 April, stated the objectives of a second IGC: the reduction in the democratic deficit, more efficient institutions, unity and coherence between the actions of the Twelve in the economic, monetary and political field, and last but not least, the development of a common foreign and security policy (CFSP).[26]

The Franco-German initiative tilted the balance in favor of those who wanted to extend treaty reform to other areas besides EMU. Thatcher was reluctant to support this initiative. Yet, she knew from her experience in 1985 that an IGC could be convened by a simple majority. During Dublin I Thatcher defined the contours of what Britain would be willing to accept on political union. First, political union should not call national identities into question. National parliaments should not be abolished and there should be no renunciation of national legal systems. Second, power should not be centralized to benefit the EC institutions. Third, the role of NATO should not be weakened. Finally, there should be no restrictions on the right of member states to direct foreign policy in the domestic context.[27]

Within the General Affairs Council, the forum where the foreign ministers had to discuss options on political union, "personal considerations and political empathy are as important as in the European Council." Genscher and Dumas got along "famously and personified the Franco-German axis at the level immediately below that of Kohl and Mitterrand."[28] The foreign ministers' excellent rapport contributed to the teamwork on issues of political union like CFSP and helped smooth over the rough areas where the two states did not always agree.

The second Kohl-Mitterrand letter, dated 6 December 1990, was the most specific one to set an overall agenda for political union. The CFSP was a key issue mentioned in that letter along with the role of the European Council. In spite of their joint letters, however, there were as many divergences between France and Germany on political union as convergence of interests. The emergence of a Franco-German strategy via-à-vis the other member states and the Community institutions was most evident on the issue of CFSP. On other issues, like a more prominent role for the European Council and creating a European citizenship, a Franco-German accord also existed. However, the two countries emphasized different aspects of democratic legitimacy, which led Germany to favor increased powers for the European Parliament as well as an increased role for the regions in Europe.

---

[26]Laursen, Vanhoonacker and Wester, "Overview of the Negotiations," in *The Intergovernmental Conference on Political Union*, 5–6.

[27]Cloos, Reinesch, Vignes et Weyland, *Le Traité de Maastricht*, 54.

[28]Desmond Dinan, *An Ever Closer Union?* (Boulder: Lynne Rienner, 1994), 248.

EMU ISSUES
This section outlines five issues which came up during the EMU prenegotiation throughout 1990. These issues are: the costs of EMU; economic coordination; the independence of the European Central Bank; budgetary discipline; and the stages of transition.

Costs of EMU
The Commission's paper, dated 20 March 1990, analyzed the costs and benefits of EMU, with emphasis on Europe's potential to coordinate macroeconomic policy with the United States and Japan and on the need for a strong ECU as a stable currency anchor to facilitate the economic exchange between Western and Eastern Europe. The paper also remarked very positively on the advantages of a single European currency and emphasized that the institutions and economic requirements for EMU, to be specified in the Treaty, should be established so that the new currency would be a stable one. Further discussions and negotiations were required, however, in order to reach a consensus on this point.[29]

The informal meeting of the ECOFIN Council from 31 March–1 April at Ashford Castle indicated the resolve of the Eleven to push forward with EMU despite the British reserve. A difference of tactics, if not strategy, between Thatcher and the Chancellor of the Exchequer, John Major, on how to approach EMU was also apparent. Thatcher was determined to resist any forward motion; Major wanted to participate constructively in Treaty negotiations with the aim of securing an "opt-in" to allow governments the choice about if, and when, to join EMU.[30]

The European Commission addressed the costs of EMU in its own study, titled *One Market, One Money*, published in Fall 1990. Its basic argument was a persuasive one that influenced key decision makers: the costs of EMU would be heaviest in the early stages. The main benefits, like the elimination of exchange transaction costs, would follow, in the last stage after the introduction of a single currency.[31] Other benefits of a single currency were, in the Commission's view, linked to the emergence of the ECU as a major world currency.

Economic Coordination
On the issue of a centralized economic policy as a counterweight to the strong independence of the ECB, a proposal favored by France, the Commission expressed important reservations. In order for such a policy to work, a political union with a strong European Parliament and a strong central government would be necessary. There was little support for this idea among the member states. Moreover, the establishment of a strong "economic

---

[29]Schönfelder/Thiel, *Ein Markt—eine Währung*, 77.
[30]Dyson, *Elusive Union*, 139.
[31]Ibid.

government" at the European level was contrary to the subsidiarity principle and ignored the historical and structural diversity among the member states. The Commission paper of 20 March did try to steer a middle course by making the proposal that the responsibility for economic and financial policy should remain with the member states but that competencies for coordination should be delegated to the Community institutions. Here the need remained to clarify issues like the extent to which the coordination should be binding on the member states and the way in which competencies for coordination tasks should be divided among the EC institutions.[32]

A significant result at Ashford Castle was the decision by ECOFIN to strengthen policy coordination procedures as the member states prepared for the beginning of Stage One in July 1990. The Committee of Central Bank Governors increased its efforts to develop its role as a Community level institution. In practical terms, this meant a more effective monitoring of national monetary policies, for example. In addition, the Committee aimed for a more visible public profile with the submission of reports to the European Parliament and the European Council.[33] Earlier, in December 1989, the Committee had agreed on a number of concrete steps designed to transform itself into the forerunner of the ESCB, to assure that it played an independent and assertive role in the EMU policy process and to coordinate monetary targets in the name of price stability. At the German level, Pöhl worked to influence the evolution of the Committee and to use its subsequent role to promote the policy interests of his institution on the road to EMU.[34]

In its basic document of 21 August, the Commission, like the Monetary Committee, did not allow any place for the General Affairs Council, COREPER or the Council Secretariat in the economic policy coordination of the Community. Instead, the European Council would "be concerned with the overall coherence of the Community economic and monetary policy." The Commission's document also proposed that ECOFIN's responsibilities should be significantly widened to include deepened multilateral surveillance exercises and major decisions concerning exchange-rate policy. In addition, the Commission sought a central role as an institution in areas like multilateral surveillance and in drawing up recommendations for economic policy.[35]

Independence of ECB
In its paper of 20 March, the Commission spoke out in favor of a federal European System of Central Banks committed to price stability and to a "high

---

[32]Schönfelder/Thiel, *Ein Markt—eine Währung*, 78–79.

[33]Dyson, *Elusive Union*, 140.

[34]Ibid.

[35]Ludlow, "Launching the IGCs: July-December 1990," 424.

degree" of independence from national governments and European institutions. Likewise the Commission argued that as a counterweight to its independence, the EuroFed should also have a democratic responsibility for its actions. The wording of the paper struck the Germans as somewhat strange, indicating that a difference of view still existed regarding the meaning of independence of monetary policy. For example, the Commission paper stated: "The Community monetary institution will also need to be democratically accountable for its actions. This is a necessary complement to its independence in order to make its policies acceptable to the public at large." In practical terms, the Commission wanted the EuroFed to hold hearings on its activities before the European Parliament.[36]

Budgetary Discipline

One of the main issues raised in the Monetary Committee's report of 23 March was budgetary discipline. The report proposed that three principles regarding budgetary discipline should be incorporated in the Treaty: (1) no monetary financing of public deficits or market privileges for public authorities; (2) no bailing-out of member states which had run into budgetary difficulties; (3) excessive deficits should be corrected even if there was no monetary financing, and their avoidance should become "a key principle of EMU."[37] Only the third principle brought out different viewpoints among the member states. For example, the question of defining what constituted an "excessive" budgetary deficit came up. The possibility that the Council could be legally empowered to decide by qualified majority vote that a given deficit was "excessive" was considered by the Eleven with only the British dissenting. The type of sanctions to be exercised against member states was also subject to some disagreement among the Twelve.[38]

Stages of Transition

The Monetary Committee's submission of its report, "Economic and monetary union beyond stage one—orientations for the preparations of the intergovernmental conference" to the ECOFIN Council on 23 July 1990[39] was an important turning point in the EMU prenegotiation. This report was thought of as a comprehensive preparatory document for the IGC and, from the German standpoint, was considered as a constructive basis for further discussions.[40] A critical point of the report dealt with the rules of the transition phase. The Monetary Committee spoke out in favor of a transitory Stage Two. Member states entry into this stage had to be dependent on the fulfillment of

---

[36]Schönfelder/Thiel, *Ein Markt—eine Währung*, 79–80.

[37]Ludlow, "The First Phase: January-April 1990," 397.

[38]Ibid., 397–398.

[39]Cloos, Reinesch, Vignes et Weyland, *Le Traité de Maastricht*, 41.

[40]Schönfelder/Thiel, *Ein Markt—eine Währung*, 96.

objective criteria.[41] If these criteria were met, then Stage Two could be relatively short. If not, then the transition to Stage Three would be delayed. This proposal raised a political dilemma: it was hardly feasible, given the dynamic nature of the integration process, for the Twelve to wait until a day, far in the future, when all Community member states fulfilled the convergence criteria before starting Stage Two. Instead it was wiser to allow all member states to work toward improving their chances of fulfilling the criteria while in Stage Two. The question of a two-speed Europe could then be posed upon entry into Stage Three depending on the number of member states ready to participate in EMU.[42]

In its Communication of 21 August, the Commission set out a timetable for EMU and the type of decision making to achieve the transition to Stage Three. The Commission proposed 1 January 1993 as the date to begin Stage Two. It also advocated a short transitional stage with a "substantial content." The Commission argued that the creation of a central monetary institution and its governing bodies before it takes up its full powers was in line with "the thinking and practice of the Rome and Paris Treaties." One of its main objectives was for the institution to create a climate of confidence among its members before it enters into full operation.[43] The Bundesbank and the federal ministry of finance thought differently. From a psychological standpoint, a monetary institution that did not have full operational responsibilities would give a weak signal to public opinion.[44]

The Commission also proposed that the transition to Stage Three should occur as a result of a decision by the European Council. This issue posed a problem to the extent that some member states saw the possibility of the European Council deciding on entry into Stage Three without making this final transition dependent on clearly defined convergence criteria written in the Treaty.[45]

The most significant results of the Rome I European Council dealt with the political decision to begin Stage Two of EMU on 1 January 1994, following the completion of the internal market and the national ratification

---

[41]These objective criteria included a high degree of price stability, budgetary discipline (no monetary financing of state debts and no excessive deficits), currency participation in the close bands of the EMS, a positive evaluation of economic convergence and the completion of the internal market including the transposition of directives into national law.

[42]Schönfelder/Thiel, *Ein Markt—eine Währung*, 97.

[43]Commission of the European Communities, *Intergovernmental Conferences*, 36.

[44]Interview, Günter Grosche, Federal Ministry of Finance, 26 April 1993.

[45]Schönfelder/Thiel, *Ein Markt—eine Währung*, 98.

procedures of the Treaty on European Union. Rome I emphasized the following points, which, in turn, influenced the future course of negotiations on EMU:

- a market-based economic union combining price stability with growth, employment and environmental protection and dedicated to sound financial and budgetary positions and economic and social cohesion. To achieve this goal the scope of action of the Community institutions would be reinforced;

- a monetary union with a new, independent[46] monetary institution responsible for a single monetary policy based on a single currency with price stability as the primary objective;

- the start of Stage Two on 1 January 1994 and the obligation on the part of member states before that date to have the largest possible participation of their currencies in the ERM, to start a process leading to the independence of their national central banks, to prohibit monetary financing and not to assume responsibility for each other's debts;

- during Stage Two, the obligation of the new monetary institution to reinforce the coordination of monetary policies, to prepare for the single monetary policy and to supervise the development of the ECU;

- within three years after the start of Stage Two, the Commission and the Council of the new monetary institution would report to the ECOFIN and the General Affairs Council on the implementation of Stage Two and on the progress made in the area of convergence in order to make a decision on the start of Stage Three, which should begin within a reasonable time thereafter. The General Affairs Council would submit the dossier to the European Council for a decision;

---

[46]There is a subtle difference between the words "autonomous" and "independent" when talking about the introduction of a new monetary institution. Autonomy suggests the possibility, however slight, of government influence on the monetary institution. In this sense, no central bank is ever totally independent of government influence as the case of the Bundesbank during German unification illustrates. Interview, Jean-Victor Louis, National Bank of Belgium, 1 July 1992.

In the EMU context, the German delegation did consider the notion of autonomy as a relevant one to describe the status of the European Central Bank during Stage Three. The essential point for the Germans is that the ECB retains a say in the determination of exchange rate policy. Interview, Günter Grosche, Federal Ministry of Finance, 26 April 1993.

- the possibility of derogations both in Stage Two and Stage Three for those member states in need of more time to fulfill certain criteria.[47]

Chancellor Kohl, in order to satisfy the requirements of the Bundesbank and the ministry of finance, made sure the provision was included that "...in order to enter Stage Two other satisfactory and durable progress toward real and monetary convergence, in particular price stability and the consolidation of public finances, should have been made."[48] Immediately after Rome I, different interpretations among the member states arose regarding the need for further lasting and satisfactory progress toward convergence prior to the start of Stage Two. Some member states interpreted this as implying a conditional, as opposed to an unconditional, start of Stage Two, depending on further achievements in the field of convergence.[49] A second difference of interpretation, particularly significant from the German viewpoint, involved the question of whether the "new institution for Stage Two" should be the European Central Bank or another institution.[50]

After Rome I two other documents were completed. The first dealt with the statutes of the European System of Central Banks and the ECB as proposed by the central bank governors. The principal features of the draft embodied price stability, independence and a federal structure. The second document included the Commission's proposals of 21 August. These were translated into a draft treaty, which, in turn, was the initial text for negotiations on EMU.

ISSUES OF POLITICAL UNION
After Dublin I, the discussions to shape an agenda for political union were entrusted to two permanent EC committees: COREPER and the Political Committee.[51] The purpose of work at this level was to outline options for the foreign ministers. In addition to recommendations on ways to foster democratic legitimacy, institutional efficiency and coherence of external action, general objectives of political union were also raised.

---

[47]Cloos, Reinesch, Vignes et Weyland, *Le Traité de Maastricht*, 41–43.

[48]Dyson, *Elusive Union*, 145.

[49]Italianer, "Mastering Maastricht," 64.

[50]Schönfelder/Thiel, *Ein Markt—eine Währung,* 107.

[51]The Political Committee is comprised of senior officials from national foreign ministries who prepare the agenda for their ministers in the area of European Political Cooperation or, in the aftermath of the Maastricht Treaty, CFSP. Their role in the Maastricht process was taken on by the personal representatives in May 1990.

OBJECTIVES OF POLITICAL UNION

The overall objectives of political union included proposals to enlarge the scope of the Community's competencies to areas like social policy, the environment, culture, education, consumer protection and telecommunications. Institutional questions also came up, especially the role of the European Council, and the idea to introduce a European citizenship. For the first time, the issue was raised whether to integrate areas of intergovernmental cooperation, like judicial and police cooperation, within the Union.[52]

The prenegotiation revealed this chapter of political union to be an open-ended one. By the time of the Presidency's summary of 30 November the list of new subjects to be considered as Community competencies was still growing. On subsidiarity, there was general agreement on the need to include the principle in the Treaty. Most of the member states insisted, however, that the *acquis communautaire* should not be called into question, that the subsidiarity principle should not encourage a "government by judges" and that the effectiveness of the Community decision-making process should not be reduced.[53]

Democratic Legitimacy

Issues pertaining to democratic legitimacy were grouped into three main areas: increased powers for the European Parliament and more democratic control exercised by the European and national parliaments; reinforcing the democratic nature of the Community institutions; and improvements in the position of the individual citizen. The Danish delegation, for example, proposed the establishment of a Community ombudsman under the auspices of the European Parliament to address citizens' concerns.

By December 1990 there was support among the member states for an extension of the existing cooperation procedure, but less enthusiasm for the German proposal to introduce a co-decision procedure between Council and Parliament in the making of Community legislation. There were also proposals made to create a body to represent regional and sectoral interests.

Efficiency

On efficiency, the personal representatives discussed an enhanced role for the European Council, a stronger Presidency system, wider use of qualified majority voting and a more effective coordination function for their foreign ministers in the General Affairs Council.

The Presidency's 30 November paper spoke of efficiency of the Community institutions and actions in terms of the role of the European Council in general, the type-classification of Community acts, and a

---

[52]Cloos, Reinesch, Vignes et Weyland, *Le Traité de Maastricht*, 55–56.

[53]Ludlow, "Launching the IGCs: July–December 1990," 442.

strengthening of the powers of the Court of Justice and the Court of Auditors with a view to assuring better implementation of Community decisions and laws.[54]

External Action/CFSP
The clearest advances were made in this area. These were motivated in turn by events taking place in the external environment as a result of the Iraqi invasion of Kuwait in August. Among the issues discussed in the CFSP context were widening the scope of the debate to include a common defense policy, the possibility of establishing links between the EC and the Western European Union (WEU) and the launching of what subsequently became known as the concept of "joint action." Possible areas that would be appropriate for "joint action," the so-called Asolo list,[55] included disarmament negotiations and confidence-building measures in the CSCE framework, EC involvement in UN peace-keeping operations and transatlantic relations.[56]

The Presidency's paper of 30 November set the agenda for negotiations on CFSP. The paper illustrated that the Presidency had been able to register "a broad majority approach" on several important points: the purpose of the Union was to deal with all aspects of foreign and security policy; there would be a single decision-making body, the Council, with jurisdiction over all aspects of foreign policy with preparations harmonized where possible; the Commission would have a greater role and a non-exclusive right of initiative; the EPC Secretariat would be enlarged and integrated into the Council Secretariat, while maintaining a specific nature reflecting its functions.[57]

INTERPRETING THE MAASTRICHT PRENEGOTIATION: THREE APPROACHES TO THE IGC PROCESS
Putnam's Two-Level Games
This approach highlights the relevance of French and German domestic institutions, as well as Mitterrand and Kohl's strategies at the European level, to the formulation of win-sets. The domestic level preferences and coalitions of French and German politico-administrative hybrids and civil servants are dealt with under Aberbach, Putnam and Rockman's four images of civil servants. The differences between the new breed of actor this study identifies as the Image IV hybrid and the other civil servants working on Maastricht are then highlighted in view of their respective inputs into internal bargaining and external negotiations throughout the IGC process.

---

[54]Ibid., 442–443.

[55]The Asolo list bears the name of the town near Venice where the EC foreign ministers met for informal talks on security issues on 6 October 1990.

[56]Ludlow, "Launching the IGCs: July-December 1990," 431.

[57]Ibid., 443–444.

Domestic Institutions

Two-level games allow for an emphasis on alliances among actors at the domestic level (Elysée and Quai d'Orsay; Chancellor's Office and *Auswärtiges Amt*; federal ministry of finance and Bundesbank; federal ministry of economics and Bundesrat), but does not consider the role of additional sub-national levels (Länder) in the formulation of strategy or the need to adopt certain tactics to achieve diplomatic and domestic goals. An equally important point which Putnam's approach brings out is the relative lack of transnational alliances on political union and the lesser degree of transnational activity overall compared with that prevalent during negotiations leading up to the Single European Act. Thus, the reader has a means of comparison to judge the extent to which Maastricht was a closed process of transgovernmental elite communication.

French Institutions

In the Vth Republic, the institutions and the political process assure that the President remains atop the pyramid in the formulation and direction of French diplomacy.[58] Christian Lequesne asserts that after Mitterrand's re-election as French President in May 1988, his autonomy in Community affairs was preeminent.[59] He also explains that the negotiation of the Maastricht Treaty, considered a "*sujet présidentiel*" because of its Franco- German dimension, was supervised closely by the Elysée from December 1990-February 1992.[60] In diplomatic affairs, Mitterrand's right to speak for the sovereign interests of the French people rests on a conception of "order" which dates back to Bodin.[61] As de Gaulle once wrote: "The function of the state consists in both assuring the success of order over anarchy and reforming that which is no

---

[58]The rational for the institutional set-up of the Vth Republic is provided by General de Gaulle in his *Mémoires d'Espoir* (Paris: Plon, 1970), 7–40; Olivier Duhamel explains the institutional evolution of the Fifth Republic in *Le pouvoir politique en France, droit constitutionnel, 1* (Paris: PUF, 1991), 5–46.

[59]Christian Lequesne, *L'appareil politico-administratif de la France et la Communauté Européenne Mai 1981-Mai 1991* Thèse de Doctorat (Paris: FNSP, 1992), 357–380. The return of a Gaullist majority in the Parliament, introducing a second period of "*cohabitation*" in March 1993, presented the possibility of shared responsibilities in European Community affairs between President Mitterrand and Prime Minister Balladur.

[60]Lequesne, *Paris-Bruxelles*, 179.

[61]Nannerl O. Keohane, *Philosophy and the State in France* (Princeton: Princeton University Press, 1980), 68.

longer in accordance with the demands of the era."[62] In spite of his own earlier reservations about de Gaulle's extensive use of presidential powers[63] or questions about the syndrome of presidential omniscience,[64] Mitterrand directed French diplomacy at Maastricht without any internal constraints. His ministers, Dumas in charge of foreign affairs, Guigou responsible for European affairs and Bérégovoy in command of the financial portfolio, were all loyal to Mitterrand. This was especially true of Dumas, one of the President's inner circle of political allies and friends. Gabriel Robin, in his book on French diplomacy during Mitterrand's first term, explains: Roland Dumas is "the President's man as a result of long familiarity; the two men are like intellectual blood brothers."[65]

The traditional powers of the French President in the areas of defense and diplomacy, otherwise known as the *domaine réservé*, are stated in Article 5 of the Constitution of 4 October 1958.[66] These powers are extensive and not subject to parliamentary accountability. Political parties do not play a dominant role in the institutional system of the Vth Republic, a set-up which reflects de Gaulle's distrust of them. In any case, prior to the Maastricht ratification in France, Community issues did not provoke much internal debate among French parties.[67]

Unique among contemporary Western democracies owing to the extent of presidential supremacy in foreign policy, France has been described as *la monarchie nucléaire*.[68] Royal decision making predominates due to a rich heritage of authoritarian thought. In theory, the old image of the king as "the one who sees the whole good of the commonwealth" was "extended by the provision of the best possible counsellors." As Nannerl Keohane writes,

---

[62]Charles de Gaulle, *Lettres, notes et carnets Juillet 1966-Avril 1969* (Paris: Plon, 1987), 265. The translation is the author's.

[63]François Mitterrand, *Le coup d'etat permanent* (Paris: Plon, 1964).

[64]Samy Cohen, "Diplomatie: le syndrome de la présidence omnisciente," *Esprit* 164 (1990): 55–64.

[65]Gabriel Robin, *La Diplomatie de Mitterrand* (Paris: Editions de la Bièvre, 1985), 10.

[66]R. Barrillon, J.M. Bérard, M.H. Bérard, G. Dupuis, A. Grangé Cabane, A.M. Le Bos Le Pourhiet and Y. Mény, *Dictionnaire de la Constitution* (Paris: Cujas, 1986), 162–163.

[67]The 1980s saw the rise of the right-wing Front National on the national political landscape and the decline of the French Communists, after their early success in alliance with the Socialists. The gradual evolution of Socialist party thinking on Europe lagged somewhat behind Mitterrand's own views. Colette Ysmal, *Les parties politiques sous la Ve République* (Paris: Montchrestien, 1989), 119–154.

[68]Samy Cohen, *La monarchie nucléaire* (Paris: Hachette, 1986).

"those who perform this function inevitably share in the king's decision, and leave their impress deep on his commands. But the formal point of decision remains focused in one will; and the monarch's dependence on his counsellors is hidden by the impressive and satisfying fiction that the law is handed down by one benevolent, absolute, superhuman will rather than being the product of negotiation, compromise or conflict."[69]

German Institutions

The legacy of the Nazi period left the Germans distrustful of centralized power. The institutional structure is defined in part by Article 65 of the Basic Law (*Grundgesetz*) which assures that a spirit of cooperation and competition exists among the Chancellor's Office and the federal ministries.[70] This constitutional requirement, and Chancellor Kohl's more relaxed approach to delegating authority in Community policy making, made flexibility in internal bargaining and constant, open channels of communication necessary during the Maastricht process. A further element of decentralized power is the strong position of the Länder in their individual areas of competence like culture, education and health. The Bundesrat, in which the Länder are represented, was dominated by the SPD-Opposition during the entire Maastricht process. This fact, and the constant input of the Länder into the internal bargaining in Bonn, further complicated the formulation of German diplomacy during the prenegotiation.

The Bundestag's strong position in the German political system, owing to the influence of German political parties, made its assent, along with that of the Bundesrat, necessary to any eventual treaty ratification. The Bundestag, led by its newly created EC Committee (*EG-Ausschuß*), demanded more rights for the European Parliament to address the democratic deficit in the Community. The issue of 18 extra seats for German parliamentarians in the European Parliament, to represent the additional population in the Federal Republic as a result of unification, was another requirement the Bundestag called for in order to ratify any eventual treaty. Additional energy and time, both of which were in short supply, were necessary to assure that the Bundestag remained informed about progress of the prenegotiation and that its demands were being adequately taken into account in Brussels. Finally, the Bundesbank, as guardian of price stability in the domestic monetary context, called for progress on political union commensurate with bold steps on EMU.

---

[69]Keohane, *Philosophy and the State in France*, 75. Lequesne emphasizes the point of decisional focus in the will of the President during the March 1983 devaluation of the franc as follows: "...Whatever the determining influence exercised by counsellors at the Elysée and certain members of the "outer" circle, the power to decide among different proposed options returns to the President and to him alone." Lequesne, *L'appareil politico-administratif de la France*, 299–300. The translation is the author's.

[70]Interview, Ursula Seiler-Albring, *Auswärtiges Amt*, 16 April 1993.

The ministry of finance was in overall charge of formulating German diplomacy on EMU. During the prenegotiation Günter Grosche worked closely with officials from the Bundesbank, the Chancellor's Office, the *Auswärtiges Amt* and ministry of economics to define the German interest in EMU. These officials contributed ideas to define German diplomacy in what was a collective effort at the domestic level throughout the negotiations. Together these men made up the so-called "Gang of Five" on EMU.[71] On occasion, Rolf Kaiser from Department 411 in the Federal Chancellor's Office, a member of the "Gang of Five,"was present with finance minister Theo Waigel's personal representative to the EMU conference, State Secretary Horst Köhler, during EMU talks in Brussels. To ensure Länder participation in these talks, representatives from Hamburg and Munich were included in the German delegation during the prenegotiation.

The *Auswärtiges Amt* was in overall charge of formulating German diplomacy on issues of political union. It was concerned about the extent to which the Länder wanted a voice in the integration process.[72] Throughout the negotiations and national ratification, the *Auswärtiges Amt* remained somewhat suspicious of Länder demands.[73] The Länder wanted more voice at the table on specific Community policies. During the prenegotiation, representatives from North-Rhine Westphalia and Baden-Württemberg were included in the German delegation sent to Brussels.

Throughout the IGC's prenegotiation, the Kohl government was obliged to present an account of progress made to the Bundesrat and the Bundestag. After Rome I the representative of the federal government, State Minister for European affairs Adam-Schwaetzer, engaged in a debate with members of the SPD-Opposition in the Bundestag. Among the main topics discussed were the results of the European Council and the state of IGC preparations. On EMU, the emphasis was clearly on an independent central bank to ensure price

---

[71]Interview, Wilhelm Schönfelder, *Auswärtiges Amt*, 6 May 1993. The role of these individuals is discussed in more detail in Chapter IV.

[72]Interview, Bavarian State Representation for Federal and European Community Affairs to the German Federal Government, 18 February 1993.

[73]In fact, the ministry of economics, not the *Auswärtiges Amt*, is in charge of Bund-Länder relations in the daily context of European integration. Throughout the Maastricht process, the Länder sought an ally in Department EB7 of the ministry of economics. This department was created under the direction of Dr. Jürgen Kuhn, during his tenure as Head of the European Division (1987–1993), to deal with Federal-State relations in the aftermath of the Single European Act. Interviews, Dr. Jürgen Kühn and Wilhelm Kaiser, Federal Ministry of Economics, 30 March 1993 and 2 July 1993.

stability in a federal system on the basis of the subsidiarity principle. No financing of budgetary deficits by the central bank was tolerable. What emerged during the debate was a clear consensus on the priority of strengthening the European Parliament in the Community system. In the words of FDP parliamentarian Irmer: "The European Union will be parliamentary and democratic, or there will not be a European Union."[74] Other important issues included a concern for developments in central and eastern Europe and the need for a Community response, the status of 18 extra seats for Germany in the European Parliament as a result of unification, and the increased use of German as a working language in the Community institutions alongside French and English.[75]

Thus, Kohl's constraints outside his coalition government included the SPD-led Bundesrat, the Bundestag and the Bundesbank.[76] Each of these institutional constraints would shape Kohl's IGC diplomacy, although perhaps not to the extent that the actors involved originally envisioned.

Level I Negotiators' Strategies

The French and German styles of negotiation during the Maastricht process provide an interesting study in contrasts. For France a strategy for EMU and political union was evident. Mitterrand sought to accomplish a few specific, priority goals. His strategy, and that of French negotiators working at other levels, was to keep the focus of the talks on these key issues. Kohl had a basic strategy of *Parallelität* which involved a link between EMU and political union. His domestic requirements favored an emphasis on tactical moves at the official level to "manage uncertainty" and "reduce complexity" in the internal bargaining process.[77]

French Strategy

As previously stated, French strategy was defined in the context of a highly centralized institutional set-up which placed Mitterrand in the position of chief protagonist. The French emphasized relatively few agenda items. These were, however, key to the entire Maastricht process: an early and quick transition to EMU; strengthening the role of the European Council with the specific responsibility to define and implement the CFSP including defense issues; establishing a European social policy; introducing a

---

[74]Deutscher Bundestag, 11. Wahlperiode, 233. Sitzung, Bonn, Dienstag, den 30.Oktober 1990, s. 18544.

[75]Ibid., s. 18546.

[76]Interview, Federal Ministry of Economics, 30 March 1993. Within the federal government the interests of the various ministries also influenced Kohl's strategy formulation.

[77]Gilbert R. Winham, "Negotiation as a Management Process," *World Politics* 30 (1977): 93–96.

Congress of Parliaments to involve national legislatures more in the integration process; and, lastly, the creation of a European industrial policy.

Final preparations in Paris for launching the IGCs took place in the second half of 1990. The domestic structure there was set up to deal with a high-pressure weekly routine of negotiations throughout 1991. The negotiators directly involved in the Maastricht process were few. At the political level, there were four: Mitterrand, Dumas, Guigou and Bérégovoy.[78] At the administrative level, Pierre de Boissieu and Jean-Claude Trichet were responsible to communicate progress made during talks in Brussels back to Paris so that internal bargaining positions could be modified. De Boissieu and Trichet were both based in the French capital at their respective ministries. They would return there each week after talks in Brussels. This kept both men out of the "hands" of the European Commission's influence.[79]

The Secretary General at the Quai d'Orsay at the time, François Scheer, explained that de Boissieu would write up résumés of the meetings in Brussels and then circulate them. These memos would form the basis for further discussions among a very limited number of persons.[80] The challenge for de Boissieu was to keep the focus on French goals during early discussions on political union. The difficulty was the open-ended agenda which just kept growing, despite the fact that key topics for discussion were organized by the end of November. De Boissieu pointed out that there were long discussions in Paris on the competencies of the Union, but this was clearly not a French priority. The subsidiarity principle was one which the French quickly understood was essential for the Germans, something which they could not live without. Therefore, the French accepted it as an essential part of the prenegotiation, although they did not quite know what subsidiarity would mean in practice. On democratic legitimacy, Dumas made the case for the idea of a Congress of Parliaments, or Senate, composed both of members of national parliaments and the European Parliament. Dumas and de Boissieu were of one mind on the need to strengthen the input of national parliaments, if need be, at the expense of the European Parliament. De Boissieu also quickly perceived that the proposed Committee of the Regions, to represent regional interests, was a must for the Germans. This, too, was accepted by the French with the knowledge that the Committee's strength would be determined by the quality of its national representatives.

French strategy was at its finest during talks on the efficiency of the institutions. Each level of negotiation was constructively engaged in

---

[78]Lequesne, *Paris-Bruxelles*, 179.

[79]Interview, Quai d'Orsay, 8 March 1993.

[80]Interview, French Permanent Representation to the European Communities, 25 November 1992.

articulating the goal of strengthening the European Council, to which the French President brought the full prestige and weight of his office. On EMU, Bérégovoy argued tirelessly for a *gouvernement économique*. On political union, Dumas would advocate a common foreign and security policy directed by the heads of state and government. Elisabeth Guigou would make the case for the European Council as the necessary organ of political impulse in the Union given its ability to advance Community dossiers as diverse as EMS and the Budgetary Compromise of 1988.

The CFSP dossier enabled French diplomacy to exhibit its special flavor. To some member states, the French recipe for CFSP provided something more than a light touch of sherry in a *bisque de homard*. France again advocated centralized decision making in the Council structure on all aspects of foreign and security policy including defense. The key aspect of this chapter was establishing a link between the Union and WEU, on the one hand, and retaining a role for NATO in an evolving European security environment, on the other.

German Strategy

Kohl's ability to work with different officials in his government, some of whom had a more thorough mastery of the complex details of EMU than he did, in part defined German strategy. The Chancellor had to balance and weigh the *Auswärtiges Amt*'s more liberal negotiating line with that of the ministry of finance's orthodoxy on EMU. His strategy to establish a political union along federal lines reflected his own convictions as much as Länder demands to incorporate the subsidiarity principle in the Treaty, to establish a Committee of the Regions and to ensure that the Länder could negotiate in Brussels on issues within their domestic competence. Kohl's basic strategy was a simple and straightforward one: step-by-step progress on EMU only with substantial achievements on political union. However, his domestic constraints, and the decentralized nature of IGC diplomacy in Bonn, made tactics more likely than strategy in order to accomplish fixed goals.

Kohl's strategy during the Maastricht process was supported by the tacit alliance between the Chancellor's Office and the *Auswärtiges Amt* as promoters of European unity. Civil servants in the *Auswärtiges Amt* kept in close contact with the Chancellor's Office and provided Genscher's personal representative, Ambassador Jürgen Trumpf, with general guidelines on German administrative positions as he negotiated in Brussels. Trumpf, however, was responsible only to Genscher and Kohl.[81] His relations with both political leaders are excellent; Trumpf could count on their support in times of crisis. Moreover, Genscher trusted his personal representative's

---

[81]Interview, *Auswärtiges Amt*, 30 July 1993.

instincts during negotiations on the more sensitive issues like democratic legitimacy.[82] Another advantage in terms of strategy formulation is that Trumpf's negotiating style has been likened to Kohl's in that his sense of timing enables him both to detect potential areas for compromise solutions and to wait until a dossier is mature in order to achieve a desired objective. This was important because Kohl's strategy of *Parallelität* encountered difficulties in the prenegotiation phase when it became clear, early on, that few national delegations supported increased powers for the European Parliament.

Franco-German Strategy

On EMU the acceptance of 1 January 1994 as the date to start Stage Two was a triumph of politicians over technical experts, a demonstration of the European Council's predominance over ECOFIN, and a clear indicator of the strength of the Bonn-Paris-Brussels triangle.[83] As a result of this decision at Rome I, by which the Franco-German tandem and the European Commission aimed to give EMU yet another element of automaticity, the domestic position of Prime Minister Thatcher was no longer tenable. The arrival of John Major would signal a change in style, if not substance, but this was not without significance for Franco-German cooperation during the intergovernmental conferences.[84]

On political union, informal talks among the foreign ministers in Asolo on 6 October revealed that the EC member states were not ready, in the short term, to make a big leap forward. Instead Dumas, supported by Genscher, considered that the content of CFSP should be determined by the European Council "on the basis of common values and interests." These decisions, taken at the highest level, could then be implemented by the ministers on the basis of qualified majority voting. It was agreed that the Commission should receive the right of initiative.[85]

On 6 December, Kohl and Mitterrand sent the second of three letters to the Council Presidency outlining their views on political union. The accent placed by the two leaders on the European Council caused a strong reaction from their Dutch colleague and his foreign minister. The Dutch concern was

---

[82]Interview, German Permanent Representation to the European Communities, 18 May 1992.

[83]Ludlow, "Launching the IGCs: July-December 1990, " 425.

[84]As one British official at the Commission explained, while Major's manner and style seemed less abrasive, it was likely that his bargaining skills could be compared to those of a hard-driving labor negotiator. This would pose even greater problems for the other members of the European Council than those of Thatcher. Interview, John Fitzmaurice, Secretariat General, Commission of the European Communities, 10 May 1992.

[85]Laursen, Vanhoonacker and Wester, "Overview of the Negotiations," 9.

two-fold: at the domestic level, each minister in the Dutch government is responsible for his own portfolio limiting the Prime Minister's power; at the European level, the Dutch saw the European Council as an intergovernmental non-Community organ and, therefore, as a threat to the European Commission. The message was clear: Franco-German cooperation was no substitute for European integration on the basis of strong Community institutions.

Aberbach, Putnam and Rockman's Four Images of Civil Servants

The emphasis on four images of civil servants is essential in the Maastricht context due to the increasing politicization of bureaucratic issues in the European Community. As Helen Wallace points out, "effectiveness" in European Community negotiations "is constrained by the negotiators' domestic level of negotiation."[86] This is because in Brussels the formation of package deals and the coalitions which sustain them are determined by what national institutional systems, legislatures and interest groups will allow. This is especially true of intergovernmental conference negotiations since Article 236 EEC stipulates that amendments to the Paris and Rome Treaties must be ratified by national parliaments. The novelty of Community affairs in the past decade is that the member states have been engaged in almost continuous negotiations on Treaty reform.[87] In other words, the agendas of IGCs are shaped by the on-going dynamics of an evolving European polity and by the domestic requirements of its member states. This fact, and changes in the international system, require national civil servants to operate in a highly fluid political context. At the working level, national civil servants in administrative hierarchies must make complex policy decisions, political in nature, to concretize their leaders' vision.

During the past decade, subtle changes have taken place in the administrative structures of France and Germany as they adapt to the integration process. It is undoubtedly true that, in general, bureaucratic influence still predominates in France whereas the presence of parliamentary and party politicians manifests itself more visibly in the Federal Republic.[88] The changes introduced by the Maastricht process attest to the fact that French and German bureaucrats can no longer content themselves with "efficient problem solving." The calls for referendums on Maastricht in France and

---

[86]Helen Wallace, "Negotiations and Coalition Formation in the European Community," *Government and Opposition* 20 (1985): 459.

[87]Interview, John Fitzmaurice, Secretariat General, Commission of the European Communities, 10 May 1992.

[88]Aberbach, Putnam and Rockman, *Bureaucrats and Politicians in Western Democracies*, 251.

Germany sparked a confrontation between bureaucracy and direct democracy.[89] As Community policies penetrated even further into domestic areas, civil servants were performing increasingly political tasks. The French and German bureaucratic contexts of the Maastricht prenegotiation are a study in contrasts, but each illustrates this phenomenon quite well.

French Civil Servants

The highly centralized nature of the French state, and the politico-administrative tasks of its higher civil service,[90] assured that IGC preparations would remain in the hands of no more than a dozen officials. At the working level, the two civil servants most directly involved were the finance minister's personal representative, Jean-Claude Trichet, aged 48, and Pierre de Boissieu, aged 45.[91] Interestingly, the two men were classmates, graduating from ENA, France's elite school of public administration, as members of the class "Thomas-More" in 1971.[92] Moreover, their participation in preparatory discussions on EMU dated back to 1989 when both men represented France in talks with other high-level civil servants in the Guigou Group. Their long association facilitated ease of communication and information exchange under the high pressure conditions and rigid time constraints of the prenegotiation.[93]

In regular Community affairs, the role of personalities is key at each level of negotiation in the Council. In IGC diplomacy, personalities were of even greater significance at the working level, where the personal representatives meticulously outlined the agendas. In his capacity as Dumas' personal representative, de Boissieu also played an influential role during negotiations on EMU. His remarkable negotiating abilities enabled de Boissieu to make the most of his contributions to issues involving both IGCs. The centrality of his

[89]John T. Rourke, Richard P. Hiskes and Cyrus Ernesto Zirakzadeh, *Direct Democracy and International Politics* (Boulder: Lynne Rienner, 1992).

[90]Suleiman, *Les hauts fonctionnaires et la politique,* 86–148; Quermonne, *L'appareil administratif de l'etat*, 224–249; Ziller, *Administrations comparées*, 321–327.

"CEE: dans l'ombre, les bâtisseurs" *L'Express*, 28 décembre 1990 outlines the roles of de Boissieu and Trichet. However, Jean Vidal, the French Permanent Representative to the European Communities, who is also mentioned in the article, was not as closely involved in domestic bargaining on the IGC negotiations as either of his colleagues.

[92]All background information on French higher officials, ministers and politicians is taken from *Who's Who in France, 1992–1993*. Another member of the class "Thomas-More" was Jean-Louis Bianco who served as Secretary General at the Elysée for ten years until May 1991. Christine Mital, "C'est l'homme le plus puissant de France," *Le nouvel observateur*, 19–25 mai 1994, 90.

[93]Interviews, Quai d'Orsay, 8 March 1993

role at the European and domestic levels, and his direct access to the President, were advantages for the implementation of French diplomacy. De Boissieu is a man of strong will and tremendous energy. He also possesses an innate sense of the weight of French history and the significance of the Gaullist tradition to the Vth Republic. In this sense, de Boissieu is a striking example of the classical nineteenth-century European diplomat confronted with the changes the power of public opinion threaten to bring to the integration process.[94]

De Boissieu's counterpart, Jean-Claude Trichet, also personifies the French higher civil servant, or *grand fonctionnaire*, as defined by Bernard Gournay. As such, Trichet belonged to that distinguished group of men who "work in constant relationship with political personnel and who play an intimate part in the preparation and application of major decisions affecting the nation."[95]

Significantly both Trichet and de Boissieu served as *chef de cabinet* during their respective careers. Trichet was director in the Cabinet of economics and finance minister Edouard Balladur from 1986–87 just prior to his appointment as director of the Trésor. De Boissieu served as director in the cabinet of European Commission Vice-President François-Xavier Ortoli, who was responsible for economic, monetary and financial questions. His post there lasted from 1978–84 after which he returned to the Quai d'Orsay. De Boissieu became director of the powerful economics division at the Quai in 1989.[96] Thus, prior to the Maastricht negotiations, both men obtained valuable experience operating in the grey area between the political and administrative worlds.

In terms of their preferences, it is important to underline the presence of de Boissieu, an ardent Gaullist, as chief negotiator at the official level for a Socialist president. This attests to de Boissieu's skills as a negotiator, through which he displays a remarkable *esprit de synthèse*, and his intimate knowledge of Franco-German relations. It also signalled that there would be a subtle tension between the Elysée and the Quai d'Orsay owing to differences of view within the latter institution. Guigou, a Socialist, with her office in the Quai, did not always agree with the highly Gaullist views of de Boissieu on issues like the extent of powers for the European Parliament.

---

[94] One of the more memorable remarks de Boissieu made during our discussion was "Je suis la France." ("I am France.") This statement reminded me very much of the General's writings, in which de Gaulle identifies himself with France.

[95] Bernard Gournay, "Higher Civil Servants in France," in *European Politics*, eds. Mattei Dogan and Richard Rose (London: Macmillan, 1971), 501.

[96] William Wallace, "Old States and New Circumstances: The International Predicament of Britain, France and Germany," in *Foreign Policy Making in Western Europe*, eds. William Wallace and W.E. Paterson (Great Britain: Saxon House, 1978), 43.

Early in his career as a diplomat, from 1973–77, de Boissieu served as First Secretary at the French Embassy in Bonn. This undoubtedly provided him with the opportunity to consolidate an already influential network of personal contacts through the use of his excellent command of the German language. Interviews with German officials in Bonn and Brussels revealed that de Boissieu is genuinely liked and respected by his colleagues. Moreover, when one speaks with de Boissieu, one is immediately struck by two qualities: his presence, which is commanding and elegant, and his communication skills, which reveal a quick analytic mind. Both qualities stood out given the dominant role of personalities at the official level.

In his work for Balladur, a Gaullist known for centrist policies, Trichet places the interest of the French state above all else. As director of the Trésor at Finance, Trichet worked at a ministry noted for its "interdepartmental vocation." This translates into immense bureaucratic power of a horizontal, not vertical, type which cuts across policy sectors.[97] The higher civil servants at the Quai de Bercy are reputed to be the most competent in France.[98] This is significant in a country which recruits its bureaucratic elite on the basis of highly competitive and rigorous exams.[99]

Trichet's commitment to serve the French state is clearly demonstrated by his dedication to his work.[100] He is noted for his views on the necessity of the policy established during the 1983 currency crisis in France, the *franc fort*.[101] He also negotiated to establish the independence of the *Banque de France* as a prerequisite for EMU. This indicates his belief in the necessity of a monetary policy considerably more independent from political influence than is the tradition in the French state.[102] As a finance ministry official, Trichet was head of the Monetary Committee, which assists the ECOFIN Council with

---

[97] Quermonne, *L'appareil administratif de l'etat*, 77.

[98] Ibid., 78.

[99] Suleiman, *Les élites en France*, 25–93.

[100] Twice the author had interviews scheduled with Trichet but both interviews were postponed. The first interview was scheduled just as Trichet was assisting finance minister Alphandéry during a currency crisis in the EMS. "European System Tying Currencies Faces A Rupture," *New York Times*, 31 July 1993. At the time of the second one, Trichet, *Inspecteur général des finances* since 1989, was preparing to leave his ministerial position to take over as governor of the *Banque de France*. "Europe Picks Money Chief," *New York Times*, 5 October 1993, D16.

[101] "Defenders of a "franc fort," *Financial Times*, 6 January 1994, 2.

[102] Mital, "C'est l'homme le plus puissant de France," *Le nouvel observateur*, 82–90.

currency alignment decisions. This kind of consistent proximity to political power distinguishes Trichet and de Boissieu from other civil servants.

In terms of "policy-style" during the internal bargaining process,[103] it was clear that the politico-administrative elite decided what the general interest was in defining strategy. There would be little, if any, indication of extensive discussions with interest groups over French negotiating positions. A pyramidal authority structure, with the state institutions superimposed upon society, gave a greater margin of maneuver to define strategy, but at the cost of openness. As a result, the French people discovered Maastricht after the Treaty's signature.[104]

Elisabeth Guigou's successor, responsible for European affairs at the Elysée, was Caroline de Margerie, a young woman of 34 with little experience. Described by one participant as a "reserved" individual,[105] de Margerie would play only a limited role in the decision making on Maastricht. This supports the point sometimes made that as Mitterrand's tenure in office lengthened, his desire for experienced counsellors on matters within his *domaine reservé* diminished.[106] This would seem to indicate a deliberate maintenance of the "court politics" atmosphere of a French President, who is partially secluded from the turbulent socio-political environment.[107]

At the Quai d'Orsay, Elisabeth Guigou's *chef de cabinet*, Pierre Vimont, played an important role during internal bargaining, both in terms of relations with the political establishment and the public. Vimont was Guigou's administrative and political right-hand in her varied activities to "educate" the French about Europe.[108] In his explanation of the internal bargaining process, it was clear that Vimont did not make a sharp distinction between administration and policy making. As Cabinet director, he was obliged to keep the political implications of various options in mind while advising his minister.[109] In terms of accountability, Vimont underlined a hierarchical and personal commitment to executive authority, namely, to his own minister and to the French President.

---

[103] Jeremy Richardson, Gunnel Gustafsson and Grant Jordan, "The Concept of Policy Style," in *Policy Styles in Western Europe*, ed. Jeremy Richardson (London: Allen & Unwin, 1982), 1–15.

[104] Lequesne, *Paris-Bruxelles*, 179.

[105] Interview, Quai d'Orsay, 8 March 1993.

[106] Lequesne, *L'appareil politico-administratif de la France*, 377.

[107] Jack Hayward, "Mobilising Private Interests" in *Policy Styles in Western Europe*, 124.

[108] Some examples are found in *Politique etrangère de la France*, novembre-décembre 1991; *Journal Officiel de la République Française*, Débats Parlementaires, Assemblée Nationale, 27 novembre 1991.

[109] Colin S. Campbell, *Governments Under Stress*, 301–302.

Vimont also quite candidly described himself as "de Boissieu's humble servant" during domestic bargaining on Maastricht.[110] Significantly, Guigou's personal links to the Quai d'Orsay were as strong as those to the Elysée. This fostered the tacit alliance that was established during the prenegotiation between the Elysée and the Quai with Guigou continuing to play a pivotal role during both IGCs and the French ratification debate. Her background and training in the French administration enabled Guigou to deal with the technical aspects of dossiers on EMU and political union whereas her experience as Minister for European affairs placed her in the position of direct contact with the people during the French ratification process.

Trichet and de Boissieu, on the other hand were not directly involved in the ratification. Vimont focused on the internal bargaining and domestic ratification but was not directly involved in the external negotiations in Brussels. As Guigou's right-hand, Vimont displayed a sensitivity to the mood of the French people throughout the Maastricht process. At one point during our interview he explained: "In light of the slim margin of approval in the referendum campaign, it was fortunate that French insistence on a pillar structure for the Treaty heeded popular sentiment." The striking aspect of Vimont's remarks though was his demonstration of a high awareness, or public conscience, about France's role in Europe.

In comparative terms, the influence which the *chef de cabinet* can wield has no real equivalent in the German system.[111] No evidence suggests that Vimont used his position to make relations between his minister and the French administration difficult during internal bargaining. On the contrary, he quickly pointed out the dangers of the Cabinet system in France. This is due to the fact that the Cabinet is in a position to serve as a "screen" between the minister and the administration to the detriment of both accountability and coherent policy making.[112]

In her writings on French ministerial staffs, Jeanne Siwek-Pouydesseau states that ministerial Cabinets are simultaneously "the product and the reflection of the French administrative system as a whole." She cites the "system" of ENA as "one of the present factors in their development." Siwek-Pouydesseau goes so far as to maintain that "ENA has trained ministerial assistants and even ministers rather than administrators...since the sons of the good Parisian bourgeoisie have never dreamed of becoming civil servants."[113]

---

[110] Interview, Quai d'Orsay, 8 March 1993.

[111] Ziller, *Administrations comparées*, 324–326.

[112] Interview, Quai d'Orsay, 8 March 1993; R. Barrillon et al., *Dictionnaire de la constitution*, 44–45.

[113] Jeanne Siwek-Pouydesseau, "French Ministerial Staffs," in *The Mandarins of Western Europe*, 208.

The key actors at the official level during internal bargaining throughout 1990 were all educated at ENA. Trained as "superbureaucrats," at least three, de Boissieu, Trichet and Vimont had developed "ministerial" abilities, or an ability to perform on behalf of ministers with ease and effectiveness.[114] Evidence also suggests that de Boissieu was always listened to by his minister, Dumas, although not always by Guigou.[115] De Boissieu also stressed the importance of smooth-flowing communication among the different ministries and the Elysée and Matignon.[116] His role in this regard was to perform the "switchboard" function. This entails the "maintenance of the links of vital communication" from the Quai d'Orsay to the Elysée and the other ministries, by circulating his reports on the nature of discussions during the prenegotiation sessions in the Council. In this way, those individuals involved in internal bargaining in Paris were kept informed and de Boissieu was given instructions on his input into the prenegotiation talks in Brussels.[117]

In short, the Maastricht process tends to confirm the thesis that more recently, in critical ways, the "elite has become indistinguishable from the political class in France." As Suleiman argues, "the barriers between serving the state, serving one's personal interests, and serving political interests have been blurred to the point of becoming, for all practical purposes, nonexistent."[118]

German Civil Servants

The two German personal representatives during the prenegotiation were Horst Köhler and Jürgen Trumpf, Ambassador at the German Permanent Representation to the European Communities. As state secretary, Köhler was no ordinary civil servant. His position is described as one which links politics and the administration. The tasks of a state secretary include: assuming the leadership of various ministerial departments; offering advice to the minister; implementation of personnel policy; giving and receiving political impetus in

---

[114] Colin Campbell and George Szablowski, *The Superbureaucrats*, 156.

[115] Interviews, Quai d'Orsay, 8 March 1993; German Permanent Representation to the European Communities, 11 June 1993; "Paris prêt à accepter un renforcement des pouvoirs du Parlement européen," *Les Echos*, 29 octobre 1991; "Mind over Maastricht," *The Economist*, December 7, 1991.

[116] Interview, Quai d'Orsay, 8 March 1993.

[117] Campbell and Szablowski, *The Superbureaucrats*, 54; Interview, French Permanent Representation to the European Communities, 25 November 1992.

[118] Ezra Suleiman, "Change and Stability in French Elites," in *Remaking the Hexagon*, ed. Gregory Flynn (Boulder, San Francisco and Oxford: Westview , 1995), 161.

dealing with coalition or party politics as the "alter ego" of the minister; paying attention to evolving specialist knowledge in policy making which often requires teamwork to implement; controlling the efficiency of the ministry.[119] Berndt von Staden, a former state secretary at the *Auswärtiges Amt*, explains the position in simpler terms: "A state secretary is a *femme de menage* who must accomplish the tasks which the minister cannot."[120] Therefore, the state secretary is also responsible to represent his minister at those meetings which the minister cannot attend.

Köhler participated in talks with Trichet, the other 10 personal representatives and Commission representatives to draft the EMU agenda. He received guidelines on German positions from his assistants at the ministry of finance, Gert Haller and Günter Grosche. Both men are civil servants noted for their politico-administrative competence. In the German administrative system, all three men had the status of *politische Beamte*.[121] In the implementation of their tasks, it is imperative that their views be in political accord with those of the federal government.[122] The characteristic trait of officials at this high administrative level, essentially head of division and head of department, respectively, is that they can be asked to resign at the discretion of their minister.[123]

One of the administrative characteristics of the German state is the cooperation and rivalry between the ministries of economics and finance whose styles have contrasted regarding economic policy.[124] Finance has traditionally had the "good housekeeping" function in support of the stability policies of the Bundesbank. In the Maastricht context, this was also the case. The role of the ministry of economics was a strong second to finance on EMU and the *Auswärtiges Amt* on political union. However, this did not prevent Germany from speaking with one voice at crucial points during the prenegotiation.[125]

---

[119] Ulrich Echtler, *Einfluss und Macht in der Politik: Der beamtete Staatssekretär* (München: Wilhelm Goldmann Verlag, 1973), 120–145.

[120] Interview, Berndt von Staden, Ambassador's Residence, 5 December 1992.

[121] Thierry Pfister, *La république des fonctionnaires* (Paris: Albin Michel, 1988), 171–173.

[122] Jacques Ziller, "Hauts fonctionnaires et politique en République fédérale d'Allemagne," 33.

[123] Interview, Wilhelm Schönfelder, *Auswärtiges Amt*, 6 May 1993.

[124] William Wallace, "Old States and New Circumstances," 45.

[125] It did create some tensions during negotiations on political union though given the social market orientation of the ministry of economics as developed under Erhard and Schiller. Kenneth Dyson, "West Germany: The Search for a Rationalist Consensus," in *Policy Styles in Western Europe*, 34–35. Aside from its desire to retain a privileged voice in the domestic structure of Community affairs, a position which IGC diplomacy threatened owing to the lead role of Finance, the ministry of economics was also not in favor of a European industrial policy.

It is important to emphasize that as the country with the strongest currency in Europe, the Federal Republic has a great deal to lose in a weak economic and monetary union. The sacrifice of the D-mark was an influential factor during the prenegotiation given the psychological impact of such a dramatic change on the German people. It is therefore no surprise that the ministry of finance, supporting the Bundesbank position, was initially reluctant to advocate economic and monetary union.[126] "We are a conservative ministry in a strong position, so we did not see why we should share power in the form of the D-mark," Grosche explained. "But the Chancellor wanted it, so we worked extremely hard," he added. The reaction of then finance minister Stoltenberg to the Genscher Memorandum on EMU in 1988 underlined the ministry of finance's lingering doubts about the plan. Stoltenberg would eventually move over to the ministry of defense.[127] Thereafter, at the ministerial and administrative levels directly involved, care was taken to assure that key players in the EMU prenegotiation were advocates of monetary integration.

At the domestic working level, Grosche did have some contact with interest groups representing civil society as German interests on EMU were being defined.[128] This is significant given civil society's relative lack of presence in the European polity, described as "popular indifference" about Community affairs,[129] in comparison with citizen involvement in the United States.[130] On EMU matters, it is certain though that German banking, industrial and trade groups found their point of access initially at the head of department and eventually at the state secretary levels in the finance and economics ministries. Among those active included the BDA (*Bundesvereinigung der Deutschen Arbeitgeberverbände*), representing German employers' associations, and the BDI (*Bundesverband der Deutschen Industrie*), supporting German industrial interests. Both groups also expressed

---

[126] Interview, Günter Grosche, Federal Ministry of Finance, 26 April 1993.

[127] Interview, Reimer von Borries, Federal Ministry of Economics, 14 June 1993.

[128] Interviews, Günter Grosche, Federal Ministry of Finance, 26 April 1993; Wolfgang Neumann, Association of German Savings Institutions, 30 April 1993.

[129] Martin Slater, "Political Elites, Popular Indifference and Community Building," *Journal of Common Market Studies* XXI (1982): 69–87.

[130] Sidney Verba, "The 1993 James Madison Award Lecture: The Voice of the People," *Political Science and Politics* XXVI (1993): 679.

their views at the European level just prior to the opening of the IGCs. This was done via UNICE, the Union of Industrial and Employers' Confederations of Europe. This is an employers' union speaking on behalf of over 30 industry and labor groups in 19 European countries. In addition to its firm support of EMU as a means "to gain full benefit from the single market," UNICE spoke out on the need for political union. References were made to strengthening the Community institutions, ensuring a clearer division of competence between member states and the Community and respecting Europe's diversity in accordance with the principle of subsidiarity.[131]

Although not as intense as the lobbying by agricultural interest groups in normal EC affairs, there was nonetheless more societal "voice" on EMU than on political union.[132] At the national level, interest groups like the BDA and BDI expressed a concern for an independent organ, the Eurofed, which would assure price stability as well as the need for member states to observe strict convergence criteria in EMU. At the European level, German interests expressed their views on the IGCs as members of the ETUC, European Trade Union Confederation, and UNICE. Significantly, two points were emphasized to a greater extent at the European level than at the German one: the need for economic and social cohesion, implying large transfers of structural funds to the poorer states of the Community; and the need for political, translated as democratic, control over the Eurofed, a position that the French would maintain throughout the negotiations.[133] Both French and German domestic interests did use umbrella organizations at the European level to voice their concerns about the Treaty negotiations. Both domestic interests, and the transnational groupings in which they found representation in Brussels, would benefit from Treaty provisions like those on European citizenship, cohesion, education, EMU and social policy.

Genscher's personal representative on political union, Dr. Jürgen Trumpf, initially served as the German member of the Antici Group[134] in Brussels

---

[131] UNICE Presse, Déclaration des milieux d'affaires européennes: la "Nouvelle Europe" entre en action, 4 décembre 1990.

[132] Joseph H. H. Weiler, "The European Community in Change: Exit, Voice and Loyalty," *Irish Studies in International Affairs* 3 (1990): 15–25.

[133] Déclaration de la Confédération Européenne des Syndicats, Union Economique et Monétaire, adoptée par le Comité Exécutif de la C.E.S. 19 et 20 avril 1990; Christopher Brewin and Richard McAllister, "Annual Review of the Activities of the European Community in 1990," *Journal of Common Market Studies* XXIX (1991): 407.

[134] The Antici Group originated during the Italian Presidency of the Council in 1975. The Ambassador at Italy's Permanent Representation to the European Communities during that time, whose last name was Antici, created the group to coordinate the details of preparations for the European Council. Mary Troy Johnston, *The European Council* (Boulder & Oxford: Westview, 1994), 28.

during Kohl's early years as Chancellor. Trumpf's reputation as Genscher's man in Brussels[135] was built on a solid knowledge of Community dossiers, a shrewd assessment of political realities and a superb sense of timing in negotiations. His friendly and low-key manner make Trumpf an approachable individual. This was most helpful in coalition-building on the numerous dossiers of political union. A career foreign service officer, Trumpf is noted for his *Sachkenntnis*, or knowledge of EC affairs, in spite of the fact that he does not have the legal training which characterizes many top civil servants in the German administration. Instead, Trumpf's detailed knowledge was acquired by spending over two-thirds of his career working in Bonn and Brussels since 1970. This is more the exception than the rule in a ministry which prides itself on generalists. Yet, in European affairs, it is necessary given the years required to learn the technical aspects of Community business. Also, the small number of people involved in the domestic administrative network contributes to a trust factor. As one official explained, "In Community affairs, we always know with whom we are dealing in the different ministries."[136] The familiarity is helpful owing to the complex and stressful nature of the work.

One of the essential coalitions in German IGC diplomacy, established during the Maastricht prenegotiation, was the solid alliance between the civil servants in the *Auswärtiges Amt* and the Chancellor's Office. Joachim Bitterlich, Kohl's point man on Franco-German relations and European Community affairs studied at ENA before making his career as a diplomat. His experience as a career diplomat in the *Auswärtiges Amt*, prior to his job at the Chancellor's Office, ensured that lines of communication would remain open. In addition, Bitterlich's pro-French attitudes and creative initiatives would promote an active Franco-German line during the prenegotiation and throughout 1991.[137] The second official in the Chancellor's Office assisting Bitterlich with the IGC on political union, Friedrich Löhr, was also on loan from the *Auswärtiges Amt*.[138] Löhr, in turn, had excellent relations with Eckart Cuntz who would play the key role at the domestic working level throughout the Maastricht process.

As ambassador and permanent representative to the Community institutions, Trumpf worked in Brussels. The civil servant responsible for the interministerial coordination in Bonn was the head of the economics division

---

[135] "Die Drahtzieher," 173–174. All other information on members of the German administration is taken from *Handbuch der Bundesregierung* 12. WP (Mai 1993).

[136] Interview, Rose Lässing, *Auswärtiges Amt*, 21 April 1993.

[137] Interview, Federal Chancellor's Office, 16 June 1993.

[138] Ibid.

at the *Auswärtiges Amt*, Dietrich von Kyaw. Already in the prenegotiation phase, his job was in some respects one of the most challenging. As he explains, "One had to deal with personalities, and to make clear repeatedly which positions one could and could not present in Brussels."[139] Given the open-ended nature of the political union agenda, individuals representing almost all the federal ministries took part in domestic bargaining. Different ministries were involved according to the dossier in question. The most significant, in addition to the *Auswärtiges Amt*, were Economics, Finance, Interior and Justice.

Kyaw is a man of intense convictions about the nature of European integration and particularly about the need for democratic legitimacy in the form of parliamentary control at the European level. He was ably assisted by Werner Kaufmann-Bühler, head of department 410, the communications hub of the departments in the *Auswärtiges Amt* involved with Community affairs. Kaufmann-Bühler was admirably suited for this job because of his penchant for detail and precision in the drafting of instructions for the other ministries and the Chancellor's Office during internal bargaining. In Autumn 1990, a sub-department, department 410–8, was created to deal specifically with the IGC on political union and the subsequent treaty ratification process in the Bundesrat and the Bundestag. The individual responsible for the direction of 410–8, Eckart Cuntz, distinguished himself under Genscher early in his career. He was subsequently named the youngest ambassador ever to represent the Federal Republic of Germany abroad. Cuntz is a highly energetic individual with a friendly and open manner in his dealings with others. His intellectual ability to deal with a broad agenda of issues, combined with the quick implementation of assigned tasks, distinguished his work throughout the Maastricht process.

Thus, on political union three individuals inside the *Auswärtiges Amt* were the principal organizers at the official level during the prenegotiation. This fact reveals that, in spite of the decentralized nature of Germany's administrative system,[140] the number of key civil servants involved in the Maastricht prenegotiation at the *Auswärtiges Amt*, and in the other ministries, was quite limited. This demonstrates that Maastricht, like the process of German unification was, in the words of Stephen Szabo, "a case of elite diplomacy carried out by a few officials with little engagement of the vast bureaucracies in these large nations."[141]

In the second half of 1990, Kyaw led the internal ministerial bargaining on issues of political union. The results of these talks enabled Kaufmann-Bühler to organize the issues around the key themes of the prenegotiation.

---

[139] Interview, Dietrich von Kyaw, German Permanent Representation to the European Communities, 11 June 1993.

[140] Renate Mayntz and Fritz W. Scharpf, *Policy-Making in the German Federal Bureaucracy* (Amsterdam: Elsevier, 1975), 165–174.

[141] Szabo, *The Diplomacy of German Unification*, 117.

This was useful for the meetings of European State Secretaries who later discussed areas of disagreement among the federal ministries in search of solutions acceptable to all involved. It also served as a basis for coalition talks which Kohl held with the FDP in November.

French and German Civil Servants

Although the French and the Germans did act in unison to advance the aims of the IGCs, much compromise on both sides was required throughout the Maastricht process. From the outset, during the prenegotiation phase, good working relations at the official level was necessary as well as evident. The glue which held many of the pieces together was the rapport between de Boissieu and Trumpf. This was based on a mutual respect for each other's abilities as negotiators and genuine liking. Their cooperation was helpful on one of the most important dossiers of political union, CFSP. As another personal representative to the IGC on political union explained, "the Franco-German tandem, strengthened by the teamwork of de Boissieu and Trumpf, served as a focal point on the CFSP." As the prenegotiation wore on, the other delegations used the Franco-German line as a way of establishing their own positions on this dossier. Often the accord between the two countries was strained, however, in part due to differing conceptions of political union and, more importantly, of the role of NATO in European security.

There was a need for patience and mutual understanding at the official level between the personal representatives working on EMU, Köhler and Trichet. The French representative, although advocating a monetary policy of *franc fort* essentially in line with German thinking, also had to defend his minister's ideas concerning a *gouvernement économique*. These ideas were not well received by the Germans, who believed that the proposed ECB had to retain the autonomous right to fix exchange rate policy independent of political authority.

The preceding consideration of the officials involved in the Maastricht prenegotiation reveals that the four images of civil servants approach is a linchpin among the different approaches in an analysis of the Maastricht process. During this phase of the process, national civil servants and central bankers were working steadily to enable the two IGCs to open in mid-December 1990. Unlike their political masters, these officials working at a lower level of discussions were able to identify points of agreement and were not operating under a rule of consensus. On EMU, their task was to limit and define the precise issues that remained to be negotiated; on political union their talks were of a more general, open-ended nature with the basic problem clear to all at the table: the inability of the political leadership to agree on a common conception of political union. This difficulty at the top would lead to an imbalance in the discussions at all levels. The untidy agenda on political union, stemming in large part from a desire on the part of member states to advance their own interests, made integrative bargaining impossible. The lack of a thoroughly prepared text, like that of the Commission's draft treaty on

EMU, hindered attempts at joint problem solving and limited the influence of the Delors Commission during the prenegotiation on political union.

This state of affairs should be viewed in light of the personal influence which Delors was able to exert during the EMU prenegotiation. His ability to develop a good working relationship with Chancellor Kohl throughout the process of German unification attests to the importance of personal links in relations between member states and Community institutions. These links at the top motivate discussions at lower levels and are therefore crucial to the success of the IGC process. Here it is also necessary to stress the limited participatory nature of the Maastricht process which was evident from the start of the prenegotiation. The large bureaucracies of the member states and the European Commission were excluded from the process; only a small number of individuals, chosen for their familiarity with Community affairs, took part.

The exclusive nature of participation is in line with Monnet's overall approach. However, unlike in earlier times, this aspect of his approach is ill suited to modern governance in an age of information technology and increased public skepticism about the role of bureaucracies in democratic governments. In this context, politico-administrative hybrids would be judged as much on their ability to facilitate joint problem solving as to articulate to the masses the essence of the issues on the table.

The Maastricht prenegotiation illustrates the difficulty of both these tasks. As Putnam's approach shows, the differences in French and German domestic structures made it difficult for the two sides to understand each other. As a centralized state, France had more in common administratively and politically with Great Britain and Spain. The fact that France and Germany were able to agree at all and move the process forward at various points in the prenegotiation attests to the strength of the "privileged partnership" and the limits of a purely intergovernmentalist approach to explain the dynamics of the IGC process. Difficulties in joint problem solving arose most clearly when there was a lack of adequate preparation of dossiers. Insufficient preparation and time to discuss issues not only hindered joint problem solving, it made the clear articulation of the issues on the table to those outside the IGC process impossible.

During the prenegotiation, the excessive complexity of the IGC agenda, with its multiple levels, images and bargains, was readily apparent. This complexity was due to the tremendous ambition to include EMU as part of a larger whole, European political union, and to the reluctance to reconcile state sovereignty with Community interest in the quest for political union. However, it is not possible to stop at this point in time and evaluate the entire Maastricht process on the basis of the prenegotiation. Instead, it is necessary to use this initial phase to shed light both on the learning experience shared by the various actors involved, and on the political nature of the issues which they confronted, as the IGC process began to unfold.

Monnet's Approach

The Commission's Communication of 21 August on EMU and its draft treaty of December were constructive and influential texts during the prenegotiation. It was a tactical advantage for the Commission to be first with a draft on the table and, unlike in the IGC on political union, to have that draft taken as the basis for negotiations by the Luxembourg Presidency.[142] Here Delors' initiative to involve the Commission in the prenegotiation best illustrates Monnet's approach; in fact, his personal input into the entire EMU process typified this approach.

The member of Delors' Cabinet who was his right-hand man on EMU, Joly Dixon, was in a more direct relationship with the President than most of his Cabinet colleagues. Dixon, the sole Briton in the Cabinet, had a clear sense of the origins of strategic leadership: "The President is the source of everything, the creator of our lines," he said.[143]

The EMU prenegotiation gave Delors the opportunity to use his skills as an intellectual, strategist and politician to the fullest. His hard-won eminence in the European Council and his special relationship in the triangle with Kohl and Mitterrand led, over time, to a *de facto* change in the workings of the Community institutions. Delors' use of personal contacts and his meticulous attention to detail, while retaining a vision of the larger picture, concretized Monnet's approach on EMU. He relied on his *chef de cabinet*, Pascal Lamy, to maintain an open dialogue with confidants around both Mitterrand and Kohl "to fine-tune the Franco-German couple to the melodies the Commission hoped to play."[144]

Above all, Delors wanted those who worked around him to "implicate" themselves in their work on European integration. Like Monnet, he had a tremendous personal commitment to a strategy for unity. Delors worked with a small team, which is a trademark of the Monnet approach. These individuals, chosen for the most part by Lamy, had inner-directed moral convictions. It was the teamwork of these persons, all devoted to a *grande mission*, which helped Delors to take the initiative on Maastricht and to exert an influence beyond the scope of a purely technocratic organization. The skill of the Delors-Lamy team enabled the Delors Commission, in the tradition of Monnet, to play the role of a policy entrepreneur on EMU.[145]

---

[142] Dyson, *Elusive Union*, 147.

[143] George Ross, "Inside The Delors Cabinet," *Journal of Common Market Studies* (December 1994): 506.

[144] Ibid., 514.

[145] Ibid., 515–516.

For example, the Commission fought off the French government's proposal that member states should be given the right to centralize economic policy in the European Council. The key point here in terms of Monnet's approach is Delors' focus on the use of the Community institutions and decision-making procedures to drive the EMU process. Delors argued for EMU to be placed within the European Community competencies. He believed that the creation of a "new institution" would redefine existing monetary relations among the member states. That he succeeded was no small victory given the sharp distinction already evident between Community and intergovernmental decision making in the context of talks on political union. Delors' success owed a great deal to the existing momentum generated by the Single European Act and Chancellor Kohl's willingness to blend the contents of the Delors Report, containing Monnet's step-by-step design, with German priorities on EMU.

Throughout the Maastricht process, the Delors Commission spoke on behalf of the "general interest" of the Community. The isolation of Thatcher at Rome I was an illustration of her determination to defend national sovereignty at all costs. But the entry of the British pound into the ERM weeks before discredited British opposition to EMU. After the European Council, Thatcher could no longer defend her distinctive position on the issue. As Ludlow notes, in a political system like the Community, based on the consensus principle, no one government can maintain a position of reserve indefinitely without breaking either the system or itself.[146] It was a lesson that John Major, despite a new approach, found as difficult to learn as his predecessor.

Time and again, the confrontation between the Delors Commission and Great Britain would illustrate the need for a flexible approach in the face of entrenched opposition by one member state on issues like EMU and social policy. The Maastricht process illustrated that variable geometry provides this flexibility within well-defined limits. In legal terms variable geometry can work in a positive sense by introducing Treaty provisions which let certain states move ahead with cooperation in specific areas or in a negative sense to the extent that other states are granted opting out clauses. Another way in which variable geometry functions is by offering a number of states the possibility to proceed with a degree of cooperation outside the Treaties in areas like EMS since 1978–1979 or Schengen from 1985–1990.[147] The Maastricht process would eventually bring these areas of cooperation into the framework of the Treaty on European Union.

---

[146] Ludlow, "Launching the IGCs: July-December 1990," 428.

[147] Charlemagne, "L'équilibre entre les etats membres," in *L'Equilibre Européen*, Etudes rassemblées et publiées en hommage à Niels Ersbøll Secrétaire Général du Conseil de l'Union Européenne (1980–1994) (Bruxelles: Edition provisoire, 1995), 69–78.

In order not to call into question Monnet's approach to European construction, however, it is important to take certain precautions in the use of variable geometry. The definition of a "basic common foundation" is necessary, including a group of fundamental policies. All member states must agree to participate in these policies. In other words, all member states must abide by the rules of competition policy because this is necessary for the functioning of the internal market. Any non-participation by member states in certain policies which could lead to significant distortions of competition, i.e., transport policy, fiscal policy, environmental policy or industrial policy, should be ruled out. Even for optional policies, which only certain member states participate in, there should be a minimum number of common rules which all member states must follow. The *acquis communautaire* must be respected and adhered to in its entirety. A level of solidarity must be maintained which is sufficient enough to reinforce economic and social cohesion among the member states.[148]

Significantly, the Maastricht prenegotiation revealed that key member states were unwilling to agree upon a minimum number of common rules which each would be obliged to follow. This was most obvious in the context of political union; instead member states kept submitting proposals for new policies to include in the Community competencies. The Community's quest for political union was strongly influenced by the Iraqi invasion of Kuwait on 2 August 1990. The call for a security component within the Community was made by those member states in favor of increased integration. This issue raised once again a longstanding debate on integration and security. The defeat of the European Defense Community (EDC) on the floor of the French National Assembly on 30 August 1954 loomed large. Delors, supported by the Italian Presidency, called for a federalist solution in line with Monnet's approach of increased powers for the Commission in the area of foreign affairs. However, several member states were content to wait-and-see how the Gulf Crisis affected their national interests.

Most importantly, France and Germany, whose leaders had made a joint plea for political union, did not throw their combined weight on the side of the Italians and the Commission. Although Bonn gave its full support, Paris appeared more aloof and noncommittal. The French attached primary importance to EMU in a Community framework, which it regards as a *sine qua non* for political union. Moreover, the Gulf War gave Paris an opportunity to boost its international standing by taking advantage of its permanent membership on the UN Security Council.[149]

---

[148] Ibid.

[149] Panos Tsakaloyannis, "The 'Acceleration of History' and the Reopening of the Political Debate in the European Community," *Journal of European Integration* (1991): 92.

Still at the heart of the European Commission's Opinion of 21 October was the notion that the separation between Community affairs and European Political Cooperation should be ended. The success resulting from the institutional reforms introduced by the Single European Act contributed to a sense of confidence within the Delors Commission about the revival of Monnet's approach. This sense of confidence led some Commission officials, including President Delors, to underestimate the opposition on the part of member states like France and Britain to relinquish sovereignty in policy areas within the scope of political union.

The Delors Commission encountered difficulties using Monnet's approach during the prenegotiation on political union mainly because France and Great Britain challenged the notion that the European institutions should be involved in EPC matters to any great extent. Monnet's approach emphasized integrative bargaining in order to define a Community interest in political union. The approach broke down in the face of individual member states' determination to preserve national sovereignty in line with the domestic interests highlighted by the two-level games approach. No common definition of political union emerged among the Twelve and the European Commission at any level during the prenegotiation. Although the personal representatives did register progress on a draft treaty text, there was no lengthy prenegotiation to enable them to arrive at an agreement on the major issues in the text or to establish a sense of how to work on joint solutions to common problems. Nor was there an attempt made to create a new European institution in the area of security and defense policy. Instead the prenegotiation on political union illustrated that some member states were adamant about reasserting their sovereign interests to counter the use of the Monnet approach to create EMU.

SUMMARY

The Maastricht prenegotiation enables us to identify the different actors at the political and politico-administrative levels who played a decisive role in the IGC process. The organization of personnel at the domestic and European levels was key to the success of the entire endeavor. The prenegotiation reveals a clear distinction between the organization of the EMU conference and that of political union. In the French case, this was not a serious problem because of the centralized nature of French diplomacy and the dominance of de Boissieu as a personality at the domestic and European levels. In the German case, the domestic requirement to link the two conferences made for organizational difficulties among the different ministries and political problems for the Chancellor's Office in its relations with the Bundesbank, Bundesrat and Bundestag.

The three approaches used in this analytical framework illustrate various aspects of these organizational difficulties. The latter can be explained in large part by the differences between French and German domestic structures and institutions (two-level games) and the types of personalities, and their interrelationships, at and among the various levels of negotiation (four images of civil servants). The multifaceted nature of the internal bargaining and external negotiations within each conference, and their impact on the domestic ratification processes (Monnet's approach), are of equal importance in any consideration of the ways in which organizational difficulties influenced the IGC process.

On EMU, the prenegotiation illustrates the importance of thorough preparation of issues on the table in view of elements of distributive bargaining among member states, i.e., Great Britain on the issue of a single currency, the cohesion states on increased funds from their richer neighbors, as well as attitudinal structuring, i.e., Köhler's presentation of the German interest in his discussions with Trichet and the other members of the Monetary Committee, and intraorganizational bargaining, i.e., Kohl's need to consider the Bundesbank's requirements on strict convergence criteria and the need for a stronger political union. The role of Delors as a policy initiator who, through a strategic alliance with Kohl and Genscher, skillfully advocated the Community interest in the Commission's draft treaty accepted as the basis for negotiations, is also highlighted by the prenegotiation.

The teamwork at the politico-administrative level, particularly that between Köhler and Trichet, emphasizes the central role of France and Germany in the overall process as well as the input and weight of these officials in political discussions. Their presence as personal representatives of their finance ministers and as members of the Monetary Committee, and the contributions of the central bank governors, were key elements of the prenegotiation and shaped the character of discussions at the table. The main issues on which France and Germany had to reach agreement were the deadline to start Stage Two, the independence of national central banks, precise convergence criteria and rules concerning budget deficits. On each issue, integrative bargaining was not as apparent as either distributive and intraorganizational bargaining or attitudinal structuring as the member states continued to adjust their diplomacy to each others' domestic interests and positions.

On political union, a Franco-German strategy to launch a second intergovernmental conference became apparent early in the prenegotiation, but the domestic interests of each state made the search for a common definition of the final goal of political integration an elusive one. The work of the politico-administrative hybrids was key to the success of the entire prenegotiation; unlike their ministers, these officials strove to identify points of agreement and were not operating under a rule of consensus. Their task was to elaborate the contents of a Treaty on political union. In conjunction with Cabinet members of the Secretary General in the Council Secretariat and, at times, President Delors, the personal representatives sketched out the contours of a draft treaty. The four main issue areas, identified by the Franco-German letters to the Council Presidency, were retained: objectives of political union; democratic legitimacy; efficiency; and external action/CFSP.

Whereas the French strategy emphasized a limited number of well-defined goals, the German ambitions for political union were much broader, owing in large part to the decentralized nature of its domestic structure and the concerns of many in the political establishment regarding the speed of national unification. All the member states kept contributing non-papers regarding the extent and nature of Community competencies well beyond the time frame of the prenegotiation; this made drafting any coherent text difficult and the use of integrative bargaining impossible. During the prenegotiation, the Commission made the first of several attempts to present a draft treaty on political union, but key member states like France and Great Britain were unprepared to envisage even a non-exclusive right of initiative for the Commission in sensitive areas like foreign and security policy. Here Delors' presence as a linchpin at different levels of negotiation was not as strong as that on EMU. His influence was considerably less important than the input of Mitterrand and Kohl or the work of Dumas' and Genscher's personal representatives.

As the prenegotiation came to a close, many individuals involved in the IGC process were concerned about the uneven progress made on the political union agenda, as compared to that of EMU. Few questioned the wisdom of convening a second conference, however, or entertained any thoughts that the IGC process could fail. Most were caught up in the whirlwind of events taking place on the international scene to be overly preoccupied with the internal dynamics of the Maastricht process. The heads of state and government and the finance and foreign ministers clearly could not devote the majority of their time to the two conferences. This fact alone placed the ministers' personal representatives under the greatest burden to keep the momentum of the negotiations going in the months to follow.

CHAPTER IV

Bringing Monnet Back In: France, Germany, EMU and Integrative Bargaining on "Steps in Time"

Experience has taught me that we cannot pretend to know the problems of others before making sure that we give the same meaning to words and use the same definitions. For this, I always came back to the method of seating people around a table.

It is often futile to attack problems which do not exist by themselves, but which are the product of circumstances. It is only by modifying these circumstances that one can unblock the situation of which they are the cause or the opportunity. Instead of using my strength on that which resists, I am accustomed to looking for that which, in the environment, creates the fixation and to change it: this is sometimes a secondary point and often a psychological climate.

Jean Monnet, *Mémoires*

Much of the credit for success during the EMU prenegotiation has been attributed to the personal contributions of Delors and the diligent efforts of finance ministers and their personal representatives. This would also be the case throughout the IGC as ministers and civil servants worked together to define precisely the more technical issues which their leaders in the European Council did not always grasp. These officials were presented with a unique opportunity to direct the course of integration. They used their collective talent to "seize the moment" of change.

This chapter opens with a focus on the working methods of the IGC. The goals of France and Germany, as stated in their proposals for draft treaties on EMU, and their bilateral consultations on specific negotiation issues follow. The main issues are then outlined prior to an analysis of the IGC using the three approaches presented in this book.

ORGANIZATION AND WORKING METHODS

The number of issues on the table that were already the subject of frank and open discussion defined, in large part, the Presidency's task. The Luxembourg Presidency's main objective was to help bring the EMU conference to a close by producing a Treaty which could be implemented.[1] To accomplish this, the Presidency focused on proposing solutions to resolve differences of opinion among the member states on various issues at each level of negotiation. This change from the previous IGC in 1985 marked an evolution in the leadership function of the Presidency. It was due in part to the increased role played by the Commission during the IGCs. In the past, the Commission was a compromise maker and tried to fill a role as mediator. Instead, throughout the IGCs, the Commission presented its own proposals which were discussed alongside those of the Twelve. For the other parties involved, there was nothing "way out" about the Commission's role as a thirteenth participant during the EMU conference.[2] As the next chapter reveals, political union was a different story.

In terms of the organization of the conference negotiations, the role of the finance ministers was a crucial one. These ministers met ten times during the course of 1991 to deal with IGC issues on the margin of their regular meetings in the ECOFIN Council. Their personal representatives met twice a month to prepare the issues on the IGC agenda. In addition, four ministerial meetings with the European Parliament were scheduled.[3] At no stage did the heads of state and government have to intervene directly in the negotiations. The Dutch Presidency also decided to place EMU as the first agenda item at Maastricht in order "to create a positive mood for what was to follow." This was one indication of the careful preparation which distinguished the entire negotiation process from that of political union.[4]

When the personal representatives had their first meeting on 15 January, they had before them a draft treaty of the Commission on EMU.[5] This text,

---

[1] Ambassador Joseph Weyland, "Strategies and Perspectives of the Luxembourg Presidency" in *The EC Council Presidency*, eds. E.J. Kirchner and A. Tsagkari (London: Association for Contemporary European Studies, 1993), 15.

[2] David Buchan, "EMU Train Stopped in its Tracks," *Financial Times*, April 8, 1991, 2–3.

[3] Cloos, Reinesch, Vignes et Weyland, *Le Traité de Maastricht*, 98- 99.

[4] Richard Corbett, *The Treaty of Maastricht* (Essex: Longman Group, 1993), 41.

[5] European Commission, *Intergovernmental Conferences*, 13–62.

which was the result of cumulative efforts over two years, clearly stated many of the objectives on which consensus among Eleven of the Twelve had been reached. Negotiations on EMU under the Luxembourg Presidency consisted initially of a close reading of the Commission's draft treaty. Alternative plans to the Commission text, based on submissions from the member states, included a British proposition for a "hard ECU," a Spanish proposal for a "hard-basket ECU," and complete draft treaties from France and Germany.[6] In terms of the final outcome at Maastricht, it is important to focus on the Commission text and the French and German texts to assess their influence on the negotiations. The British proposal did not favor a commitment to a single currency. Although it was taken seriously, particularly by the French who saw it as a way to strengthen the ECU in Stage Two,[7] the British plan was never an alternative to monetary union.

The Presidency proposed its first draft treaty on 17 April. About 80% of the final text agreed on in Maastricht was already on the table. The Presidency acknowledged that this was testimony to the successful team work of the groups of personal representatives. Three issues brought out the element of diversity among the Twelve as they strove to negotiate the steps to a single currency: the British problem; the contents of Stage Two; and economic convergence.

In contrast to his Luxembourg counterpart, Dutch Prime Minister Lubbers, whose country assumed the Presidency on 1 July, was very anxious about the results of both IGCs after the Luxembourg European Council. Lubbers believed that most of the work still had to be done and that the Maastricht Treaties were not yet ready. On EMU the Dutch Presidency aimed to build on two concrete achievements of the Luxembourg Council: the confirmation of 1 January 1994 as the beginning of Stage Two; and the intention of several member states to present specific programs, with precise quantitative objectives and means, destined to assure progress on convergence.[8]

As established by the Presidency in its calendar for the EMU conference, a working group of experts met on 17 October to examine aspects relative to the roles of the Commission and Parliament, relations between the central bank governors and the Economic and Financial Committee of the Union and the statutes for the future European Central Bank. In the last months of the conference, the working group, comprised of deputies of the personal

---

[6] Italianer, "Mastering Maastricht," 68–70.

[7] Agence Europe, 12 janvier 1991, 10. Information on the negotiations presented in this chapter is taken from daily reports of Agence Europe throughout 1991 unless otherwise indicated.

[8] "Le Sommet Européen a confirmé les divergences sur l'Union," *L'Echo*, 2 juillet 1991, 3.

representatives, sorted out the details of the more technical issues.[9] Their meeting was followed by that of the personal representatives on 22 October to examine two draft protocols to annex to the Treaty on excessive budgetary deficits and transition to Stage Three. After these meetings the Dutch Presidency submitted a revised draft treaty on EMU to the member states on 28 October. The final negotiations prior to the Maastricht European Council were based on this draft treaty.

French and German Goals

France chose to focus its EMU diplomacy on a few simple goals. The most important one was the establishment of a *gouvernement économique* by which the European Council would set the guidelines for economic and monetary policy in the Union. Economic policy had to be as fully defined at the European level as monetary policy. The creation of the ECB at the start of Stage Two in January 1994 was another French priority. Third, a fixed timetable with established deadlines for each stage of EMU was essential with the decision on transition to the final stage taken by qualified majority vote.

Germany, on the other hand, was much more concerned with strict adherence to precisely defined convergence criteria than any arbitrarily set dates in the EMU process. The Germans also favored a role for the ECOFIN Council, consisting of economics and finance ministers who were technically competent, in the decision making on EMU. Finally, the Germans were against an automatic transition to the final stage of EMU by a fixed date. The Federal Republic also insisted that a unanimous decision be required.

Franco-German Consultations

During the informal ECOFIN meeting of 11–12 May the Luxembourg Presidency tried to deal with Franco-German differences on Stage Two and the timing of the creation of the ECB. The Presidency aimed to present a draft treaty acceptable to both France and Germany, a treaty which would allow the German government to strike a bargain on this issue with the Bundesbank. The Presidency's proposal envisaged two subperiods to Stage Two. The first (1994–1995) would feature something like the German proposal for a Council of Central Bank Governors. The second (1996-Stage Three) would begin with the establishment of the ECB. Having made a concession to Germany, including the idea of sanctions against countries with excessive budget deficits, the Luxembourg draft proposed that a decision to move to Stage

---

[9] Interview, Alexander Italianer, Commission of the European Communities, 25 May 1994.

Three, and to set a date for this final stage to begin, could be taken by the end of 1996.[10]

Both the French and German finance ministers showed signs of willingness to compromise. Waigel was pleased that the agreement implied that the ECB would be modelled on the Bundesbank and that there would be a deferral of the date for the establishment of the ECB. Bérégovoy was convinced that the German government was preparing to accept a timetable. The other new idea was that each country should prepare convergence programmes to submit to ECOFIN, before Stage Two, to affirm their will to achieve economic convergence.[11]

Just prior to the Luxembourg European Council, President Mitterrand used his contacts with Santer, Kohl and Major to stress the need for a European Council "without surprises" based on the Presidency's approach "which coincided with French views." The French President and the German Chancellor shared the same views on the Luxembourg Council, namely, to preserve the progress already made, to confirm points of agreement, but without taking any decisions on the conferences. In the eyes of some observers, however, harmony was more apparent than real. Throughout the Luxembourg Council a certain ambivalence in French views was detected on a number of important issues including Stage Two of EMU.

In Mitterrand's view, what did occur at Luxembourg was "two hours of discussions in circles" on EMU owing to the British reserve. This forced the leaders to return to the point of departure with no change in positions. Mitterrand finally stated: "I think Major's decision to maintain his reserve for as long as he is not satisfied with the agreement is perfectly understandable. My experience of these matters is that we will have an agreement—in the last five minutes."[12]

Kohl's wish to treat Major gently and to sign two Treaties or none at all made him opt for ticking off the dossiers at Luxembourg where broad agreement was reached like EMU without closing those files. In this way, member states which might already be satisfied would have an incentive to play along until Maastricht brought the conferences to a conclusion. On EMU, discussions revealed that the main disagreements still existed among the Eleven on the transition phase between the present and Stage Three, the economic content of EMU, notably on the issue of budgetary constraints, and the role of the ECU. On institutional issues, the potential of member state divergences on the role of the European Parliament regarding questions of national budgets and public deficits concerned the Presidency. Both the Luxembourg and Dutch Presidencies had to bear in mind, however, that the

---

[10]Dyson, *Elusive Union*, 156.

[11]Ibid.

[12]John Palmer, "Political Union Casts Long Shadow over Monetary Accord Progress," *The Guardian*, 1 July 1991, 11.

Germans did not want too much political interference in monetary matters.[13]

In early November a difference of opinion between France and Germany emerged over the role of the European Monetary Institute (EMI) in Stage Two of EMU. During a meeting of the personal representatives on 4 November, Jean-Claude Trichet argued for a EMI which would be the true embryo of the future ECB with all its prerogatives. Horst Köhler made clear the German preference that the Institute should not have any power to make monetary policy in the transition stage. The differences in views involved two questions. In terms of capital, how should the Institute be endowed? Who should head the Institute? Regarding this second question, the Germans believed that the President of the Institute should come from the circle of the twelve central bank governors whereas the French wanted a president and a vice-president from outside this circle.

As the personal representatives and group of experts worked out the finer technical details, Bérégovoy and Waigel talked during the 10th Franco-German Economic and Finance Council meeting the next day. Although differences remained, the two ministers affirmed that their countries' positions on EMU were "very close." Although several points like the composition of the European Monetary Institute's administrative council remained open for discussion, a common Franco-German position on EMU at Maastricht was not impossible.

During a ministerial meeting on 11–12 November, the personal representatives, Trichet and Köhler, hinted at a possible Franco-German compromise on the role and tasks of the EMI in Stage Two. This was not explained to the Presidency, however, which drew the opposite conclusion.[14] Negotiations during this meeting served as a basis for the Presidency to prepare a set of "overall findings" for the "conclave" of finance ministers on 1–2 December in Scheveningen.

KEY ISSUES

To facilitate an analysis of the EMU conference, four main issues are considered: political control, including institutional questions; budgetary discipline; the transition to Stages Two and Three of EMU; and economic convergence criteria including cohesion.[15]

Political Control and Institutional Questions

Early in the EMU conference, Bérégovoy reiterated the French draft treaty's idea of a *gouvernement économique* by explaining that it was not possible to

---

[13]Interview, Peter Jabcke, German Permanent Representation to the European Communities, 24 July 1992.

[14]Interview, Commission of the European Communities, 25 May 1994.

[15]Buchan, "EMU Train Stopped in its Tracks," 2–3; this section relies heavily on Schönfelder/Thiel, *Ein Markt—eine Währung*, 127–143.

completely subordinate economic policy to monetary policy. He further stated that it was necessary to distinguish between monetary policy and exchange rate policy, the latter to be determined by political leaders in the European Council. Köhler underlined the importance of the subsidiarity principle, to which Germany attached great importance. The Federal Republic was not in favor of a common economic policy as introduced by the French.[16]

With regard to the European Council's role in EMU, three key questions were posed during the IGC. Should the heads of state and government be able to give instructions only for economic policy or also for monetary policy? Should these guidelines be binding? Should they be agreed upon by the European Council or the ECOFIN Council? During negotiations the member states realized that only unbinding instructions for economic policy would be enforceable. Some states wanted the orientation for monetary policy also to be decided by the European Council. But the German delegation pointed out that this would run counter to the independence of the ECB. In its view, the competence to give economic guidelines should lay at the ministerial level in the ECOFIN Council.[17]

The question of which institution should be responsible for external monetary policy, the Council or the ECB, remained open throughout the conference. The majority of delegations, including the French, believed that the ECOFIN Council should be allowed to determine the "major guidelines" of external monetary policy. Yet, it remained unclear to some delegations, like the German, what "major guidelines" meant. "Three areas of responsibility were defined: that for daily interventions on foreign exchange markets; that of rulings on the exchange rate regime and, if need be, the fixing of price values against third currencies; that of exchange rate policy in intermediate areas, for example, informal agreements on exchange rate policy target zones between the main currencies in the international system."[18]

Already in the prenegotiation, there was agreement among the Twelve that the ECB should be responsible for daily interventions on the exchange markets and that the ECOFIN Council should be responsible for the exchange rate regime. The Council's responsibility was later qualified so as to indicate that decisions on the exchange rate regime had to be in accord with the goal of price stability. The responsibility in intermediate areas was disputed until the end of the negotiation. A solution had to be found at the highest level in Maastricht which guaranteed that the efficiency of the ECB to lead a price

---

[16]Wolfgang Neumann, *Auf dem Weg zu einer europäischen Wirtschafts- und Währungsunion* (Stuttgart: Deutscher Sparkassenverlag, 1991), 61–65.

[17]Schönfelder/Thiel, *Ein Markt—eine Währung,* 127–128.

[18]Ibid., 128–129.

stability-oriented monetary policy was not infringed upon by exchange rate policy tasks of the Council.[19]

Budgetary Discipline

At the start of negotiations, the personal representatives attempted to define what constitutes an "excessive" budgetary deficit. The work of the Monetary Committee on this crucial issue in the area of economic discipline was helpful. In addition to the French draft text, a contribution by the German delegation, based on Article 115 BL, served as a basis for negotiations. The German "golden rule" states that the budget deficit should not exceed government investment.[20]

The different member states' conceptions about measures to take to ensure budgetary discipline were quite different. Most delegations acknowledged that the Council must have the power to fix, if need be, binding upper limits on public borrowing by member states. The basic criteria which the Council should use to fix these limits, as well as the question of possible sanctions for states in violation of established limits, remained open. The definition of an "excessive budget deficit" was already difficult as there was little scientific information on the issue.

On the question of sanctions, the French and German delegations proposed in the last instance to suspend payments out of EC funds to member states running excessive budget deficits. This provoked resistance notably on the part of the poorer member states. In their view, a state's financial situation should not be aggravated through additional financial sanctions from the Community if, in an emergency, it runs an excessive budgetary deficit.[21]

Stages of Transition—The Design of Stage Two

In the German view, the strengthening of convergence was the crucial point in the transition between stages. Other member states, including France, interpreted the Rome I Conclusions to mean that the "new institution" should be called the European Central Bank and that it should be assigned substantial tasks during Stage Two. In the course of negotiations, the Luxembourg Presidency put forward a compromise proposal in the form of a non-paper[22] which stated that Stage Two should be divided into four phases:

---

[19]Ibid., 129.

[20]*The Basic Law of the Federal Republic of Germany* (Bonn: Press and Information Office of the Federal Government, 1987), 75–76.

[21]Schönfelder/Thiel, *Ein Markt—eine Währung,* 130.

[22]A non-paper is a handy diplomatic device which facilitates precise discussion on an issue. It avoids labeling a working paper as official so that participants can more easily modify positions in the course of discussion. George P. Schultz, *Turmoil and Triumph* (New York: Scribner's, 1993), 141.

- "At the start of 1993, with the coming into effect of the Maastricht Treaty, a new Council of National Central Bank Governors should be charged to strengthen the cooperation among the Central Banks and promote the development of the ECU;

- On 1 January 1994 the ESCB should be established if sufficient progress on convergence is achieved;

- On 1 January 1996 at the latest the ESCB should be in operation. Its tasks in this phase should be a closer coordination of monetary policies and the preparation of a common monetary policy in the final stage of EMU. All member states should by this time participate in the close exchange rate band of the EMS. Additional convergence demands were again not formulated for this phase.

- Prior to 1 January 1997 the results on convergence should be reviewed and a decision by the European Council on the start of Stage Three of EMU should take place. As soon as this deadline is set, other tasks should be transferred to the European Central Bank including the administration of national foreign currency reserves."[23]

The Presidency's goal was to facilitate a constructive dialogue marked by questions about how best to proceed on this issue instead of forcing the rejection of a position which member states obviously could not agree upon. However, the Luxembourg proposal did not achieve a consensus and was not followed up. Instead of establishing clear demarcations, i.e., the transfer of sovereignty for monetary policy to the ESCB "in one step" at the start of the final stage of EMU, the grey zone between national and ECB competencies would be larger in each of the four phases in the proposal.[24]

During informal discussions among the economics and finance ministers and central bank governors at Apeldoorn on 20–21 September, finance minister Kok invited his colleagues to focus on the following points regarding the establishment of the "new institution," to be called the European Monetary Institute, in the transition stage to begin on 1 January 1994. Since a consensus had emerged in favor of the Institute, its principal tasks, according to the Presidency, should be to assure the coordination of monetary policies, the surveillance of the European Monetary System, the promotion of the ECU, and the technical preparation of Stage Three in terms of the ECB and the single currency. In addition, Kok asked his peers in which manner the autonomy of the Institute could be envisaged during a period when national

---

[23]Schönfelder/Thiel, *Ein Markt—eine Währung,* 131–132.
[24]Ibid., 132.

competencies in the area of monetary policy should not be altered. Regarding the composition of the EMI Council, there were differences of opinion as to whether the Council should consist exclusively of the twelve central bank governors or another person from a circle of independent personalities.

The Transition to Stage Three

"The transition to the final stage involved three problems which came up during the course of negotiations: Who should decide on the entry into Stage Three and with which voting procedure (unanimity or majority vote)? On the basis of which convergence criteria should the suitability of member states to participate in Stage Three be measured? Should a minimum number of states be required to begin Stage Three and, if so, how many?"[25]

The question of voting procedures for entry into Stage Three was particularly complicated. All member states wanted to be involved in the decision on the transition to the final stage of EMU. Likewise, it was necessary to prevent member states which lacked sufficient economic stability to participate, or Great Britain which did not want to participate, from maintaining a veto position. In the course of negotiations, different proposals were contributed to ensure that those member states which did qualify could, in any case, establish a single currency.[26]

"In accordance with a model developed by France and the European Commission, the Luxembourg Presidency envisaged a three-stage voting procedure:

- By a "test date" prior to 1 January 1997 the European Council should decide by the usual consensus procedure on the timing of the transition to Stage Three.

- The ECOFIN Council should then decide, by qualified majority, but with the agreement of at least eight of the twelve member states, on the practical rules of transition as well as on the design and duration of rules of exception for those member states which did not fulfill the conditions for participation in Stage Three.

- Afterwards those states participating in Stage Three should settle by unanimous vote the irrevocable fixing of exchange ratios between their currencies and the necessary measures for the adoption of a single European currency."[27]

---

[25]Ibid., 133.
[26]Ibid., 133–134.
[27]Ibid., 134.

The informal ministerial session, including the central bank governors, at Apeldoorn on 20–21 September marked "an important step forward" for the EMU conference. The ministers considered draft treaty texts prepared by their personal representatives. On the transition to Stage Three, an agreement was reached that convergence criteria proposed by the Dutch Presidency should be utilized. Accordingly the member states should fulfill four conditions for a period of at least two years before moving on to Stage Three:

- "Their rates of inflation must lie close to that of the EC member state with the highest level of price stability.

- Their budget deficit should not be excessive (from the start an upper limit of over 3% of Gross Domestic Product was discussed).

- They should take part in the close exchange rate band of the EMS.

- Their interest rates should be close to those states with the highest level of price stability."[28]

These criteria still had to be defined and quantified in order to be able to have an objective basis for a decision. On the more general rules of transition, the Presidency asked the member states to retain the approach founded on: objective convergence criteria which should not be "utilized in a mechanical manner"; and dispensations permitting the weaker countries to join at a later date on the basis of the same criteria. Minister Kok also called for reflection on the respective roles of the ECOFIN Council, the European Council and the member states to apply three basic principles that the decision to begin Stage Three should respect: no veto; no obligation to participate; and no discrimination. A decision-making procedure based on a Belgian compromise proposal was retained. Three years after the beginning of Stage Two, the Council, based on a report by the European Commission and the EMI, would take stock of the progress on convergence. This evaluation would be founded on objective criteria; it would determine if transition to the final stage is possible and which member states fulfill the set conditions. The analysis of the situation would be adopted by the classic decision-making procedures of the Community in which majority voting in the Council was employed. It would then be transmitted to the European Council whose task it is to make the final decision. For those states which would not be able to participate immediately at the start of Stage Three, special temporary dispensations would be granted which would enable them to rejoin the train on the basis of the same criteria retained for the first group of countries.

---

[28]Ibid., 135.

The question of the minimum number of member states which should be necessary to enter into Stage Three was not yet fixed. The number under discussion ranged from six to eight on the basis of a Community comprising twelve member states. Other issues which remained unclear were the extent to which member states not participating in Stage Three right from the start wished to be involved in the EMU institutions, particularly in the European System of Central Banks and sessions of the ECOFIN Council about special questions relating to EMU.[29]

Economic Convergence Criteria Including Cohesion

The German draft treaty, which was submitted to the IGC in late February, asserted a strict view of convergence In response to the harder tone of the German text, Delors noted that in an effort to have the most precise type of convergence, the Community ran the risk of never achieving EMU. In the spirit of Monnet, Delors spoke of the necessity to create EMU on the basis of "a dialectical impulse among politics, institutional change and the realities of the present situation." During the meeting, Köhler confirmed that German authorities were prepared to share "monetary sovereignty." Yet, the convergence criteria for passage to Stage Three implicit in the German text indicated that the strictest conditions would have to be fulfilled by EMU participants.

Unlike the Commission draft treaty, the German text stipulated three precise conditions to fulfill the convergence criteria in order for member states to make the transition from Stage Two to Stage Three of EMU: a high level of price stability; national budgetary deficits reduced to a "tolerable level"; a broad convergence of interest rates. The German text also indicated that the European Council should take measures to define the eventual participation of those member states unable to make the initial transition to Stage Three.

Cohesion was discussed again during a meeting of the personal representatives in early June. The Spanish delegation reiterated its point of view on the need to include in the new Treaty elements to stimulate convergence. An instrument above and beyond structural funds was required which would assure a transfer of financial resources to poorer member states. In the Spanish view, the assets which price stability and the disappearance of exchange rate risks represent might be sufficient to prevent regional disparities among rich and poor member states. However, these assets would be insufficient to allow the poorer states to catch up to their wealthier neighbors in order to achieve cohesion within the Community. During a general debate on the issue, the Greek, Irish, Portuguese personal representatives approved this vision of things. This pressure was not enough though to convince the

---

[29]Ibid., 136.

Luxembourg Presidency to change its project for a draft treaty. Instead, a compromise envisaged by a majority of the member states assured the Mediterranean countries that the cohesion dossier would be dealt with seriously during talks on the Community budget the following year.

Spain and Greece made their position clear during the EMU conference that they were against signing a Treaty which did not establish a "cohesion fund" to provide Community financing in areas like transeuropean networks and environmental protection. In their view, this would help the poorer member states in their goal to achieve the economic convergence criteria necessary to participate in EMU. Due to the sharp divide of eight to four on cohesion, this issue had to be resolved at the highest level in Maastricht during negotiations on political union.

The Problem of the British "Opting-Out" Clause

The Dutch draft treaty, submitted to the conference on 28 October, aroused the concern of the Commission and several member states due to Article 109 which allowed a member state to "opt-out" of Stage Three. This Article was interpreted by those concerned about its presence in the Treaty as a possible dangerous precedent in light of future enlargements. In their view, this reference to Great Britain's special status regarding EMU should be included in a footnote or a protocol annexed to the Treaty so as not to introduce a general rule on "opting-out" in the Treaty text. Of significance in the draft treaty were several passages within parentheses to indicate the open discussion on text Articles which remained. The most important issue concerned the number of member states necessary to make the transition to Stage Three—six, seven or eight.

The Ministerial "Conclave"

A marathon session of the ECOFIN Council took place from 30 November to 2 December. Important results were registered on issues of institutional questions, budgetary discipline and the transition to Stage Three.

Political Control and Institutional Questions

Regarding the EMI's tasks and administration, an agreement was reached that the EMI should hold the currency reserves of member states which transfer them willingly. There should be restrictions on the utilization of these reserves, however. The currency reserve role of the EMI should have no influence on national monetary policies, for example. The EMI should also have no privately owned capital, only working funds. The President of the EMI should come from outside the circle of central bank governors, but should be suggested by them, whereas the vice-president should be nominated by them. On the question of external monetary policy, it was agreed that the ECOFIN Council could give only general instructions on exchange rate policy but should give no directions on this matter.[30]

Budgetary Discipline
An understanding was reached that, in the context of sanctions taken to implement budgetary discipline, there would be no curtailment of payments from the EC structural funds. A comprehensive set of sanctions was agreed upon that goes from admonitions to interest-free compulsory payments. A certain cooperation was demonstrated to the poorer countries whereby, alongside "hard criteria," like the extent of public deficit and national debt, the overall fiscal policy development of a country should be strictly taken into consideration.[31]

Transition to Stage Three
On the basis of a proposal from Pierre Bérégovoy, if the European Council could not achieve a consensus by 1996 on the start of Stage Three, it should take a decision by simple majority once again in 1998. In this context, the European Council would meet as the "Council," which would enable the heads of state and government to make a decision by simple or qualified majority. In Community parlance, this special meeting of the European Council is known as the Stuttgart Formula.[32]

The marathon ministerial session ended in the early morning hours of 3 December. According to European Commission Vice-President Christophersen, four themes remained for the heads of state and government at Maastricht: a final discussion of the transition to Stage Three of EMU; the "opt-out" clauses for Great Britain and Denmark; economic and social cohesion; and several "defined institutional aspects." In his opinion, none of these difficulties was insurmountable.

On the advice of the ECOFIN Council, the Dutch Presidency proposed to the Maastricht European Council on 5 December the following deadline for the transition to Stage Three:

- By 31 December 1996 at the latest, the EMI Council and the European Commission should report to the ECOFIN Council on the member states' progress in achieving the convergence criteria.

- Afterwards the ECOFIN Council assesses, on a recommendation from the Commission, which member states fulfill the requirements for the transition to Stage Three and delivers a qualified majority vote to the European Council. The ECOFIN Council consults the European Parliament beforehand and transmits Parliament's position to the European Council.

---

[30]Ibid., 142.

[31]Ibid.

[32]Ibid.

- The European Council, according to the Stuttgart Formula as "Council" of the heads of state and government, meets together and decides unanimously, with due regard for the Commission and EMI reports as well as the positions of the ECOFIN Council and the European Parliament, if entry into Stage Three is "reasonable" and establishes by unanimous vote if the majority of the member states fulfill the requirements for Stage Three.

"If the European Council achieves a positive decision on both counts, it subsequently fixes the date for the start of Stage Three. Only in the two votes taken by unanimity, should a member state have a right to veto this decision. Member states that can not yet participate in Stage Three, should not prevent the decision on a deadline. This no-veto principle had yet to be drawn up. If, in the course of this procedure, a starting date for the transition to Stage Three cannot be fixed, the European Council should settle the decision by simple majority in a second round of voting. The following procedure should be valid:

- Prior to the end of 1998, the first two procedural steps on the review of achieved convergence should be repeated.

- The European Council, again meeting in accord with the Stuttgart Formula, assesses by simple majority which member states fulfill the necessary requirements for the transition to Stage Three and fixes by a simple majority vote a starting date for Stage Three of EMU."[33]

INTERPRETING THE EMU CONFERENCE: THREE APPROACHES TO THE IGC PROCESS

Putnam's Two-Level Games

This approach identifies the unit level of analysis, which is defined as states and individual political leaders during the intergovernmental conference process. Two-level games highlight the extent to which heads of state and government were autonomous from their ministers and bureaucracies in their definition of strategy and use of tactics to conclude the IGCs and parliamentary ratifications of Maastricht. In the case of the Dutch Presidency, Putnam's approach illustrates ways in which domestic institutions can complicate European diplomacy. This approach also shows how ministers responsible for advancing the conference negotiations took an independent line vis-à-vis their domestic institutions in order to bring the negotiations to the point where the European Council could then make the final decisions.

---

[33]Ibid., 143.

The influence of French and German domestic institutions on EMU conference diplomacy demonstrate different domestic priorities. In France, the goal of the President was to assert his dominance over monetary policy. Here the triumph of politics over technocracy was evident. In Germany, Kohl had to contend with the powerful position of his finance minister, Theo Waigel, who was an influential politician in the CDU's sister party, the Bavarian CSU. The Chancellor also had to satisfy the requirements of the Bundesbank, the Bundesrat and the Bundestag, all institutions which demanded an EMU treaty written "in German script."

In terms of strategy formulation at Level I, the French approach was a highly centralized one with Mitterrand, Guigou and Bérégovoy all playing significant roles, supported by the work of Trichet and de Boissieu. Yet, the responsibility for decision making remained Mitterrand's alone. He was not inclined to share it with monetary authorities like the head of the *Banque de France*. Kohl, on the other hand, operated in an environment which assigned considerable responsibilities to his finance minister and the Bundesbank President. These individuals also had to work with Genscher whose approach tended to favor compromise solutions with France.

Domestic Institutions

One example of the practical difficulties inherent in the strategy of *Parallelität* involved domestic institutions. These difficulties were rooted in differences existing among domestic bureaucracies and in the fact that mechanisms for coordinating the two IGCs were rather weak. Two sorts of competence were needed at the EMU conference: technical-economic and legal-institutional. The first was in abundant supply, but the second was scarce due to the secondary role of officials from foreign ministries.[34] In concrete terms, this problem was illustrated by the initial formulation of the Dutch Presidency on the decision-making procedure in the Council on the transition to Stage Three. Specifically, this initial formulation eliminated any idea of a political commitment taken in signing and ratifying the Treaty. In other words, the Treaty risked being downgraded to a mere declaration of intent. Here the lack of coordination between the two IGCs proved deleterious: a combination of skepticism and inexperience with institutional issues risked jeopardizing the whole endeavor.[35]

The three approaches, used together, provide an explanation of the ways in which domestic institutions, and the individual actors working within them, complicated both the internal bargaining and external negotiations which took place during the EMU process. Different points of view among domestic

---

[34]Lorenzo Bini-Smaghi, Tommaso Padoa-Schioppa and Francesco Papadia, *The Policy History of the Maastricht Treaty: The Transition to the Final Stage of EMU* (Rome: Banca d'Italia, 1993), 25.

[35]Ibid., 27.

bureaucracies, at the ministerial and official levels, complicated a situation prevalent throughout the conference: namely, the weakness of the mechanisms meant to ensure coordination between the two IGCs. This weakness impacted on the subsequent ratification debates; the number of decision-making procedures and large scope of policy changes mentioned in the Maastricht Treaty baffled the average citizen.

At the ministerial level, the role of the Dutch Presidency of the Council was particularly instrumental in its focus on the necessity to conclude negotiations in Brussels at the expense of domestic agendas. For instance, during the Dutch Presidency, Kok departed from the views of his advisers in the Dutch finance ministry. Their positions were influenced by a hidden domestic agenda which in part aimed to get a grip on budget deficits in the Netherlands. Instead, Kok used his political skills and "feeling" for the EMU conference discussions to advance dossiers.[36] In terms of Putnam's approach, his actions illustrate the influence of negotiators below the chief of government which contributed significantly to the final results obtained at Maastricht and the independent line taken by these same negotiators in Brussels from their domestic ministries. At crucial points during the multilateral negotiations, domestic agendas had to give way to the requirements of bringing the EMU conference to a close.

Ministers and politico-administrative hybrids were so influential throughout the conference that political leaders in the European Council intervened rarely, if at all. This suggests an external negotiation process whose technical details went beyond the understanding of most heads of state and government. These leaders indeed found themselves confronted by central bankers and politico-administrative actors who had influence on internal bargaining and external negotiations within their limited area of expertise. The close link between the two IGCs implied, moreover, that economic and financial influence could be translated into political influence. The Bundesbank's insistence on the need for a strong political union to complement EMU attests to this fact.

The French Case

Throughout the IGC process Bérégovoy, with the full support of Mitterrand, advanced the idea of a *gouvernement économique*. Clearly he respected the right of the President to dictate the terms of monetary policy and tried to transfer this institutional set-up to the European level. There was bound to be tension, however, because the Treaty being negotiated contained provisions calling for the independence of the *Banque de France* from the government. In the monetary sphere, this was a challenge to the President's political authority.

---

[36]Interview, Commission of the European Communities, 25 May 1994.

In an attempt to shape the Treaty provisions under negotiation, Dumas described an alternative plan in his address to the National Assembly on 24 October. Regarding EMU he clarified the actual French concern at that point in the conference to compensate for the power which would be given to a relatively independent ECB by a political counterweight which would decide on the economic and financial policy in the Community. France maintained that this role should not only belong to the Commission, but to the European Council as well. In the latter, a forum for discussion among elected leaders, efficiency would be reconciled with respect for national sovereignties.[37]

Ironically, the French emphasis on the role of political leaders in the European Council as a way of addressing the democratic deficit in the European Community came at a time when the French public, and publics in other European countries, were suspicious of domestic political establishments. In France the phenomenon of a popular loss of faith was striking. Part of the difficulty was the length of the President's tenure in office. With the passage of time, he had become more out of touch, less willing to consult and more prone to mistakes. The French did not doubt Mitterrand's intellectual capabilities but rather his powers of leadership. The closed circle with the President at its center was far removed from the popular imagination. Most people were quite preoccupied with their own daily problems in an era of high unemployment and doubts about the national identity in the face of immigration on a massive scale. For the man in the street, politics had become boring. The French ratification process subsequently demonstrated that a national political renewal at the elite and societal levels was an urgent necessity.[38]

The German Case

Internal bargaining on IGC diplomacy in Bonn throughout 1991 was shaped by several factors. Two of the more significant ones were the autonomy of the ministries involved and the nature of the SPD-Opposition in the Bundesrat and the Bundestag. On EMU, the ministry of finance took the lead in active consultation with the Bundesbank and the Chancellor's Office. The Chancellor established the link between EMU and political union early on and the SPD-Opposition insisted that any Treaty which did not make significant advances in political integration would not be ratified by either the Bundesrat or the Bundestag.

In Germany, more so than in other Western European governments, the role and position of the minister of finance is a particularly strong one in

---

[37]Ministère des Affaires Etrangères, *La politique etrangère de la France*, Textes et Documents, Septembre-Octobre 1991, 146–147.

[38]"The Thinker Who Ran out of Ideas," *The Economist*, October 19, 1991, 31–32.

relation to the other members of the Cabinet.[39] In the Maastricht context, this was because of the common understanding between the finance minister and the Bundesbank President, the position of Waigel as an influential member of the CSU and the involvement of the finance minister in the internal bargaining on all IGC issues with financial implications.

The position of ministry of finance civil servants working on the EMU conference was heavily influenced by the status of the D-mark as the strongest and most stable currency in the EMS. In order to assure that a single European currency would be just as stable, the future ECB had to be taken seriously by citizens, firms and investors. The German view on a low-profile monetary institution in Stage Two came to the fore at a session of the personal representatives in April. When it became clear in early July that a Belgian compromise proposal to create a European Monetary Institute in Stage Two would be acceptable, officials in the ministry of finance, with the staunch backing of the Bundesbank, adopted a minimalist position as to its future responsibilities. By the time of the informal meeting in Apeldoorn in late September, the German position was somewhat at variance with the French particularly on such issues as the composition of the EMI's Board, the source of its capital and the extent of its tasks in the management of foreign exchange reserves.[40]

Internal bargaining on the issue of the nature of the monetary institution took place among the "Gang of Five," namely, Günter Grosche at Finance, Peter-Wilhelm Schlüter from the Bundesbank, Rolf Kaiser from the Chancellor's Office, Ralf Zeppernick from Economics and Wilhelm Schönfelder from the *Auswärtiges Amt*. The bargaining involved a great deal of flexibility, give and take, and the search for common ground in the joint elaboration of German positions. This was especially true given that the Bundesbank's position on EMU was expressed with unusual directness prior to the Luxembourg European Council by Vice-President Hans Tietmeyer. The Bundesbank Vice-President was a participant on occasion with Schlüter during the internal bargaining process. Tietmeyer clearly stated that a united Germany had much to lose in EMU, namely "one of the most successful and best monetary structures in the world."[41] His views were counterbalanced at times by those of an influential advocate of monetary integration, State

---

[39]Torbjörn Larsson, "The Role and Position of Ministers of Finance," in *Governing Together*, eds. Jean Blondel and Ferdinand Müller- Rommel (New York: St. Martin's, 1993), 207–222.

[40]Bini-Smaghi, Padoa-Schioppa and Papadia, 16–19.

[41]David Marsh, *Die Bundesbank* (München: C. Bertelsmann, 1992), 312.

Secretary Werner Lautenschlager from the *Auswärtiges Amt*[42] who participated at times in internal bargaining on EMU with Schönfelder.

Discussions on German positions throughout the IGC were held weekly at the ministry of finance. Grosche organized the information gleaned from these sessions in preparation for the conference sessions in Brussels. He was in direct contact with his immediate supervisor, Gert Haller, and with Horst Köhler. Both Köhler and Haller represented German interests at EMU conference meetings. Despite this collective input during internal bargaining, some officials from the *Auswärtiges Amt* still spoke of an unwillingness on the part of Finance officials to allow others to influence decision making in general on matters related to EMU.[43] This suggested a tension between the two ministries for influence in the sphere of monetary policy. The *Auswärtiges Amt*, in particular, was keen to assure its minister's decision-making input in the General Affairs Council on a wide range of policy matters in the proposed Union. These differences point to the relevance of bureaucratic politics at the level of internal bargaining among domestic ministries and "turf-fighting" which describes conflicts within the Council structure (ECOFIN and Monetary Committee versus General Affairs and European Council) during EMU negotiations at the European level. The impact of these differences on the formulation of strategy and tactics is considered in the next section.

Negotiators' Strategies
The use of strategy, as opposed to tactics, was more prevalent during the EMU conference than during negotiations on political union. The small number of precise, technical issues made strategy formulation less complicated, particularly for the French. German goals were extremely well defined throughout the IGC. Since the other states were the "askers" on EMU, in the sense that they had more to gain, the German position was predominant. Still tactics were necessary to bring about compromise solutions with the French on key issues like the institutional content of Stage Two and decision making on the transition to Stage Three.

The French Case: The Triumph of Politics and Hierarchy Inside the President's Circle
The EMU conference took place during a period when the costs of national unity prompted German monetary authorities to follow an expansionist policy. High German interest rates also obliged other member states to follow

---

[42]State Secretary Lautenschlager was instrumental in negotiations which led to breakthroughs during the German Council Presidencies in 1983 and 1988. Unlike State Minister Seiler-Albring who was a parliamentary state minister, Lautenschlager was a permanent civil servant with the highest rank in the ministry. Rede des Bundesministers des Auswärtigen, Dr. Klaus Kinkel, anläßlich des Abschiedsempfangs für Staatssekretär Dr. Lautenschlager auf dem Petersberg am 28. Januar 1993, Mitteilung für die Presse Nr. 1017/93 (Bonn: *Auswärtiges Amt*, 1993).

[43]Interview, *Auswärtiges Amt*, 29 January 1993.

rigorous monetary policies. French strategy on EMU was ambitious in its aim to counter German monetary dominance in the Community.

The triumph of political will as opposed to technocratic expertise was the goal of Mitterrand's IGC diplomacy.[44] French domestic bargaining on positions taken during negotiations took place in a highly centralized politico-administrative environment. A small team consisting of individuals in the Elysée and the Quai d'Orsay served as coordinators for both conferences. Bureaucratic politics was not a relevant aspect of internal bargaining in Paris. Yet, the French were playing a shrewd game of turf-fighting at the European level by insisting on the primacy of the European Council, not the ECOFIN Council, in the EMU process.

As seen from the Elysée, one idea marked French diplomacy on EMU: it would be a positive development for the international monetary system and advantageous for France. Therefore, its quick realization with wise convergence criteria was a French goal. In the French view, the use of tactics to deal with the main problems during the conference, namely, defining the convergence criteria, determining the use of sanctions to counter excessive budgetary deficits and monetary transfers in the context of the debate on cohesion, was necessary.[45]

On EMU issues, there were technical meetings at the Elysée and at Matignon which included President Mitterrand's counselor for European affairs, Caroline de Margerie, Dumas' counselor for foreign affairs, Jean-Michel Casa, and the personal representatives, Trichet and de Boissieu. During general meetings with various ministers in the French government on the different issues which arose on the agenda of the EMU conference, the same individuals were involved: Mitterrand, Dumas, Guigou, Bérégovoy, and Trichet and de Boissieu.[46] The small number of individuals made strategy formulation easier given the absence of domestic constraints. Yet, Mitterrand himself acknowledged that an agreement on the two Treaties would most likely be achieved in the last five minutes at Maastricht. The President was taking into account British intransigence on social policy and immigration issues, key dossiers in the conference on political union. A British veto on any significant issue at one table threatened to jeopardize an accord on EMU at the other.

---

[44]Jean-Michel Lamy, "Mitterrand parie sur le duo franco-allemand pour conduire l'ambition européenne commune," *Les Echos*, 8 octobre 1991, 7.

[45]Interview, Quai d'Orsay, 8 March 1993.

[46]Ibid.

The German Case: Chancellor Diplomacy, Ministerial Autonomy and SPD-Opposition

The German interest in EMU was first articulated by Genscher with the active support of Kohl. Administrative officials indicated that it was Kohl's insistence on the need for EMU that guided German diplomacy. Given these political developments, the Bundesbank had adopted its own subtle strategy since the early days of the Delors Committee. Instead of a counterproductive and outright opposition to EMU, the establishment of the strictest possible conditions for the entry of member states into its final stage could undermine its realization.[47] The emphasis on strong convergence as a required task of Stage Two was clearly spelled out by Bundesbank representative to the EMU conference, Peter-Wilhelm Schlüter.[48] In late June, Kohl stated the German position on the necessity to insure a stable currency with characteristic frankness: "No one is ready to give up the stable D-mark in favor of an unstable currency. That is after all a major foregone conclusion."[49] The SPD-Opposition, in its inquiries to the federal government also showed concern as to the standards set for convergence and the methods by which economic disparities among the member states would be addressed.[50] Its insistence on a voice in the transition to the final stage would be a major issue in the ratification debate.

The issue which perhaps best illustrated Kohl's strategy to achieve EMU was the type of decision making to use in the transition to Stage Three. In late September, the Presidency's formulation of the procedure on the transition to Stage Three was reworded to emphasize a Community-based procedure. This was done since the decision to move to Stage Three had to be taken by Community bodies not by individual member states. However, it still contained a clause which enabled countries to decide freely whether to participate or ask for a derogation. By November a form of wording was proposed to limit the opt-out clause to specific countries which had declared at the time of ratification their unwillingness to move to the third stage. In the last meetings of the EMU conference before Maastricht, the procedure for the third stage was substantially strengthened.[51]

---

[47]Marsh, 324–325.

[48]Peter-Wilhelm Schlüter, "Die Europäische Wirtschafts- und Währungsunion: Anmerkungen zur Regierungskonferenz," *Integration* 3/91 (Juli 1991): 106–114.

[49]Marsh, 301. The translation is the author's.

[50]Deutscher Bundestag, 12. Wahlperiode, Kleine Anfrage der Fraktion der SPD, Stand der Verhandlungen der EG-Regierungskonferenzen und Verhandlungsstrategie der Bundesregierung zur politischen Union und zur europäischen Wirtschafts- und Währungsunion, Drucksache 12/833, 6; Deutscher Bundestag, 12. Wahlperiode, Antwort der Bundesregierung auf die Kleine Anfrage der Fraktion der SPD, Drucksache 12/1068, 18–20.

[51]Bini-Smaghi, Padoa-Schioppa and Papadia, 28–29.

First, the opt-out clause was eliminated from the main text of the Treaty and the British problem was left for the heads of state and government to settle in Maastricht. Second, it was decided that *de facto* and *de jure* the decision would be taken by the European Council, which would adopt the voting rules of the Council of Ministers. Third, unanimity was required to take a decision in 1996. Lastly, the decision would be taken in 1998 by simple majority, if in 1996 the decision for a majority of member states to move to Stage Three was not taken.[52]

Technically, the decision-making procedure had some loose ends, but it clearly reflected the principle that Waigel, Köhler, Bérégovoy, Kok and others had stressed with particular emphasis in the closing days of the EMU conference: "Maastricht is irreversible." To participants in the IGC process, it was clear that the new, forceful push was influenced by the active interest taken by the heads of state and government, Mitterrand and Kohl in particular, during their preparations for the Maastricht European Council.[53] This issue illustrates the will of both leaders to work together to push the Maastricht process forward and to move beyond exclusive formulations of individual nation-state preferences. The intergovernmentalist framework of analysis does not explain why this type of decision-making procedure was accepted, particularly by Germany, whereas two-level games, in tandem with the four images and integrative bargaining, stress the influence that individuals below the head of state and government had on shaping a common approach to bargaining on EMU within the Council structure.

The Council is emphasized in the Maastricht process as a Community institution capable of collective decision making. As Hayes-Renshaw and Wallace point out "the term 'intergovernmental' implies that there is some definable boundary between...the national polity and the transnational arena." This volume argues that this boundary was not always clear during the Maastricht process. "Ministers and their officials meeting in the Council are both national and Community actors, carrying double affiliations and responding to prompts and pressures from both sides."[54] This fact, which was also true during the Maastricht process, gives us reason to try to explain that process in a way which departs from a classical intergovernmentalist framework.

During the IGCs and domestic ratifications, there was a need to structure the monetary policy debate at the domestic and European levels. This attitudinal structuring on monetary policy among the actors involved can be considered more thoroughly by looking at transnational politics, i.e.,

---

[52]Ibid., 29.

[53]Ibid.

[54]Fiona Hayes-Renshaw and Helen Wallace, "Executive Power in the European Union: The Functions and Limits of the Council of Ministers," *Journal of European Public Policy* 2 (December 1995): 563.

the impact of the "1992" process, and cross-table alliances, i.e., Dumas-Genscher, Trichet-de Boissieu-Köhler, than by single nation-state preferences. It was also clear that among the levels of internal bargaining and external negotiation, politico-administrative hybrids understood the psychological views of their cross-table counterparts better at times than their ministers. For example, Trichet and de Boissieu both sensed that the German reaction to the idea of a *gouvernement économique* would not be a positive one. Their political feeling for this situation ran counter to Bérégovoy's insistence on a *gouvernement économique* and on the issue of the independence of the *Banque de France* throughout the Maastricht process. The capacity of individual negotiators to come to terms with the views of their counterparts impacted on the extent to which integrative, as opposed to distributive, bargaining could take place in Brussels. Köhler's capacity to empathize with the efforts of other states like Italy to cut budget deficits in order to meet the convergence criteria subtly influenced the way in which Maastricht was presented to the Bundestag, Bundesrat and to the German people.

Clearly Kohl's strategy during the EMU conference had to take into account the interests of the Länder and the Bundestag. His finance minister was responsible in large part to present the government's views. The German delegation's emphasis on precise, objectively definable and strict criteria had to be thoroughly presented by representatives from the ministries of finance and economics to members of the Bundesrat and Bundestag during a meeting of the *EG-Ausschuß* on 25 September 1991. After the informal meeting of the ECOFIN Council in Apeldoorn days before, Länder politicians and national parliamentarians were particularly concerned about the progress registered in the IGC on the content of Stage Two and tasks of the EMI, the convergence criteria for the transition to the final stage, the budgetary sanctions mechanism in Stage Three, relations among member states making the transition to the final stage and those remaining in Stage Two, and the ECB's competencies in the domain of exchange rate policy.[55]

Aberbach, Putnam and Rockman's Four Images of Civil Servants

As the negotiations advanced, the role of the personal representative became increasingly important. Aberbach, Putnam and Rockman's approach identifies a new breed of actor introduced by the IGC process, the politico-administrative hybrid. This actor's role can be situated between the state and

---

[55]Interview, *EG-Ausschuß*, 29 April 1993. In the last phase of the EMU conference, the German position on the substantial issues was stated in a press document released by the Ministry of Economics. Bundesministerium für Wirtschaft, Pressestelle, Überlegungen zum gegenwärtigen Stand der Verhandlungen über die europäische Wirtschafts-und Währungsunion, Bonn, 22. Oktober 1991.

political leader level of analysis identified by the two-level games approach and the internal bargaining and external negotiations processes emphasized in light of Monnet's approach. The EMU conference reveals the special role these actors played between the national and European levels, and the political and administrative worlds, as they defined interests and positions throughout the IGC process.

During the conference, compromises made on the basis of Presidency non-papers and drafts had to be struck. Trichet was particularly instrumental during the discussions on the transition to Stage Three. In early April, he proposed with Cartesian clarity three basic principles for the procedure on the passage to the final stage: no veto in the sense that no country could prevent the others from moving to the third stage of EMU if this was desired; no coercion whereby no country should be obliged to participate against its will; and no arbitrary exclusion in the sense that insufficient economic convergence would be the only other reason which could prevent the participation in the Union of a willing member state. These principles, and the idea that the European Council should in substance take the decision while the ECOFIN Council would implement it, were accepted following the endorsement of President Delors as the basis of the conference discussions. The precise interpretation to be given to these principles was then thoroughly debated.[56]

From the vantage point of de Boissieu, who was actively involved in both conferences, the gravity of negotiations on EMU involved the positions of certain key member states. Italy took a maximalist position vis-à-vis the center which was occupied by France and Germany. Spain, negotiating for the cohesion states, was closer to France although slightly off-center and Great Britain took a minimalist position. Italy allied with France on several key issues of the conference especially the timing of transition stages. Great Britain, despite its general reserve on Stage Three, otherwise followed the German line.

In the Fall the Dutch Presidency, represented by finance minister Kok, prepared the ground for a satisfactory compromise on the functioning of the EMI in Stage Two: the idea that the EMI should have an external president, a limited amount of capital and some ability to manage reserves. The German delegation, led by Horst Köhler, showed some flexibility on all these points and recognized the importance of the task of preparing the instruments for the single monetary policy. Overall the risk of an excessively weak monetary institution in Stage Two was avoided. The responsibilities attributed to the EMI in the field of monetary policy coordination remained quite limited, however. The risk of an inconsistency developing between the stability of exchange rates in the ERM and the autonomous conduct of monetary policies

---

[56]Bini-Smaghi, Padoa-Schioppa and Papadia, 26.

in the transition was not really confronted.[57] In the German view, this was due in part to a lack of time and an exhausting agenda for officials at the working level who bore the brunt of the work throughout the EMU conference.[58] In the end, the weakness of the coordination function of the EMI is one reason why some observers conclude that it eventually resembled more the monetary institution favored by the Germans and the British than that envisaged by the French and the Italians.[59]

By many accounts, the key intellectual contribution and impact on the EMU conference came from the Germans in combination with the Dutch Presidency. As German personal representative, Köhler played a decisive role. He carried the persuasion that derives from a clear conception of the German interest, both in terms of what the German government wanted and what the Bundesbank would wear.[60] Many EMU conference participants found the state secretary to be a combination of openness and charm as well as a talented negotiator capable of enforcing the German negotiating line. The other participants also realized that ultimately his government had the one veto that mattered. Köhler's influence was replicated in the Monetary Committee, of which he was a member with Trichet. His position at the official level, and oftentimes at the ministerial level negotiating in place of Waigel, was a pivotal one around which a balance had to be found. Köhler's work was consistently supported by that of Grosche, who in the last months of the IGC participated at the level of negotiation below that of the personal representatives, the group of experts. Unlike Trichet, Köhler was vocal in his support of EMU, speaking out along with Waigel to members of the German press and public on the advantages of a single currency. The combination of his presence negotiating at the ministerial level and his public articulation of the advantages of EMU for Germany, during the negotiations and subsequent parliamentary ratification debate, characterized the state secretary as a new breed of actor emerging from the Maastricht process. As a politico-administrative hybrid, Köhler was one of the most important actors linking political leadership at the state level of analysis with the types of bargaining and negotiation processes during the conferences and Treaty ratifications.

As a group, the personal representatives wanted to keep monetary affairs within the competence of the ECOFIN Council instead of leaving such decisions to the heads of state and government in the European Council. This was one issue on which a decision was necessary in order to make the project for a draft treaty in the EMU conference conform with that of political union. It was also an issue where the leaders in the European Council would assert their authority vis-à-vis ministers and civil servants in the form of "an

---

[57]Ibid., 19–22.

[58]Interview, Federal Ministry of Finance, 26 April 1993.

[59]Bini-Smaghi, Padoa-Schioppa and Papadia, 22.

[60]Dyson, *Elusive Union*, 155.

independent political will in the name of integration and union."[61]

In terms of EMU, all three levels—from the group of experts, up through the personal representative to the ministerial—made crucial political decisions that enabled the process to flow, if not always smoothly, then consistently over time. Although compromises were struck that were not always satisfactory to all parties concerned, the goal of creating a single currency was accepted by all with the exception of Britain. At each level, matters which pertained to essential decisions on key issues were debated. Finance ministers were engaged in the decision-making process up until the few final decisions that remained for the heads of state and government in Maastricht.

The personal representatives' role as joint problem solvers is a difficult issue on which to generalize, however. During the IGC, these national administrative elites functioned as the two-faced gatekeepers of European policy, looking toward their national as well as the European arena and conducting negotiations between the two. These officials took the Commission's draft treaty and proposals quite seriously and respected Delors' contributions. Although the German delegation remained adamant on key issues like central bank autonomy and strict convergence criteria out of an interest to ensure price stability, Köhler was open to solutions which would promote joint gains among the member states. There was a certain amount of understanding voiced for the poorer member states as well as a willingness to give them every opportunity to improve their economic situations so as to be eligible for Stage Three of EMU. The Community interest was viewed through the prism of German monetary stability with the central bankers in all member states attaining a certain legitimacy in policy making in order to promote stability in the European system.

At the official level, Köhler and Trichet worked together closely and participated in key ministerial sessions alongside the ministers. Trichet's understanding of German thinking on monetary policy was helpful in the search for solutions to common problems like the content of Stage Two. Compromises were struck which were acceptable to both parties in large part because French and German officials, like their leaders, wanted to make EMU a reality. Their mutual commitment to the irreversible nature of the EMU process prepared the way for a series of bargains to be struck on the decision-making procedure to begin Stage Three during the last months of the EMU negotiation. The acceptance of qualified majority voting to make this decision is a striking example of the use of joint problem solving to achieve a result in the Community interest.

Waigel's noted absence at times from the table in Brussels may reveal more about the nature of the EMU conference than his presence there. Köhler's input attests to the influence of the new breed of actors identified

---

[61]Ibid., 159.

here as joint problem solvers on crucial issues like the definition of convergence criteria and the timing of the transition to Stage Three. Although the final decision on the transition to Stage Three was taken by Kohl in Maastricht, Köhler's voice was useful to keep domestic constituents (ministry of finance, Bundesbank, German public opinion) on board throughout the IGC process. His style of bargaining and negotiation was one which stressed German interests while remaining open to creative solutions to foster a Community spirit.

The EMU conference also gave Delors an opportunity to demonstrate his abilities as a natural strategist and negotiator who thinks in terms of integrative bargaining and the general interest. Delors made use of his expertise in monetary matters to facilitate joint problem solving on EMU. He then translated this know-how into negotiating influence among the heads of state and government. Delors' role can be described as that of a linchpin holding together different bargaining relations[62] while suggesting creative solutions like having the British opt-out on EMU and the cohesion fund. His public role as a defender of a federal Europe, a Community based on institutions as well as on Franco-German relations, is another illustration of the new breed of actor emphasized here. As the highest ranking politico-administrative representative of a European institution, Delors, even more than Köhler, could be situated between the state/political leader level of analysis and the internal bargaining and external negotiations during the IGC process. More than any other leader, besides Mitterrand and Kohl, Delors identified himself personally and politically with Maastricht.

Delors' presence throughout the IGC process in discussions with central bankers, administrative officials, ministers and political leaders in the European Council placed him in the best position to serve as the bridge between the administrative and political levels on EMU. No other individual was so well placed at so many different levels of negotiation to contribute decisively to the final outcome. In discussions among leaders in the European Council, Delors spoke out in favor of a link between EMU and cohesion in such a way as to promote the strategic role of the Commission as an institution capable of bargaining and mediating on behalf of the poorer member states within the Community. His efforts, and those of Kohl and Gonzalez, to get beyond purely distributive bargaining tactics on cohesion and to reach an agreement which would benefit the general interest were clear. Many Germans felt that this agreement went against German domestic interests, given the difficult economic conditions in the Federal Republic after unification. Here Kohl's tactics paid less attention to distributive and intraorganizational bargaining than to integrative bargaining and attitudinal structuring. His focus was clearly a European one even if this meant overruling his own administrative officials and societal interest groups.

---

[62]Ibid., 171.

Monnet's Approach

The French draft treaty on EMU, introduced on 28 January, not only brought up the issues of economic convergence, political control via the institutions and the transition phases; the text also raised questions about the approach to negotiations during the EMU conference. President Delors expressed his own fears about "opening Pandora's Box" as delegations brought up new issues and questions instead of concentrating on those already on the table. This was a particularly important point regarding institutional issues given the demands imposed by the parallel nature of the two IGCs. The French draft text did not only propose changes to specific chapters of the Commission's draft treaty. It represented an alternative institutional plan for EMU which also caused conflicts during the political union negotiations. In terms of using the Monnet approach to achieve integrative bargaining, the task at hand was to stick to the Commission text as the basis for negotiations during the EMU conference.

After the ministerial meeting on 28 January, Delors sought to remind the Twelve of the questions which were left outstanding at the Rome European Council. On issues of economic discipline, Delors signaled that the French draft text gave considerable substance to economic union. By going further than the Commission regarding budgetary constraints, the text constituted an important element of compromise. In the context of political control and institutional issues, Delors noted that differences still existed among the proposals on relations between the ESCB and the Council. Although the French text conserved the "classical institutional triangle," Council and Monetary Committee plus European Parliament and Commission, Delors distanced himself from the French idea of a Congress of Parliaments. He reasoned that this attempt by Paris to strengthen the association of national parliaments and the European Parliament could undercut the other Community institutions by creating a new duo: European Council-Congress. Delors' comments on these issues illustrate the way he used Monnet's approach to preserve the institutional balance in the Community.

On the convergence conditions required to make the transition to the final stage, the German delegation attributed high importance to the reference values defining the convergence criteria which, it argued, should be utilized in an objective way. From this vantage point, the fact that only three countries qualified in 1991, namely, France, Luxembourg and Denmark, was not an argument against strict criteria. It rather indicated that convergence conditions were not yet ripe for a move to the final stage. The German delegation supported the view that convergence criteria should be inscribed in the Treaty. In this way, the criteria could only be modified by a unanimous vote of the member states. This point was one on which there was disagreement with the French delegation. A compromise solution which was the result of classic distributive bargaining was adopted after the French agreed with the German delegation on this point.[63] This issue highlights the strength of the Franco-German tandem and the use of distributive bargaining during the EMU conference. Integrative bargaining was evident to the extent that all the participants were engaged in the process to find a way to achieve a single currency. How to do so was the problem which required a common solution. In this sense, the EMU conference illustrated Monnet's maxim that the goal was to line all the negotiators up on one side of the table and the problems, or issues, to be tackled on the other. The cohesion issue, in which a way was found to integrate the interests of Spain, Portugal, Ireland and Greece, is just one example of the efforts to keep all the member states on board.

One convergence criterion introduced by the German delegation, participation in the Exchange Rate Mechanism, aimed to insure that economic agents and policy authorities would become acquainted sufficiently in advance with the constraints of a fixed monetary system. This proposal was accepted by the other delegations in part because it attributed to the EMS the "institutional" role of preparing the road toward full monetary union. The Germans also proposed the convergence of long-term interest rates as a criterion, arguing that "the durability of the convergence achieved (must be) reflected in the markets' verdict, as well, i.e., in a virtual harmonization of capital market rates." Eventually, this criterion was included in the Treaty despite Italian and French opposition.[64] Here the weight of the German delegation was evident. Its emphasis was less on fixed timetables, characteristic of Monnet's approach, than on a clear conception of the national and regional interests, as defined in a thorough preparation for Stage Three. The insistence on these points was necessary in light of the domestic ratification, which Köhler made clear throughout the Maastricht process.

During negotiations, President Delors suggested the idea that it might be possible, in order to get around a possible British veto, to imagine a "unilateral declaration" by which London would emphasize during the Treaty ratification that its acceptance of the common currency in Stage Three would require the formal agreement of the House of Commons. Delors underlined that given the United Kingdom's active participation in the conference, this idea might be premature. However, if during the Maastricht European Council, the United Kingdom could not accept the idea of a single European currency, the Treaty must be agreed on by the other member states. Here Delors showed his ability to serve as a mediator among the member states reconciling divergent positions based on his conception of the general Community interest.

During the ministerial meeting at Apeldoorn, general agreement was reached on the following: the EMU Treaty must be signed by the Twelve so as to reject, at least in theory, the notion of a "two-speed Europe;" a balance must

---

[63]Bini-Smaghi, Padoa-Schioppa and Papadia, 33.

[64]Ibid., 35.

occur between the economic and monetary poles of EMU; the procedures to follow for the decision on transition to the final stage, a decision which must be made by the European family; and the institutional provisions which must be finalized. The informal meeting at Apeldoorn was significant in terms of Monnet's approach because of the commitment to using Community decision-making procedures to achieve the final stage of EMU. This procedure included the suggestion of qualified majority voting by the heads of state and government on the transition after input from the Commission and the EMI, in the form of reports, and a consultative role for the European Parliament in the process.

Under the Dutch Presidency, the basic negotiating text of the EMU conference was modified from that of the Commission text, particularly regarding the introduction of the EMI in Stage Two. Nonetheless, the Commission was influential when it gained a greater role for the European Parliament in EMU. In accordance with Article 109b of the Treaty, the ECB is to present an annual report to the European Parliament and may be requested to appear before its competent committees. The Commission also influenced proposals on capital liberalization with third countries. Again, with strong Commission support, the proposal of the French and German governments that, as a sanction for excessive budget deficits, EC structural fund aid should be withheld, was defeated.

Delors' personal influence was apparent throughout negotiations concerning the Protocol on Economic and Social Cohesion, including its provision for the new cohesion fund to support environmental projects and transeuropean networks. Fundamental to this Protocol, agreed on in Maastricht, was the idea of matching support for weaker EC countries that were fulfilling programs of economic convergence as part of EMU. Throughout the IGC Delors put his political weight behind what he regarded as a key linkage between EMU and cohesion. He was also concerned about the Commission's competencies in EMU, particularly in the field of multilateral surveillance as a means to measure progress on convergence. Here the Commission was given a role to play as stated in Article 103 of the Maastricht Treaty.[65] In each case, Delors focused on the role of institutions as a means to define the context for state action and on the positive gains which could be achieved from integrative bargaining on issues which divided the richer and poorer member states within the Community. In the final remaining weeks of EMU negotiations, Delors and the French consistently emphasized the Monnet approach in the form of a timetable for the transition to Stage Three. This set the scene for integrative bargaining on EMU between Mitterrand and Kohl at Maastricht.

---

[65]Dyson, *Elusive Union*, 147–148.

SUMMARY

Throughout 1991, the EMU conference was able to deal with many of the important issues on the table in the four key issue areas considered in this chapter: political control, including institutional questions; budgetary discipline; the transition to Stages Two and Three of EMU; and economic convergence criteria including cohesion. In terms of the multilateral negotiation process, it is essential to underline that by the time the Luxembourg Presidency proposed its first draft treaty on 17 April about 80% of the final text agreed in Maastricht was already on the table. This was clearly due to the work of the personal representatives as the key actors in the EMU process. At the state level of analysis, highlighted by two-level games, the French representatives, Trichet and de Boissieu, went back to Paris weekly for internal discussions. Köhler, Haller and Grosche were also based in Bonn giving them ready access to other federal ministries that had to be involved in domestic bargaining. Whereas the French achieved internal consensus easily on the diplomacy of EMU, the Germans took much more time in internal bargaining, remaining for nine hours in continuous discussion at one point on the transition to Stage Three.[66] This point highlights the relevance of bureaucratic politics in the German case. It also illustrates the great efforts that went into achieving a consensus position among the federal ministries on different issues.

Three concrete issues dominated discussions throughout the EMU conference: the British problem; the contents of Stage Two; and economic convergence criteria. The Dutch Presidency began its work on the basis of at least two solid accomplishments by its Luxembourg predecessor: a decision by the European Council to begin Stage Two on 1 January 1994 and a willingness on the part of all member states to demonstrate progress on convergence in the form of written reports to the Council. As the conference entered its final phase, a fourth level of negotiation, the technical experts, was added to facilitate discussions. Since these experts were removed from the political levels of negotiation, it was easier for them to reach decisions. These decisions were then passed up to the personal representatives for review. This illustrates the bottom to top nature of the Maastricht process. In many respects while the highest political leaders set the guidelines, the working level civil servants bore the brunt of the task implementation during the negotiations and ratifications. This was particularly true in the German case where no domestic referendum occurred.

The use of several approaches brings out the nature of the work performed by a new breed of actor situated between the highest political leadership and the civil servant level throughout the IGC process. This actor had to confront tensions existing at different levels of domestic bargaining and external negotiations and tried to deal with them, if possible, in a

---

[66]Interview, *Auswärtiges Amt*, 27 December 1994.

constructive and creative manner. Here the level and nature of the different domestic institutions involved (executive versus ministerial, political versus technical), the types of individuals participating (political versus politico-administrative), and the type of bargaining (distributive, integrative or intraorganizational) all contributed to the ways in which attitudes were influenced or structured as the processes of internal bargaining in Paris and Bonn and the external negotiations in Brussels interacted.

CHAPTER V

France, Germany and Negotiations on Political Union: Questions of Definition and Balance

> Union between persons or groups is not natural; it cannot be the result of an intellectual process. The essential is that there is, between persons or groups, a common interest.

> The veto is the profound cause and, at the same time, the symbol of impotence to get beyond national egoisms. But it is only the expression of more profound and often unavowed blockages.

> Jean Monnet, *Mémoires*

The IGC on political union was marked from the start by classical negotiating techniques which illustrated the extent and number of divergences among the Twelve. The fact that no common definition of political union could be agreed upon, despite the contents of the Franco-German letters to successive Council Presidencies, made the likelihood of integrative bargaining remote. This chapter focuses initially on working methods of the conference. An outline of French and German goals and consultations during the multilateral negotiations follows. Key issues are then explained prior to an analysis of the IGC in terms of the book's three approaches.

ORGANIZATION AND WORKING METHODS

Through skillful management of its Presidency, Luxembourg wanted to achieve a single negotiating text on political union.[1] It began its work by establishing an IGC agenda and a calendar of meetings at different levels of negotiation. The Luxembourg Permanent Representative to the European

---

[1]Colette Flesch, "La diplomatie luxembourgeoise: nécessité, réalité et défi," *Studia Diplomatica* XXXVI (1983): 145–162; Helen Wallace, "A Critical Assessment of the Styles, Strategies and Achievements of the Two Presidencies," in *The EC Council Presidency*, 47–48.

Communities, Ambassador Joseph Weyland, chaired the meetings of the personal representatives each week starting in January. He was ably assisted by his deputy, Jim Cloos. As Minister Poos' personal representative, Ambassador Weyland was responsible with his minister for the coordination of horizontal questions linking political union to EMU.

In January, the personal representatives approved a CFSP questionnaire for their ministers. An official closely involved in the Presidency's work considered the questionnaire approach to be a very practical way to solicit information from the member states. This approach had the tactical merit of obliging all member states to play with their cards on the table.[2]

Poos chaired ministerial sessions which took place about once a month at the margin of the General Affairs Councils beginning in February. The introduction of the Luxembourg draft treaty on 16 April was the first concrete result of these initial sessions. It was a document of about 95 pages, which, under the roof of the "Union," established a distinction among Community policies, CFSP and cooperation in justice and home affairs. These three pillars were linked together by the *chapeau*, a series of introductory Articles which established the Union. De Boissieu suggested the pillar structure to an informal working group known as the "Friends of the Presidency."[3]

This group, already established under the Italian Presidency, consisted of the personal representatives' assistants. It was chaired by Jim Cloos and met two or three times a week. The "Friends of the Presidency" were responsible for preparing the groundwork for the personal representatives by clarifying points of debate and posing questions for response by the national delegations on key issues.[4]

In July the Dutch Presidency inherited a full agenda from its Luxembourg predecessor. Much of the daily responsibility for the Presidency fell on Minister van den Broek.[5] The Dutch Presidency's closest ally among the member states was Belgium. It also had the Commission's full support.

---

[2]The CFSP questionnaire was subdivided into three sections, namely, policy objectives, the procedure to put common policies in place and operational modalities like how to integrate progressively European Political Cooperation into the mechanics of Community decision making. Interview, Jim Cloos, Luxembourg Permanent Representation to the European Communities, 23 November 1992.

[3]Enrico Martial, "France and European Political Union," in *The Intergovernmental Conference on Political Union*, 124.

[4]Under the Dutch Presidency, the "Friends of the Presidency" met with Guus Borchardt as chair. Since most of the preparatory work had been accomplished, it met fewer times.

[5]Pietro Sormani, "All' ambiziosa Olanda il timone della CEE," *Corriere della Sera*, 2 luglio 1991, 7.

The Presidency's main concern was to limit the extent to which intergovernmental procedures could interfere with integrationist decision making.

International events delayed the work of the IGCs in early September. The initial two meetings of the personal representatives had to be cancelled owing to time constraints. The delay caused concern at the official level because there was so little time left to conclude the negotiations. As their schedule grew tighter in October, no less than eight sessions at the working level were assigned by the Presidency. Papers sent from ministries in national capitals were of little use at this late date. The time had come to bring the negotiations to the point which would enable the European Council to reach an agreement on 9–10 December.[6]

French and German Goals

French IGC diplomacy concentrated on five main issues. The strengthening of the European Council as the Union's main decision-making body was at the top of the list. The development of the CFSP, including a defense dimension incorporating the WEU, was another high priority advanced in tandem with the Federal Republic. The establishment of a Community social policy was essential for the Socialist President. With the naming of Edith Cresson as Prime Minister in May, a Community industrial policy was added to the French list of *desiderata*. Finally, the idea of a "Congress" which would involve national parliaments more closely with the integration process was advocated.[7]

The Germans had three goals on institutional matters that were absolutely essential during the IGC. These were the inclusion of the subsidiarity principle in the Treaty text, the creation of a Committee of the Regions to address Länder interests and strengthening the powers of the European Parliament. These aims were meant to address the democratic deficit in the Community. The third pillar involving judicial and internal affairs cooperation was Kohl's personal initiative. Here the Chancellor aimed to address the burning issue of immigration on the domestic scene by Europeanizing asylum policy. Kohl was also worried about the transnational spread of crime and drugs accompanying the fall of internal borders within the single market. Finally, Germany favored the Dutch Presidency's approach of a unitary structure for the Treaty which, unlike the three pillars, subjected CFSP and judicial and internal affairs to Community decision-making procedures.

---

[6] Interview, French Permanent Representation to the European Communities, 25 November 1992.

[7] Yves Doutriaux, *Le traité sur l'Union Européenne*, 15–78.

Franco-German Consultations

Bilateral inputs by the two countries served as an impetus to multilateral negotiations on Treaty reform in several ways. Early during the conference on political union, they proposed to establish a Council comprising interior and justice ministers to deal with matters like immigration and visa policy at the European level. The British considered any debate on this idea premature stating that "a case has not been made" for such initiatives.

On CFSP, the Genscher-Dumas paper outlined a proposal that aimed to increase Europe's ability to act in security and defense matters. The ideas presented in the five-page paper included the establishment of a European defense identity in the long-term, the creation of a European pillar within NATO, the integration of WEU into political union by 1997, and the definition of security objectives by the European Council with the WEU serving as a channel of cooperation between political union and NATO. The French position on security differed significantly from that of the Commission in that it envisaged keeping security and defense policies firmly in the hands of the member states with a restricted role for the Community institutions.[8]

At the end of February, the Genscher-Dumas paper on European security policy underwent two important revisions. First, although it confirmed that links between the European Parliament and the WEU Assembly should be established, the paper no longer mentioned any role for the "Congress" which included representatives of national parliaments. Paris also accepted a transfer of the WEU Council from London to Brussels in order to facilitate contact between that organization and NATO. In the French view, the transfer of WEU to Brussels made sense only if the organization was to be inserted into the context of political union under the direction of the European Council. This was by no means a point of agreement among the Twelve with the Netherlands, in particular, dissenting.

The Genscher-Dumas paper served as a point of reference to further orient the debate around the table. The Franco-German position was warmly supported by Italy, Spain, Belgium, Luxembourg and Greece. Ireland maintained its habitual reserve, but would offer some signs of flexibility if, when a defense policy was put into place, it was not called upon to participate in decisions to implement the policy. Denmark showed some more openness on the issue as compared to its previous position. Great Britain, while confirming its concern for maintaining the Atlantic Alliance intact, admitted the need for "a more coherent and visible European defense identity" which "could under certain circumstances act in an independent manner."

---

[8] Philippe Lemaitre, "Le projet de la Commission sur l'union politique européenne diffère de celui de la France," *Le Monde*, 24 octobre 1990, 8.

During the ministerial meeting on 15 May, Guigou explained that although France was not totally satisfied with the most recent Luxembourg "non-paper," it was necessary to guard against an "all or nothing" attitude. France, like the majority of conference participants, aimed for a federal Union as stated in the Kohl-Mitterrand letters. However, this perspective could not take place in the immediate future. Moreover, the question of the unity of the Treaty structure was not new. It had already been posed during the 1985 IGC negotiations on the Single European Act.

As Guigou explained, the solution proposed by the Luxembourg Presidency was an attempt to create a mixed domain for certain policies which were no longer intergovernmental, but not yet communitarized. In other words, the proposed structure aimed to introduce a progressive communitarization of policies which still remained outside the traditional Community decision-making procedures. Guigou also pointed out that although the decision-making procedures were adapted to a variety of domains in political union, the three institutions, Commission, Council and Parliament were present in all areas. To underline the evolutionary character of the Community, Guigou took note of the German proposal made by State Minister for European affairs Seiler-Albring to reinforce the *chapeau* at the beginning of the Treaty by specific reference to all the Community institutions and by the introduction of a general evolutionary clause. Guigou thought this idea deserved the attention of the conference participants.

Prior to the Luxembourg European Council on 28–29 June, foreign minister Poos indicated that discussions at the highest level would be limited to a small number of issues in order to give the "clear political direction" necessary to enable the leaders to reach an accord at Maastricht. The talks would focus on four key issues: co-decision; cohesion; social policy; and defense. However, it seemed that Chancellor Kohl did not intend to have an in-depth discussion at Luxembourg on the most contentious issues. In this way, he hoped to avoid isolating his colleague and friend, John Major.

The Chancellor was expected to call for a clear Community line by December on fighting drug-traffickers and on handling asylum seekers. This personal initiative of Kohl's had Mitterrand's conditional support provided that these policies remained in the realm of intergovernmental cooperation in the short-term.[9] Although Kohl was seeking to extend Community decision making into these areas, he did in turn agree to back his French colleague's wish to include a social component in the new Treaty. Here German business leaders were against the Community having more powers. Social harmonization would tend to follow economic and political integration; setting minimum standards would suffice, in their view.[10]

---

[9] Interview, Council Secretariat, 27 May 1992.
[10] Interview, Rainer Eberle, *Auswärtiges Amt*, 16 April 1993.

Despite their differences on issues like the nature of democratic legitimacy in the Community or the extent to which a European security identity should rely on NATO, France and Germany tried to further the integration process in ways that Britain was clearly not prepared to endorse. This was evident after the Luxembourg European Council. The Federal Republic offered Great Britain an equal role with France in preparing an initiative to relaunch CFSP. The offer, disclosed by Lutz Stavenhagen, State Minister in the Federal Chancellery, was for Britain, France and Germany to draw up a joint paper in the autumn which would form the core of negotiations.

Clearly Germany was sounding out prospects, but the idea was seen by senior British sources as almost too visionary because of the differences among the three partners about common foreign and defense policies. Nonetheless, Stavenhagen made plain Germany's determination to reach formulas that would not put Britain out on a limb or face it with "harrowing" choices.[11] This attitude did not alter the belief in Bonn, however, that only when France and Germany act together, can the Community progress. "The alliance with France is still the cornerstone of Germany's European policy— and will remain so," remarked a government planner. "In a 20-country Community, north-south conflicts would be harder to manage, so compromises between France, representing the south, and Germany, representing the north, will be more essential than ever," he added. As one of Germany's negotiators explained, "We cannot count on Britain's interests being European, as we can with the French. Only if Britain overcame its problems with the Atlantic link and its reluctance to give up sovereignty could we have a triple alliance."[12]

During the IGCs, both partners had to establish a working relationship in the new European context after unification. In order to include the new Länder into the network of Franco-German relations, Mitterrand visited the former German Democratic Republic on 16–20 September.[13] In a speech in Berlin, he stated that the EC must include countries of "the whole democratic Europe." However, if the Community should be opened to the whole of Europe, and France engaged herself in this endeavor, this should not be "at the price of the destruction of the Community." Berlin was also chosen as the location for a conference on clandestine immigration proposed by the French and German interior ministers. Countries from central and eastern Europe were also invited to participate with a view to the Europeanization of this issue.

The bilateral relations between France and Germany were instrumental as negotiations on political union drew to a close. A compromise between the

---

[11]David Gow, "UK Offered Special EC Role," *The Guardian*, July 5, 1991.

[12]"A German Idea of Europe," *The Economist*, July 26, 1991.

[13]Pierre Haski, "Visite de rattrapage de Mitterrand dans les Länder de l'Est," *Libération*, 18 septembre 1991, 20.

two was struck on co-decision which facilitated multilateral negotiations on democratic legitimacy. Even though history has shown Franco-German leadership is a prerequisite for Community agreements, the tactics on CFSP used by Dumas and Genscher after the informal ministerial session in Utrecht during early October were risky. Their intention to call a special meeting in Paris to advance the CFSP negotiations angered the smaller states and risked isolating Britain. The Dutch Presidency was strongly against the initiative to call a Paris meeting, viewing it as an arrogant display of power.[14]

The objective of the Paris meeting was to win over a clear majority of Community member states in favor of bringing defense fully into the Union sooner than Britain and Italy had suggested in their joint paper.[15] Prior to the Anglo-Italian paper, Hurd had argued strongly for the Community to maintain European Political Cooperation which the British always supported.[16] In their view, EPC held up well under the strain of Yugoslavia and other crises. But the shift of opinion among most member states toward taking low-level foreign policy decisions by majority vote was evident. A number of delegations believed that, as in internal market legislation, few foreign policy decisions would be taken by majority vote, but its very threat would help the Twelve reach consensus quicker.[17]

Dumas and Genscher were joined in Paris by their Spanish counterpart. The following week Mitterrand and Kohl submitted the last of three Franco-German letters to the Council Presidency. The letter's aim was to translate the Franco-German proposals on security and defense into Articles to be inserted into the Luxembourg-Dutch draft treaty. The Articles included provisions stating that CFSP would in the long term include a common defense. The WEU would become an integral part of the integration process in the defense area with the Council organizing relations between the Union and WEU. This arrangement was not to interfere with the obligations of member states in the context of the Atlantic Alliance. The entire CFSP chapter in the Treaty would be reviewed no later than 1996.

Kohl and Mitterrand also declared that Franco-German military cooperation on the 5,000 man military brigade stationed in Baden-Württemberg would be strengthened. The joint brigade was meant to serve as

---

[14]Interview, Dutch Permanent Representation to the European Communities, 23 November 1992.

[15]John Palmer, "Paris Talks Raise Stakes in EC Drive for Union," *The Guardian*, October 7, 1991.

[16]Simon Nuttall, *European Political Co-operation* (Oxford: Clarendon , 1992) gives an excellent overview of both British interests in EPC and the mechanics of the process.

[17]David Buchan, "EC Divided over Future Plans for Defence," *Financial Times*, October 7, 1991.

the core of a future European army which other member states might eventually join. Although the declaration was somewhat vague, observers believed it recommended the establishment of common military corps stationed in Strasbourg consisting of 50,000 to 100,000 men. The reaction of the Commission and most of the other member states, with the exception of Britain, to the declaration was positive. Soon after WEU Secretary General Wim van Eekelen remarked that he considered it possible to a find a compromise between the Anglo-Italian and Franco-German proposals on security and defense. In his view, the idea of a European pillar in NATO must be emphasized and a declaration on the role of WEU attached to the Treaty negotiated in Maastricht. The Secretary General also stressed the provisionary role of WEU in the Union until the next Revision Conference in 1996.

On 14–15 November Mitterrand, Cresson and 13 members of the French government had a series of consultations with their German counterparts in the context of the 58th Franco-German summit in Bonn. The preparation of the Maastricht European Council on 9–10 December was at the center of the talks which also included discussions on the situation in central and eastern Europe and Yugoslavia. The Franco-German corps, mentioned in the last Kohl-Mitterrand letter, was on the agenda as well. The Ministers of Defense, Pierre Joxe and Gerhard Stoltenberg, presented a report on the Franco-German Defense Council which would be responsible for "reflections on the missions and the calendar for implementing the Franco-German corps."[18] French sources indicated that the organization of the corps would develop progressively "over the three or four years to come." A *communiqué* specified that the missions of the brigade would take place with a perspective toward a commmon European defense. The one issue on which the French and the Germans were not on the same wavelength in Bonn was industrial policy with the Germans against the inclusion of an Article in the Treaty.[19] Nonetheless, both leaders identified Britain as the main obstacle to an accord at Maastricht.

KEY ISSUES
In order to facilitate analysis of the negotiations on political union, four main issue areas are considered: institutional matters including democratic legitimacy, European citizenship, extension of Community competencies and subsidiarity; the third pillar, or cooperation in justice and home affairs like asylum, immigration and visa policy; the Treaty structure including the

---

[18]Philippe Lemaitre, "M. Kohl et M. Mitterrand mettent la dernière main à la préparation du conseil," *Le Monde*, 15 novembre 1991, 7.

[19]Claire Tréan, "MM. Kohl et Mitterrand mettent en garde contre un échec à Maastricht," *Le Monde*, 18 octobre 1991, 4.

relationship of the European Community to the proposed Union; and CFSP.[20]

Institutional Matters

There was a certain flexibility to the early discussions, but one of the main issues of the conference emerged during the early meetings: the powers of the European Parliament. Regarding democratic legitimacy, there was general agreement that the right of co-decision for the Parliament with the Council of Ministers on Community legislation was an essential element of talks. Other themes debated were nomination of the Commission, Parliament's rights of petition and inquiry, and assent.

The discussion on the right of co-decision for the European Parliament was based on a German proposal. Most delegations expressed the conviction that it was advisable to go beyond the actual cooperation procedure in order to involve Parliament more closely in the Community decision-making process.[21] Cooperation was introduced as a decision-making procedure by the Single European Act and requires two parliamentary readings. Majority voting always applies in the Council. This procedure was applicable originally to Treaty Articles which led to the completion of the internal market. Discussions to expand its use were also part of negotiations on political union. In the co-decision procedure, some delegations wanted Parliament to have the right to make legislation on an equal footing with Council.[22]

Denmark, however, took exception to the idea of introducing co-decision. Instead the Danish representative argued that the cooperation procedure was sufficient despite the fact that its scope of application was not extensive. The debate on this issue dealt mainly with the problem of the efficiency it was necessary to maintain in Community decision making and the question of institutional equilibrium. Several delegations indicated that the co-decision procedure could result in a loss of influence for the Commission and underlined the likely negative consequences for the institutional balance. An official closely involved in the Luxembourg Presidency explained the fear on the part of several delegations that Parliament would produce too many resolutions and thereby paralyze Community decision making.[23] Among the

---

[20]Philippe de Schoutheete, *Rapport sur l'Union Politique* (Bruxelles: Université Libre de Bruxelles, 1992), 2–3 (mimeo).

[21]*The New Treaty on European Union* Volume 2: Legal and Political Analyses (Brussels: Belmont Policy Center, 1992) give an account of the extension of the European Parliament's competencies and an explanation of new decision making procedures introduced by the Maastricht Treaty.

[22]The cooperation and co-decision procedures are defined in the Appendix.

[23]Interview, Luxembourg Permanent Representation to the European Communities, 23 November 1992.

proposals on co-decision submitted by the member states, only the German one envisaged a "Committee of Arbitration" made up of representatives of Council and Parliament.

Democratic legitimacy was at the top of the foreign ministers' agenda during their third meeting. In terms of co-decision, efficiency was the main issue particularly with regard to the time delays between deliberations in Council and Parliament during which decisions must be made. During the debate, Genscher and Seiler-Albring defended the German interest to go very far on co-decision. Unlike Italian and Belgian proposals, the German plan suggested that the Commission share with Parliament its right to initiate Community legislation.[24] The German delegation also envisaged some influence for the European Parliament on issues falling within the scope of CFSP.[25] This proposal provoked the opposition of the smaller member states which had little to gain owing to their small representation in Strasbourg. The United Kingdom, with the support of Denmark, Ireland and Portugal, agreed to reinforce the political control of Parliament, but was against any increase in its legislative powers. The French delegation, represented by Dumas and Elisabeth Guigou, suggested limiting co-decision to normative and legislative acts. In the French view, the Council should vote at qualified majority on amendments from Parliament at the end of the co-decision procedure. The idea of a final rejection of legislation, or veto, by Parliament and the introduction of co-decision progressively by sectors also came from the French.[26] France occupied a middle of the road position on co-decision which could tilt the balance of the negotiations either way.[27]

In April Genscher and his Italian counterpart, Gianni de Michelis, issued a joint declaration calling for the European Parliament to have an equal say with national governments in Community decision making.[28] This marked one of the rare occasions on which Germany signed a formal statement on a

---

[24]David Buchan, "German Plan to Widen Powers of MEPs Upsets EC Partners," *Financial Times*, 19 February 1991; "Vermittlungsausschuß für Rat und Europaparlament," *Handelsblatt*, 19 February 1991, 5.

[25]Interview, State Secretary Jürgen Trumpf, *Auswärtiges Amt*, 30 July 1993.

[26]Rat der Europäischen Gemeinschaften, Generalsekretariat, Mitteilung an die Presse 4863/91 (Presse 25), Dritte Ministertagung der Regierungskonferenz über die Politischen Union, Brüssel, den 4./5. März 1991, 3–5.

[27]Interview, French Permanent Representation to the European Communities, 22 June 1992.

[28]Julie Wolf, "Bonn and Rome Unite to Set EC Union Agenda," *The Guardian*, 11 April 1991.

multilateral Community issue with a country other than France. This reflected a fundamental divergence of interests between Bonn and Paris concerning the democratic deficit.[29]

Three issues which revealed serious differences among the Twelve at the personal representative level, namely, citizenship, economic and social cohesion and social policy, were discussed by their ministers in May. On European citizenship, the discussion revolved around the direct applicability of the rights inherent in the concept. In other words, to what extent could a European citizen seek redress in a court of law in order to make these rights prevail? Denmark, and to a lesser extent, Britain were totally against direct applicability. The right of a citizen of any member state to vote in the municipal or European elections taking place in a state of residence other than the individual's state of origin, posed the greatest constitutional problems. Dumas underlined this point which would become a major focus of the French ratification debate.[30]

On cohesion the Spanish idea to create new funds to finance new Community policies, in addition to the already existing structural funds, was refused by France and Germany. This debate was further complicated by the fact that the "cohesion states," led by Spain, wanted to include mention of future Community financing in discussions on this issue. A redistribution of Community resources in the name of solidarity via "interstate funds," or large transfers of monetary resources from richer to poorer member states, was also suggested during the EMU conference. The majority of member states wanted this issue resolved in Community discussions about the revision of structural funds after the conclusion of the intergovernmental conferences.

Regarding social policy, Belgium, France and the Commission showed reluctance, and Denmark and Spain indicated their outright refusal, to consider a German proposal which aimed to replace unanimity voting by a reinforced qualified majority, 66 of 74, in the Council. This position reflected a German preoccupation with its own high standards in social policy and the reluctance to be bound by what might turn out to be insufficient European social legislation.[31] Seiler-Albring explained that her government was prepared to compromise on the number of votes required in the Council to make social legislation. The criticisms tabled revealed an unwillingness to complicate an already tortuous decison-making procedure and to run the risk, under the

---

[29]David Buchan, "Germany and Italy Draw up Plan on EC power," *Financial Times*, 11 April 1991.

[30]Jean Quatremer, "La citoyenneté devise les Douze," *Libération*, 15 mai 1991, 32; Elisabeth Guigou, *Pour les européens* (Paris: Flammarion, 1994), 49.

[31]Interview, Rainer Eberle, *Auswärtiges Amt*, 16 April 1993.

pretext of limiting unanimity, of encroaching upon the domain already covered by qualified majority voting.

Delors underlined that the Community had arrived at the breaking point of relations between economic and social Europe. He argued for a change in the institutional provisions which would finally allow the application of the European Social Charter. Minister Guigou indicated that "the Presidency's proposals on social policy were at the absolute limit of that which France could accept. Any further toning down of the text on social provisions was unacceptable." To avoid a stalemate, France was prepared early on in the negotiations to offer Britain an opt-out on social policy.[32]

At the beginning of September, the Dutch Presidency circulated a non-paper aimed to reinforce the Community character of the Luxembourg draft treaty by affirming the prerogatives of the Commission and the Parliament. To take into consideration the events occurring in eastern Europe, the non-paper proposed the extension of a reinforced cooperation procedure and qualified majority voting to domains like transeuropean networks, research and information technology and environmental protection. Each of these issues was seen as relevant across the Continent.

During a ministerial meeting in late October, Guigou indicated that France accepted the application of the co-decision procedure to Community decisions in the areas of research, environment, consumer protection and eventually transeuropean networks. In the case of an inability to reach agreement with the Council in the proposed conciliation committee, the European Parliament would have the last say to reject a text as long as this was expressed by a qualified majority of its members. In exchange for the softening of the French position on co-decision, Germany agreed to support the French idea of a "Congress" reuniting national and European parliamentarians three times yearly.[33]

At the foreign ministers' session in November two divisive issues dominated the agenda: social policy and cooperation in interior and justice affairs. The negotiations on social policy illustrated the gulf which still divided Great Britain and the other member states. The British foreign minister was opposed to any "communitarization" of third pillar competencies. During negotiations on this issue, a distinction was made between "strengthened cooperation," in areas listed in an annex to the Treaty including asylum policy, immigration policy, and the fight against drug-trafficking and terrorism, and "communitarization" by which an area like visa policy would be introduced in the Treaty through an Article "x" and eventually included in the Community competencies by a qualified majority

---

[32] Interview, Quai d'Orsay, 8 March 1993.

[33] Jacques Docquiert, "Paris prêt à accepter un renforcement des pouvoirs du Parlement européen," *Les Echos*, 29 octobre 1991, 4.

vote of the Council. Great Britain was the only delegation against a common visa policy.

During the conclave at Noordwijk on 12–13 November, the foreign ministers negotiated on the basis of a new Presidency draft treaty which reflected "majority tendencies." In the new draft treaty, co-decision was envisaged in 10 cases, 3 in the area of competencies including Article 100a relating to the internal market. Great Britain gave its approval of the co-decision procedure, as outlined in Article 189b of the draft treaty, but much depended in its view on the scope of application. Douglas Hurd suggested the use of co-decision in areas relating to the completion of the internal market and, if need arises, in environment and research and development. Dumas insisted on adding industry, health, culture and social policy. Genscher suggested the idea of an evolutionary clause permitting the extension of the scope of co-decision at a future date.

Clearly the British concession on co-decision fell short of Germany's ambitions for Parliament, however, with Genscher saying: "If I wanted a car, I would not settle for a bicycle—and here we are being offered a snail."[34] The German foreign minister also reminded the others of the link which his government established between advances on EMU and progress on political union. Not surprisingly, the cases listed requiring the assent of Parliament were less numerous than those requiring co-decision. The Presidency did reinforce the role of the Committee of the Regions though which had to be consulted in 7 cases instead of the 3 mentioned in the Luxembourg draft treaty.

Third Pillar Issues

During their early meetings, it was necessary for the personal representatives not to lose sight of the larger objectives of political union by getting lost in excessive attention to detail. A certain sense of balance was also necessary to realize the political significance which lay behind the legal and somewhat technical questions involved in enlarging the scope of Community competencies under Article 235 EEC, for example. This was true during initial discussions about intergovernmental cooperation on judicial matters like asylum, immigration and visa policy and whether or not to include these issues within the scope of Community decision making.

In the context of extension of competencies, the personal representatives also briefly discussed intergovernmental cooperation on the fight against terrorism and judicial affairs. Several member states believed that the issues under discussion should be regrouped into three categories: Community competencies; classical intergovernmental cooperation, with the possibility of inclusion in the Community decision-making procedures under EEC 235; and an intermediary system which accommodated both CFSP and justice and home affairs.

---

[34]Rory Watson and Nicholas Comfort, "Major Bites the Bullet to set Maastricht Deal," *The European*, October 15, 1991.

During the Luxembourg European Council in late June, Chancellor Kohl proposed, and his counterparts supported, an initiative by which the conference on political union would consider clauses relative to the harmonization of the asylum and immigration policies of the Twelve and the creation of a Europol to fight against crime and drug-trafficking across borders. On the harmonization of asylum and immigration, the Commission and the member states would have a right of initiative. Decisions would be taken unanimously with the eventual implementation of measures decided by qualified majority voting. Kohl suggested that the Maastricht European Council should receive a report from the ministers responsible for immigration on concrete measures of harmonization and an analagous report on the fight against crime and drugs.

This matter was discussed by the personal representatives during their last meeting before the summer break on 25 July. The question on the table was in which part of the Treaty to place judicial cooperation. Two camps opposed each other. Germany, Belgium, the Netherlands and the Commission wanted these issues in the Community domain whereas Denmark, Ireland and the United Kingdom defended the idea of a third pillar. The question also remained open as to whether the member states should retain a right of initiative in this area, which Germany advocated, or if the orthodox Community approach should prevail. The procedure was that the goal of those states which supported the Community approach inserted their point of view in parentheses so that the foreign ministers could make a decision on this purely political matter.

Treaty Structure

During their meeting in Dresden on 2–3 June, the foreign ministers openly differed on the Treaty structure. The sympathizers which stood behind the European Commission's initiative to retain a unitary structure were the Netherlands, Belgium, Italy, Greece, Spain, the Federal Republic and Ireland.[35] Although the United Kingdom, Portugal and Denmark remained firmly in the the other camp, it was France, supported by the Luxembourg Presidency, which set the tone for the opposition.[36] Minister Poos said after the meeting that the two sides had understood each other's views and that a compromise was possible. Such a compromise likely would involve a Treaty clause indicating that the new structures were temporary. The Treaty could also state that the eventual aim is a more federalist system. As Poos explained, "Even the most federalist member states among us agreed that you can't treat foreign policy and cooperation among police in the same way we now deal

---

[35]Mark M. Nelson, "EC Officials Fail to Agree on Plan for Political Union," *The Wall Street Journal*, 4 June 1991, 4.

[36]Philippe Lemaitre, "La France s'oppose à la Commission de Bruxelles sur le partage des pouvoirs dans une Communauté renforcée," *Le Monde*, 5 juin 1991, 4.

with the internal market."[37] Germany was indeed prepared to consider this alternative but not in the face of staunch opposition from both France and Great Britain. The divergent views between France and Germany on this significant point were highlighted in the German press.[38]

At their June session in Luxembourg, the ministers examined three aspects of the draft treaty: the *chapeau*; the function of the institutions; and Community competencies. To assuage fears aroused by the structure of the Luxembourg draft treaty, the Presidency included in the *chapeau* a reference to the "federal finality" of the Union and the possibility to pass from intergovernmental to Community decision-making procedures for some Union policies. The Presidency also insisted on the unity of the Union institutional framework even though the structure comprised three pillars. Hurd voiced his objection to the term "federal." Minister Ellemann-Jensen stated a more nuanced position. Denmark could accept reference to "an ever closer Union of States."

In late September, the personal representatives had a first exchange of views on a new draft treaty introduced by the Dutch Presidency. At least seven member states did not understand how the Presidency could devote almost three months to a new draft treaty which left only five weeks to negotiate the remaining substantial issues. De Boissieu underlined the fact that a new text required another year of negotiations. The Commission and Belgium gave the Presidency full support for its new draft text. Most of the other delegations supported the Luxembourg draft treaty. The Federal Republic took a median position indicating a German willingness to negotiate on one or the other text as long as negotiations progressed.

The fact that the Dutch text favored an increased role for the European Parliament initially secured the support of Kohl.[39] As other member states voiced their opposition, however, Germany started to edge away from the Presidency's position. "We were not really supporting the Treaty," one official said, "we just favor some of the ideas and want to get on with the work."[40] The atmosphere the next day, later referred to as "Black Monday," was tense. The assault on the Presidency, represented by Hans van den Broek, was unprecedented in Community history. Ten of the Twelve attacked the Dutch text during a heated exchange. Only Belgium openly sided with the Presidency.

As the meeting continued late into the evening, it became clear to several delegations, notably France, that the price the British might have to pay for the

---

[37]David Buchan, "EC Presidency Seeks to End Political Union Row," *Financial Times*, 4 June 1991, 1.

[38]"An der Leine," *Der Spiegel*, 10 Juni 1991, 160.

[39]George Brock, "Federal Camp Wins First Round," *The Times*, September 26, 1991, 11.

[40]_____, "Dutch Challenged over Draft for Union Treaty," *The Times*, September 29, 1991, 20.

abandonment of the Dutch text included concessions on the scope of common decision making and majority voting in the Council of Ministers, joint policy making in social affairs, and the extent of co-legislation powers for the European Parliament. The Dutch plan for a stronger European Parliament did receive heavyweight backing from Hans-Dietrich Genscher.[41] He shrewdly waited until after his colleagues had voiced their opinions to give his views on the Dutch text. Genscher was trying to judge whether his vote could influence the outcome in one way or another.[42] The final outcome of the meeting was that the Luxembourg text remained the reference point for the negotiations, although it could be amended with some of the ideas put forward by The Hague.[43]

CFSP

During their early talks, a debate arose among the personal representatives over three points. The first and second dealt with a case scenario in which one or several member states wished to take some distance from a common position on a foreign policy issue. Would this be possible and under which set of circumstances? France stated that it was out of the question to insert a clause in the Treaty permitting disassociation from common policies. A majority of delegations did agree though that a procedure could be established to allow a member state to take distance with the consent of its partners. The third point concerned the obligation of the member states to speak with one voice. The majority of the personal representatives decided that while a unity of view was necessary, unity of expression was not. Although the Presidency and the Troika would present the Community view, the member states should be able to express their own national sensitivities. France, Ireland, Denmark and the Netherlands presented different reasons why this option should be retained in view of their perceived individual vital interests.

In light of tragic events in the Gulf War, the foreign ministers used their February meeting on CFSP to indicate the path for their representatives to follow. Their responses to the Presidency's questionnaire allowed the personal representatives to present a first draft treaty at the next ministerial session in early March. The points on which there was disagreement remained in brackets. There were two tours of the table in response to the Presidency's

---

[41]John Palmer, "EC ministers Sink Dutch Union Effort," *The Guardian*, October 1, 1991; David Usborne, "Dutch EC Plans Rejected," *The Independent*, October 1, 1991.

[42]Interview, *Auswärtiges Amt*, 21 July 1993.

[43]Julie Wolf, "Netherlands Retreats from Sweeping Plan on EC Political Union," *The Wall Street Journal*, October 1, 1991; Rat der Europäischen Gemeinschaften, Generalsekretariat, Mitteilung an die Presse, 8400/91 (Presse 155), Siebte Ministertagung der Regierungskonferenz über die Politische Union, Brüssel, den 30. September und 1. Oktober 1991, 4–5.

questionnaire which examined the objectives, the content and the institutional framework of CFSP.

On 26 March the foreign ministers and Delors met informally at the Castle of Senningen in Luxembourg to discuss the future role of CFSP. Minister van den Broek went even further than his British counterpart with his plea to maintain European security by preserving the Atlantic engagement and the American presence on the Continent. Genscher reckoned that the Franco-German proposals be viewed in light of an unprecedented historical context. A unified Germany had confirmed its intention to integrate in as extensive a manner as possible into the Community. Was not this engagement the best response to concerns shown by the Hague toward German unity and to the hopes placed by the countries of central and eastern Europe in the Community?

During the ministerial session in April, Poos indicated that the member states made an effort at "balanced compromise" on the issue with a majority in favor of the Franco-German initiatives. He also suggested that the next step was to "try to raise the level of compromise" by examining several points in greater detail. These points were the general problems in relation to the defense dimension in the Treaty, qualified majority voting, and the active role of the Commission at each stage of definition, coordination and implementation of CFSP. The Luxembourg non-paper suggested that the implementation of the security policy be made by the foreign ministers at qualified majority. Four countries, Great Britain, Denmark, Ireland and Portugal, preferred that unanimity remain the rule. This was the first important cleavage among the Twelve. The Spanish foreign minister described the results as "a completely minimal compromise." Moreover, the link established between the WEU and political union for the envisaged defense policy was the weakest possible. Seven member states, led by France, wanted the Treaty to make explicit mention of the defense dimension. In a general manner, these states viewed the Luxembourg text as too timid on defense.[44] Guigou, the only Minister representing France at the meeting, explained, "We would like the Treaty to specify that the WEU can apply the decisions on defense matters taken by the political union, but other than that the draft takes up the essential of that which we consider important."[45] Britain, Denmark, the Netherlands and Ireland rejected the idea of a European defense.[46]

During a weekend meeting at the site of the Luxembourg thermal spa Mondorf-les-Bains weeks later, the foreign ministers held a "frank and very

[44]Philippe Lemaitre, "Les Douze restent divisés sur l'union politique européenne," *Le Monde*, 17 avril 1991, 6.

[45]Isabelle Marchais, "CEE: la marche vers l'union politique," *Le Figaro*, 16 avril 1991, 3. The translation is the author's.

[46]"Les Douze divisés sur l'essentiel," *Le Quotidien*, 16 avril 1991, 15.

technically informed" discussion on CFSP. The established cleavages among the member states remained, but the British presented a nuanced position on a European defense identity. In the British view, "two cardinal ideas" had to be respected: "NATO should remain the central place" for defense consultations; and the integrated command structure should be retained. On this basis, Douglas Hurd developed a vision based on three zones of geographic competence: the NATO area, in which there could be consultations among the Europeans with respect for Atlantic decisions; the NATO "out-of-area," in which a non-permanent autonomous European intervention force, in concertation with NATO, would be called in cases of emergency; the zone of central and eastern Europe, in which the European pillar of the Alliance might have to play a specific card in case of problems.

Given the impasses on the links between the Community, WEU and NATO, Gianni de Michelis adopted a mediatory position between the British and the French, advocating an approach in phases. The first phase would end in 1998, with the expiration of the Treaty establishing the WEU, thus allowing it to become a "bridge" between NATO and the Community. During the second phase, over the next five years, WEU would become an organ of the Community. The third phase would view a political development in the direction of a federal state.

An informal foreign ministers' meeting in October near Utrecht allowed for a "very constructive discussion" on CFSP. Delors believed that an Anglo-Italian joint paper on security represented a compromise which could serve as "a good basis for an approach to the defense issue in the short term." Britain and Italy's contribution to the conference stated that WEU should be entrusted with the task of developing the European dimension in the field of defense. Its role would be developed in two complementary directions: as the defense component of the Union and as the means to strengthen the European pillar of the Alliance.[47] The Anglo-Italian paper went a little further toward the French insistence on a role for the Union in defense while retaining the NATO framework. In part their joint position was meant to take some of the momentum away from the Franco-German initiative on defense.[48] However, it was also part of British strategy to seek common ground when possible. The British government was determined to sign a Treaty in Maastricht, believing delay would only make negotiations more difficult.

Three themes dominated the ministers' discussion: the "Asolo" list which dealt with areas in which to define common action; the procedure to apply in

---

[47]Europe Documents, 5. Oktober 1991; George Brock and Michael Binyon, "Britain Accepts EC Goal of a United Policy on Defense," *The Times*, October 5, 1991.

[48]Colin Brown, Sarah Helm and David Usborne, "Rifts with Europe Healing," *The Independent*, October 4, 1991.

the implementation of common action; the place in the Treaty where Articles relating to security and defense should appear. This discussion on the first theme was the shortest with mostly technical questions being delegated to the personal representatives and the political directors in the national foreign ministries. These two groups of officials also had the task of specifying the "Asolo" list of areas involving common action.

The second theme was the most intensely debated of all. The Twelve were divided into "four schools" on voting procedures: qualified majority with some distinction made among the proponents of this rule "in principle"; qualified majority adapted to the evolution of a particular situation (in other words, it would have to be decided which part of the action would be voted on by a qualified majority); a declaration annexed to the Treaty stipulating that a "member state would abstain to the extent possible from preventing a unanimous consensus in the Council when a qualified majority of states are favorable to the adoption of a mode of common action"; and unanimity.

On the last theme, the important point was that for the first time Britain accepted the perspective of a common defense policy. Hurd pointed out that it was necessary to find a balance in the Treaty Articles between the long-term perspective of a European security policy and the short-term necessity to do nothing which would weaken the Atlantic link. France, Germany and Spain continued to support the Genscher-Dumas paper. For Dumas, three fundamental differences separated the two approaches. First, the Franco-German proposals favored European integration whereas the Anglo-Italian paper relied on NATO. Second, the Franco-German text assigned the responsibility for defense issues to the European Council. Third, Paris and Bonn indicated the eventual fusion of WEU and political union. In order to explore this issue in greater depth, Dumas and Genscher invited those member states on the same wavelength to a meeting in Paris.

The Presidency indicated that its objective for the Noordwijk conclave on 12–13 November was to concentrate the negotiations on problems considered essential by each member state with the goal of submitting to the European Council at Maastricht a limited number to be decided at the highest political level. The CFSP was high on the list of agenda items for Noordwijk. Horizontal issues, including institutional questions, were left for the foreign ministers' conclave.

Yet progress at Noordwijk was least visible on the issue of security and defense. Britain, Denmark and Portugal continued to show reluctance to use qualified majority voting in this sensitive area. According to Guigou, the debate on this issue revolved around the question of whether the Twelve wanted a common defense or a common defense policy. France and Germany argued for the first option. Other delegations supported this initiative. In their view, since President Bush had given the "green light" during the NATO Summit in Rome, it was not necessary to be "more catholic than the Pope." Discussions seemed to focus on the exact links between political union and

WEU with a tendency to favor a separate declaration on WEU in an annex to the Treaty.

The Foreign Ministers' Conclave

At the end of negotiations on the first day of the foreign ministers' conclave in early December, Gianni de Michelis announced that the only concrete decision that had been taken was that after Maastricht the Community would be called the European Union. As for the rest of the issues on the IGC agenda, differences in national positions remained. Six problems were outstanding: the Treaty structure and "federal vocation"; the CFSP especially with regard to decisions taken by qualified majority; defense with the majority of member states advocating a common defense policy as opposed to the Franco-German proposal of a common defense; new competencies; social policy; and cohesion. The last two issues were the most difficult to resolve. De Michelis described the cohesion dossier as "explosive."

After the second day of the conclave, President van den Broek confirmed the maintenance of the term "federal vocation" in the Treaty as part of a package which must be closed in Maastricht. There would be a price for its removal. Debates on the Treaty structure and the *chapeau* were closed although the Commission wanted to use the *chapeau* to prevent a contamination of the Community by the intergovernmental nature of CFSP. Hurd believed that a compromise still had to be reached on this issue whereas on defense Genscher stated that the relations between WEU and the European Union were no longer in question and corresponded to the French-German proposals. Dumas confirmed that CFSP would be the first issue on the Maastricht agenda. In his view, during the conclave a more "Atlanticist" draft text, based on a British-Dutch note, had less support than a Belgian draft which incorporated the Franco-German proposals.

INTERPRETING THE CONFERENCE ON POLITICAL UNION: THREE APPROACHES TO THE IGC PROCESS
Putnam's Two-Level Games

This section considers the changes in domestic structures brought about by the IGC and the strategies employed by Mitterrand and Kohl. Aberbach, Putnam and Rockman's approach and Monnet's approach are used in conjunction with two-level games to analyze the role of civil servants in the political union negotiation process.

Domestic Institutions

The Maastricht process introduced the potential for changes to domestic structure. The French case illustrates attempts to use the negotiations as a means to strengthen statist institutions. The case of Germany suggests the opposite scenario: a desire to increase the influence of European institutions via deeper integration. Domestic structural changes were implemented to increase efficiency and legitimacy and thereby facilitate the integration process.

The French Case

During the Maastricht negotiations, the French aim to increase the role of the European Council in all aspects of Community business was clear. The French President, in his capacity as head of state, would be predominant. Important decisions in CFSP should be taken by him alone. However, in other areas, particularly EMU, the French were not as successful at reinforcing state power over Community decision making.

In addition, the French were determined to strengthen the role of national parliaments in European integration at the expense of the powers of the European Parliament. The French wanted the European Parliament to remain divided as an institution among three cities: Brussels, Luxembourg and Strasbourg. In a budgetary debate before the National Assembly on 5 November, Guigou explained that of the funds allocated for Community affairs, almost 50 million francs involved the defense of Strasbourg as a European capital. This investment demonstrated French determination to prevent the transfer of the European Parliament's plenary sessions to Brussels.

The proposed relocation of France's elite school to train top civil servants, the Ecole Nationale d'Administration, or ENA, to Strasbourg by the Cresson government on 7 November 1991 also meant to emphasize the importance of the Alsacian capital. Here French European interests were a reflection of its domestic priorities. The relocation of state institutions to cities in several parts of France was a goal of several Socialist governments. The transfer of ENA had a dual aim best understood in terms of domestic institutions and the training of national civil servants. First, the school's transfer was part of a government program that aimed to move institutions with significant adminis-trative tasks outside Paris.[49] Second, the transfer aimed to Europeanize the school's curriculum by establishing a center for training in European law in the same physical complex as ENA in Strasbourg.[50] This center's task would be in part to prepare French civil servants and politico-administrative hybrids for work related to Community negotiations.

The German Case

One of Chancellor Kohl's first speeches before the Bundestag on 30 January highlighted German goals on political union. Kohl highlighted German diplomatic objectives with direct relevance to domestic politics. Maastricht was presented as an opportunity to consolidate and build on the completion of the internal market. The removal of internal border controls under the Schengen Accord was described as a German priority. The Chancellor

---

[49]Patrick Lemoine, "L'ENA entre deux sièges," *La Croix*, 7 juin 1993.

[50]Interview, Ambassador François Scheer, French Permanent Representation to the European Communities, 25 November 1992.

emphasized the inextricable link between the two intergovernmental conferences by which progress on EMU must accompany greater control by the European Parliament over Community decision making.[51]

During the negotiations, Cuntz circulated status reports to different divisions in the *Auswärtiges Amt.* The Committees in the Bundesrat and Bundestag were also informed on a regular basis throughout 1991. After the Luxembourg Presidency submitted its draft treaty, there was a meeting on 24 April of the Bundestag's Foreign Affairs Committee with federal officials working on political union. This meeting dealt with the general status of the intergovermental conference. The difficulties with Great Britain on issues like co-decision, social policy and the defense dimension of CFSP were emphasized. Much of the discussion involved CFSP. The Bonn government considered the Luxembourg draft to be a good working basis for further talks on this issue.

The fact that the daily work on the IGC was in the hands of national civil servants was a source of frustration for parliamentarians. The SPD spokesperson for European political affairs, Heidemarie Wieczorek-Zeul, called for a greater public debate on the content and goals of German IGC diplomacy. As an expression of her dissatisfaction with the federal government's answer to an inquiry on CFSP, Wieczorek-Zeul accused administrative officials of treating the work on the negotiations like some type of "secret command."[52]

Moreover, although Genscher had obtained the approval of the other member states for an increase in German representation in the European Parliament prior to the opening of the conference,[53] this goal was proving more elusive than ever as negotiations wore on. In October Renate Hellwig, chairperson of the *EG-Ausschuß* in the Bundestag, said she expected the German government to reject any deal which failed to meet her committee's demands. "We do not expect to have to reject it ourselves," she said.[54] The *EG-Ausschuß* was particularly insistent on a power of co-decision in new policy fields for the European Parliament and on the bolstering of foreign and

---

[51]Deutscher Bundestag, 12. Wahlperiode, 64. Sitzung, Bonn, Mittwoch, den 30. Januar 1991, 84–85.

[52]"SPD will Diskussion der Europa-Verträge," *Frankfurter Allgemeine Zeitung*, 9. September 1991, 8.

[53]Erich Hauser, "Deutsche Ernüchterung und ein zerknirschter Kanzler," *Frankfurter Rundschau*, 7. Februar 1992, 5.

[54]Quentin Peel, "Bonn Warning on Political Union Treaty," *Financial Times*, 18 October 1991.

security integration within the Community.[55]

Prior to the Noordwijk ministerial conclave, Seiler-Albring addressed the Bundesrat on the status of the IGCs. She assured the Länder politicians that the federal government was fully aware of their demands which were taken very seriously during negotiations in Brussels. Seiler-Albring affirmed the Bonn government's intent to push through the negotiating line agreed on during internal bargaining among the ministries, the Bundesbank and the Länder.[56]

After the conclave, problems with the Bundestag and the SPD remained. According to Wieczorek-Zeul, the Treaty revisions on the table "could not be approved without substantial modifications." She reproached the Bonn government for not "investing all of its force for the rights of the European Parliament." German parliamentarians also began to realize, however, that if the European Parliament's powers did not increase, it would be necessary to strengthen the influence of the Bundestag on European policy making. This points to an increased role for national parliamentarians in the integration process. The Bundesrat's wish to have a say on issues within its exclusive competence, if these came up in Council negotiations, also indicates a strengthening of the influence of state civil servants within the European negotiation process.

In terms of bureaucratic structural changes, there were suggestions to create a European ministry in Bonn to deal with Community affairs. However, in the context of domestic politics, this would not be feasible since there is a delicate political balance in the distribution of ministerial portfolios within the Bonn coalition government. Also from the administrative point of view, European policy making is made in terms of individual competencies like environment and agriculture, for example. No ministry would want to surrender its policy competencies to a separate European ministry given the loss of bureaucratic and political influence involved. Instead, existing ministries like the *Auswärtiges Amt* contemplated creating a European Division, in which Community affairs would be dealt with alongside policies in the CFSP and third pillars.

---

[55]Deutscher Bundestag, 12. Wahlperiode, Antrag der Fraktion der SPD, Verhandlungen der Bundesregierung in den EG-Regierungskonferenzen zur Politischen Union und zur Wirtschafts- und Währungsunion, Drucksache 12/1434, 1–6; Deutscher Bundestag, 12. Wahlperiode, Entschließungsantrag der Fraktionen der CDU/CSU und FDP zur Erklärung der Bundesregierung, Gipfeltreffen der Staats- und Regierungschefs der EG in Maastricht sowie der Staats- und Regierungschefs der NATO in Rom, Drucksache 12/1476, 1–8.

[56]Debattenbeitrag der Staatsministerin im Auswärtigen Amt, Ursula Seiler-Albring, in der Sitzung des Deutschen Bundesrats am 08. November 1991, Mitteilung für die Presse Nr. 1239/91, 2–7.

Negotiators' Strategies

The negotiations on political union relativize the notion of strategy. The use of tactics by national leaders to advance national goals during the conference was evident. Tactics were also necessary owing to the lack of definition and the broad agenda for political union. Coherent strategy was formulated by those states with limited and precise objectives and a small number of individuals at all levels of negotiation like France. The German strategy of *Parallelität* proved difficult to implement owing to the overwhelming opposition to increased powers for the European Parliament. It is also important to underline the interplay of domestic and European goals in the implementation of the Dutch Presidency's strategy to introduce a unified Treaty structure. Here we realize that the role of individuals other than the head of state or government can be relevant to the outcome of negotiations at different levels in the Council.

The central role of Hans van den Broek during the Council Presidency, and the institutional set-up of the Dutch political system which buttresses the position of the foreign minister, left Prime Minister Ruud Lubbers in a somewhat strained relationship with his colleague. Both men belonged to the same political party, the Christian-Democrats (CDA), and both had international ambitions. To complicate matters, the CDA was in coalition with the Social Democrats (PvdA) which favored relations with eastern Europe over the traditional transatlantic links of the Christian Democrats. A key actor, the State Minister for European affairs in the foreign ministry, Piet Dankert, was a former President of the European Parliament and a staunch federalist. His ambition to limit the role of the European Council and to push through a unified Treaty structure strongly influenced the IGC negotiations. In terms of domestic politics, both parties were advocates of reforming the financial situation of the Dutch state. This influenced the work of the Social Democratic finance minister Wim Kok regarding the Presidency's position on cohesion within the context of political union and other issues on the EMU agenda.[57]

Not surprisingly, the Dutch text was controversial even before it left The Hague. Dankert, a powerful player in the Dutch coalition government, belonged to a new continental breed of "European affairs ministers" who wield enough power to coordinate European policies across several government departments.[58] With the foreign minister bogged down in Yugoslav diplomacy, the job of steering the Treaty was given to Dankert, who was close to Lubbers and a Socialist member of the coalition. The Socialists were under pressure to bring down the coalition over disputes about Dutch disability benefits. To keep the government together, the Cabinet gave Dankert most of his own way.[59]

---

[57]"Die Niederlande auf der Suche nach ihrem Platz in Europa," *Neue Zürcher Zeitung*, 2. Juli 1991, 4.

[58]Brock, "Federal Camp Wins First Round," 11.

[59]———, "Dutch Challenged over Draft for Union Treaty," 20.

Moreover, the Dutch believed that there was German support for their text which would tilt the balance among the member states in its favor. There was German backing, but at the level below Genscher. The individual who initially supported the Dutch draft was Dietrich von Kyaw. However, the weekend before the ministerial meeting, Dumas convinced his German counterpart that the Dutch were showing *trop de zèle fédéraliste*. The difficult relations between Genscher and van den Broek did not help the Dutch initiative.[60]

The "Dankert plan" had encountered initial opposition at the level of the personal representatives who did not want to start work on the basis of a new text. Peter Nieman, the Dutch Ambassador in the Presidency chair during the conference, relayed this information to his government, but Dankert persisted. The fact that Nieman was unable to convince his government that its actions were heading right into a brick wall illustrates the broad influence that national ministers for European affairs can wield. In this context, the Dutch case demonstrates how the requirements of domestic coalition politics can complicate negotiations at the European level. It also shows how transnational alliances can bring out differences of opinion within a member state's government, i.e., the initial support of the *Auswärtiges Amt*, at the level below Genscher, of the Dutch foreign ministry's initiative.

The French Case

As viewed from the Elysée, two ideas marked French diplomacy during the negotiations on political union. First, in terms of a strategic line, the French negotiating position emphasized no transfer of sovereignty on CFSP. It was to be intergovernmental in nature. Since the political maturity among the member states to act as a unit in matters of "high politics" was not yet evident, a gradual approach marked by flexibility dominated French thinking on this issue. French proposals on the CFSP did resemble the Fouchet Plans of the 1960s. However, its evolutionary nature and the inclusion of the Commission in CFSP matters leave its ultimate definition as a policy, and not just as a process, open to question.[61]

Second, in terms of European policies and institutions, the French saw the necessity to diversify Europe and democratize its problems. Although several personal representatives stated repeatedly that the extension of the Community's competencies was not a major issue of negotiations on political union,[62] certain issues like social policy and industry were significant to Mitterrand and Cresson. From the French standpoint, Europe most definitely had a role to play in these areas. With regard to the democratic deficit, it is

---

[60]David Buchan, *Europe: The Strange Superpower* (Aldershot: Dartmouth, 1993), 40.

[61]Interview, Quai d'Orsay, 8 March 1993.

[62]Interviews, Quai d'Orsay, 8 March 1993 and *Auswärtiges Amt*, 30 July 1993.

important to underline that the French emphasized the democratic legitimacy of the European Council as the body in which elected political leaders defined and dealt with the issues on the Community's agenda. This body gave the French President the greatest opportunity to exercise his wide range of powers.

According to participants at the Elysée and the Quai d'Orsay, the Prime Minister did not try to obstruct French internal bargaining during the conference. About a dozen people were also involved in the IGC process at Matignon.[63] After her appointment in May 1991, Cresson played an active role in placing industrial policy on the conference agenda. On many issues, there were technical meetings at the Elysée. These meetings were organized by the President's counselor for European affairs, Sophie Caroline de Margerie, and included Dumas' counselor for foreign affairs, Jean-Michel Casa, and the personal representatives, Trichet and de Boissieu among others.

The individual responsible for the coordination of IGC dossiers distributed among the officials in different national ministries was Guigou's *chef de cabinet*, Pierre Vimont. He worked quite closely with the others to keep the internal bargaining process in sync with the rapid pace of political union negotiations. Here the interplay of personalities was decisive. Many of these individuals had worked together before like Guigou and de Boissieu. All of them had extensive experience in Franco-German and/or European Community affairs. This enabled the team to work well as a "network of communication."[64]

Although Mitterrand advocated a federal Europe in his joint letter with Kohl, he was no doubt aware of the danger in pushing the idea too fast and too far. Given the activities and populism of Le Pen's National Front, Mitterrand could find himself confronted at home with a widening rebellion, in defense of the values—real or supposed—of the tricolor, which could complicate the handling of both domestic and foreign policy.[65] A sign of this concern was the appointment of Edith Cresson in May 1991 instead of Michel Rocard. Cresson's mandate from the Elysée was to ready France for the single market, a daunting task given how ill-informed and ill-prepared the majority of the French people were regarding the "1992" project. The new Prime Minister's obvious qualification was that of a very robust defender of the national interest.

Despite differences which emerged between the two countries during the 57th Franco-German Summit in Lille on 29–30 May regarding a Community electronics and information policy, this in no way deterred Cresson. The Prime Minister was unyielding in her view that an industrial policy for Europe

---

[63]Interview, French Permanent Representation to the European Communities, 25 November 1992.

[64]Interview, Quai d'Orsay, 8 March 1993.

[65]Michael Sutton, "France: Who Beats the Nationalist Drum," *The World Today*, June 1991, 101–102.

was an absolute necessity. During an interview on 28 June, she argued for greater cooperation among European firms in order to prevent their disappearance on competitive world markets. In response to a question on the role of the state in the modern economy, Cresson emphasized its role in education and training. [66]

French strategy remained consistent throughout the remaining months of negotiations. Clearly there was a divergence of opinions at different levels of negotiation within the French delegation on allowing Parliament greater powers. Dumas and his personal representative were firmly against the idea. As the IGC progressed, Guigou was more amenable to compromise. [67] Her line eventually prevailed to break a deadlock in negotiations on democratic legitimacy.

The French view on the issue of the Treaty structure was articulated by Guigou during a hearing before the National Assembly on 3 October. She criticized the fact that negotiations on political union had registered no progress since the end of the Luxembourg Presidency. Three months had been lost. The focus of the Dutch Presidency was an "abstract" debate on the Treaty structure whereas, in the French view, it was the substance of the Treaty which counted. As Guigou explained, the Dutch text gave little substance to the CFSP or the third pillar and accorded too much power to the European Parliament. [68] There was also general agreement in Paris that the Dutch text aggravated the differences among the member states. A high-ranking official close to Guigou described the Dutch text as "a loss at all tables." [69]

German Priorities

The Luxembourg European Council was viewed as a success for the German negotiating line. The isolation of Britain and fixed acceptance of only partial results in the conference were avoided. Authorities in Bonn believed that progress was made in Luxembourg on the Chancellor's initiative regarding cooperation on justice and home affairs. Note was made of the fact that the final *communiqué* from the Presidency made no reference to federalism, watered down the European citizenship concept and left the European Parliament in the shadows. Consequently, German diplomacy aimed to

---

[66]Ministère des Affaires Etrangères, *La politique étrangère de la France, textes et documents*, Mai-Juin 1991, 139–142. Interestingly, Cresson would subsequently be appointed by Mitterrand as one of two French Commissioners in the European Commission under Jacques Santer in 1995. Her portfolio is Research, Education and Training.

[67]Interview, Richard Corbett, European Parliament Secretariat, 3 July 1992.

[68]Ministère des Affaires Etrangères, *La politique étrangère de la France, textes et documents*, Septembre-Octobre 1991, 92.

[69]Interview, Quai d'Orsay, 8 March 1993.

develop and refine a *Stufenkonzept* by which democratic legitimacy, citizenship, majority voting in the Council, CFSP and the third pillar competencies would evolve in the Union via revision clauses in the Treaty. Despite the "single institutional framework" contained in the *chapeau* of the Luxembourg text, Germany sought to introduce an even greater unity in the Treaty structure by binding the second and third pillars even closer to the Community. In the German view, it is questionable at best to use *passerelles*, or Treaty Articles which allow policies in the second and third pillars to be gradually included in the Community, to accomplish this task.[70]

Near the end of negotiations, it became apparent that the strategy of *Parallelität* might not be implemented. Right from the start, Kohl had insisted on linkage between progress on political union and EMU. One senior official in the *Auswärtiges Amt* explained the situation: "The problem of the Community is Britain. It is not Germany. We are on our way to solve the British problem in the new negotiations by giving a covered up two-speed Europe as a way out on monetary union. We cannot imitate the exceptional deal for Britain on EMU in the field of political union...Now we are threatened with a linkage that is so weak that the thing will not fly in domestic German politics." [71]

Cohesion was another major issue of discord prior to Maastricht. Just after the foreign ministers met in Noordwijk, Prime Minister Gonzalez visited Chancellor Kohl in Bonn. There was a misunderstanding between the Commission President and the Spanish Prime Minister who felt that Delors had not defended Spanish views on the cohesion issue strongly enough during the conclave. Chancellor Kohl understood Felipe's "problem" in terms of Spanish domestic politics and, with the assistance of the Council Secretariat, a compromise solution was sketched out.[72] Final details remained to be worked out at Maastricht in the presence of the all the leaders in the European Council. Days later Spain did threaten a veto at Maastricht if cohesion was accorded a "secondary place" in the Treaty. The cohesion issue showed that Kohl was well informed about domestic political situations in other Community member states.

At the end of November, Chancellor Kohl spoke before the Bundestag to explain his views on an increase in the powers of the European Parliament. Although Kohl believed that the political union required greater parliamentary control, this could only be realized in two stages. In his mind, two steps to achieve greater democratic control were better than none at all. So as a first

---

[70]Interviews, German Permanent Representation to the European Communities, 30 July 1992 and *Auswärtiges Amt*, 29 January 1993.

[71]Peel, "Bonn Warning on Political Union Treaty."

[72]Interview, Peter Ludlow, Center for European Policy Studies, 15 May 1992.

step, Kohl proposed a strengthening of the Parliament's authority at the beginning of the 1994 legislative period and the granting of additional rights for European parliamentarians from the start of the next legislative period in 1999.

The Chancellor also put forward a tactical maneuver to avoid an eventual stalemate in Maastricht. In a declaration attached to the Treaty, all those member states wanting to advance the integration process could state: their will to construct a Union with a "federal vocation"; their acceptance of a Revision Conference in 1996 to strengthen the communitarized policies in the Treaty; their desire not to profit from any "opt-out" clauses; that only those countries applying for admission would be accepted which agreed to the declaration's provisions. In Kohl's view, the agenda for 1996 would include an extension of the co-decision procedure, the competencies in social policy, CFSP and the communitarization of some policies in judicial affairs.

During the foreign ministers' conclave on 2–3 December, German priorities were a precise formulation of the subsidiarity principle, with regard for the Länder and the departments responsible for different European competencies within the various federal ministries, industrial policy, bearing in mind the position of the ministry of economics, on the one hand, and the French position on the other, and a visible result on CFSP, with an eye on the balance between progress on EMU and political union. On the industrial policy dossier, officials in the *Auswärtiges Amt* had to strike a delicate balance: domestic objectives as outlined by the ministry of economics weighed in alongside the need to make Franco-German relations the motor for political union.

Other issues which were particularly important for Germany included a time link between the Commission's term in office and the election of the European Parliament, the assent of the Parliament on decisions to amend the Treaty (Article 235 EEC) and on future Treaty changes (Article 236 EEC), the extension of co-decision to social policy and internal market affairs (particularly 100c, visa policy, border controls) and the inclusion of justice and home affairs matters in the Community competencies. The French proposal for a Conference of Parliaments was acceptable as a declaration as long as this did not weaken the role of the European Parliament.

In internal debates just before the Maastricht European Council, the strategy of *Parallelität* was extremely important. Although the SPD was for EMU, and would not accept "populistic headines with a nationalistic backdrop," Wieczorek-Zeul stated that the acceptance of further moves toward EMU in 1996 by the Bundestag should be made dependent on progress obtained in rights for the European Parliament.[73] Speaking in the Bundestag,

---

[73]"Warnungen vor übereilter Währungsunion," *Frankfurter Allgemeine Zeitung*, 9. Dezember 1991, 17.

after the foreign ministers' conclave on 5 December, Genscher admitted that the gains for the Parliament were insufficient. He, like Kohl, spoke of accomplishing this task in a series of steps. However, the SPD insisted that without the aforementioned coupling of EMU and political union, Maastricht could not be a success. Domestic actors understood that compromises among leaders in the European Council would be necessary, but in the essential area of democratic legitimacy the Federal Republic could not be "weak-kneed."[74]

Franco-German Strategy

Just about a week prior to Maastricht, in bilateral talks between Mitterrand and Kohl in Paris, the remaining differences between the two countries were discussed. Elisabeth Guigou and Joachim Bitterlich, who kept the lines of communication open between the Quai and the Chancellor's Office, were also in contact. President Mitterrand was less interested in the "conveyor belt" toward federalism than Chancellor Kohl. French priorities at Maastricht were more or less assured in terms of a pillar structure for the Treaty, but much work was necessary to create a common European defense, to preserve controversial Articles on social policy in the Treaty and to achieve agreement on an industrial policy for the Community. It was agreed that at Maastricht the French were prepared to accept a declaration on the "Congress," or Conference of Parliaments.[75]

The industry issue had first to be discussed at the ministerial level. Cresson's resolve on this issue meant that only discussions in the European Council could bring about an accord. France was also prepared to accept a German compromise formula on subsidiarity and evolutionary clauses on the European Parliament and justice and home affairs. The main French concern was CFSP.

Aberbach, Putnam and Rockman's Four Images of Civil Servants

During the IGC, national civil servants played a crucial role in the day-to-day preparation of dossiers. Negotiations at different levels were noteworthy for a hasty and intense preparation by civil servants owing to the late decision to convene a second conference. Significantly, the personal representatives wrote much of the text of the eventual Maastricht Treaty. One highly placed Commission official described an almost excessive attention to detail with the personal representatives "dotting every i and crossing every t" in the text. The foreign ministers, on the other hand, had a difficult time making crucial decisions on the essential issues. The end result was that the Maastricht

---

[74]Deutscher Bundestag, 12. Wahlperiode, 64. Sitzung, Bonn, den 5. Dezember 1991, 5431–5434.

[75]A declaration was not as binding on member states as a protocol. The latter was the equivalent of text written in the Treaty, but protocols appeared after the text so as to make the document look more presentable.

European Council was left with a large number of agenda issues to settle in two days.

The fact that essential decisions would be taken by the European Council is quite understandable from a democratic standpoint. It consists of the highest level of democratically elected leaders in the Community member states. However, the fact that the text which these leaders decided upon was written for the most part by highly placed civil servants with limited decision making by foreign ministers implies an extraordinary degree of political influence for unelected diplomats in the entire Treaty-making process. Minister Ellemann-Jensen did admit that some of the problems to be encountered later, during the national ratifications of the Maastricht Treaty, were more the responsibility of the foreign ministers than President Delors. As Ellemann-Jensen explained, "We foreign ministers should be blamed more because we had the contact with our constituencies. We should have started to realize that the Community looked like a centralized bureaucratic monster....We were so busy trying to understand the new situation in eastern Europe that we didn't listen to the signals."[76]

It is necessary though to ask whether the foreign ministers really had sufficient contact with their domestic constituencies to understand the nature of public opinion on European affairs, in general, and Maastricht, in particular. In most respects, the foreign ministers have the crucial organizational role, and burden of the work, during each six-month Council Presidency. There is a tremendous amount of pressure and routine tasks involved just to conduct normal Community business and the other demands of world diplomacy, not to mention IGC negotiations. Are individuals whose daily work involves a great deal of international travel in the conduct of foreign affairs constantly in touch with the domestic mood? The foreign ministers' key position at the crossroads of decision making on European policies, which have domestic implications, means that these individuals must be plugged into the domestic scene or risk the alienation of publics that can no longer follow their policy making at the European level.

The foreign ministers' personal representatives during the Maastricht negotiations were meant to assist the ministers with the daily business of the two conferences. This fact assured the centrality of these officials in the negotiations. As most negotiators admit, there is no substitute for a hands-on knowledge of the minutest details of a text. Given their astute understanding of the political significance behind their decisions on technical points, the personal representatives exerted a profound influence on the final Treaty. This is in spite of the fact that their negotiating style was one of "behind closed doors." This style is reminiscent of the distinction made by Aberbach, Putnam and Rockman in Image III between politicians and bureaucrats. The personal representatives were less politico-administrative hybrids than extremely well-placed politico-administrative civil servants. These officials influenced the

---

[76]Grant, *Delors: Inside the House That Jacques Built*, 235.

decisions of their political masters because of their extraordinary contribution to the drafting of the Treaty eventually agreed on in Maastricht.

The personal representatives' role as joint problem solvers is another issue. During the conference on political union, there was no common conception at any level of negotiation on the definition of the final goal. This made the civil servants' role as joint problem solvers from the Community standpoint difficult at best and impossible at worst. The Commission, acting much more like a thirteenth member at the table than during the 1985 IGC negotiations, clearly overplayed its hand from the start. This damaged the spirit of the negotiations in a striking way. Moreover, it is universally recognized that the provisions on political union were not well drafted owing to a messy and unwieldy agenda, the excessive number of compromises that had to be struck on minute details and the large number of languages used during negotiations and draft translations.

In the French and German cases, the negotiations on political union illustrate the essential role of civil servants working at the official level to draft the Treaty. The conference also illustrates, however, that most important decisions were made not by ministers, but by political leaders at Maastricht, with the civil servants remaining behind the scenes. For this reason, the image of politico-administrative hybrids does not explain their role during the Maastricht process.

The French Case

The central figure at the official level, Pierre de Boissieu, was linked in a relatively free fashion to the chain of command: Mitterrand, Dumas, Guigou and Bérégovoy. De Boissieu's room to maneuver within the scope of instructions on his negotiating line was great. And he made the most of this advantage.[77] De Boissieu's negotiating line was never overruled by his minister, indicating their accord on the essential issues. From de Boissieu's vantage point, French diplomacy must emphasize the strong role of the state. The entire Maastricht process was viewed as "an intergovernmental negotiation which must lead to a culture of compromise." De Boissieu explained that the gravity of negotiations during the conference involved the positions of certain key member states. France and Germany occupied the center ground with Spain taking a maximalist position on most issues, and Great Britain leading supporters of the minimalist position.[78] The full extent of de Boissieu's influence can be viewed by assessing his contributions to the debate on the Treaty structure. His influence was exerted behind the scenes through coalition building among those member states and institutions with a

---

[77]Interview, Secretariat General, Commission of the European Communities, 11 June 1993.
[78]Interview, Quai d'Orsay, 8 March 1993.

preference for the pillar structure. Moreover, it is clear that de Boissieu was following the strict line of Mitterrand and his minister on this issue.

The German Case

When the Dutch Presidency submitted its alternative draft treaty to the conference in September, the German negotiating position, formulated in the *Auswärtiges Amt*, was to support the Dutch text. There was a difference of opinion between Trumpf and Kyaw over the German response to the Dutch draft treaty. Trumpf believed the opposition, including France and Great Britain, to be too great and the timing not right to introduce the Dutch text. Kyaw felt that the Germans should have held out longer in support of the Presidency's initiative. Kyaw based his judgement on the already existing democratic deficit in the Community and the wide agreement within the Bonn government and the SPD-Opposition on the need to increase the European Parliament's powers. Yet, he also acknowledged that his role as a civil servant was not to make public statements on how to address the democratic deficit in the Community. This is the task of the political leadership.[79]

Clearly the judgement call was Genscher's to make, but Kyaw's concern was that support for the Luxembourg draft treaty would have a negative impact on the German ratification debate. This was especially true since the French persisted in refusing to grant Germany 18 additional seats in the European Parliament without a corresponding increase for the other large member states. Genscher explained his decision, based in part on Trumpf's assessment of the situation at the official level, in an interview with a Dutch newspaper. He emphasized the German commitment to political union for which elements of the Dutch text would be useful in future negotiations.[80]

Monnet's Approach

Early in negotiations on political union, the Dutch expressed irritation about the unilateral nature of French diplomatic initiatives during the Gulf Crisis. Mitterrand expressed the French viewpoint, namely, that political union did not yet exist but that this crisis indicated how badly Europe needed to advance its construction. Although the fundamental positions of the member states were the same regarding the Gulf War, the practical responsibilities were not. Contrary to Monnet's approach, which envisaged a role for the European Commission, the French view was that the smaller states would have to allow

---

[79]Interview, Ambassador Dietrich von Kyaw, German Permanent Representation to the European Communities, 11 June 1993.

[80]Interview des Bundesministers des Auswärtigen, Hans-Dietrich Genscher, mit der niederländischen Zeitung Algemeen Dagblad (Ausgabe vom 16. Oktober 1991) zu Fragen der europäischen Integration, Mitteilung für die Presse Nr. 1221/91, 1–2.

the larger countries to speak on their behalf as a European security and defense identity evolved.[81]

Delors' attempts to implement Monnet's approach during the IGC on political union were less successful than those during the EMU conference. The notion of "family spirit," often stressed by Monnet, was not very present. The Community had grown too large. Given that an influential personal representative like de Boissieu worked out of his national capital, there was little time to meet or discuss viewpoints about issues on the table with Commission officials or personal representatives from other member states like Greece and Portugal.[82]

Delors' presence during the negotiations was influential in discussions on cohesion, at the Luxembourg European Council, for example, precisely because he could explain in a succinct manner different national positions. This talent was helpful in the search for compromise solutions. President Delors always looked to link issues on the table during the IGCs to the momentum of progress completing the internal market. Thus, he emphasized the fact that the social dimension of the internal market was the one point in which significant progress was not made. Yet, Delors did not think it wise to spend too much time on this issue, or any other, at Luxembourg. Any aim to ambush a country on an isssue was not a good approach. It was better to bring positions together with a view toward discussions in Maastricht. This maxim could also be applied to the debate on the Treaty structure. Undoubtedly, de Boissieu's idea to introduce a Treaty structure with pillars featuring intergovernmental cooperation posed the greatest threat to the Community, or Monnet, approach in the form of decision making in the emerging Commission-Council-Parliament triangle. The Commission's draft text, largely ignored by the Luxembourg Presidency, appeared in sections between February and June. Its most provocative section was on foreign policy. In this area, the right of initiative would no longer remain with individual governments; the Commission, the Council Presidency or a grouping of at least six member states would have that right. The Commission, the Council Secretariat and the permanent representatives of the member states in Brussels would prepare and implement common policies. This would effectively limit, if not eliminate, the role of political directors in national foreign ministries in the CFSP process.[83]

"The Commission's chief concern seems to have been to give itself more power," said Carlos Westendorp, Spain's Minister for European affairs. "The Commission's role should be to search for common ground, but in taking an

---

[81]Ministère des Affaires Etrangères, *La politique étrangère de la France, textes et documents*, Septembre-Octobre 1991, 114–116.

[82]Interview, Quai d'Orsay, 8 March 1993.

[83]Grant, *Delors: Inside the House That Jacques Built*, 189.

extreme position, it behaved like a thirteenth member."[84] Although Delors and his advisers had worked with the Luxembourg Presidency and Council Secretary General, Niels Ersbøll, in 1985 during the drafting of the Single European Act, in 1991 relations among the three were strained. In the Commission's view, the Luxembourg Presidency was "in the pocket of the French and the Council Secretariat." This was a direct reference to the enormous influence exerted by de Boissieu and Ersbøll, highly competent negotiators who were determined to limit the Commission's power.[85]

Ersbøll was long regarded by many insiders as an *eminence grise*, owing to his political weight as an adviser to the heads of state and government regarding Community affairs. During the initial Maastricht ratification debate in Denmark, Ersbøll stepped into public view to give some interviews in which he argued for the Danish ratification of the Treaty. Unlike Delors, the Secretary General of the Council was not extremely well-known by the public at large nor did he seek out that kind of role. However, his contacts with the press, speaking out on political issues, illustrate his role as a politico-administrative hybrid.

On the issue of the Treaty structure, Delors' behind the scenes campaign included writing letters to the heads of state and government warning that Luxembourg's draft treaty represented a dangerous departure from the institutional framework that had evolved in the Community over the past forty years. By speaking personally to a number of political leaders, Delors managed to convince seven member states, including Germany, to address the issue in Dresden. However, the Commission's strategy of openly siding with the Presidency in September on this same issue was an error. The end result was not only the failure of the Dutch draft treaty but a loss of credibility for the Commission in the eyes of the member states for the remainder of the negotiation.

Some delegations did judge the Treaty structure in the Luxembourg text as too intergovernmental. Only 10 pages dealt with institutional questions, a fact which drew criticism in the press.[86] Another long-time observer of Community affairs declared that the pillar structure was a return to the Fouchet Plan of the 1960s.[87] Moreover, the French delegation's proposal of 1996 as the date for a Revision Conference to examine the Treaty provisions on political union aroused certain suspicions. This was true in part because this deadline indicated less Monnet's approach of fixed timetables and more a

---

[84]Ibid.

[85]Ibid., 190.

[86]"Unscharfe Konturen einer europäischen Union," *Neue Zürcher Zeitung*, 22. April 1991.

[87]Emanuele Gazzo, "L'Union (politique) européenne (1)—Une manoeuvre à déjouer," *Agence Europe*, 22 et 23 avril 1991, 1.

French unwillingness to consider substantial institutional reforms during the actual conference.

On these issues, Delors ran up against the entrenched positions of at least four member states which fought to retain intergovernmental cooperation to defend their national interests. These states were determined to resist Commission influence in this area. It is also questionable as to whether Monnet would have employed such a confrontational approach on this important issue.

During the IGC, a broad array of policies including research, energy, health, culture, transeuropean networks, civil protection and tourism were specified as new Community competencies. Delors spoke of a "shopping list" instead of an insistence on certain priorities for the Community. Each country insisted on its own individual hobbyhorse. Germany even put in a proposal for an Article on animal protection. This speaks to the diversity of the numerous issues the personal representatives had to prepare for ministerial sessions. One German civil servant described their efforts as wanting to get "as much as possible for Europe." De Boissieu lamented the lack of " balance" during the entire negotiation.[88] Clearly little attempt was made to negotiate on the basis of a text that was throughly prepared by a committee like the Delors Committee on EMU. And after the introduction of the Luxembourg draft treaty in April, the personal representatives immediately began to discuss its contents Article by Article instead of concentrating on its larger principles to achieve a *vue d'ensemble*.[89]

Clearly the way in which the draft text on political union was negotiated did not reflect Monnet's approach with its emphasis on integrative bargaining. Instead classical techniques of distributive bargaining, in which compromises are made among states with widely divergent national interests, were the norm. Most importantly, no one definition of political union was shared by the member states that could enable negotiators at different levels to establish a workable agenda or emphasize joint efforts to address commonly understood issues.

SUMMARY

The negotiations on political union were given a strong impetus as a result of the three Franco-German letters addressed to successive Council Presidencies. Despite these obvious bilateral initiatives, however, France and Germany remained divided on the definition of political union. Moreover, each member state had its own interests to pursue, based in part on the domestic requirements of Treaty ratification. Four main issues dominated the discussions throughout 1991: institutional matters, including democratic legitimacy, European citizenship, extension of Community competencies and

---

[88]Interviews, German Permanent Representation to the European Communities, 11 June 1993 and Quai d'Orsay, 8 March 1993.

[89]"L'union politique en discussion," *Libération*, 16 avril 1991, 21.

subsidiarity; the third pillar or cooperation in justice and home affairs like asylum, immigration and visa policy; the Treaty structure, including the relationship of the European Community to the proposed Union; and CFSP. Throughout 1991, the personal representatives were faced with an unwieldy conference agenda that hindered their ability to draft a coherent text. The foreign ministers' preoccupation with external events in central and eastern Europe left the heads of state and government with many decisions to make during the Maastricht European Council.

The three approaches used in the context of the political union negotiations shed light on the obstacles to integrative bargaining and the ways in which the debate on the Treaty structure linked each of the main issue areas together during the IGC process. The emphasis of Putnam's two-level games on domestic institutions explains the unwillingness of several of the member states to agree on the extent of power to be given to the European Parliament. This unwillingness in turn produced a complicated and cumbersome co-decision procedure which was necessary to include in the Treaty to satisfy the domestic requirements of German ratification. Moreover, two-level games' focus on negotiators' strategies, provides an illustration of the ways in which Dutch coalition politics complicated van den Broek's role during the Maastricht negotiations as well as how transgovernmental alliances brought out different viewpoints on an issue among Genscher and Trumpf, on the one hand, and Dankert and Kyaw, on the other.

Aberbach, Putnam and Rockman's approach complements two-level games in this context initially by emphasizing the input of well-placed civil servants, under the ministerial level of negotiation, into strategy formulation. On the issue of Treaty structure, Genscher's decision not to support the Dutch draft treaty was clearly the decisive one during the General Affairs Council meeting on 30 September. Both Kyaw and Trumpf acted within the limits of their administrative roles with Genscher taking the full responsibility to defend his action to the press and public opinion. However, the debate on the Treaty structure, particularly as it related to greater powers for the European Parliament, impacted on the German ratification debate in the Bundestag. It also figured prominently in the proceedings and ruling of the Constitutional Court regarding the compatiblity of the Treaty on European Union with the Basic Law.

Aberbach, Putnam and Rockman's approach also points to the influence which different politico-administrative hybrids brought to bear on the debate over the Treaty structure. Whereas President Delors openly sided with the Dutch government's plan, Secretary General Ersbøll, in tandem with de Boissieu, successfully defended the Treaty's pillar structure. On this issue, classic distributive bargaining was evident. Moreover, the threat to several of the most crucial aspects of Monnet's approach was clear in the form of maintaining intergovernmental decision making in two of the three pillars of the Treaty on European Union. Significantly, the debate about the Treaty structure concerned each of the other dominant issues of the IGC; institutional issues, third pillar issues and CFSP were all linked in the Maastricht Treaty's structure.

The insights provided by Monnet's approach tie into those of the other two approaches to the extent that it emphasizes the ways in which the lack of a common definition of political union, and the inability of the member states to speak a Community language during the negotiations, hindered integrative bargaining on the part of the personal representatives or foreign ministers. Guigou's openness to the proposal made by Seiler-Albring concerning stronger provisions in the *chapeau* of the Treaty was an attempt to get beyond purely distributive bargaining and to focus more on attitudinal structuring. The German idea behind the reinforced *chapeau*, agreed to by Guigou, was to underline the evolutionary character of the Community and to allow for a mixed domain in which some policies which were no longer intergovernmental but not yet communitarized could exist.

Here Guigou had to consider the impact of a unified Treaty structure, with all policies subject to traditional Community decision-making procedures, in terms of the French ratification debate. Finally, the use of Monnet's approach to explain the IGC process illustrates the changes in the European environment since the founding of the Communities. Specifically, this approach makes the reader sensitive to the fact that problems arose during the national ratification debates because a substantial number of citizens in the member states were not willing to accept a Treaty negotiated behind closed doors.

CHAPTER VI

Mind over Maastricht: Leadership and Negotiation in the European Council[1]

For the politician, the constant aim is to be in the Cabinet, and to be the first there. This exercise is inevitably linked to a certain presentation of things, and the presentation counts as much, if not more, than the things themselves. Everything revolves around the struggle for nomination; and the object of power, the problem to settle, is forgotten. I have not known a great politician who is not highly egocentric, and for reason: if he had not been, he never would have imposed his image and his person. I could not be so, not because I was modest, but because one cannot concentrate on a thing and on oneself. This thing was always the same for me: to make men work together, to show them that beyond their differences and over their borders, they have a common interest.

Men accept change only in necessity; they see necessity only in crisis.

Jean Monnet, *Mémoires*

The Maastricht European Council took place on 9–10 December 1991 in a small Dutch town at the crossroads of Europe. The agenda was full despite the fact that civil servants, central bankers, finance and foreign ministers had discussed the finer points of the texts on EMU and political union. Only the decisions that had to be made at the highest political level to reach an accord on the Treaties remained. During the negotiations, nine larger issues dominated the agenda. As always, the devil was in the detail. In this sense, the Maastricht European Council could be likened both to a 12-dimensional game of chess and a family tug of war.[2] The nine agenda issues left for the European leaders to settle were: 1. the transition to the final phase of EMU; 2. decision

---

[1] Some of the ideas for the contents in this chapter are taken from Barbara Kellerman and Jeffrey Z. Rubin, eds., *Leadership and Negotiation in the Middle East* (New York: Praeger, 1988).

[2] Boris Johnson, "Small Room That Could Shut the Door on Plans for Europe," *The Daily Telegraph*, December 12, 1991.

making on the CFSP; 3. the defense dimension of the CFSP; 4. the powers of
the European Parliament; 5. the inclusion of the term "federal vocation" in the
chapeau or general provisions common to both Treaties; 6. new Community
competencies; 7. interior and justice affairs including the contentious issue of
whether or not to place Article 100c in the first pillar; 8. cohesion; and 9.
social policy. [3] All of these issues came up on the first day of negotiations, but
some were discussed more thoroughly than others. The night between the first
and second days of the Council was used by the Presidency to rewrite Treaty
Articles and to craft compromises often in bilateral or trilateral talks with
member state leaders. The remainder of the second day was devoted to
bringing negotiations on political union to fruition which was a delicate task
given the intransigence of Major on social policy.

In the multilateral context of negotiations at Maastricht, the bilateral input
of France and Germany was crucial to the final outcome. In concrete terms,
the success of the Franco-German negotiating line can be seen by comparing
the Luxembourg draft treaty in June with the final results obtained in
Maastricht. On EMU, no fixed date for the transition to Stage Three appeared
in the June text. Nor were there any provisions on a European defense or a
Community Article on immigration and visa policy like 100c. In the final
treaty text each of these issues is specifically mentioned: EMU in the first, or
European Community, pillar; defense in the second, or CFSP, pillar; and 100c
as the *passarelle* in the first pillar which relates to issues in the third, or justice
and home affairs, pillar. On each issue, the role of the Franco-German
partnership, tilting the balance of the negotiations in a positive direction, was
decisive. In this chapter, the three approaches presented in the Introduction are
used to illustrate this fact and to analyze the roles of Kohl, Mitterrand and
Delors during the Maastricht European Council. The decisions taken by
Mitterrand and Kohl in order to conclude the negotiations are then linked to
the domestic ratification processes explained in subsequent chapters. [4]

SUNDAY NIGHT'S MEETINGS

Arguably some of the most important meetings in Maastricht took place
before the official opening of the European Council. On the evening of 8
December, shortly after their arrival in Maastricht, Mitterrand and Andreotti
met to discuss the decision on the passage to the final stage of EMU. Prior to
Maastricht, the finance ministers were convinced that EMU should have

---

[3]Baudouin Bollaert, "Les neuf 'mines' qui peuvent faire tout exploser," *Le Figaro*, 9
décembre 1991, 6.

[4]Most of the information about the Maastricht European Council was obtained in numerous
confidential interviews over a three-year period.

strong criteria to fight against inflation, a firm commitment to price stability, and that the proposed ECB should be independent from national governments. These requirements were necessary to retain the support of the Kohl government and the Bundesbank for EMU. The German reluctance to accept any strict timetable for the establishment of a single currency was also well known.[5]

During their meeting, the French and Italian leaders decided on a proposal that would require the European Council to set a deadline of 1999 for creating the European Central Bank even if a majority of member states did not yet fulfill the convergence criteria to make the transition to the final stage of EMU. Both men were concerned that the proposal on the transition to Stage Three put forward by the finance ministers the week before could allow a "loophole" delaying establishment of the ECB well into the next century. That draft would have allowed some European countries to adopt a single currency as early as 1997 only if there was unanimous agreement that economic conditions in a majority of member states were favorable.[6] As an alternative plan, Bérégovoy proposed to his colleagues in ECOFIN a procedure that combined a firm timetable for Stage Three with qualified majority voting in the European Council to determine whether sufficient states had met the convergence criteria. This plan, which corresponded to Mitterrand's and Andreotti's line of thinking, underlined the irreversibility of EMU. This principle was key to the negotiation, and to the Franco-German negotiating line, in large part because Kohl wanted an irreversible process as much as his French counterpart. Mitterrand and Andreotti's compromise was designed to overcome Bonn's fears that other European leaders, in their eagerness to gain influence over German monetary policy, might be tempted to play down economic performance as a criteria for membership in the future currency union. By proposing that the European Council decide by majority vote that EMU would start in 1999 even if only three member states fulfilled the necessary convergence criteria, the two leaders were ensuring a deadline for the transition to EMU before the end of the century. Implicitly understood in the proposal, however, was that France and Germany would have to be able to fulfill the strict criteria by the 1999 deadline. Without these two countries, EMU would make no sense. To join, a country would have to focus on achieving at a minimum two essential criteria. It would have to ensure that its inflation rate did not exceed 1.5% of the average of the three lowest member states and hold its budget deficit to within 3% of GDP.[7] The French and Italian leaders were certain that the European Council would open the next morning with a serious consideration of their proposal.

---

[5] Marsh, *Die Bundesbank*, 313.

[6] Tom Redburn, "EC Agrees on a Single Currency," *International Herald Tribune*, December 10, 1991.

[7] Marsh, *Die Bundesbank*, 314.

The other important meetings that evening were those that Gonzalez held with Kohl and Lubbers, respectively. The Spanish goal was to achieve a clear Treaty commitment on cohesion funds to help the poorer EC countries to make the final transition to EMU. An early solution to this problem, in light of Gonzalez's promise to veto any Treaty lacking provisions on cohesion, threatened to put Britain under even greater pressure to make concessions on EMU. From Major's standpoint, cohesion, social policy and the use of the term "federal vocation" in the Treaty were all issues which could prevent a positive outcome at Maastricht.[8]

MONDAY'S AGENDA

The Presidency, with Ruud Lubbers in the chair, opened the European Council by welcoming Enrique Baron Crespo who spoke briefly about the need to involve the European Parliament more in the decision-making process of the Union. Lubbers thanked President Crespo for Parliament's involvement in the three years of work leading up to Maastricht and for its participation in the dialogue during the interinstitutional meetings. In the Presidency's view, Crespo's appearance at Maastricht illustrated that his institution was acting in a parliamentary fashion. From Crespo's standpoint, "Parliament had no desire to be an onlooker in a Community devoid of enthusiasm. On the contrary, it wished to be one of the key actors...." [9] After Crespo's departure, the Dutch Prime Minister turned to the agenda set out in his letter to the other heads of state and government. Lubbers called for understanding among the participants. He also asked that no conclusions be reached that day. New proposals were to be worked on by the Presidency overnight.

EMU

This was the first issue to be addressed. Lubbers commented on the good progress made in previous negotiations. Further discussion was necessary at the highest political level, however, before the ECOFIN Council met again to draft the final Treaty provisions. The political leaders had to concentrate on two questions from the Presidency's standpoint: how to guarantee the passage to Stage Three; and how many states were required to make the transition to the final stage?

Chancellor Kohl argued that Stage Three was crucial and should be made "irreversible." There should be no discrimination and no first- and second-class countries. In Kohl's view, adherence to the convergence criteria was

---

[8]"Major and Kohl Risk Isolation at Maastricht," *Financial Times*, December 9, 1991.

[9]"Summit Sound-bites," *Financial Times*, December 10, 1991.

fundamental in order for the EMU process to be credible and acceptable. The balance on convergence criteria agreed by the finance ministers must not be altered. The transition to Stage Three should be made in 1996–97 if a majority of states fulfilled the criteria for convergence. For the Chancellor, this majority would represent a critical mass. On the other hand, Kohl stated that in 1998 only those states that fulfilled the convergence criteria would make the transition even if this number did not constitute the majority. [10]

Like Kohl, President Mitterrand insisted that the Community must agree on the irreversible nature of a single currency. He also staunchly supported the Chancellor's demand that the convergence criteria be met. The President then proposed that a date be fixed to start Stage Three probably at the beginning of 1999. By suggesting the proposal that he and Andreotti had already discussed, Mitterrand combined irreversibility with acceptance of a two-speed EMU. This procedure made it easier for Kohl and Waigel to argue that a key concern of the Bundesbank had been met: namely, that not all states were likely to be ready for EMU at once. [11] Mitterrand also argued that the opt-out clause should not be general or indefinite. There were reports, denied by French spokesmen but confirmed by others, that Mitterrand had suggested the need for a time limit on Britain's exemption from EMU. Both the British and Minister Kok dismissed this idea. [12]

Prime Minister Major called for no coercion and no Stage Three. In his view, any text insisting that all member states participate in the transition to the final stage of EMU was going backwards. Major essentially wanted to get an opt-out clause because Britain was not ready to agree to a single currency. He thought the EMU text was dangerous. Major also expressed fears about the disruptive effect of "too small a group" of countries entering EMU. The Prime Minister argued against a two-speed Europe, in which the poorer EC countries like Portugal and Greece and the political recalcitrants such as Britain, would be left potentially in the slow lane of a fast-track design. [13]

Gonzalez essentially agreed with Kohl and Mitterrand that the transition to EMU should be irreversible. However, he insisted that no move be made without a cohesion instrument in the Treaty. The Spanish position on this issue was reiterated by the Portuguese, Irish and Greek leaders who all

---

[10] Redburn, "EC Agrees on a Single Currency."; David Buchan and David Marsh, "Currency Union Likely to Be a Tier-full Affair," *Financial Times*, December 10, 1991; Boris Johnson and George Jones, "Kohl 'Wants to Start Train Now'," *The Daily Telegraph*, December 10, 1991.

[11] Dyson, *Elusive Union*, 157.

[12] Buchan and Marsh, "Currency Union Likely to Be a Tier-full Affair."

[13] Johnson and Jones, "Kohl 'Wants to Start Train Now'."

otherwise accepted the proposed text on the final transition.

As the twelve leaders voiced their positions on EMU, Prime Minister Lubbers took notes. In his summary, Lubbers noted that the Spanish and Greek leaders raised the cohesion issue which would be discussed that evening during negotiations on political union. Prime Minister Schlüter stated that Denmark was prepared to participate fully in Stage Three but that he could not predict the results of the referendum on Maastricht. The Portuguese Prime Minister had brought up the issue of cooperation among the participant countries in Stage Three, on the one hand, and the other member states remaining temporarily outside of EMU on the other. In Lubbers' view, this issue would have to be discussed among the finance ministers later in the day. He also emphasized the crucial nature of the convergence criteria for Stage Three and noted the divergences of view on the decision to make the transition. There were those leaders like Kohl and Mitterrand who wanted the European Council to take the decision. Major suggested the possibilities of a general opt-out clause or for the member states to decide on participation in Stage Three when national parliaments agreed.[14]

Kok pointed out that in view of the differences between Major and some of the other member states on this issue, a unanimous accord on the EMU Treaty was unlikely during the European Council. As he put it, "You cannot find a compromise between 'yes' and 'no'."[15] Lubbers asked the ECOFIN Council to prepare a new draft on the transition which essentially meant a review of Article provisions 109f and g. The Dutch Presidency then turned to a discussion of CFSP.

CFSP/Defense

There were sharp divergences on the use of qualified majority voting and the defense dimension of the CFSP. Genscher argued that the proposals on qualified majority voting made by the Presidency were the minimum acceptable. He also recalled the suggestions for joint action by the Twelve submitted by France and Germany. In his view, this list could evolve over time subject to suggestions made by the foreign ministers. On defense, Genscher noted that the ministers' meeting in WEU had to adopt a declaration later that afternoon. The Community had to make a decision that day for which Genscher advocated a "common defense" with WEU as "an integral part of the Union." Instead of the pre-Maastricht draft that stated the European Union was able to "request" WEU to implement its decisions, Genscher wanted the WEU to act "in conformity" with EU decisions.[16] He also supported the Greek goal of membership in the WEU.

---

[14]Agence Europe, 9 et 10 décembre 1991, 3–4.

[15]"Summit Sound-bites."

[16]Robin Oakley, "Britain Sees Gaullist Trick on Defence," *The Times*, December 10, 1991.

President Mitterrand also recalled the Franco-German text of 15 October. Like Genscher he advocated that WEU be subordinate to and take instructions on defense policy from the Union. The French President further argued that the Union needed some autonomy from Washington.

Although Major voiced support for CFSP, he was not in favor of qualified majority voting in this area. As one British official succinctly put it, "We do not want QMV on CFSP."[17] On defense, Major stated that Britain could agree to the prospect of common defense policies but not to their immediate introduction. Under no conditions, however, should the WEU be under the direction of the European Union. Major was supported by Prime Minister Andreotti and by the Dutch Presidency on the defense issue. France and Germany received the solid support of Felipe Gonzalez who wanted the CFSP to be a step forward compared to European Political Cooperation. He argued for the need to simplify the decision-making procedure and agreed with the Belgian Prime Minister's defense proposal. This was essentially a compromise by which a common defense policy would be developed leading eventually to a common defense. No reference should be made in the Treaty to a limitation of national prerogatives in this area.[18]

Lubbers remarked on the differences among the member states. In his view, these would remain well into the negotiations. The Presidency stuck to its proposed text and waited to review the WEU ministers' declaration presented later in the afternoon. The declaration was prepared by the political directors from national foreign ministries for review by their ministers.[19] Its adoption was a "pre-condition" for an accord at Maastricht.[20] The declaration would specify WEU's relations with the European Union and the Alliance, its operational role, and the relocation of the institution's Council to Brussels. The heads of state and government then broke for lunch until mid-afternoon.

EP, Community Competencies, QMV
When negotiations resumed at about half past three, the Presidency laid out the agenda for the rest of the day. Negotiations initially focused on specific points regarding a broad range of interconnected issues: the powers of the European Parliament; the inclusion of the term "federal vocation" in the Treaty; new Community competencies with reference to the use of QMV; the contentious Article 100c and related matters in internal and justice affairs.[21]

---

[17]"Summit Sound-bites."

[18]Agence Europe, 9 et 10 décembre 1991, 4.

[19]The defense ministers did provide input into the contents of the declaration, but the drafting was done by the political directors in national foreign ministries.

[20]Agence Europe, 9 et 10 décembre 1991, 4.

[21]Ibid., 11 décembre 1991, 3–6.

Chancellor Kohl was virtually isolated in wanting more powers for the European Parliament than most other Community leaders were willing to concede. Nonetheless, the Bundestag and Bundesrat insisted on greater powers for the European Parliament in the proposed Union as a *quid pro quo* for EMU. Kohl could not afford to look "weak-kneed" on this issue at home. To make matters more difficult, he had to contend with increasing skepticism on the part of German public opinion about the surrender of the D-mark.[22] Kohl made his position clear that he wanted changes in the power of the Parliament before the end of the century. It was essential for the EP to begin legislating with the co-decision procedure before its 1994 general elections. Kohl wanted co-decision used in areas of new Community competence like transeuropean networks, environment and social policy. In his view, the third reading in the co-decision procedure should be dropped. This would leave Parliament the right to co-legislate with the Council instead of merely brandishing a veto. The latter result would leave a negative impression of the EP's contribution to decision making on Community legislation. Moreover, Kohl argued for an extension of the assent procedure by which Parliament had to agree to any future Treaty revisions.

Kohl fought hard to include as much substance in the Treaty as possible in the form of new Community competencies. He wanted a reference to the "federal vocation" of the proposed union in the Treaty but realized this was a question of differing interpretations of the phrase's meaning by Britain. In Kohl's view, the substance of the text would steer the course toward the goal of a federal union even if there was no explicit mention of the term in the Treaty. This was one of the reasons why he stood firm on the inclusion of Article 100c concerning visa policy in the Community sphere.

Genscher argued for the EP's right to assent on any future Treaty revisions. He also insisted that the subsidiarity principle had to be as firmly defined as possible in the Treaty. The Presidency's text on subsidiarity would not be acceptable to the Bundesrat. Genscher reminded the other leaders that the Bundesrat threatened to veto any Treaty that did not respect the federal nature of the Basic Law and its exclusive competencies in areas like culture, education and health.

Mitterrand supported the inclusion of 100c in the first pillar competencies. The combined Franco-German weight behind the proposal was necessary to achieve this negotiating objective against the staunch opposition of Major. Mitterrand also understood the German interest in subsidiarity for reasons of internal political structure and domestic ratification. Clearly the French President was more comfortable with a looser definition of subsidiarity given the centralized structure of his own state and the relatively weak position of the regions in France. He supported the German text though. This

---

[22]"Major and Kohl Risk Isolation at Maastricht."

was an example of the Franco-German axis at work during the Maastricht Council.

Mitterrand's main goal at this point in the negotiations was the introduction of a European industrial policy. The President, with the strong and outspoken support of Cresson at home, asked for qualified majority voting on industrial policy. He argued that a precedent existed for QMV on this issue in the Treaty of Paris that established the European Coal and Steel Community in 1951. In the Colbertist tradition, national leaders used the state to support industry. In the Maastricht context, industrial rhetoric was but a symptom of a larger crisis of sovereignty. The crisis focused on industrial objectives because of their important contribution to the influence exercised by a great power.

The French state true to its Jacobin heritage used the discourse of industry obeying the state as a response to encroachments on French sovereignty.[23] Here the state was able to assert its authority in a key policy sector as a response to the limitations imposed on its margin of maneuver by economic interdependence. In the overall context of interdependence, two phenomena are striking: the emergence of an embryonic European government in Brussels; and the larger role accorded to legitimate regional authorities, some of which are forming transnational alliances below the level of the state as part of the integration process. Both phenomena can be perceived as threats to the French state. However, as is sometimes the case in European integration, there is a clear contradiction in the French position of support for QMV in decision making on industrial policy. This is because in such a situation the French could be outvoted on issues of vital interest. Yet, it is also true that French diplomacy could be successful in this area with QMV, if majority coalitions can be formed with other states in support of its position.

Prime Minister Major was in full agreement with the Germans on the introduction of the subsidiarity principle albeit for different reasons. In the British view, subsidiarity had nothing to do with a federal constitution. Instead it would effectively weaken the power of Brussels at the center by insisting that the Community only act in matters which could not be handled more efficiently at a lower level of government. The fact that this principle makes more sense in a federal system of government did not seem to deter Major from arguing for its presence in the Treaty.

At this point in the negotiations, the British Prime Minister considered the Presidency text as the basis for a deal. He strictly defended the minimalist position on more rights for the European Parliament and the extension of Community competencies.[24] Major also argued for an intergovernmental chapter, or third pillar, in justice and home affairs. The bottom line was that

---

[23]Elie Cohen, "Dirigisme, politique industrielle et rhétorique industrialiste," *Revue Française de Science Politique* 42 (avril 1992): 197–218.

[24]References to the British position on these issues are made in Chapter V.

Major could not accept the inclusion of visa policy, as stated in Article 100c, in the Community competencies as proposed by Kohl and Mitterrand. Major also stated that the mention of a "federal vocation" for the proposed union in the *chapeau* of the Treaty had no chance of acceptance during the British parliamentary ratification. A clause stipulating the need for a revision of the Treaty in 1996 was acceptable to Great Britain, however.

Delors contributed to the negotiations on the extension of Community competencies by arguing for the inclusion of consumer protection which France, Belgium and Spain supported. Delors also negotiated on the environment issue which was particularly delicate at this point in negotiations. Environment was introduced as a Community competence under the Single European Act. Negotiations on this policy during the IGC were meant to strengthen existing Community provisions. Germany, Denmark and the Netherlands were especially keen on improvements in environment. In its opinion of 21 October 1990, the Commission had indicated its support for the increased use of QMV in this area to make the decision-making process more effective. At Maastricht Delors negotiated on the basis of this position shared by Genscher and Elleman-Jensen.

Gonzalez and Portuguese Prime Minister Cavaco Silva led the offensive for unanimity on matters of a fiscal nature in the environmental field as specified in Article 130s.2.[25] These leaders pushed for an environment fund to be established as part of the cohesion aid package to make monies available for EC environmental policies in poorer member states.[26] This point was left open pending decisions the following day.

Cohesion

The Presidency then turned to negotiations on cohesion. Gonzalez insisted on clauses in the Treaty creating a new "cohesion fund" to help poorer states prepare for currency union. Spain also wanted to ensure that the EC budget

---

[25]This Article in Title XVI on the environment states: "By the way of derogation from the decision-making procedure provided for in paragraph 1 and without prejudice to Article 100a, the Council, acting unanimously on a proposal from the Commission and after consulting the European Parliament and the Economic and Social Committee, shall adopt: provisions primarily of a fiscal nature; measures concerning town and country planning, land use with the exception of waste management and measures of a general nature, and management of water resources; measures significantly affecting member states' choice between different energy sources and the general structure of its energy supply. The Council may, under the conditions laid down in the preceding subparagraph, define those matters referred to in this paragraph on which decisions are to be taken by a qualified majority."

[26]David Gardner, "Cohesion Becomes Less of a Sticking Point," *Financial Times*, December 10, 1991, 2.

was adequately supplied by progressive taxation levied according to the "relative prosperity" of member states. "There can be no route to EMU without an instrument in the treaty which guarantees cohesion," Solchaga reportedly told his colleagues. Delors tried to forge a compromise between the Spanish position and that of the Germans on cohesion.[27] He argued that the budgetary requirements of the member states left only a very narrow margin of maneuver for the Community. EMU could help all the member states. Delors explained that cohesion funds would address two problems: transeuropean networks and environment. Such funding would help the poorer member states participate in the progressive implementation of Community policies in the two areas. The cohesion issue gave Kohl the opportunity to illustrate his commitment as a "true believer" in European integration. In spite of a severe socio-economic situation in eastern Germany, and a possible recession, Kohl was prepared to accept the establishment of a cohesion fund in the Treaty to which German financial contributions would be substantial. In the words of one top Commission official, "Kohl showed himself to be very European on cohesion." [28] Minister Hurd, however, argued that Britain was already the second largest net contributor to the EC budget. The British, and to a lesser extent some members of the German delegation, were willing to accept a non-binding declaration on cohesion annexed to the Treaty as opposed to a protocol. This was a significant distinction because protocols attached to the Treaty were just as binding legally as Treaty Articles. Less than a protocol would have represented a potentially damaging political climbdown for Gonzalez, even if the non-binding declaration referred in some detail to the budget and cohesion package that the Commission was preparing for the following year. [29] This stand-off among the member states left the Presidency with the task of redrafting the provisions on cohesion during an all-night session of bargaining.

Social Policy

The Presidency left the sensitive issue of social policy until the end of the first day. Major explained that the British position on this issue was often misunderstood. In his view, the social chapter was not an "attractive proposition in any way." The gainers would be the industries of Japan and America, not the workers of Europe. The British were diligent in their critiques of the draft treaty. Major could therefore deal confidently with technical clauses that some of the other leaders might not have thoroughly read. The majority of European leaders, including Kohl and Mitterrand, were in a "visionary" mood. Major instead placed an emphasis on devotion to detail, a trait that also characterizes the British civil service. The social chapter

---

[27]Ibid.

[28]Interview, David Williamson, Commission of the European Communities, 11 June 1993.

[29]Gardner, "Cohesion Becomes Less of a Sticking Point."

more than any other issue was intractable for Major. He could not betray the Thatcherite revolution.[30] With France, Denmark and Luxembourg all indicating that the Presidency text was minimal on social policy, Lubbers decided to redraft the provisions and try another round of negotiations the next day.[31] The importance of this issue to the outcome at Maastricht was hinted at by Danish Prime Minister Schlüter who unequivocally indicated that social policy was essential to the balance of the final Treaty text.

Just prior to the close of the first day of negotiations, the heads of state and government discussed the finance ministers' demand to take part in future discussions on EMU at the highest level in the European Council. Whereas some of the political leaders emphasized retaining their decision-making capacity, others thought there was a good reason to study the finance ministers' proposal. President Mitterrand was quite adamant in his statement that the French finance minister should not be asked to make a decision in the name of France. Major underlined that as Prime Minister he could take decisions contrary to his finance minister but that it would be important for the European Council to be informed about financial matters. Kohl insisted on the necessity for discussion between the heads of state and government and the finance ministers on cost questions, but did not advocate placing clauses as such in the Treaty. Lubbers suggested that the opinion of the finance ministers on matters of EMU be asked during future preparations of the European Council. The Presidency set the time for negotiations to resume the next morning at 9:30.

DRAFTING OVERNIGHT BARGAINS
During the night, the Presidency modified several key clauses in the proposed Treaty on Political Union as a result of concessions made during the day's negotiations and bargains struck that night.[32] This technique had evolved into an essential aspect of diplomacy during the European Council long before Maastricht. In the IGC context, it was particularly arduous, however, due to the complex and detailed technical nature of Treaty reform.

---

[30]Philip Stephens, "Major Approaches Moment of Truth on British Concessions to Partners," *Financial Times*, December 10, 1991.

[31]The Presidency's watered-down version of the social chapter proposed "a modest extension of qualified majority voting to the right of information (but not consultation) for workers, and to health and safety aspects of working conditions. It retained the provision for the "social partners"—employers and trade unions—to make agreements which could become Community law." Grant, *Delors: Inside the House That Jacques Built*, 201.

[32]Agence Europe, 11 décembre 1991, 5.

EMU

During a press conference just before midnight on Monday, Chancellor Kohl confirmed German resistance to the idea that the Maastricht Treaty should automatically signal the end of the D-mark. "One does not baptize a child before it is born," Kohl remarked. The Chancellor also took aim at the French and Italian suggestion to name the single currency the ECU or European Currency Unit. Peter-Wilhelm Schlüter, the Bundesbank observer in the German delegation at Maastricht, was present at the hotel where Kohl spoke. A staunch supporter of EMU, Schlüter was involved during much of the internal bargaining in Bonn to develop the German negotiating line. As he listened to Kohl, his eyebrows raised. The Chancellor's words indicated future differences of opinion among the member states on EMU which successive Presidencies would have to mediate.

This was also a memorable spectacle of political theatre with Kohl astutely reacting to the German news coverage of the impending accord on EMU.[33] The news was on the cover of *Der Spiegel,* Germany's pre-eminent weekly news magazine, with a picture of a battered silver mark coin on the blue background of the 12-star European flag. The reaction showed that months of half-hearted media coverage, combined with a German predisposition to follow the government line, had effectively hidden the European Council's issues from the popular consciousness. *Der Spiegel* pointed out that "the German parliament remained suspiciously silent" about Maastricht,[34] a claim contradicted by parliamentary debates and numerous newspaper articles published during the IGCs.

The hard facts remained, however. The first day of the European Council had produced a "breakthrough" on EMU. The final formula for decision making on Stage Three emerged from last-minute discussions among France, Italy and Belgium but most importantly supported by Germany. Kohl was given assurances notably by the French that decisions on which states qualify for the demanding disciplines of an irrevocable monetary union would follow strict convergence criteria.[35] In the words of Bérégovoy's spokesman, the finance minister had led "a very well-conducted tactical battle" to convince other ministers in ECOFIN of the plan.[36] Kohl then backed Mitterrand and Andreotti's presentation of this decision-making procedure for the transition to Stage Three when he understood that there would be strict implementation of the convergence criteria for countries to participate in EMU. Free of the

---

[33]Marsh, *Die Bundesbank*, 319.

[34]Robin Gedye, "'End of Beautiful Mark' Rouses Germans at Last," *The Daily Telegraph*, December 10, 1991.

[35]Robin Oakley and George Brock, "Major Stands Firm on EMU Opt-out Clause," *The Times*, December 10, 1991.

[36]David Buchan, "'Fast Forwards' Relish Their Victory in Battle over EMU Timetable," *Financial Times*, 11 December 1991.

bureaucratic baggage that so weighed down his British counterpart,[37] Kohl appeared ready to acquiesce in the inherent contradiction of a treaty that would set both strict economic criteria and firm dates for the move to a single currency.[38] At the same time, Germany hardened its stance that the future ECB be sited in Frankfurt.[39]

The Dutch Presidency accepted the majority view on the need for a timetable on EMU. "There was a general acceptance of the need for irreversibility," Kok explained. Britain did not share this view but was in a weak position to resist because Major had obtained an opt-out clause. By late evening, the realization had set in that the deal that would emerge from Maastricht on EMU looked likely to be an amalgam of many things which Britain did not like. The argument was made that this reflected a failure of British negotiating strategy. Had London concentrated less on an opt-out clause, it might have been able to fight for better terms on the transition to a single currency.[40] Not surprisingly, it took the Presidency until the end of the second day of negotiations to iron out all the details regarding Great Britain's opt-out clause on EMU.[41]

CFSP/Defense

The Presidency's new draft of clauses on CFSP stipulated that upon adoption of a common action the Council would decide at each stage the questions on which it would decide by qualified majority vote. The Commission in particular was not deceived by the continued use of unanimity in decision making on this crucial issue of political union. Delors was still concerned about the complexity of the decision-making process in spite of the planned inclusion of Declaration 27 stating that "with regard to Council decisions requiring unanimity, member states will avoid preventing a unanimous decision where a qualified majority exists in favor of that decision."[42]

On defense, the Presidency redrafted clauses treating relations with NATO to indicate that the specific security and defense policies of certain member states would be respected. The Presidency's new drafts indicated that these states' obligations stemming from NATO membership would be

---

[37]Major's domestic constraints included individuals in his own party and in his Cabinet who were hostile to European integration as well as his dependence on the civil service owing to its thorough preparation of the dossiers on the table at Maastricht.

[38]Stephens, "Major Approaches Moment of Truth on British Concessions to Partners."

[39]David Marsh, "Germans Press for Central Bank in Frankfurt," *Financial Times*, December 10, 1991.

[40]Andrew Marshall, "Single Currency Comes a Step Closer," *The Independent*, December 10, 1991.

[41]Agence Europe, 11 décembre 1991, 6bis.

[42]*The New Treaty on European Union*, 149.

honored due to the compatibility of CFSP with NATO policies. The eventual framing of a common defense would be subject to an evaluation. The Presidency did not retain, however, the *passerelle* suggested by Belgium that would have allowed the gradual transfer of parts if not all of the CFSP to first pillar, therefore making it subject to Community decision-making procedures.[43]

In comparison to the Luxembourg draft treaty, both Kohl and Genscher did obtain from the Dutch Presidency a slightly closer association for the European Parliament in security and defense matters. However, when viewed alongside provisions in the SEA, this step in the direction of closer association was not the significant improvement for Parliament that the Germans wanted in security matters. Draft clauses did emphasize that the EP would be consulted, its views on CFSP duly taken into consideration and that Parliament would have to be regularly informed by the Presidency and the Commission about the CFSP. A footnote also indicated that in CFSP matters the linguistic rules that applied in the Community would be respected. The implication here was that all CFSP texts would be translated into each of the official Community languages. This was a step in the direction of the greater use of the German language in Union affairs. For the moment, however, COREU, the network of information that linked the Twelve member states foreign ministries, would only be translated into French and English as had been the customary practice in EPC matters.[44]

In the final Treaty provisions, the Presidency revised the text to read that Treaty amendments would enter into effect only after having been approved by an absolute majority of the European Parliament and ratified by the parliaments of all the member states. The final provisions also indicated that another IGC would be called in 1996 to examine dispositions in the proposed Treaty on CFSP and other policies for which revisions were envisaged.

EP, Community Competencies, QMV

In accordance with Major's wishes the phrase "federal vocation" was taken out of the text. Instead in Article A of the *chapeau* the Presidency made reference that the present Treaty marked "a new stage in the process to create an ever closer Union among the peoples of Europe, in which decisions are taken as closely as possible to the citizen." This Article also specified that the "Union shall be founded on the European Communities." Three tasks assigned to the union were specified: namely, the implementation of a CFSP, including the framing of a common defense policy; close cooperation in justice and home affairs; and the integral maintenance of the *acquis communautaire* with the goal of developing it and subjecting policies and cooperation to Community institutions and mechanisms of decision making.

---

[43] Agence Europe, 11 décembre 1991, 6.
[44] Ibid., 6bis.

A clearer definition of subsidiarity was also redrafted to accommodate German and British interests. The new Article 3b indicated that the Community should only act on matters that cannot be sufficiently achieved by the member states. There was a certain ambiguity, however, as to the definition of areas in which the subsidiarity principle would apply.

On Article 100c regarding visa policy, the Presidency deferred to British sensitivities by proposing a new procedure in which the Council would act unanimously to determine those third countries whose nationals must possess a visa in order to enter the Community. Qualified majority voting was only foreseen in an extreme case of emergency during which the Community was threatened by a large influx of immigrants from any third country.

On industry, the Presidency's new draft reflected its own bias as well as that of the Federal Republic and Great Britain in that the proposed Article was not to serve as a basis for the Community to introduce subsidies or measures to distort free competition.

The Presidency also drafted clauses by which the Community funds to finance environment and transeuropean networks would be replaced by the cohesion fund. Moreover, on environmental policy, the Council would decide unanimously those aspects of the policy to which QMV would apply.[45]

Cohesion
On this issue, the Presidency took Spanish interests into account by proposing in Article 130d "that the Council...create prior to 31 December 1993 a cohesion fund to contribute financially to the realization of projects in the areas of environment and transeuropean networks." The Presidency also suggested a study of ways to correct certain elements in the Community system of own resources that were not in the interests of the poorer member states.

Social Policy
Lubbers also forged a compromise proposal on social policy by which certain areas of EC labor market regulation included in the Treaty would be dealt with by unanimous rather than qualified majority voting in the Council of Ministers. He reportedly had the backing of his Christian Democratic counterparts in the European Council including Kohl, Andreotti, Mitsotakis, Martens and Santer. Lubbers hoped that concessions on social policy would give Major a deal he could sell to his Conservative party and the House of Commons without enraging Mitterrand who indicated that he would not sign a Treaty that did not include provisions on social policy.[46]

TUESDAY'S DECISIONS
The second day of negotiations at Maastricht were marked by difficulties on the issue of social policy which threatened results made in other areas and a

---

[45]Ibid., 6.

[46]David Buchan, "Lubbers Puts Faith in Social Policy Compromise," *Financial Times*, December 10, 1991.

breakthrough on EMU. The inclusion of visa policy within the Community sphere of decision making was another important gain for the Franco-German negotiating line.

EMU

The finance ministers had agreed the previous day on a procedure for the transition to Stage Three that reflected the wishes of the heads of state and government. The Maastricht text had already stipulated that not later than 31 December 1996 the European Council should vote on whether a majority of the member states fulfill the conditions for a single currency and should then vote on proceeding with setting a date for the irrevocable fixing of exchange rates. In previous drafts, this vote was to be unanimous, a condition insisted on by the Germans. The draft on the table during the second day suggested that the vote be taken by qualified majority, which in practice normally required the agreement of eight member states in a Community of Twelve. The conditions required for EMU to take place in 1997 were, therefore, a qualified majority vote by the European Council that successfully determined a critical mass of states ready for the transition to a single currency. This critical mass had to contain at least seven member states to constitute a majority.

This draft also stipulated that when finance ministers report to the European Council on the preparedness of the member states for a single currency, they should look at each country on the basis of the criteria, which cover inflation, budget deficits, government indebtedness and currency stability. In light of the proposed procedures for moving from Stage Two to Stage Three, these criteria were all the more important.

The Treaty had always emphasized that the convergence criteria were not mechanical things; there was a strong element of interpretation involved, and the criteria are not the same as immutable conditions. "Decisions will be made on 'the basis of an overall judgement'," Kok was reported to have said the day before. "We're not going to be governed by computers."[47]

---

[47]Marshall, "Single Currency Comes a Step Closer." There are numerous references in the Treaty text that support this view. For instance, Article 1 of Protocol 6, Protocol on the Convergence Criteria referred to in Article 109j of the Treaty establishing the European Community states: "The criterion on price stability referred to in the first indent of Article 109j(1) of this Treaty shall mean that a Member State has a price performance that is sustainable and an average rate of inflation, observed over a period of one year before the examination, that does not exceed by more than 1 1/2 percentage points that of, at most, the three best performing Member States in terms of price stability. Inflation shall be measured by means of the consumer price index on a comparable basis, taking into account differences in national definitions."

The decision to institute majority voting for the first try at EMU in 1996 accentuated the political elements of decision making. By placing more weight in the hands of the European Council, it emphasized the horse-trading that might take place in the immediate run-up to a single currency.[48] However, unless the heads of state and government could reach a bargain to strengthen political integration, Kohl would refuse to sign a treaty on EMU at Maastricht. Few member states had heavier domestic stakes in success at Maastricht than the Federal Republic. Kohl, like all of his counterparts, had promised national gains in a stronger Union. Beyond that, most Community officials were convinced that the proposed Treaties probably offered the Twelve's last realistic chance to make progress before the deteriorating situation in eastern Europe had to be tackled.[49]

In light of the tough compromises yet to be made on political union, one of the first things the Presidency did as negotiations opened was to schedule a review of key EMU provisions on the opt-out for Great Britain until after lunch. At that time, each political leader received a text of the protocol on the transition to Stage Three. Lubbers read the protocol aloud, stressing the irreversible character of movement to Stage Three. The leaders then agreed on the text. Schlüter mentioned the special problem of a Danish referendum on the transition to the final stage. He emphasized Denmark's desire to participate from the start of Stage Three and his unequivocal support for the protocol on transition. To address its domestic constitutional requirements, an additional protocol was granted to Denmark that considers its need for a referendum on the final transition stage.

Major recalled the British position. He thought that the no coercion clause on EMU was a good solution. Unlike Denmark, there was no problem with a referendum on the transition to Stage Three. However, the British could not be bound to move to the final stage. A separate protocol was necessary to address this issue. That protocol, largely inspired by Delors, was attached to the end of the Treaty and only applied to Britain. It would allow the British parliament to decide, independently of the European Council, whether it was going to take part in Stage Three of EMU. This solution on Tuesday evening resolved what Minister Kok called "one of the most important subjects at Maastricht."[50]

CFSP/Defense

The Presidency also scheduled negotiations on CFSP and defense issues for later in the afternoon on Tuesday. A quick lunch was set for 12:30 during which the heads of state and government and the foreign ministers ate separately. This gave the WEU foreign ministers, who were also meeting under the Presidency of Genscher at the margins of the European Council,

---

[48]Ibid.

[49]Joseph Fitchett, "Halfway Home in Maastricht," *International Herald Tribune*, December 10, 1991.

[50]Corbett, *The Treaty of Maastricht*, 42.

some time to discuss last points on the WEU Declaration.[51] The two key issues of security, namely, the nature of the WEU's relationship to the proposed Union and majority voting on implementing joint action, continued to be the subject of intense negotiations that resulted in further modifications.[52] Talks among the heads of state and government and foreign ministers that afternoon focused on the scope of QMV and how to word provisions on a "common defense." Some progress was made in both areas and it was agreed to let Greece accede to the Western European Union. Genscher played an influential role in this last agreement by using his position as WEU President to support strongly Greek admission to the European defense organization. The Presidency then suspended the negotiating session on CFSP until later that evening in order to address other issues.

Franco-German solidarity was quite evident during the more difficult moments of the 31-hour marathon session of negotiations at Maastricht. This was most especially the case on Tuesday afternoon. On each difficult issue Kohl and Mitterrand met to coordinate their actions. Although this exasperated some other member states at times, it was generally acknowledged that the Franco-German impulse was necessary to bring negotiations to a successful conclusion.[53] France and Germany used their combined weight to force an accord on defense at Maastricht. Later Tuesday evening, Major acquiesced to the ideas stated in the Franco-German paper dated 15 October and agreed to establish a European defense organization, the WEU, as a "component of European Union" that would also "reinforce the European pillar of the Atlantic Alliance."[54] The achievements in the defense area were considered by many involved to be second only to the agreement on EMU at Maastricht. The results on CFSP were more modest by comparison, with little to cheer about in the area of decision making. Unanimity remained for all intents and purposes the rule with only a limited scope for initiative by the Commission and even less participation by the Parliament. France and Germany did obtain agreement on the inclusion of the CFSP among the issues on the agenda of the Revision Conference in 1996, however. [55]

EP, Community Competencies, QMV

On Tuesday negotiations focused on the extension of the scope of co-decision to strengthen the European Parliament. Major was willing to accept the application of co-decision in areas like the environment provided that

---

[51] Agence Europe, 11 décembre 1991, 3–4.

[52] Corbett, *The Treaty of Maastricht*, 48.

[53] Alain Dauvergne, "Les six acquis de Maastricht," *Le Point*, 14 décembre 1991, 16.

[54] Craig R. Whitney, "Britain's Way: A Qualified Agreement," *New York Times*, December 11, 1991, A20.

[55] "The Deal is Done," *The Economist*, December 14, 1991, 30.

unanimity voting remained the rule in the Council. Delors reiterated his view that co-decision making in the Parliament would not work with unanimity voting in the Council. Throughout the day, however, Major showed a greater reluctance than other European leaders to surrender sovereignty on sensitive areas including a code of work laws, a strengthened European Parliament and greater competencies for the Commission bureaucracy in Brussels. By trying to reconcile co-decision with unanimity, he attempted to slow down the integration process by complicating its decision-making procedures. During the negotiations, certain Community competencies were among the last issues to be resolved. As one Commission official explained, "This is a poker game where players don't show their final cards until the showdown."[56] In the face of British resistance, it is not surprising that only limited progress could be made on increasing the scope of QMV. One Commission official did express satisfaction with the end results on QMV because Maastricht was only meant to be a first step.[57] Another German official was more cautious about overall results. "We need to get enough clear progress on unity so that we don't have to spend weeks back-pedaling and explaining that Maastricht wasn't a dead end," he said. But he also agreed with a French official's opinion of the emerging Treaty: "We are going to get just enough done to keep Europe from falling apart," the Frenchman remarked.[58]

The compromise achieved at Maastricht on industrial policy again illustrated the Franco-German axis at work.[59] Mitterrand obtained a Treaty Article on industry while the Germans insisted on, and were granted, unanimity in decision making. As an official in the Council Secretariat put it: "The French got the symbolism, the Germans won the substance."[60] Still the compromise did not please all parties involved as the French bemoaned the lack of QMV and the federal ministry of economics objected to a Treaty Article on industry policy.[61] Arguments against interventionist tendencies at the European level, owing to the creation of this new Community policy, came up later during the German ratification of Maastricht.

One of the most sensitive issues that came up during the second day of negotiations was the inclusion of Article 100c in the first pillar or Community competencies. In the words of one high-ranking Commission official,

---

[56]Fitchett, "Halfway Home in Maastricht."

[57]Interview, Alain van Solinge, Commission of the European Communities, 26 July 1992.

[58]Fitchett, "Halfway Home in Maastricht."

[59]"Für eine europäische Industriepolitik," *Frankfurter Allgemeine Zeitung*, 9. Dezember 1991, 11.

[60]Interview, Poul Christophersen, Council Secretariat, 27 May 1992.

[61]Interview, Prof. Dr. Gerhard Rambow, Federal Ministry of Economics, 21 July 1993.

discussions at Maastricht ended on this issue.[62] Major maintained his reserve on this Article. Genscher argued for its inclusion so as to open a small door for the gradual communitarization of immigration and visa policies. Elisabeth Guigou supported Genscher's position. Although the French policy on asylum differed substantially from that of the Germans, French leaders understood the explosive nature of the issue in German domestic politics. Their support of German goals on this Article indicated French intentions to proceed gradually in the transfer of internal and justice affairs policies from intergovernmental cooperation to Community decision making. The combined weight of France and Germany, plus Major's desire not to be isolated more than once at Maastricht, led him to concede this issue later on Tuesday. The issue of social policy was yet to be resolved and the British Prime Minister had already used up a lot of his European capital on EMU. His friendship with Chancellor Kohl was advantageous for Major, but it was clear that Germany and France were determined not to leave Maastricht without a Treaty. This fact illustrated that the British strategy of holding out until the end had its disadvantages especially since the other European leaders were not as easily swayed by the British position as Major originally thought possible. Playing for time clearly had its limits.

Cohesion

On this issue Gonzalez argued clearly for a protocol establishing a cohesion fund to provide financial assistance to the poorer member states. There was some debate among the Germans and the Spanish on the policy areas to which the cohesion fund should be applied. With some helpful mediation from President Delors, however, Lubbers did obtain an agreement among the Twelve on the establishment of a fund for monetary assistance to Spain, Portugal, Ireland and Greece. This agreement meant that a legally binding protocol was attached to the Treaty committing the Union to increase the already existing structural fund resources and to create a new cohesion fund to aid the poorer member states in the areas of environment policy and transport infrastructure.[63]

Social Policy

This issue caused the greatest concern among the participants at Maastricht. Some leaders and officials thought the entire negotiation could fail if an accord could not be reached on social policy. Throughout the day on Tuesday Lubbers tried to reach an agreement acceptable to Major and the other eleven political leaders. Each time he failed. Delors tried to break the deadlock with a proposal which would allow Britain to opt out of particular social laws and

---

[62] Interview, Secretary General David Williamson, Commission of the European Communities, 11 June 1993.

[63] Alan Riding, "Europeans Agree on a Pact Forging New Political Ties and Integrating Economies," *New York Times*, December 11, 1991, A26.

then, if it wished, to opt back in. But Major rejected all varieties of opt-out. Meanwhile, behind the scenes, Pascal Lamy considered the possibility that if the British would not accept an opt-out, because of the negative connotations, Major might buy the idea of eleven countries "opting-in" to the social chapter. Lamy and his team worked on this idea and prepared some documents. Their concern was to safeguard the role of the Community institutions, particularly the Commission, in any social policy provisions in the Treaty.[64]

Meanwhile, the argument on the social chapter dragged on and seemed likely to wreck the negotiations. "The hour of truth is approaching," Mitterrand's spokesman said impatiently as Tuesday night wore on, threatening that France would refuse to sign any Treaty that did not contain a social charter. Kohl called Delors over to make the suggestion that it might be better to postpone the application of the social charter for a few years. Delors convinced Kohl that postponing an agreement on social policy would damage the Community; an Eleven-country opt-in would be a better idea. In a series of bilateral and trilateral meetings Delors, Lubbers and Kohl saw Major several times. "By then there were only four people...around the table: Lubbers, Major, Kohl and myself," according to Delors. The Commission President's powers of persuasion helped bring Major around to the idea of an Eleven-country opt-in.[65]

Rather than water down their social plan to suit Britain, the Eleven agreed to go ahead on their own, outside the Treaty on Political Union, leaving the British out. The social chapter was excised from the body of the Treaty and called an "agreement." It would be signed by eleven governments. A protocol in an appendix to the Treaty stated that the Eleven would make social policy according to the rules of the "agreement" and authorized the member states to use the Community institutions and procedures to do so.[66] "I hope in not too long a time the UK will join again," Lubbers remarked early Wednesday morning. "We did the best we could."

The reaction to Major's intransigence was one of surprise. Still he was preferable to Thatcher. During a pause in tough negotiations that night, Kohl was heard to remark, "Say what you want—the lady isn't there anymore." Even Mitterrand, who was playing poker at least as tough as Major's over the social policy issue that night, didn't wish Thatcher back. "Maybe she's beginning to be missed, but it's a mistake," his spokesman said. During two days of intense negotiations, Major did show, however, that he could be as tough, if not tougher, a classic labor union negotiator as the Iron Lady herself. His hard bargaining did conceal one fundamental change though. Thatcher

---

[64]Grant, *Delors: Inside the House That Jacques Built*, 201.
[65]Ibid., 202.
[66]Ibid.

would never have agreed to EMU, as she made clear before she was ousted the year before.[67]

INTERPRETING THE MAASTRICHT EUROPEAN COUNCIL: THREE APPROACHES TO THE IGC PROCESS
Putnam's Two-Level Games

Intergovernmental conference negotiations in the European Council accentuate the role of state leaders emphasized in two-level games. This approach enables us to focus on the ways in which Mitterrand and Kohl had to reconcile their individual interests at the state level of analysis with the dynamics of the IGC process at the Community level. The presence of Image IV hybrids was particularly significant on EMU in the case of Delors, Guigou and Köhler. At Maastricht, their intimate knowledge of the issues on the table was influential during the crisis points when the negotiations almost broke down. The contributions of these politico-administrative hybrids, particularly Delors, serve to highlight the manner in which different sub-processes of negotiation took place during the Maastricht European Council on issues like EMU, social policy and the third pillar.

The Maastricht process allows us to test empirically several of Putnam's observations about two-level games. In his focus on the strategies of Level I negotiators, Putnam states that they are often badly misinformed about Level II politics. Uncertainties about the size of a win-set can be both a bargaining device and a stumbling block in two-level negotiation. In purely distributive Level I bargaining, negotiators have an incentive to understate their own win-sets. This is plausible since each negotiator is likely to know more about his own domestic level than his opponent does. On the other hand, uncertainty about the opponent's win-set increases one's concern about the risk of involuntary defection. Deals can only be struck if each negotiator is convinced that the proposed deal lies within his opposite number's win-set and thus will be ratified.[68] In the Maastricht context, it is necessary to emphasize that Mitterrand was quite aware of Kohl's domestic situation, particularly with regard to the Chancellor's constraints on EMU.

Putnam's two-level games points to two strategies which leaders can employ, namely, "tying hands" and "cutting slack."[69] A strategy of "tying hands" attempts to constrict the domestic win-set. A leader may adopt this strategy to induce his counterpart across the table to compromise at a point closer to the first statesman's preference. Heads of state who adopt the second strategy, "cutting slack," try to expand the domestic win-set to accommodate

---

[67]Whitney, "Britain's Way: A Qualified Agreement."

[68]Ibid., 452–453.

[69]Evans, "Building an Integrative Approach to International and Domestic Politics," 399–403.

an international agreement that might otherwise be rejected.[70] Both strategies can be applied to the Maastricht negotiations while bearing in mind that tactics, not strategy, were decisive in the final outcome.

The French Case

The predominance of the head of state illustrates Putnam's emphasis on a single leader and his ability to define strategy. Although Dumas, Bérégovoy and Guigou all took part in the European Council, François Mitterrand was the main protagonist. Mitterrand's main concerns were to fix a date for EMU and to define the role of the European Council in CFSP. Although he had considerable autonomy from domestic pressures, Mitterrand's relative bargaining position at the table was by no means weaker than either Kohl's or Major's. IGC negotiations during the Maastricht European Council illustrate that Putnam's discussion of state strength has to be modified in order to take into account French leverage in the Franco-German relationship.

Clearly Mitterrand was aware of Kohl's desire to strengthen the integration process before leaving office. The French President also knew that Kohl was concerned about the commitment of future generations of leaders in a unified Germany to European construction. Mitterrand counted on Kohl's determination to make German unity and European unity two sides of the same coin. This determination made Kohl take courageous choices in the face of domestic opposition. Some of these choices, particularly on EMU, supported the French negotiating line. This was a strong line despite the fact that Mitterrand had no domestic constraints.

The EMU dossier was thoroughly prepared by civil servants and central bankers with extensive input by Delors. However, the final political decisions were made at the highest level among the heads of state and government. With Mitterrand taking the initiative to assure his German counterpart of the need to respect strict economic convergence criteria, the ball fell into Kohl's court either to accept or reject a fixed timetable. Here it is important to underline that the French President showed astute understanding of the Chancellor's domestic situation. At Maastricht there was no uncertainty regarding the level of apprehension and misgivings about a European currency in Germany. Thus, Mitterrand and Bérégovoy, in an astute tactical move, assured Kohl that strict convergence criteria would be achieved by all participants that met fixed deadlines on EMU.

Interestingly, the strategy of "tying hands" in Putnam's approach runs counter to the expectation that leaders desire a maximum level of executive autonomy. Major, for instance, relied on his knowledge of the fact that the constraints of party politics would prevent him from signing any agreement for Britain at Maastricht that included a European social policy. His

---

[70]Moravcsik, "Integrating International and Domestic Theories of International Bargaining," 28.

counterparts around the table were aware of this as well. Mitterrand was open to allowing Major an opt-out on social policy at a very early stage in negotiations on political union because he wanted to avoid an obstacle to signing a treaty in Maastricht. The result was a stalemate until Major agreed to a proposal which allowed him a graceful way out of a no-win situation.

Mitterrand's proposal on the decision-making procedure to make the transition to Stage Three of EMU put Kohl in the position of "cutting slack" or trying to expand his domestic win-set, in order to accommodate an agreement at Maastricht that both leaders clearly wanted. This was especially true since Kohl was unable to attain much increase in powers for the European Parliament, the *quid pro quo* for agreement on EMU demanded by the Bundestag.

Mitterrand was obviously using Maastricht as an opportunity to enhance his standing at Level II. The Socialists' lack of popularity at home led Mitterrand to try to reduce potential losses by achieving an accord on social policy. He blatantly pursued his own conception of the national interest in the European context by decisively influencing the CFSP dossier. By fighting to retain its intergovernmental character, with the locus of decision making in the European Council, Mitterrand emphasized his personal influence on any subsequent policy making. Only on industrial policy did the French President come up short although cooperation with Bonn on this dossier illustrated the workings of the Franco-German axis. In the final hours of negotiation at Maastricht, a lot of give and take was required to allow everyone to leave with a Treaty that could be sold to domestic publics during ratification processes.

On three crucial issues in which a potential surrender of sovereignty was implied, namely, EMU, the common visa policy and European citizenship, Mitterrand played a key role. The French president, in tandem with Kohl, supported the concept of European citizenship at Level I in order to push through his objective of obtaining the vote for foreigners living in France at Level II. Although Mitterrand realized that these Treaty objectives would require constitutional amendments, he also knew that Maastricht had the potential to divide the political Right at home which would be caught between a desire to preserve national sovereignty and yet not appear anti-European. The main contours of the French leader's win-set were defined by the need for a pillar structure to the Treaty in which the CFSP and justice and home affairs pillars were subject to intergovernmental cooperation. This was necessary in order to secure domestic ratification.

The German Case

For Kohl the most pressing issue at Maastricht was the link between EMU and substantial progress on political union. There were a number of domestic pressures that Kohl had to contend with. First, his leadership role at Maastricht, while crucial, was one he shared with his experienced foreign minister. As explained previously, Genscher's pan-European emphasis stood in contrast at times to Kohl's more Atlanticist orientation. Moreover, the foreign minister's ambition to seek a high political profile for his small party, the Free Democrats, was well-known.[71] Second, Kohl was facing a Social Democratic majority in the Bundesrat that demanded integration in line with an unambiguous federal vocation for the proposed Union. Third, an overwhelming majority in the Bundestag, that cut across party lines, favored a greater transfer of powers to the European institutions. Contrary to Putnam's suggestion of an inverse relationship between autonomy from domestic pressures and relative bargaining position internationally, Kohl's vulnerability to domestic pressures did not strengthen his hand at the table in Maastricht. Relatively speaking, his bargaining position during negotiations was weaker than those of his counterparts in the face of British intransigence on issues like EMU and social policy and French reluctance to concede too much on the crucial dossier of increased powers for the European Parliament. To explain the Chancellor's actions at Maastricht, in the face of domestic constraints, Putnam's approach must be refined. It should take into account factors like Kohl's personal convictions about European unity owing to the lessons drawn from the German experience of European history and sociological influences dating back to Kohl's childhood growing up in the Rhineland near the border with France.

Nonetheless, Kohl's interests in Europeanizing issues like asylum and immigration, included in justice and home affairs, illustrate a shrewd politician at work. Always fully cognizant of an explosive domestic situation, the Chancellor literally all but wrote the provisions in the third pillar of the Treaty. Kohl also fought hard to obtain the inclusion of Article 100c on visa policy within the scope of the *acquis communautaire*. Here Kohl was "tying hands" in order to convince Major that Maastricht would not be ratifiable without this provision in the Community competencies. The fact that Kohl and Mitterrand forced a concession from the British Prime Minister on this point, in spite of Major's ability to drive a hard bargain across the board at Maastricht, shows its importance for the Germans at the domestic level. This dossier was handled directly from the Chancellor's office with Kohl evading the ministerial bureaucracy in Bonn. Clearly he shifted the balance of power at Level II away from the strict requirements of Article 65 BL, which allows for much leeway in ministerial autonomy, and concentrated the power in his own office. He also used the forthcoming Community policy on asylum to put reform of Article 16 BL, which featured the most liberal asylum policy in Europe, on the domestic agenda. This was in spite of SPD resistance to constitutional reform in the Bundestag.

It was EMU, however, more than any other issue on the table, that allowed Kohl to pursue his own conception of the national interest in the European, and international, context. Here Kohl used what Putnam terms synergy, in which European actions are employed to alter outcomes otherwise

---

[71]Both these points are developed in Chapter II.

expected in the domestic arena. The Chancellor's acceptance of a timetable with fixed dates on EMU was in all ways a personal decision which defied the views of the Bundesbank and the German bureaucracy. It was the ultimate political decision made in what Kohl perceived to be as much the German interest as the European one. By agreeing to make the European Council the ultimate arbiter of the decisions on passage to Stage Three, Kohl was countering the ambition of central bankers at Level II to control state and Community policies.[72]

At Maastricht Kohl had leeway to accept the timetable in the face of negative press and public opinion owing to the strict economic convergence criteria which would be difficult for most member states, including Germany at that point, to meet. The difficulties he expected to encounter with the Bundesrat and the Bundestag over his inability to secure greater powers for the European Parliament were another matter entirely, however. The link between the two separate but parallel intergovernmental conferences was a *sine qua non* for Kohl right until the final weeks in December. Despite his modest success at Maastricht, his overall long-term strategy was to approach this issue in steps, by obtaining more and more powers for the European Parliament as EMU progressed in successive stages. The unexpected domestic result would be a call for an increase in the powers of the Bundestag on European legislation in order to counter the European Parliament's insufficient input in the policy process. As the chair of the *EG-Ausschuß* in the Bundestag, Renate Hellwig, explained, this outcome was not entirely satisfactory in terms of integration. It was necessary, however, to address the democratic deficit at the national level if sufficient steps were not taken at the European one.[73]

Aberbach, Putnam and Rockman's Four Images of Civil Servants

For both Mitterrand and Kohl, the Maastricht European Council illustrated a clear independence from domestic bureaucracies. Key decisions like EMU, the CFSP and provisions on third pillar issues were taken at the highest level with the politicians taking responsibility for their actions in the subsequent ratification debates.

The only exception to this rule of politicians bearing the responsibility for Maastricht in the public perception was that of President Jacques Delors. He perhaps more than any other individual involved in the IGCs most closely resembles an Image IV hybrid in the Aberbach, Putnam and Rockman mold.

---

[72]Kenneth Dyson, Kevin Featherstone and George Michalopoulos, "Strapped to the Mast: EC Central Bankers between Global Financial Markets and the Maastricht Treaty," European Consortium for Political Research Workshop: The Single Market and Global Economic Integration, Madrid, 17–22 April 1994, 9.

[73]Interview, Renate Hellwig, *EG-Ausschuß*, Bundestag, 29 April 1993.

However, Delors' possible emergence as a politico-administrative hybrid, in which he sought to inform the general public about Maastricht, must be viewed in contrast to his work behind the scenes in the technical work of negotiations in the Council. Clearly Delors was perceived by other heads of state and government as a technocrat who sought to transcend the limits of his role. This was obvious initially in light of Thatcher's criticisms of the Commission President. During the Maastricht European Council, Council President Lubbers would often interrupt a debate and ask Delors to explain a problem and summarize the positions of the different member states. Delors would respond with short, unbiased summaries of each country's position. At one point Major was said to have remarked to an aide that Delors was playing the role of a consultant to the Community's heads of state and government.[74]

Given Delors' unique mix of behind closed doors influence and publicly expressed commitment to European integration, perhaps it is fairest to say that the same remarks made of Monnet could also be applied to him. He was "neither a civil servant nor a politician. He was in a category of his own."[75] Delors' contributions to the Maastricht process on issues with high visibility in the public eye, like EMU and social policy, illustrate his commitment to European unity as a type of mission to improve the everyday lives of citizens. His influence on the cohesion dossier, in tandem with that of Kohl's, illustrated that he has a vision of how relations among states could be, a vision that transcends power politics. His comments at European Council meetings on foreign policy issues, while angering some heads of state and government, demonstrated his determination to make the Commission an actor in "high politics." Here Delors treaded on ground well beyond the boundaries of technocratic circles. To his credit, it can be said that he, like Monnet, is a born teacher. Yet Delors had a finer instinct than Monnet for projecting an aura to the public. He used this instinct during his tenure as President both to promote the interests of that institution and to influence the French domestic debate on European integration. For this reason, it can be argued that Delors best fits the Image IV mold of a politico-administrative hybrid. His role was more than just that of a higher civil servant but yet less than that of a democratically elected national politician.

Delors' role in the Maastricht context promoting integration by means of revisions to the original Treaties makes the further emergence of Image IV hybrids likely. This is significant because the phenomenon of the civil servant acting like a politician *manqué*, eager to promote a personal strategy, is less relevant in most European countries than in the American context. Here the case of Guigou is also illustrative. Although she represented France as a Minister for European affairs at Maastricht, Guigou's civil-service training

---

[74]Grant, *Delors: Inside the House That Jacques Built*, 200–201.
[75]Duchêne, *Jean Monnet: The First Statesman of Interdependence*, 21.

would be in a constant state of tension with her political skills when she later presented the Treaty to the French public.[76] The exact nature of her influence on the Maastricht process is difficult to discern. This is because, on the one hand, her responsibilities as Minister for European affairs cut across the EMU and political union negotiations. On the other, her presence was felt in several different places owing to her previous responsibilities as Mitterrand's counselor at the Elysée and as head of the SGCI. [77] Minister Guigou's pedagogical talents in explaining the relevance of European integration for France were colored by a highly technical grasp of complex dossiers. Yet, despite this technocratic background, she was perhaps the most eminently qualified among those in the French political establishment to engage herself in the popular debate on Maastricht because of her intimate knowledge of the Treaty negotiations working at the official and ministerial levels.

Horst Köhler was the higher civil servant in the ministry of finance whose negotiating skills shaped a Treaty text written in German script for the heads of state and government to review at Maastricht. The qualities that distinguished Köhler as a politico-administrative hybrid were both his influence negotiating at the ministerial level, in Waigel's absence, and his adeptness as a communicator explaining the EMU Treaty to the German public. At Maastricht, however, Kohl made the decision on the transition to Stage Three against the judgement of finance ministry officials. This was both an indication of the inherently political nature of the EMU process and the limits to the influence that politico-administrative hybrids possess.

Monnet's Approach

The decisions on EMU taken at Maastricht traced in a bold manner the line drawn by Monnet's approach. The decision by Kohl to accept a fixed deadline for EMU has been described as a "significant tactical negotiating victory" for the French, "a victory that in turn owed much to Chancellor Kohl."[78] This book argues that the Mitterrand-Andreotti initiative on the basis of Bérégovoy's idea and Kohl's decision to accept it provide an example of integrative bargaining in the Monnet tradition. The conditions of motivation, information, language and trust were all present between Mitterrand and Kohl. Both leaders had the motivation to try to make the integration process irreversible. The two leaders each aimed to give the other enough information about domestic interests to enable each to strike a "yesable" bargain on EMU: in other words, a deal that could be ratified. Mitterrand and Kohl, as bilateral

---

[76]Lequesne, *Paris-Bruxelles*, 75–76.

[77]The SGCI (Secrétariat général du Comité interministériel pour les questions de coopération économique européenne) is the central administrative apparatus to prepare French negotiating positions regarding Community dossiers on the Council agenda.

[78]Dyson, *Elusive Union*, 156–157.

partners, both spoke the Community language on EMU emphasizing it as an endeavor for the European family. And Mitterrand sought Kohl's trust by assuring him that a timetable for EMU would not prevent the achievement of strict convergence criteria.

The blend of convergence criteria and fixed dates is an attempt to achieve a synthesis, or integration, in a bargain which brings together two seemingly irreconcilable ideas. There is a creative tension in the combination "convergence-dates" and the potential for an *élan* to drive the EMU process in a non-linear series of "steps in time." In the Maastricht context, this bargain is more than a compromise in the sense of classic distributive bargaining. It is also more than a "victory" for the French or a "concession" by Chancellor Kohl. The German Chancellor was quite conscious of his own power to conclude, or not conclude, the Maastricht European Council with a decision on EMU. His use of his own power at Maastricht, in the context of both EMU and cohesion, showed him to be a responsible European whose words are backed by deeds.

Kohl may not have been thinking of Monnet the man as he made his decision to accept the 1999 deadline. However, it is clear that there is a Monnet equation in Community affairs of which Kohl was well aware. This equation may be simply stated as "institutions + fixed dates = politics."[79] Without a doubt the compromise tactics so illustrative of distributive bargaining were also present at other moments during the Maastricht negotiations. The opt-out for Major on Stage Three was just one example of distributive bargaining on the same issue of a fixed date.

Perhaps Horst Teltschik's comments provide some insight into the relations among the three individuals who worked so hard to achieve integrative bargaining on EMU. He says: "The triangular relationship of Kohl-Delors-Mitterrand was pivotal. Delors mediated between Kohl and Mitterrand and, never afraid of stating his own views forcefully, tried to influence them while doing so. He understood our domestic problems and helped Mitterrand to do so, such as when we wanted the IGC on monetary union postponed until after the November 1990 elections."[80] Given these comments, it is important to emphasize Delors' role during the IGCs from the standpoint of his commitment to the Monnet approach. On EMU, Kohl and Mitterrand, aided by Delors' initiatives, were trying to focus on the common interest, rather than on trades between conflicting interests, and to maximize the advantages of their joint undertaking rather than to exchange gains and losses with each other. The contrast with the decisions taken on political union, particularly in the areas of CFSP and justice and home affairs, was evident to all the leaders at Maastricht.

---

[79]Interview, *Auswärtiges Amt*, 27 December 1994.

[80]Grant, *Delors: Inside the House That Jacques Built*, 141.

However, it is also necessary to underline the creation of a new institution, the European Central Bank, as part of a common solution to the problem of how to create EMU. The workings of the ECB have the potential to create a new psychological situation that transcends the old one and enables the Community to define integration in a completely different context. In its emphasis on the creation of a new institution, Monnet's approach is illustrative of a perspective in international relations otherwise known as "neoliberal institutionalism." This perspective does not assert that "states are always highly constrained by international institutions." Nor does it claim that "states ignore the effects of their actions on the wealth or power of other states." Neoliberal institutionalists, like Robert Keohane, do argue, however, that "state actions depend to a considerable degree on prevailing institutional arrangements, which affect: the flow of information and the opportunities to negotiate; the ability of governments to monitor others' compliance and to implement their own commitments; (and) prevailing expectations about the solidity of international agreements."[81]

Whether the creation of a European Central Bank will actually be able to redefine the context of integration in Europe in line with the tenets of neoliberal institutionalist thought, or whether internal strife on the bank's board of governors will reflect older suspicions and a return to classical balance of power politics, are questions for the future. The attempt to use Monnet's approach in the creation of EMU illustrates just how difficult it is to achieve integrative bargaining on complex issues, like a set date for entry into Stage Three, among states with such divergent national traditions. In this regard, the German delegation's insistence on a unanimous decision in order to decide on the passage to Stage Three was at variance with Chancellor Kohl's views and those of the other leaders in the European Council. This was because the Bundesbank was quicker than the Bonn government to believe that the goal of EMU was first and foremost the undermining of German power. Wilhelm Nölling, President of the National Bank of Hamburg, stated: "Let us have no illusions—in the actual discussions over the new monetary order in Europe, at stake are power, influence and the pursuit of national interests."[82]

Yet, there is little question that the Community's member states are trying to maximize joint gains. Whether the political will exists to make the tough choices at Level II which EMU will require a few years down the road is open to question. Agreement on a fixed date is a necessary point of departure. The use of integrative bargaining to achieve an accord on this point was decisive to the final outcome at Maastricht. The fulfillment of the required convergence criteria and securing the agreement of national parliaments to move on to the final stage are other matters. Of particular relevance here is the issue of

---

[81] Keohane, *International Institutions and State Power*, 2.

[82] Marsh, *Die Bundesbank*, 311–312.

whether or not other member states, besides the Federal Republic of Germany, will agree to the significant steps on the road to political union, namely increased powers for the European Parliament, in exchange for a green light on the creation of the European Central Bank and a single currency.

SUMMARY

As a forum for intergovernmental conference negotiations, the Maastricht European Council revealed both the pressure on heads of state and government to make a series of complex decisions in only two days and the demands which the IGC process makes on the energy and time of all participants involved. It is important to underline that the nine issues on the Maastricht agenda were only one part of an overall program for the European Council, which also included other issues relevant to Community affairs and European Political Cooperation. On most outstanding issues which needed to be resolved to conclude the Treaty on European Union, the teamwork of France and Germany was necessary to sustain the momentum of the negotiations. On crucial issues like EMU, a European defense policy and Article 100c on visa policy, which was in the end included in the Community sphere, the Franco-German negotiating line stood firm.

The three approaches used in this study illustrate how on the crucial issues like EMU, the defense dimension of CFSP and Article 100c, Mitterrand and Kohl were keeping in mind the requirements of their own domestic interests while simultaneously aiming to expand the contours of each other's win-set. Mutual efforts on the part of both leaders to influence the definition of the other's win-set were particularly difficult to achieve for two reasons: the large number of interconnected issues on the political union agenda; and the inextricable link between the EMU and political union conferences which Kohl viewed as necessary to achieve German ratification. It was quite clear during the prenegotiation that, despite their joint letters to the Council Presidency, France and Germany had as many divergent as convergent interests and viewpoints on the objectives of political union. This fact alone makes the agreement achieved at Maastricht significant in terms of each country's willingness to go beyond the purely national interest in the definition of goals for the Union.

The separate preparations for the two IGCs, in terms of the bureaucratic personnel responsible for each conference, impacted on the Maastricht European Council's agenda to the extent that the links between the horizontal issues, which cut across both IGCs, were never very strong. This complicated negotiations during the European Council with numerous *tours de table* during which the Dutch Presidency had to return repeatedly to issues like social policy. Such constraints made integrative bargaining on these issues impossible because there was no common definition of the ways in which they fit into the design of political union. Although EMU was defined as part of this larger entity termed political union, it was apparent that the objectives of the part, namely EMU, were clearer than that of the whole.

Certain individuals who had a very clear idea of the issues at stake on both conference agendas, like President Jacques Delors and Minister Elisabeth Guigou, worked hard to try to keep the lines of communication open between the French and German sides and to inform citizens about the results obtained at Maastricht during the domestic ratification processes. These individuals were neither civil servants nor politicians and the tasks demanded of them during the Maastricht process fell in a grey area between two very different worlds. In the case of Delors, in particular, his presence during the Maastricht European Council was felt in the areas of EMU, regarding the opt-out for Great Britain, as well as on social policy concerning the opt-in for the eleven other member states. His role as a "consultant" to the heads of state and government is a testimony to the influence he had during IGC negotiations in the European Council. Undoubtedly, one of his most significant accomplishments is the fact that he altered the institutional balance which had existed prior to 1985, and, in so doing, carved out a role for the European Commission in the IGC process.

Nonetheless, the decisions taken by Kohl, Mitterrand and the other leaders in the European Council clearly mark the limits of the influence which politico-administrative hybrids possess in the IGC process. This volume emphasizes the presence of these new actors as linchpins in the sub-processes of IGC negotiations and subsequent parliamentary ratifications—at times serving as a bridge between the domestic and European levels as well as the elite and popular ones, in the case of Köhler and Guigou. Particularly on EMU, the role of these actors was crucial to the outcome because they, like Delors, knew the technical details, or substance of the on-going process inside out, and mastered the personal relations among different levels of negotiation necessary to facilitate a final agreement at Maastricht.

Their role set the stage for integrative bargaining to take place between Kohl and Mitterrand precisely because the careful preparation and attention to detail which characterized the EMU conference engendered the elements of motivation, information, language and trust from the lower levels of negotiation to the highest one. The task which subsequently faced leaders and politico-administrative hybrids alike was to translate these four elements of Monnet's approach to individual citizens and parliamentarians during domestic ratification processes. These same politico-administrative actors would have to be involved to bring the IGC process to its logical conclusion with the ratification and implementation of the Treaty.

CHAPTER VII

The Maastricht Debate and Ratification in France: The Power of Public Opinion and the Status of Sovereignty

Quite early, I had the instinct, which became a rule of conduct for me, that thought cannot be separated from action.

The greatest danger that Europe faces is the deterioration of the individual, who cannot include in his daily life, in his security, the means which progress would permit him to contribute. If he cannot make a contribution to his life, it is because the conditions in which we live, the conditions in which the countries of Europe live, prevent him from doing so.

Jean Monnet, *Mémoires*

On 11 March 1992 President Mitterrand submitted the Treaty on European Union (TEU) to the French Constitutional Council. Article 54 of the French Constitution obliged the Council to rule on the compatibility of the Treaty with the Constitution of 1958. The Council gave its opinion on 9 April 1992. This ruling opened both a constitutional debate and the next in a series of chapters on French national identity and the country's role in Europe. This chapter initially examines the parliamentary revision of the Constitution and the referendum debate to authorize ratification of the Treaty on European Union.[1] The power of public opinion regarding European integration, and the

---

[1] The French referendum of 20 September 1992 on the Treaty on European Union authorized the ratification of Maastricht. Article 52 of the Constitution of 1958 empowers the President of the Republic to ratify international treaties. A detailed discussion of the constitutional debate is found in Philippe Keraudren and Nicolas Dubois, "France and the Ratification of the Maastricht Treaty," in *The Ratification of the Maastricht Treaty: Issues, Debates and Future Implications*, eds. Finn Laursen and Sophie Vanhoonacker (Dordrecht: Martinus Nijhoff, 1994), 147–153.

status of sovereignty as a result of the decision to ratify the Treaty, are then considered. Finally, the national ratification is interpreted in light of the three approaches used in this book to analyze the IGC process.

THE PARLIAMENTARY REVISION OF
THE CONSTITUTION OF 1958

In the early stages of the constitutional revision, the view within established political circles in Paris reflected the wide gap between elites and the public. Individuals working in the European institutions, notably Commission and Parliament, as well as some French politicians and civil servants, had a take-it-for-granted attitude that the authorization to ratify Maastricht would pass in the French parliament like a letter in the mail. Few individuals questioned whether the postage was sufficient to deliver an extremely bulky package.

In its opinion, the Constitutional Council took the view that three Articles in the Treaty on European Union were contrary to the French Constitution because of their infringement on national sovereignty. By far the most controversial of these was Article 8b (1) concerning the right of Union citizens to vote and stand as candidates in municipal elections.[2] The Constitutional Council stipulated that this required an amendment of Article 3 of the French Constitution which gives only French nationals that right. The Council also ruled that since the French Senate was constituted by means of indirect elections via an electoral college composed of members, some of whom hold seats on the French Communal Councils, and since the French Senate, as a parliamentary body, took part in the exercise of national sovereignty, only French nationals could take part in the election of Senate members.[3] The Constitutional Council did not consider, however, that Article 8b (2) of the Treaty on European Union, regarding Union citizens' rights to vote or stand in elections for the European Parliament, required any change in the Constitution.[4] On EMU, the Constitutional Council held that implementation of the objectives of an independent European Central Bank, the irrevocable fixing of exchange rates, and the adoption of a single currency were contrary to the Constitution of 1958. Finally, the Constitutional Council considered that Article 100c (3) regarding visa policy required an amendment of the French Constitution from 1 January 1996, the date on which the Council of Ministers would start adopting decisions by qualified majority. In the view of the

---

[2]Eric Dupin "La 'citoyenneté européenne' au coeur de la révision constitutionnelle," *Libération* , 11–12 avril 1992, 16.

[3]*White Paper on Denmark and the Maastricht Treaty* (Copenhagen: Ministry of Foreign Affairs, 1992), 58.

[4]"Europe: Le Cactus Constitutionnel," *Libération*, 10 avril 1992, 1.

Constitutional Council, such decisions could lead to an infringement on French national sovereignty.[5]

Once the Constitutional Council's decision was obtained, a revision of the Constitution was necessary.[6] The revision had to be accomplished in one of two ways. Article 89 of the Constitution of 1958 stipulates that the National Assembly and the Senate, on a reference by the President, vote on an identically worded draft revision, which is then submitted to a referendum. The President can decide to forego the referendum and opt for the parliamentary route. The bill is then scrutinized by the two assemblies, meeting as the *Congrès du Parlement*, and is adopted only if accepted by three-fifths of the votes cast. A second method, involving recourse to Article 11 of the Constitution, was last used by General de Gaulle in 1969. This Article is legally disputed because it authorizes the President to submit directly to a referendum "any draft law...intended to authorize the ratification of a treaty, which, without being contrary to the Constitution, might affect the operation of the institutions...."[7]

On 12 April, a few days after the Council's ruling, President Mitterrand gave a long televised address during which he spoke about the constitutional revisions required to authorize the Maastricht ratification.[8] The President saw the problem of amending the Constitution as a parliamentary matter. As a first step, Mitterrand wanted to see if the two Houses agreed to the proposed constitutional revisions. If either the National Assembly or the Senate did not agree, Mitterrand would consult the French people on the issue. The President also explained that "France must accept the idea contained in the Treaty that we all benefit from a European Community citizenship at the same time as from a French citizenship. It is normal to demand a certain time of residency... several years. I would take precautions because certain constitutional aspects are present. In France a municipal counselor participates in the vote for senators—a strictly national election—and mayors possess police powers in the name of the French state. Therefore, it would not be possible for a

---

[5]Eric Dupin, "Maastricht Bouscule La Constitution," *Libération*, 10 avril 1992, 2.

[6]François Luchaire, "L'Union Européenne et la Constitution," *Revue du Droit Public* (1992): 589–616.

[7]This dispute concerns the powers of the president in relation to the prime minister and parliament in the matter of constitutional revisions. "L'utilisation de l'Article 11," in *Les révisions constitutionnelles de la Ve République*, Arlette Heymann-Doat, La documentation française, No 705, 28 mai 1993, 62–68.

[8]"Mitterrand ne rénegociera pas Maastricht," *Libération*, 13 avril 1992, 2.

foreigner to exercise these rights. The European Council will deal with this subject beginning in 1995."[9]

The debate that arose over Article 8b TEU was the most striking example of the tremendous impact EC affairs is beginning to have in the minds and hearts of domestic publics. In this sense, the changes introduced by Maastricht were matters of internal policy. The French debate showed that the potential for greater integration, encompassing even greater areas of domestic policy making, is evident; otherwise, the fierce resistance to change makes no sense. However, before the French would even begin to address the substantial issues on the European agenda during the Maastricht debate, their attention focused on narrow-minded quarrels of internal politics like the vote for foreigners. Early polls revealed that two of every three French voters were in favor of a referendum on the Treaty indicating the significance of the issues raised in terms of the domestic debate.

On the basis of the Constitutional Council's opinion of 9 April, the French government decided, on 22 April, to table a bill for amendment of the Constitution. Article 2 introduced a new chapter XIV in the Constitution of 1958 titled "European Union," consisting of two new Articles 88–1 and 88–2. The initial draft of Article 88–1 dealt with French consent to the transfer of powers necessary for the creation of EMU and the establishment of a common visa policy in the Union. The initial draft of Article 88–2 pertained to French consent on the right of nationals of other member states resident in France to vote and stand as candidates in municipal elections. These individuals could not serve as mayor or take part in the election of senators, however. The proposed amendments were put to the National Assembly on 22 April 1992 and then submitted to the Legislative Committee for discussion.[10]

The amendment bill was discussed for the first time in a plenary session of the National Assembly on 5 May. The French government was able to secure a comfortable majority in support of the bill in spite of serious reservations among the Gaullist rank and file about constitutional aspects relating to European citizenship and the surrender of sovereignty in monetary and visa policies. Prior to the regional elections in March, the Gaullists had served notice of their intention to campaign against the terms of the Maastricht Treaty. In mid-February Alain Juppé, the party's secretary general, addressed the issue on French radio. "It is completely out of the question to give foreigners the possibility of having municipal councillors, who could then endorse a candidate for the presidency, elect senators or become mayor," he said.[11] After several years of party acquiescence without enthusiasm to Mitterrand's European policy, the *Rassemblement pour la République*'s (RPR)

---

[9] Ibid. The translation of Mitterrand's quote is the author's.

[10] *White Paper on Denmark and the Maastricht Treaty*, 59.

[11] Ian Davidson, "French Gaullists Will Try to Block Maastricht Pact," *Financial Times*, February 19, 1992.

objections to the Treaty on European Union represented a clear-cut reversion to traditional Gaullism. However, the political debate on the Treaty placed the party's leader, Jacques Chirac, in a difficult position at best. Although favorable to the ratification of Maastricht, Chirac walked a tightrope between expressing clear support for the Treaty and sympathizing with those members of his party openly against its ratification.[12] The Gaullist party's tactics made it easier, however, for its members to adopt a frankly nationalist position during the regional elections and thus compete more openly for the popular vote swinging toward the extreme right-wing National Front.[13]

At the start of plenary talks in the National Assembly on 5 May, Philippe Séguin, a staunch Gaullist opponent of Maastricht, tabled a procedural motion to the effect that the bill should not be discussed in Parliament. Instead, he argued, there should be a referendum. The motion was rejected by 396 votes to 101 with 72 abstentions. It was supported by 126 Gaullists in alliance with all 26 Communists.[14] The fact that half of the RPR group abstained, and only one member voted against, indicated the emergence for the first time of factions within the Gaullist party on integration.[15]

A total of 97 amendments were tabled during a week of plenary discussions in the National Assembly. The Government confirmed orally that the Luxembourg Compromise, by which a state used its veto power to defend its national interest during negotiations in the Council, would continue to exist. On 13 May the amendment bill was passed by 398 votes to 77 with 99 abstentions. Those in favor included 263 Socialists, 5 *Rassemblement Pour la République*, 77 *Union Démocratie Française* (UDF), 39 Centre Union and 14 Independents.[16] Those against consisted of 4 Socialists, 31 Gaullists, 7 UDF,

---

[12]Gilles Bresson, "Quand Maastricht divise Jacques Chirac," *Libération*, 25 mai 1992, 8.

[13]Davidson, "French Gaullists Will Try to Block Maastricht Pact."

[14]*White Paper on Denmark and the Maastricht Treaty*, 60.

[15]Although Mitterrand played off various factions within the Socialist party in order to enhance his own presidential standing, these factions never emerged in response to European integration. Factions were more readily apparent, however, regarding defense issues, i.e., CERES. Colette Mazzucelli, "Comparative Dimensions of Factionalism. The French Socialists and the German Social Democrats: A Review of the Theses of Sartori, Beller and Belloni and Hine" (unpublished paper).

[16]*Rassemblement pour la République* (RPR), led by Jacques Chirac, is a party in the Gaullist tradition for which European integration has long been a sensitive subject among party militants. *Union pour la Démocratie Française* (UDF), presided over by Valéry Giscard d'Estaing, is a federation of parties made up principally of the center parties, *Centre des Démocrates Sociaux* (CDS) and the *Parti Républicain* (PR). It is a party with a strong pro-European and pro-Community tradition.

1 Centre Union, all 26 members of the Communist Party and 7 Independents. Among those abstaining were 3 Socialists, 33 RPR, 5 UDF and 3 Independents.[17]

Several substantive amendments, which emphasized nationalistic preoccupations, were added to the bill. Clearly French politicians wanted to counter the possibility that the European Union might be moving in a federalist direction. In Article 2 of the Constitution, on the flag and the national anthem, *le français* was added as the Republic's official language. The preservation of the French language and culture in the face of competition from any of the other eight official Community languages was thereby reinforced. In Article 74, on the French overseas territories, it was stipulated that their status would be determined in a special framework law. The title of the Constitution's new Chapter XIV was changed from "European Union" to "The European Communities and the European Union." Chapter XIV started with a new Article 88–1 defining the Union in the following terms: "France shall be a member of the European Communities and the European Union consisting of States which, in accordance with the Founding Treaties, have freely decided to exercise some of their powers in common." The original bill's Articles 88–1 (on EMU) and 88–2 (on the right to vote and to stand as a candidate at municipal elections) became Articles 88–2 and 88–3.[18]

In Article 88–3 it was stipulated that the rules for the exercise by EC nationals of the right to vote and the right to stand as a candidate at municipal and European Parliament elections would be laid down in a separate law. A new Article 88–4 was introduced into the Constitution stipulating that the Government would submit proposals by the European Commission involving provisions of a legislative nature to the National Assembly and the Senate at the same time as the proposals were submitted to the Council of Ministers. Each body would give an opinion on these proposals either in a special committee or in plenary session in accordance with detailed procedural rules laid down by law.[19] The legal impact of this new constitutional provision is not nearly as significant as its potential political ramifications. This is because

---

[17] *White Paper on Denmark and the Maastricht Treaty*, 60–61.

[18] Arlette Heymann-Doat, *Les révisions constitutionnelles de la Ve République*, 17–18.

[19] Ibid., 18–19.

it gives the assemblies greater legitimacy both to assert a right to be informed and to state their opinion on European integration at any time.[20]

After its reading in the National Assembly, the amended bill was then passed on immediately to the Senate. The senators argued above all for assurances from the government that the constitutional revision on the right to vote in municipal elections for non-French nationals should be voted in identical terms by both the National Assembly and the Senate.[21] One reason for this is that the senatorial majority differs from the governmental majority. Charles Pasqua, President of the RPR group in the Senate, exploited this difference. He did so by supporting the reservations of a large majority of the Gaullist electorate which feared that all foreigners, particularly North African migrants, might assert the right to vote in future local elections. Therefore, a Senate amendment was added to the constitutional bill specifying that only European Union citizens could vote and run for office in local elections.[22] A second reason is that the Senate is elected through indirect universal suffrage by a college of *grands électeurs*, nominated in part by local councillors. With reference to the Constitutional Council's decision, the constitutional bill specified clearly from the start that Union citizens cannot participate in the election of senators. However, the Senate thought it necessary to add that those citizens cannot nominate the Senate electors. It also specified that the Organic Law, defining all procedures related to application of the right to vote (including eligibility), ought to be voted in the same terms by both assemblies. This was done in order to ensure the Senate's ruling parity with the National Assembly.[23]

After discussion in committee, the bill was submitted to the plenary on 2 June. Discussions in plenary were suspended on 3 June owing to the Danish referendum. The French reaction to the Danish rejection of Maastricht was one of firm resolve to implement the Treaty before the end of the year. In a joint declaration with Kohl, Mitterrand affirmed the French commitment to ratifying Maastricht and to opening negotiations on the accession of the EFTA countries to the Community.[24] The President also announced that he would

---

[20]Keraudren and Dubois, "France and the Ratification of the Maastricht Treaty," 151.

[21]Frédéric Bobin et Daniel Carton, "Les sénateurs souhaitent des garanties supplémentaires sur la citoyenneté européenne," *Le Monde*, 22 mai 1992, 8.

[22]Françoise de la Serre & Christian Lequesne, "France and the European Union," in *The State of the European Community, Volume 2*, 152.

[23]Ibid.

[24]Jean Quatremer, "Europe: Le Non Danois provoque un electrochoc," *Libération*, 4 juin 1992, 2.

submit Maastricht to a popular referendum. [25] Most importantly, the French government did not intend to accept a renegotiation of the Treaty. Procedural arrangements would have to be discussed in the Council to accommodate the consequences of the Danish vote.

The Danish rejection of Maastricht did provoke a debate among French intellectuals who spoke of a "catharsis" for the integration process as a result of the negative vote. [26] References to the "risks of ignorance" were meant to alert the politico-administrative establishment about the urgent need to inform the French public about integration. The fact that the negotiation of Maastricht illustrated a national democratic deficit, with fewer than a dozen individuals aware of the substance and potential implications of the Treaty, would complicate efforts aimed at a positive result in the French referendum. Criticisms made about the closed nature of the bureaucracy in Brussels were no less true of politico-administrative elites in Paris. Clearly public confidence and trust in holders of political office were in large measure discredited. More importantly, the Maastricht debate showed that the government had insufficiently prepared the terrain of direct consultation with the people.

During the plenary discussions which resumed in the Senate on 9 June, Dumas made clear that if the Danish people continued to oppose the Treaty, the member states would make necessary adjustments so that Maastricht could enter into force for the Eleven. In political terms, the intention of the foreign ministers to finish all the national ratification procedures was stated a few days before during their Oslo meeting on 4 June. The Danish Minister was in agreement with this decision because time was needed for reflection on the referendum result and on the subsequent political course to follow. Guigou indicated that there was room for disagreement among the constitutional experts who argued that the Treaty was null and void after the Danish rejection. What counted above all in her view was the will of those who signed the Treaty not to modify its contents and to submit the original text to national parliaments for ratification. Citing the example of the enlargement negotiations in 1972, the Minister for European affairs noted that even though Norway refused to ratify, this did not prevent the other member states from going ahead. [27]

On 17 June the Senate, after further discussion in plenary, passed the bill approved by the National Assembly with additional substantive amendments.

---

[25]Philippe Reinhard, "Référendum: l'effet d'announce de Mitterrand," *Le Quotidien*, 4 juin 1992, 3.

[26]Alain Minc, "Not So Much a Crisis like a Catharsis," *The European*, June 11, 1992; Laurent Cohen-Tanugi, "Les leçons du syndrome danois," *Le Monde*, 11 juin 1992, 2.

[27]Pierre Haski, "Guigou: Ne plus faire l'Europe comme avant," *Libération*, 6 juin 1992, 3.

Articles 88–2 and 88–3 no longer referred to the actual Treaty on European Union of 7 February 1992 but to the content of that Treaty in case modifications became necessary as a result of one or more countries not joining the Union. The introduction of the right to vote and the right to stand as a candidate in municipal elections in Article 88–2 was changed from an obligation to an option, and it was specified that only citizens of the Union resident in France could avail themselves of such rights. It was also stipulated that citizens of the Union could not hold the post of mayor or deputy mayor or take part in the appointment of senators. The Senate was given the same weight as the National Assembly in the subsequent establishment of the specific implementing provisions as laid down in a special framework law.[28]

Article 88–4 was amended so that the National Assembly and the Senate no longer had to give opinions on proposals for Community legislative acts, but could adopt resolutions in accordance with detailed rules laid down in their respective rules of procedure. Article 54 was amended so that a minority of 60 members of the National Assembly or 60 members of the Senate could in future ask to have international legal obligations put to the Constitutional Council for its opinion as to whether these obligations were compatible with the Constitution.[29]

Since the French Constitution can only be revised on the basis of identical texts, the Senate version of the bill was sent back to the National Assembly on 18 June for a new vote.[30] The National Assembly adopted the Senate's text without amendment by 388 votes to 43 with 2 abstentions. All Gaullist party members except one walked out before the vote. Those who voted in favor consisted of 258 Socialists, 1 Gaullist, 73 UDF, 39 Centre Union and 12 Independents. For the final adoption of the constitutional amendments, President Mitterrand decided to put the bill before the members of the National Assembly and the Senate convened in Congress at Versailles on 23 June.[31]

After a short debate the Congress passed the bill without further amendment by 592 votes to 73 with 14 abstentions. Of the 875 members of the Congress, 196 Gaullists did not attend. Deeply divided between those skeptical about the Community and those totally hostile to the Treaty, these individuals saved the appearance of party unity by walking out of the parliamentary session. They declared there was no case for constitutional revision since the Danish rejection made the Treaty null and void.[32] Those

---

[28]*White Paper on Denmark and the Maastricht Treaty*, 61–62.

[29]Ibid., 62.

[30]Ian Davidson, "Vote Brings Ratification Nearer in France," *Financial Times*, June 18, 1992.

[31]*White Paper on Denmark and the Maastricht Treaty*, 62.

[32]Ian Davidson, "French Clear Maastricht Treaty Hurdle," *Financial Times*, June 24, 1992.

who voted in favor consisted of 325 Socialists, 142 UDF, 104 Centre Union, 5 RPR and 16 Independents. Those who voted against included 7 Socialists, 2 RPR, 15 UDF, 1 Centre Union, 41 Communists and 7 Independents. Three Socialists, 7 UDF and 4 Independents abstained.[33] The summoning of the two Houses of Parliament to Versailles for only the fourth meeting of its kind in the entire history of the Vth Republic strengthened the unity of the pro-Europeans.

The Gaullists, backed by Communists and the National Front, intended to exploit opposition to Maastricht to attack President Mitterrand. Chirac said that constitutional changes had been rushed through to divide the opposition and re-enforce the President's authority in the run-up to general elections. In the vote on the EDC in 1954, it was the same alliance by the Gaullists and Communists that defeated the pro-European initiative. However, unlike the situation in 1954, the Maastricht vote did more to damage Gaullist party unity than the authority of the Socialist President.

On the contrary, Socialists and Giscardian forces used Maastricht to hurt Chirac's reputation as the most popular opposition presidential candidate. His image as a credible leader was tarnished as a result of his ambivalent attitude about Europe. Throughout the parliamentary revision Chirac expressed his support for Europe in a lukewarm manner, but was also sympathetic to those Gaullists who oppose further European unity. At Versailles, he led a walk-out of Gaullist senators and deputies before the debate started. He refused to defend his decision to boycott one of the most important historical dates in the Vth Republic although the leaders of eight other parliamentary groups spoke in reply to a speech by Bérégovoy and a short message from the President.[34]

THE REFERENDUM DEBATE

The idea to bring forward the French referendum on Maastricht to July was discussed in the French Cabinet the day after the Versailles Congress. A rethink on the referendum date was confirmed by Justice Minister Michel Vauzelle immediately after the eight-hour debate in the Salle des Princes at Versailles. Deputies and more than 1,000 officials were ferried to Versailles in buses under heavy police escort because of fears that the meeting could be interrupted by demonstrating farmers. Vauzelle said the Cabinet would decide whether it was politically and legally feasible to hold the referendum in July instead of September.[35] "The essential thing is that the referendum take

---

[33] *White Paper on Denmark and the Maastricht Treaty*, 62.

[34] Paul Webster, "French Leaders Seek Early Maastricht Poll," *The Guardian*, June 24, 1992, 4.

[35] Ibid.

place...at a moment when the people can take a well-informed decision," he said.[36]

Due to the summer holidays, 12 July was considered the latest practical date for an early poll. Mitterrand was said to be in favor of bringing the date forward, to avoid a rift in an opportunist pro-European alliance between Socialists and Centrists led by former President Giscard d'Estaing. The possibility of an early referendum was considered the week before the Versailles Congress when it seemed that the pro-Maastricht alliance would break down over the dispute concerning the Senate's power to veto a Treaty clause on European citizens voting in municipal elections.[37]

"We must strike while the iron is hot," said Dumas.[38] This statement was true enough in that any delay would give Treaty opposition forces time to mobilize. On 1 July, however, the French Council of Ministers approved 20 September as the date for the popular referendum. Jacques Lang, the Minister for Cultural affairs who led the "yes" campaign in the company of Minister Guigou and the Secretary General at the Elysée, Hubert Védrine, argued in favor of an early referendum precisely because of his concern for greater indifference and hostility toward Maastricht as the summer wore on.[39] However, the government's concern not to interrupt the impending summer vacations determined the timing of the referendum. During a televised address, the President explained that the people would have nearly three months to think about and debate their choice regarding a "very simple" question: "Do you approve of the bill submitted to the French people by the President of the Republic authorizing the ratification of the Treaty on European Union?"[40]

Days after the announcement of a September date for the referendum, the leader of the Gaullists, Jacques Chirac, stated that he would vote "yes" even though fellow Gaullists Charles Pasqua and Phillipe Séguin would lead the anti-Maastricht campaign. Chirac's "yes" *à la carte* allowed the RPR "to play the game of diversity." This option also facilitated the Gaullist strategy of marginalizing the National Front by preventing Le Pen from capitalizing on the "no" vote.[41] In addition, it was generally difficult for those persons

---

[36]"French Vote on EC Treaty Could Occur Next Month," *The Wall Street Journal*, June 24, 1992, 2.

[37]Webster, 4.

[38]"French Vote on EC Treaty Could Occur Next Month," 2.

[39]Jean-Michel Thenard, "Maastricht, le référendum renvoyé à l'automne," *Libération*, le 25 juin 1992, 2.

[40]"Mitterrand pose sa question aux français," *La Croix*, 3 juillet 1992, 4.

[41]Gilles Bresson, "Maastricht: Chirac invente le oui à la carte," *Libération*, 4–5 juillet 1992, 5.

engaged in the "yes" campaign to lend credence to their arguments by reference to the Treaty. Its complicated bureaucratic jargon and the lack of readily available and complete Treaty texts until the end of August led Franco-German specialist, Alfred Grosser, to write: "a difficult treaty, but an easy 'yes.'"[42] His view reflected that of many French analysts, commentators and intellectuals who felt a positive popular response to advance the process of 40 years of European integration was not a difficult choice.

Pasqua and Séguin set out early to complicate that choice, however, with a well-led and effectively organized populist crusade. Pasqua, claiming that "the existence of the nation was in question," attacked EMU as the key to a centralized, federal Europe in which the renunciation of a system of nation-states was evident. In his view, the first danger in this scenario would be German dominance in a federal Europe. The second danger would involve a European Central Bank run by faceless technocrats. This would exacerbate the already unacceptable situation of a democratic deficit in the Community.[43] Séguin argued for a "no" vote "to awaken Europe" and to assert three principles: to relaunch European construction on the basis of the integral nature of the *acquis communautaire*; to re-establish the primacy of politics in the functioning of the European institutions; and to re-establish politics in the strategic vision of the future European architecture. Nothing short of a renegotiation of Maastricht would be necessary to correct the fundamental flaws in the Treaty, according to Séguin. For instance, it was necessary to specify more clearly in the Treaty text the distribution of competencies between the Commission and the Council of Ministers, instead of relying on the vague notion of subsidiarity. Another necessity involved taking into consideration the opening to the east of the Continent in the aftermath of the democratic revolutions there. There was little in Maastricht that acknowledged this evolving situation in the former Communist satellite countries.[44]

Pasqua's claim that the Maastricht debate threatened the existence of the nation-state could also be understood in another light. The Treaty's attempt to accentuate the role of the regions in Europe led to commentaries on the way to reorganize territories in France. As Jean-Louis Guigou argues, the French regions are not yet real regions; they are often conglomerations of departments. At various times when the regionalist movement threatened to

---

[42]Alfred Grosser, "Traité difficile, 'oui' facile," *La Croix*, 10 juillet 1992, 24; Paul Webster, "Maastricht Texts Bombard French," *The Guardian*, 19 August 1992.

[43]Jean-Philippe Moinet, "Pasqua: 'L'existence de la nation est en cause'," *Le Figaro*, 4 août 1992, 6.

[44]Philippe Séguin, "Dire non pour réveiller l'Europe," *Le Figaro*, 6 août 1992, 6.

surface in France, those in the Jacobin tradition always relied on the legitimacy of the departments in order to maintain a centralized structure within the French state. Guigou argues that the recomposition of territories around seven or eight regions can be an objective which France, integrated in Europe, should attain for two reasons. The first involves economic efficiency. Costs would be reduced and administrative services would function better. The second would be to strengthen the cultural character of the regions in an attempt to preserve French local identities.[45]

Such a territorial recomposition is anathema to Pasqua and Séguin because it defies the tradition of departments and administrative centralization. Undoubtedly, these changes would fundamentally alter the nature of the French state. However, although the territorial administrative framework has not evolved much over the past hundred years, the exclusive role of the *département* has been questioned. In the national and European contexts, with the development of rapid transport like the TGV, and transeuropean networks of high speed trains that can link up with the TGV, the *département* appears to be too small an administrative framework for economic development.[46] Examples of French regions trying to strengthen their national position by a good fit into the European context are Nord-Pas-de-Calais and Rhône-Alpes. Nord-Pas-de-Calais, along with the three regions that comprise Belgium and a region in southern England, have joined forces to create a Euro-region. All five regions plan to reap benefits for their citizens through links provided by transeuropean networks and increased investment. The goal of Nord-Pas-de-Calais is to modernize after the decline of the coal industry and to compete better in the modern economic environment. Rhône-Alpes, in addition to Baden-Württemberg, Lombardy and Catalonia, makes up one of the "four motors of Europe" in an effort to take advantage of emerging transnational economic and political ties.[47]

The theme of economic renewal is one of great significance in terms of French public support for European integration. Polls taken in early August and early September illustrated some of the reasons for "yes" and "no" votes on the Treaty. In the earlier poll, the main reasons for the "yes" vote were economic prosperity, peace, and the opening of borders, respectively. The main reasons for those voting "no" were a fear of opening borders, a worsening of the unemployment situation, and a lack of information about an overly complicated Treaty.[48] The poll in September revealed that the French

---

[45]Jean-Louis Guigou, "La recomposition des territoires," *Libération*, 24 juillet 1992, 5.

[46]Jean-François Drevet, *La France et l'Europe des régions* (Paris: Syros-Alternatives, 1991), 174.

[47]Ibid., 152–155.

[48]Eric Dupin, "57% du oui à sept semaines du référendum," *Le Monde*, 4 août 1992, 4.

found Giscard d'Estaing to be the most convincing proponent of the Maastricht Treaty, followed closely by Delors. This was the case even though Giscard's message was at times rather ambiguous as illustrated by his remark: "yes to Maastricht in spite of socialism." Guigou, despite her tremendous personal engagement in the "yes" campaign, ranked number fifteen on a list of eighteen individuals named. As for Delors, he was perceived by the French as neither a politician nor a bureaucrat. His announcement on 31 August that he would quit as Commission President if the French voted "no" to Maastricht[49] was not, however, the most striking instance of participation in the French debate by an individual outside the domestic political scene. The fear of Germany that emerged during the Maastricht debate irritated France's partner across the Rhine.[50] In an attempt to calm French fears, Kohl made a brief televised appearance during the TF1 debate on 4 September.[51]

As part of his strategy to win over skeptical voters, however, Mitterrand argued a few days later that a united economic policy would be for the leaders in the European Council to establish, with the future European Central Bank merely in charge of implementation. German civil servants in Bonn feared that this apparent threat to the independence of the planned central bank could set off a backlash in Germany, whose leaders and citizens are wary of imported inflation.[52] Mitterrand's referendum strategy to divide and conquer the Right was risky in that it exposed Maastricht's fate to the vagaries of approval ratings for the President himself. It also revealed the debate on Europe to be a pawn in the game of internal political manoeuvres. "It is Europe that one must now vote on," declared Mitterrand at the height of the campaign. The President described the Treaty on European Union as "the third stage of European construction" after the Treaty of Rome and the Single European Act. It was "a Treaty of protection for our country planned by Chancellor Kohl, Jacques Delors and myself to implement the internal market without borders," Mitterrand explained.[53] To present the Treaty as part of a historical design, the President emphasized that other steps would follow Maastricht in the same logic.

---

[49]Thierry Bréhier, "M. Jacques Delors quitterait son poste en cas de victoire du 'non'," *Le Monde*, 2 septembre 1992, 1.

[50]Eric Le Boucher, "Bonn: l'exploitation de la 'peur de l'Allemagne' dans la campagne irrite beaucoup...," *Le Monde*, 4 septembre 1992, 9.

[51]Pierre Haski, "Le 'conseil d'ami' d'Helmut Kohl," *Libération*, 4 septembre 1992, 5.

[52]Andres Wolberg-Stok, "Envoy Sees Oui Problem for Treaty," *Irish Press*, 10 September 1992.

[53]"C'est l'Europe qu'il faut maintenant plébisciter," *Libération*, 4 septembre 1992, 4.

The Power of Public Opinion

Notwithstanding Mitterrand's remarks, an analysis of the referendum results revealed ambivalent popular attitudes on both the credibility of established national political parties and the purposes of integration. The "yes" vote carried only 51.05% of the public taking part in the referendum against 48.95% for the "no" vote. Of those individuals who voted "no" to Maastricht, 39% did so to express dissatisfaction with the President himself. Another 35% voted "yes" out of fear that a "no" vote would carry the day. The ambivalence in French attitudes on European construction is obvious, however, in a closer look at the main reasons for "yes" and "no" votes. The largest percentage of "yes" votes was cast to ensure a lasting peace in Europe. Yet, in comparison to the 72% who voted along these lines, 57% voted "no" because of the loss of French sovereignty implied. Although 63% voted "yes" in acceptance of Maastricht as indispensable for European construction, another 55% voted "no" in order not to leave Europe in the hands of Brussels technocrats. Another 40% voted "no" out of fear of German dominance. Most significantly, 31% voted "no" to reject the entire French political establishment.[54]

In the view of two French political scientists, Olivier Duhamel and Gérard Grunberg, the referendum results reflect less the opposite views of two homogeneous factions than the result of the juxtaposition of several cleavages. Five cleavages have in fact been discerned.[55] The first cleavage is sociological. Two of the main factors were the level of education and the sociocultural group in which voters belonged. Evidence of primarily white-collar support for integration pointed to its elitist nature. The second cleavage is political. For the most part, centrist political parties joined forces to vote "yes" in contrast to many extremist groups, like the Jacobin CERES within the Socialist party, for example, or the National Front, which voted "no." The third cleavage is more specifically ideological. Although in need of further analysis, an inverse connection does exist in France between partisans/adversaries of European Union and partisans/adversaries of more authority in general. In other words, opposition to integration tends to be strong among those segments of the population that favor a more authoritarian attitude toward societal questions. This implies a necessity to examine French

---

[54]Eric Dupin et Pierre Giacometti, "Premier regard sur un paysage électoral mis sens dessus-dessous par le scrutin," *Libération*, 22 septembre 1992, 4–6.

[55]Olivier Duhamel et Gérard Grunberg, "Référendum: les dix France," in *L'état de l'opinion (1993)*, eds. Olivier Duhamel and Jérôme Jaffré (Paris: Editions du Seuil, 1993), 79–86.

attitudes on Europe in the context of a debate on tradition versus modernity.[56]

The fourth cleavage is geographic. The referendum clearly showed that a majority of the larger French cities voted "yes." Marseille, a National Front stronghold with problems including racist attitudes against foreigners and a high unemployment rate, was a notable exception to the rule. Many individuals living in the rural countryside were more inclined to vote against the Treaty, which undoubtedly reflected in part the farmers "no" vote to reform of the Common Agricultural Policy. The fifth cleavage is historical. Traditionally Christian-Democratic France diverges from republican-secular France on the issue of European integration. With the exception of the Paris region, a resounding "yes" for the Treaty was registered in traditionally Catholic regions where the *Mouvement Républicain Populaire* (MRP) was once strongly entrenched. However, this party had often been replaced in these regions by the Socialist party by the beginning of the 1970s. On the other hand, regions with an old Socialist or Communist tradition tended to vote "no." Nord-Pas-de-Calais, although a traditionally Catholic region with a high investment in Community policies, was pushed into the "no" camp by the traditionally leftist working-class vote in its industrial surburbs.[57]

Another French sociologist, Philippe Habert, argues that the outcome of the referendum stems from a combination, hitherto unknown in French electoral history, of "tactical voting" and the European issue.[58] On the basis of the referendum results, Habert concludes that it is no longer possible to count on voters automatically casting their votes in accordance with established political and socio-economic affiliations. It is now necessary to convince voters on each issue. Moreover, the new electors are individualists who are unstable and eclectic in their political choices. This is confirmed by the increasing volatility of the electorate, which is, as mentioned previously, connected with an acute crisis of confidence in established political parties.[59]

The French journalist, Eric Dupin, observes that the Maastricht referendum, unlike the previous referendums held during the Vth Republic, did not serve to settle a major conflict, to endorse a consensus or to hold a

---

[56]Françoise de la Serre & Christian Lequesne, "France and the European Union," 154.

[57]Ibid., 154–155.

[58]Philippe Habert, "Le choix de l'Europe et la décision de l'électeur," *Commentaire*, 60 (1992–1993): 871–880; Keraudren and Dubois, "France and the Ratification of the Maastricht Treaty," 168.

[59]Keraudren and Dubois, "France and the Ratification of the Maastricht Treaty," 168–169.

plebiscite on the French President.[60] However, although Mitterrand made it clear that he would not step down as a result of a negative vote on 20 September, poll results clearly indicated that between 30–40 percent of the voters cast their ballot that day to express their dissatisfaction with the President himself or with the entire French political establishment. The fact that Maastricht dealt with complex legal and emotionally-charged issues, like European citizenship, made it difficult for the French people to answer, in a well-informed or focused manner, the question posed about the Treaty. Instead, the referendum, called as much for reasons of internal politics as for those regarding the future of European integration, empowered public opinion in what turned out to be as much a debate concerning the state of affairs in France as about the French role in Europe.

The importance of Mitterrand's decision to consult French voters about the Treaty should not be underestimated. The referendum results suggest that the newly emerging cleavages among the French are as much a symptom of a lack of sufficient clarification about the Treaty as of popular dissatisfaction with domestic politics. The outcome on 20 September points to the need for a permanent dialogue between politicians and citizens on French involvement in integration.[61] This poses quite a different challenge than that of formulating diplomatic initiatives for negotiations in Brussels. The necessity to establish a permanent dialogue between the French people and their elected representatives regarding EC affairs is also reflective of the "changing architecture of politics" in which national sovereignty simultaneously adapts to and shapes the institutions with which the state must co-exist. The referendum illustrated that in any future dialogue the power of public opinion to shape decisively the way in which member states participate in the Community is potentially significant.

The Status of Sovereignty in Light of the Maastricht Referendum

Article 3 of the Constitution states that: "National sovereignty belongs to the people, who shall exercise this sovereignty through their representatives and by means of referendums. No section of the people, nor any individual, may arrogate to themselves or himself the exercise thereof."[62] To consider the status of sovereignty in light of the Maastricht referendum, it is important to understand the motivations behind the actions of politicians and citizens during the constitutional revisions and the political debate.

---

[60]Eric Dupin, "Maastricht, le référendum du quatrième type," *Libération*, 14 août 1992.

[61]Keraudren and Dubois, "France and the Ratification of the Maastricht Treaty," 172. These authors call for a "confrontation of opinions between politicians and citizens about France's involvement in European integration."

[62]*The French Constitution* (London: Ambassade de France, 1986), 1.

The actions of politicians across the political spectrum illustrated a strong attachment to the notion of state sovereignty. This was perhaps best understood in the context of the intense political debate over Article 8b TEU. The Senate in particular was adamant about strict conditions preventing foreign electors from taking part in either the election of senators or the prerogatives of national sovereignty. Here the Senate was also asserting its own power vis-à-vis the National Assembly. Some of the Senate's more influential members, like Pasqua, were seeking additional institutional powers enabling them to state their opinion on matters of European integration at any time. Mitterrand had reason to be concerned about a threat to the institutional balance established by the Constitution of 1958. A greater parliamentary voice aimed to limit the scope of presidential prerogatives as the assemblies augmented their own power.

As the French position on European institutional issues illustrates, there is a marked preference by both the head of state and the parliament for a Community structure that preserves to as great an extent as possible the scope of national action. Even the French goals in the EMU context aimed at increasing national leverage on European monetary policy by a seat for France on the board of the future European Central Bank. Moreover, during the Maastricht debate, anti-European personalities in both assemblies seized the opportunity to influence public opinion against the Treaty on the grounds that it constituted a threat to the sovereign nature of the French state.

As stated previously, public opinion about the Treaty was heavily influenced by the voters' limited understanding of its contents. The exercise of sovereignty by the people through their elected representatives was problematic in the case of Maastricht. This was precisely because of the wide gap between the representatives' awareness of the implications of the Treaty and the popular ignorance of its complex legal provisions and structure. One higher civil servant who worked closely with Minister Guigou admitted that the French insistence on a three-pillar structure was so strong in order to take into account popular attitudes.[63] In other words, the French public was not prepared to abandon French sovereignty to the Community institutions by accepting supranational decision making on the CFSP or other policies normally within the sovereign purview of the French state.

Significantly, the process of European integration illustrates more of a density of interaction between states than among peoples. Communication between communities as a result of new electronic technologies is just beginning in the Community member states including France. Even if this communication increases, and it most likely will, does this trend suggest the emergence of a "global civilization" beyond sovereignty? As defined by Mary Catherine Bateson, the notion of an emerging global civilization, unlike the idea of world government, suggests "a loosely integrated form of world order

---

[63]Interview, Quai d'Orsay, 8 March 1993.

that might have the following characteristics: it would develop gradually, and may already be in the process of development; it could coexist with rich cultural and political diversity; it would not rely on the centralization of power characteristic of the modern state; and it might make a virtue of ambiguity."[64]

Bateson argues that what is essential to a sense of "shared membership is a sense of the familiar, a resilient substructure of global community that will allow flexibility in tackling the vast and urgent issues that we as a species must face together. Trust and tolerance for ambiguity within some broader framework are built from the ordinary. At the local level, such a substructure is built up from day-to-day interactions. At the global level, it is more likely to develop by listening to radio and television and walking in a marketplace that draws on worldwide resources than through formal education programs."

It remains an open question as to whether, over successive generations, a viable form of European order can be pieced together from only partially shared systems of meaning, crossing over existing cultural diversity among peoples. Clearly the framework of communications in this order will be very different from the Community system developed by diplomats negotiating in Brussels. In all essential respects, however, transcending sovereignty at the popular level will be as challenging as at the governmental level. This is because of the enormous psychological adaptation required to accept a transference of popular loyalty to an entity beyond the nation-state. As the Maastricht debate confirmed, the prospect of transferring the loyalty of national publics from the legitimacy of the state to the European institutions left some French voters confused, others indifferent and still others downright hostile. On the basis of these reactions, it is possible to conclude that the status of sovereignty in France remains a prominent one, at the forefront of its increasingly interwoven domestic and European political agendas.

INTERPRETING THE MAASTRICHT RATIFICATION IN FRANCE: THREE APPROACHES TO THE IGC PROCESS
Putnam's Two-Level Games

During the national ratification processes of the Treaty on European Union, attention once again focused on the domestic level of analysis emphasized in Putnam's approach. The aim of the three approaches used together is to analyze how the IGC process brought about the emergence of a new type of actor in European integration whose role was to bridge the gap between the domestic level of bargaining on EMU and political union issues and the

---

[64]Mary Catherine Bateson, "Beyond Sovereignty: An Emerging Global Civilization," in *Contending Sovereignties*, eds. R. B. J. Walker and Saul H. Mendlovitz (Boulder & London: Lynne Rienner, 1990), 145.

sub-processes inherent in the Maastricht negotiations and national ratifications. In the French case, there was a parliamentary procedure and a popular referendum. In addition to Mitterrand, Guigou, and to a lesser extent Delors, implicated themselves in the Maastricht process as events played out in France.

Putnam's emphasis on the head of state as the nexus between the international and domestic levels in any two-level negotiation was typified by the role of the French President throughout the Maastricht process. In the politico-institutional set-up of the Vth Republic, the President has absolute power to decide the manner in which the Constitution is revised and the way in which domestic actors, whether institutional or societal, authorize the ratification of international treaties. Mitterrand made the conception, negotiation and ratification of Maastricht the core of his foreign policy during his second term. In each stage of the ratification process, his constitutional right to direct the course of events was unquestionable. The President wanted to conclude the ratification before the summer, if possible.[65] This timetable was a clear indication of just how confident he was about an early acceptance to authorize ratification of the Treaty.

Mitterrand's use of the referendum to encourage a "great debate" about Maastricht differed in one essential way from de Gaulle's use of the referendum as an instrument of direct contact with the French. Mitterrand had no intention of resigning as President in case the referendum failed.[66] The President was in a weakened position after the disastrous defeat of the Socialists in regional elections during March 1992. The replacement of Edith Cresson by Pierre Bérégovoy was a temporary fix at best.[67] For astute observers of the French political scene, the problem was more fundamental than a change in government. The real issue was the duration and extent of presidential powers and the corresponding need for institutional change in the Vth Republic.[68] Specific questions arose concerning the length of Mitterrand's presidential tenure and the ways in which de Gaulle's constitutional legacy

---

[65]"Mitterrand ne rénegociera pas Maastricht," 2.

[66]A comparison of de Gaulles's and Mitterrand's ideas about and uses of presidential authority is made in Duhamel, *De Gaulle-Mitterrand la marque et la trace*, 43–61. A study devoted to Mitterrand's leadership abilities is Alistair Cole, *François Mitterrand: A Study in Political Leadership* (London and New York: Routledge, 1994).

[67]Previous reference is made to changes within the Socialist government in Chapter V.

[68]Charles Zorgbibe, *De Gaulle, Mitterrand et l'esprit de la Constitution* (Paris: Hachette, 1993).

might be harmful to the democratic nature of the French political system.[69] By reinforcing the position of the European Council, Mitterrand was using the European context to support his own power at the state level far removed from societal interests. This led some observers to argue that the democratic deficit existed as much at the national level as at the European one.[70] Here the French case buttresses Putnam's remarks on the head of state's ability to pursue, in the international context, his own conception of the national interest.

The "great debate" on Maastricht occurred at two levels that were separated by an ever-widening gulf. Significantly, this debate exposed, for the first time, genuine cleavages on the question of European integration within established political parties. The most striking example of this phenomenon was evident within the Gaullist party, in general, and within the personage of Chirac, in particular. In this context, Mitterrand the strategist used Maastricht as a lever of influence to boost Socialist party prestige, to persuade the French people of the validity of Europe for the nation and to present his contribution to a momentous event in world history. He relied on the tremendous resonance of European integration in the domestic arena concerning a project in which no less than a fundamental change to the Treaty of Rome was at stake. Mitterrand's constitutional prerogatives in foreign policy, combined with the traditional lack of popular debate on these issues, placed the President in a formidable position.[71]

Less clear, however, was the potential success of Mitterrand's strategy. The second level, namely, the French citizens, was disenchanted with the European adventure and with the established political parties that advocated integration. The rise of the "protest" vote, on the extreme Right and in ecological and regional movements in France and other EC member states, seriously weakened European-minded political leadership. The Treaty debate was confusing and, at times, contradictory precisely because the public in France and elsewhere knew too little about the events taking place.

At the popular level, the Maastricht debate in France was one of national identity. The bond many French have with the soil, strengthened by their familial origins in the provinces, typifies *la spécificité française*.[72] Just as the

---

[69]Pierre Haski et Jean-Yves Lhomeau, "Le joker de François Mitterrand," *Libération*, 10 avril 1992, 3.

[70]Laurent Cohen-Tanugi, *L'Europe en Danger* (Paris: Fayard, 1992), 134–143.

[71]Marie Claude Smouts, "French Foreign Policy: The Domestic Debate," *International Affairs*, 53 (January 1977): 36–50.

[72]Fernand Braudel, *The Identity of France, Volume 1: History & Environment* (New York: Harper & Row , 1990). As a fifth grade student my interest to study in the provinces was strong. My language teacher, a French native, taught me that to know the country is to live outside Paris among its people.

Common Agricultural Policy provokes French fears of the loss of a "way of life,"[73] so did the fierce debate that polarized around a single Treaty Article on European citizenship illustrate the French attachment to the nation-state. Once again, however, nuances were discernible at both the level of the political establishment and that of popular debate.

In terms of the political establishment, Mitterrand had already introduced the idea of the vote for foreigners residing in France during the 1988 presidential campaign.[74] At that time, as during the Maastricht debate, this was a banner that Le Pen's Far Right, and some others within the Conservative ranks, could wave as a warning against the perceived demise of French identity in the Jacobin tradition.[75] During the Maastricht debate, Mitterrand was clear on the French obligation to adhere to Article 8b TEU. This was only normal given his early and firm support, in tandem with Kohl, for the Spanish proposal on citizenship during the negotiations on political union. At the popular level, the tone of the debate was recorded in a series of polls taken throughout the period from March-September 1992. Striking differences of opinion were evident across generations.[76] Those in the age group 18–24 were more open to the idea of a European citizenship co-existing with the national one. There was also less suspicion of foreigners among the youth and more acceptance of a place for other Europeans within the French society.[77] However, this age group was also the most critical of the lack of information available on the Community and of its distance from the majority of citizens. In spite of subsequent national derogations to the Treaty, like the inability of non-French nationals to take part in the election of senators, clearly the President was using the dynamics of negotiations at the European level to promote domestic political change.

One of the paradoxical results of the Maastricht ratification in France involves the strengthening of the parliament in the institutional set-up of the Vth Republic. As part of his aim to gain domestic support, Mitterrand accepted this constitutional modification. The new Article 88–4 demonstrates one of the ways in which the democratic deficit at the European level is being addressed at the domestic one. This change will cause greater difficulties for a future French President, particularly during periods of cohabitation, if he or she aims to shift the balance of power at Level II in favor of domestic policies

---

[73]Barry James, "Behind Farm Crisis: French Fear the Loss of a 'Way of Life'," *International Herald Tribune*, November 27, 1992, 2.

[74]Haski et Lhomeau, "Le joker de François Mitterrand," 3.

[75]Sutton, "Who Beats the Nationalist Drum," 99.

[76]Eric Dupin, "57% du oui à sept semaines du référendum," 2–4.

[77]Colette Mazzucelli, "Maastricht and the Younger Europeans: Signs of Generational Change," *International Affairs Review*, 3 (Spring/Summer 1994): 66–86.

that are preferable for exogenous reasons. Future attempts at the European level to extend the rights granted to Union citizens, for example, may be more difficult to implement at the national level owing to greater parliamentary oversight. Or, as the more perceptive members of the Gaullist party realized, even if the Treaty on European Union were to be ratified by all the member states, the final transition to EMU could not be considered irreversible. National parliaments would inevitably have the final say before exchange rates were irrevocably fixed.[78]The changes brought about by Maastricht present paradoxical consequences for a French head of state participating in two-level games. On the one hand, Maastricht enabled Mitterrand to strengthen his own position in the European polity by re-enforcing the role of the European Council. On the other, the constitutional changes at Level II, required to proceed with the authorization of Treaty ratification, complicate any future president's ability to formulate a strategy at Level I that will garner subsequent parliamentary support.

The interaction between the European and domestic levels in the Community system is not always rational. The increasing complexity of the relationships among institutional actors, European Commission, Council of Ministers and European Parliament, and a potentially larger number of member states makes policy making less comprehensible to civil servants and societal interests alike. There are clear limits to the logic of two-level games in the framework of the IGC process. This is due to the fact that political leaders are only beginning to learn about the extent of popular discontent with the lack of democratic accountability in the Community. Moreover, it is not clear that educating and informing national publics about Community affairs will be sufficient in order to convince the majority to accept the changes taking place as a result of integration. In the French case, both the power of public opinion and the prominent status of sovereignty act as constraints on the President's ability to reconcile European and domestic interests. In this context, the formulation of a "strategy" by any member state to advance European unity by means of another IGC in 1996 is questionable.

As some observers and practitioners of Community affairs argue, IGCs to reform the Treaties of Paris and Rome at frequent intervals are undesirable and could even be disastrous.[79] The Treaty on European Union needs time to be implemented, as did the SEA, before it can reveal its contribution to the integration process. At present, and for the foreseeable future, the Treaty remains the result of a clear contradiction. Although it expands the scope of significant policies that are subject to Community decision making, like EMU, other essential areas remain in the framework of intergovernmental

---

[78]"France's Road to Euro-Union," *Financial Times*, May 13, 1992.

[79]Peter Ludlow and Niels Ersbøll, *Preparing for 1996 and a Larger European Union: Principles and Priorities* (Brussels: Center for European Policy Studies, 1994).

cooperation. This is so for a specific reason: the reluctance of several states, including France, to surrender, too quickly, more sovereignty to the European institutions.

The Danish rejection of Maastricht illustrated the reluctance on the part of one member state to relinquish sovereignty. First, the Danish "no" is a most interesting exception to the requirements of Putnam's "win-set." Among the Twelve, Denmark's politico-administrative establishment was the most careful to formulate a strategy for the IGCs that reflected domestic preferences and coalitions and respected Level II domestic institutions like the EC, or Marketing, Committee of the Danish parliament. The "no" vote therefore came as an even greater surprise to Danish political leaders and negotiators who gave utmost consideration to the prospect of a referendum at the conclusion of the IGCs. The fact that the other heads of state and government intended to press ahead with their ratifications, without re-opening the IGCs to amend Treaty, illustrated the need for a solution that took into account Europe *à la carte*.[80] This fact was further demonstrated by the Danish refusal to adhere to provisions on European citizenship and CFSP.

Minister Guigou's remarks on the Danish rejection of Maastricht are relevant in terms of Putnam's remarks on the need for Level II participants to ratify a treaty or face a renegotiation at Level I owing to an "involuntary defection," or failed ratification. In several interviews after the Danes voted "no," she explained that it was necessary to make the Union the concern of citizens and not just of experts.[81] In her view, the Treaty on European Union was still valid legally and politically. In legal terms, Guigou made a distinction among the various phases of negotiation, signature, ratification and implementation. The Treaty was negotiated and signed by the Twelve. This fact was not changed by the Danish rejection; the Treaty remained on the table. It was essential to finish the third phase of ratifications in all member states in order to see how many countries ratified. Only at that moment would it be possible to see if the Treaty would be applied to the Twelve or to fewer member states. In the second case, the Treaty would be adjusted to reflect the end results.

---

[80]The conception of Europe *à la carte* comes from the writings of Sir Ralf Dahrendorf. This idea proposes that member states may choose to cooperate on some policy issues—hence *à la carte*—but the agenda should not be cast in stone. Helen Wallace, with Adam Ridley, *Europe: The Challenge of Diversity* (London: Routledge & Kegan Paul, 1985), 35.

[81]Haski, "Guigou: 'Ne plus faire l'Europe comme avant," 3; Frédéric Bobin et Claire Tréan, "Un entretien avec Mme Elisabeth Guigou," *Le Monde*, 3 juin 1992, 4.

Most classical international organizations or regimes would not try to find solutions to a failed treaty referendum by a participating state. Negotiations would have to be re-opened and a new treaty would have to be approved by all states involved. Nor would these organizations encounter the legal difficulties implied by potential Danish opt-outs to Maastricht. This makes it necessary, in light of the Danish experience, to refine Putnam's approach by acknowledging the existence of a European polity that conducts IGC negotiations and national ratifications in a *sui generis* manner. The European Council reacted to the Danish "no" by using its network of political elites at the center to sustain just enough momentum for the Treaty ratifications to continue. Thus, its leaders bought valuable time to consider a number of legal and political options to deal with the Danish dilemma. The final agreement which met Danish demands for legally binding opt-outs, described by some observers as "an exercise in legal and constitutional acrobatics,"[82] illustrates the essential and increasingly prominent role of the Council Secretariat in the IGC process. The Secretariat's Legal Service, headed by the Frenchman, Jean-Claude Piris, was able to provide the solution to a political problem at the European level which had its roots in Danish politics. Although the problem originated at Level II, a solution was required at Level I. This was a solution which member states acting individually, outside of the transnational network that defines the European polity, could not achieve.

Finally, the close personal relations between Mitterrand and Kohl in the bilateral and European Council frameworks, after the Danish "no," were illustrated by Kohl's appearance on French television during the referendum debate. Here once again it is evident that Putnam's point that Level I negotiators are often badly informed about Level II politics was not applicable. During the national ratification debates, as during the IGC negotiations, politicians and civil servants at different levels in France and Germany were well informed about each others' interests and concerns. Numerous bilateral contacts at the official level were necessary to keep the lines of communication open and to prepare for European Council meetings where decisions were taken on how to proceed with national ratification processes after the Danish rejection of the Treaty. In this context, the role of civil servants and politico-administrative hybrids was essential to the IGC process.

Aberbach, Putnam and Rockman's Four Images of Civil Servants
The constitutional revisions and the popular referendum to authorize the French ratification of the Treaty directly involved politicians more than civil servants. This approach, however, is necessary to supplement both two-level

---

[82]Lionel Barber and Hilary Barnes, "Legalistic Acrobatics Rescue Denmark," *Financial Times*, December 14, 1992, 2.

games and Monnet's approach because it highlights the role of a new actor whose influence was crucial throughout the IGC process.

In addition to the head of state, there was one other person who was as closely implicated in the referendum debate as in the IGC negotiations: the French Minister for European affairs, Elisabeth Guigou. Throughout the summer, Guigou was the main person responsible to speak to the French voters about Maastricht. As most of the political establishment left for their August vacations, she campaigned on the beaches and resorts from Normandy to the Côte d'Azur, tirelessly working for a "yes" vote. Guigou was admirably suited for the job of presenting the Treaty to the French people. Her day-to-day hands-on involvement in the Maastricht prenegotiation, as Mitterrand's counselor for monetary affairs in the Elysée and later in the negotiations on EMU and political union, as Minister for European affairs, was intense. Moreover, Guigou's role as a civil servant and minister was significant in the maintenance of close relations with the Chancellor's Office in Bonn.

Guigou's educational background at ENA and career path as an advisor to ministers and presidents, prior to becoming a minister herself, perhaps best illustrates the mix of higher civil servant training and political authority that so characterizes the French system. By all accounts Minister Guigou's enthusiasm and pedagogical talents selling the Treaty were admirable. As a Minister, she delivered a clear political message that French voters recognized, regardless of whether they agreed with that message or not. For example, in one detailed commentary for the French newspaper, *Libération*, both Elisabeth Guigou and Philippe Séguin analyzed and explained each Article of the Treaty to French voters.[83] After the Danish "no," Minister Guigou also made clear that she and Minister Dumas had held four plenary debates on European integration in the National Assembly, including two on the Maastricht negotiations. The difficulty, in her opinion, was that very few parliamentarians were interested in the proceedings.[84]

Her training as a higher civil servant was problematic only in so far as it personified for some French citizens the type of civil servant they feared in Brussels. It is possible that Guigou came across to some French citizens as the kind of removed Brussels bureaucrat that the anti-Maastricht forces claimed were taking over the Community.[85] This would be an interesting commentary on popular perceptions, however, given the fact that Guigou made her career

---

[83]"Oui Non," (supplément) *Libération*, 31 août 1992, 1–44.

[84]Fréderic Bobin et Claire Tréan, "Un entretien avec Mme Elisabeth Guigou," 4.

[85]Scott Sullivan, "Together or Not," *Newsweek*, September 14, 1992, 11.

until that time as a French, not a European, civil servant.[86] Her low rating on a list of leaders considered by the French as engaging proponents of the Treaty did nothing to help Guigou's image as she promoted Maastricht, however.

Guigou writes that, when the President suggested that she enter the government to replace Edith Cresson as Minister for European affairs in October 1990, she felt gratitude and apprehension. She had until that point never held a political office. Guigou was at ease in the higher administrative bureaucracy where she had the opportunity to deal with fascinating subjects in the service of the French state. The political world did not really attract her interest. She was proud to have contributed, in the shadows of power, to the good relations between the Socialist President and his Gaullist Prime Minister, Jacques Chirac, during the period of *cohabitation* in the mid–1980s. At once a counselor at the Elysée and Secretary General of the SGCI, Guigou worked for both men defining French positions during negotiations in Brussels. This work was sufficient to satisfy her curiosity about the world of politics, a world that she describes as "foreign."[87]

Guigou was quick to realize, however, that by accepting to serve as Minister in the government of Michel Rocard, she would have entirely new responsibilities. After previously having treated just about every conceivable issue in Community affairs from the vantage point of the administration, she would now have to introduce the French people to Europe.[88]

It remains an exceedingly difficult task to reconcile in any one individual the technical expertise of the higher civil servant in Community affairs with the political vision necessary to reach out to the people and explain the integration process. The need for both qualities to be present in certain individuals is increasing, however, in order to address in part the democratic deficit in the emerging European polity. This is particularly true in so-called "grey-area" zones in which Community competencies begin to interact more and more with classical intergovernmental cooperation. Some third pillar issues introduced by Maastricht, in particular those that may touch on the

---

[86]After the Socialists left the Government in March 1993, Guigou was replaced as Minister for European affairs by Alain Lamassoure. She subsequently went on to win a seat in the European Parliament in the June 1994 elections. In her capacity as a member of the Socialist Group, she is one of two representatives of the European Parliament in the Reflection Group responsible for deliberations on the 1996 Revision Conference agenda. Guigou continues to play a political role, but as a member of a European institution.

[87]Guigou, *Pour les européens*, 16–17.

[88]Ibid., 17. The author has translated and paraphrased Guigou's writings from the original French text.

common visa policy, are noteworthy examples. Here the democratic deficit, in the form of widespread neglect of mechanisms to ensure political and social accountability, is blatantly obvious.[89]

Guigou's role in the entire Maastricht process is illustrative of the type of politico-administrative hybrid introduced by Aberbach, Putnam and Rockman. Although her role in no way resembled that of Delors, she, like the Commission President, was more familiar with the technical dossiers treated in EC negotiations than with the world of politics. Guigou's place at the nexus between national and European affairs clearly was not that of the chief of government mentioned in Putnam's two-level games. However, her participation in the negotiation and ratification processes illustrates the need to acknowledge the presence of Image IV hybrids at levels of negotiation below the chief of state.

In the Maastricht context, there is no question that Mitterrand was the chief protagonist by virtue of his authority as President. However, Guigou's roles, first at the official and later at the ministerial levels, were an integral part of the IGCs and the two phases of constitutional revision and referendum debate prior to domestic ratification. Her participation in the implementation of Maastricht as a negotiation process, a legislative policy program and a French strategy for a lasting peace order on the Continent was decisive. Without that participation, the Treaty implementation in France would have been more difficult, if not impossible, given the close nature of the referendum results.[90]

Monnet's Approach

The relevance of Monnet's approach to the French ratification debate may be assessed by considering the role of the Action Committee for Europe during that debate and by exploring the significance of *engrenage* to the integration process. As stated previously, *engrenage* connotes the enmeshment of member units and the "locking in" of whatever integrative steps are achieved. It may somewhat reduce the alternatives for member units, in particular, making the costs of opting-out of joint policies higher than those of continued involvement. Here it is important to emphasize that the French ratification revealed the limited extent of society's participation in *engrenage*.

---

[89]Hans Ulrich Jessurun D'Oliveira, "Expanding External and Shrinking Internal Borders: Europe's Defence Mechanisms in the Areas of Free Movement, Immigration and Asylum," in *Legal Issues of the Maastricht Treaty*, eds. David O'Keeffe and Patrick M. Twomey (London: Wiley, 1994), 277.

[90]President Mitterrand publicly recognized Guigou's contribution to the IGC negotiations during an interview just weeks prior to the French referendum. "C'est l'Europe qu'il faut maintenant plébisciter," *Libération*, 4 septembre 1992, 4.

In terms of the Action Committee's activities during the debate, four pro-Maastricht Gaullist deputies, led by former Prime Minister Chaban-Delmas, took part in the vote of 23 June on the bill to amend the Constitution at Versailles. As President of the Action Committee for Europe, Chaban-Delmas worked very hard to secure the passage of Maastricht throughout the debate. In this sense, the French members of the Action Committee worked to achieve its main goal of influencing opinion within the national parliaments that had to ratify changes to the Treaty of Rome.

However, the fact remains that the Action Committee's endeavors were quite distant from the daily preoccupations of ordinary citizens. The French public knew little of its existence. Moreover, in the referendum phase, the Delegation of the European Commission in France, which has an office in Paris, was able to play a more central role than the Action Committee. The Delegation's task was to provide answers to specific questions about Maastricht made by those individuals in the French government working to inform the public.[91]

Ironically, Chaban-Delmas' remarks during interviews and radio speeches when questioned about the significance of the Maastricht Treaty for integration suggest less the views of Monnet than those of General de Gaulle. One interview just before the French referendum on 20 September illustrates the Gaullist nature of Chaban-Delmas' position. In his words, Maastricht allows for "the creation of a system in the same manner as the Common Market." This is to say "an interstate system in which each state retains its full independence, its sovereignty and pools sovereignty on certain specific goals according to a unanimous contract."[92] The rejection of Maastricht as a first step to a federal Europe is quite clear. Also evident in the text of the interview is Chaban-Delmas' opinion on the risk taken by the President in his decision to call a referendum on Maastricht.

In Chaban-Delmas' view, the first error made by the leaders responsible for the referendum campaign was to think that Maastricht would pass easily. The second error was committed by certain individuals engaged in favor of the "yes" vote. Instead of starting the main information campaign in August, the tendency was to wait until September. This allowed the advocates of the "no" vote time to plead their case to an ill-informed French electorate.[93] Minister Guigou was the main exception to this rule. As part of the Socialists' local campaign, she engaged in a valiant personal effort for the "yes" vote throughout the summer vacation.

---

[91] Interviews, 8 March 1993 and Ephräim Marquer, 6 July 1993.

[92] "J. Chaban-Delmas invité de France-Inter," *Politique Intérieure*, 19 septembre 1992, 15.

[93] Ibid., 18.

An early referendum would have reflected Monnet's approach. This approach is noteworthy in two ways. First, in order to convince others to support his many projects, Monnet was present everywhere. This meant extensive travel which he undertook well into his seventies. Second, and of particular relevance in the Maastricht context, Monnet had an uncanny knack for never allowing the opposition sufficient time to mobilize.

The French attempt to ratify and implement Maastricht as policy indicated an alarming reality in the Monnet approach: support for European integration in Community member states had been taken for granted by political leaders and administrative bureaucracies. The functionalist idea of an ever greater interlocking of Community institutions and national competencies that generated its own momentum was still valid, but public support was necessary to advance the integration process. Popular resistance could, and would, slow the pace of integration in order to allow for societal adjustment. In this sense, the Maastricht process illustrated that *engrenage* was still an integral force in European construction. Monnet's step-by-step approach was arguably still a viable one particularly in the area of EMU. There was one crucial difference, however. Psychologically, the loss of national currencies was a powerful signal that Europe was moving ahead at a more rapid pace. The establishment of a single European currency was as much a *saut qualitatif* as another step on the road to Union.[94] The changes taking place in the Community since 1985, although reported in the press, went relatively unnoticed by national publics until the ratification debates. In 1992, all at once, citizens began waking up to a reality that was far out in front of events in their everyday lives.

In this context, however, *engrenage* should be distinguished from notions like "spillback," a form of resistance based on the expectation of an ever smaller piece of the economic pie. Spillback is not a credible explanation for the French reserve at either the elite or popular levels regarding Maastricht. On the contrary, a majority in the French elite and populace felt the need for a strong Europe to compete economically with Japan and the United States. There was also the sentiment at both levels that French monetary policy had been hostage long enough to the dictates of the Bundesbank. The Treaty on European Union was meant to address these issues.

Societal resistance can be understood in that the Maastricht Treaty, with its mix of integrative and intergovernmental policies and grey areas in-between, is inherently a more complex and potentially confusing reality than anything foreseen by the Founding Fathers of the Community. *Engrenage* can and does take place in specific areas relating to the internal market. A concrete

---

[94]Ephräim Marquer, *L'Europe en poche. Quelques réflexions sur la méthode et le coût du remplacement des monnaies manuelles nationales par des pièces et billets en ECU*, Mémoire de fin d'études à l'Institut Supérieur du Commerce, Promotion 1992.

example in the Maastricht Treaty is Article 100c pertaining to the common visa policy. The falling of barriers as a result of the completion of the internal market called for a common visa policy vis-à-vis the outside world in order to prevent illegal smuggling across borders in the emerging transnational polity. This policy is to be decided on within a Community decision-making framework. Other fields, in particular CFSP, however, remain equally resistant at present to the intermeshing of Community decision making and national competencies. This resistance reflects in part the inability of society to adjust to the prospect of supranational decisions in this pillar.

To promote support for integration "from the grass roots up," and thereby mitigate societal resistance to change, calls for more than a monumental effort in education and information. It necessitates a change in mentality and an adjustment to a new context. This type of attitudinal structuring at the societal level requires a significant amount of time and a persistent learning effort. The ratification debate offered a valuable opportunity to introduce French voters to the changes taking place in a new context. This opportunity also represented, in a democratic polity, the minimum basic requirement to inform citizens about changes impacting on their daily lives.[95] Guigou explained that the idea of the French trying to learn about Maastricht weeks prior to the referendum was "like a student who crams for an exam."[96] Obviously this way of learning about the Treaty is not suited to promoting sustained support for integration at the grass roots level.

The process of learning about Maastricht is difficult for citizens to tackle under pressure precisely because the Treaty's legislative procedures are complex and numerous. Legislation is made at various levels behind closed doors via negotiations in the Council structure. This is why educating the masses about European laws, in the face of criticisms by Treaty opponents like Séguin and Pasqua, is not easy. For example, the question of how to explain to ordinary citizens about the type of negotiations that could arise in the Union, whereby intergovernmental policies previously discussed in groups like TREVI would henceforth be negotiated within the institutional structure of the Council, presupposes a certain level of knowledge about European policy making which most French citizens do not possess. By stating "more and more our adventure is too elitist and technocratic, and people are not

---

[95]Robert A. Dahl, "A Democratic Dilemma: System Effectiveness versus Citizen Participation," *Political Science Quarterly*, 109 (Spring 1994): 23–24.

[96]Thomas Ferenczi et Jean-Pierre Langellier, "Un entretien avec Mme Guigou," *Le Monde*, 16 septembre 1992, 1.

comfortable with it," Jacques Delors captured the essence of the real threat to integration in his own native land.[97]

Delors' role in the ratification debate once more illustrated his status as a politico-administrative hybrid who passionately advocated Monnet's approach. His role can also be understood as a way of presenting the European Commission to national publics that are often suspicious of its motives as an institution. Days after the Danish rejection of Maastricht, the French sociologist, Michel Crozier, defended the European Commission as "an enormous advance over national bureaucracies, the French one in particular." He reminded his audience that the Commission proposes policies but that national politicians and ministers decide on these proposals.

Crozier also believed that the concern shown by Commission civil servants for European issues was superior to that manifested by French bureaucrats for the public good.[98] Crozier was trying to explain to citizens the necessary role of the Commission in the *engrenage* process. This information effort is essential. However, the ratification debate illustrates that the distance between the working methods of a supranational institution and the subnational politics emphasized in the ratification debates is difficult to bridge. This is one of several reasons why the French ratification highlighted the effects of distributive bargaining. The lack of popular knowledge about the IGC process made it possible for opponents of Maastricht to present the ratification of the Treaty as a zero-sum game: a win for a European Community run by faceless technocrats in Brussels was a loss for the sovereign French state.

Not surprisingly, *engrenage* also poses a challenge at the elite level. The corresponding change in mentality, or attitudinal structuring, required on the

---

[97]Grant, *Delors: Inside the House That Jacques Built*, 213. During my time as a Fulbright Fellow in Paris, many individuals explained to me that the French were largely unprepared to cope with the changes brought about by the completion of the internal market or "1992" program. This lack of preparedness reinforces feelings of insecurity among the people in the face of perceived dictates from "faceless bureaucrats" in Brussels or dominance from the partner across the Rhine. In this way, Maastricht complicated the domestic landscape by aiding politicians on the Far Right, like Le Pen, who can and do play on these fears in order to advance their own populist political agendas.

[98]Bernard Bonilauri, "Crozier: éloge de la Commission de Bruxelles," *Le Figaro,* 9 juin 1992, 6. Another article in defense of the Commission appeared soon after. Giles Merritt, "Making Brussels a Scapegoat for Failed European Leadership," *International Herald Tribune*, June 25, 1992, 6. Elisabeth Guigou also makes reference to the absurd pretensions of ENA graduates who believed themselves to be the "sole possessors of the national interest." Guigou, *Pour les européens*, 104.

part of national civil servants negotiating in the Council is hard to achieve. This is particularly true for those civil servants from proud nation-states with long traditions of sovereignty like France or Great Britain. Through its success during the past decade in pursuing a policy of *franc fort* and bringing inflation below the German rate, France invested more economic and political capital in European union than any other member state. The painful transition to Europe after 1983 in part explained why the debate in France on Maastricht was so grudging; it also explained why the French government could least afford to allow Maastricht to fail.

The emphasis on German power during the Treaty debate was a prominent sign of the intense preoccupation the French have with rank in the world. It also illustrated that the French and German elites base their European policies on different foundations. For the French, entrusted with a universal mission, the Community is a tool to serve the national interest. For the Germans, out of consideration for the lessons of history, the national interest must be cast in the Community mold.[99] The geopolitics of a post Cold War Europe has disturbed the old "balance" among the Community's member states. The French are particularly sensitive to the fact that the voice and influence of German policy makers has been altered.[100] This sensitivity and the lack of trust in political elites at the societal level were two of the greatest obstacles to integrative bargaining during the ratification debate.

The reaction of the French voters was a shock to most individuals in the politico-administrative elite who do not have a strong tradition of educating society about Community affairs. The increased use of opinion polls, and possibly referendums, on Europe allows the French people to know their attitudes and feelings better than before. But the French institutions, and particularly the administrative elite working inside, have yet to catch up with this new popular self-awareness. The task of the politico-administrative hybrids identified in this study is to serve as the link between the world in which technical negotiations take place during the IGC process and that of popular sentiment. Information by these individuals, gleaned from their unique experiences at both the domestic and European levels, needs to be made available to ordinary citizens. Without such an effort, many people will continue to feel that issues essential to their daily lives, like EMU, are presented to them only after decisions have been made behind closed doors. To take the logic of two-level games one step further, it is necessary for politico-administrative hybrids to communicate with citizens. It is their task to make clear that domestic structures as well as societal expectations influence

---

[99]Daniel Vernet, "L'Allemagne par-dessus tout," *Le Monde*, 23 mai 1992, 3.

[100] Hayes-Renshaw and Wallace, "Executive power in the European Union," 576.

European strategies and to point out the ways in which the integration process, particularly *engrenage*, impact on national systems.

SUMMARY

The French ratification of the Treaty on European Union illustrates the relative ignorance of national publics regarding the IGC process, in particular, and European integration, in general. The constitutional changes required to ratify Maastricht in France, as well as the popular reaction to the Article on European citizenship, indicate the strength of national sovereignty in the face of an increasingly transnational integration process. The three approaches used in this volume permit an analysis of the IGC process by defining one of two principal units, i.e., the French state represented by its President, and identifying a new breed of actor, i.e., the politico-administrative hybrid. This actor's participation in the Maastricht process linked France's domestic politics and the debate within its society about Maastricht to its European diplomacy.

The significance of Putnam's two-level games is its emphasis on domestic level actors who, along with the strategy formulated by the head of state and the structure of domestic institutions, influenced the IGC process. In the French case, the Maastricht process once again revealed the dominant position of the President of the Republic as "master of the game." However, the national ratification also revealed a deeper political malaise in the French political system in which presidential tenure and influence were called into question. Under the Constitution of 1958, Mitterrand's authority in foreign affairs is unassailable. However, his use of the referendum to allow for popular approval of the Treaty on European Union was motivated as much by a Machiavellian sense of power politics, i.e., to divide the French Right prior to regional elections in March 1993, as it was to involve, or implicate, French citizens in the integration process.

The fact that so few citizens knew anything about Maastricht made Guigou's work selling the Treaty as indispensable a part of the IGC process as her numerous contributions to the negotiations on EMU and political union. As an Image IV hybrid, Guigou had to implicate herself publicly in the ratification debate. To do so, she had to familiarize herself with a world beyond that of negotiations in the Council. As the Maastricht process illustrated, European integration has become increasingly complex. Heads of state and government and ministers do not have the time to devote their attention exclusively to European Community affairs. Therefore, the role and influence of Ministers for European affairs are bound to expand over time. The blurring of political and administrative roles in the French elite during the past decade makes it more than likely that politico-administrative hybrids will continue to wield influence in future IGC processes.

A more difficult issue raised by the Maastricht process, and the corresponding role of Image IV hybrids, is the extent to which the gap which has emerged between the European and domestic levels can be bridged by the participation of politico-administrative actors in public information campaigns. The Maastricht process indicated the enduring attachment of citizens to the nation-state as the primary means of political and social identification. To complicate matters, the opaqueness of Community policy making was reinforced by a cumbersome co-decision-making procedure introduced by the Treaty on European Union. The resilience of sovereignty and the complexity of integration, make the participation of Image IV hybrids essential in societal debates on the future of integration. An important question remains the extent to which their knowledge of distributive and intraorganizational bargaining could facilitate attitudinal structuring or integrative bargaining at elite and popular levels. Theodore Zeldin writes: "The interesting prospect is that Europe—with still only a vague idea of what its great principle of subsidiarity means—will have to develop a new way of using referendums and polls, which does not just tell the losers to go to hell."[101] This statement is relevant to the framework used in this analysis of the French ratification. Specifically, it illustrates that politico-administrative hybrids do have a specific role to play facilitating greater understanding between elites and citizens in the integration process. Only in this way can *engrenage* remain a viable approach to European construction by means of further Treaty reforms at the European level and domestic ratification debates that reflect a consistent popular involvement in integration policies.

---

[101] Theodore Zeldin, "France's Murmuring Heart," *The Guardian*, September 17, 1992.

CHAPTER VIII

The Maastricht Debate and Ratification in Germany: The "Psychology of the Mark" and the Role of Civil Servants

I have never missed an opportunity to act in life. The point is that one should be prepared. For this, it is necessary for me to have a conviction shaped by a long reflection. When the moment arrives, everything is simple because necessity no longer leaves room for hesitation.

The resistance of men and things is on the scale of the change we seek to bring. It is in fact the surest sign that we are on the road to this change.

Jean Monnet, *Mémoires*

Almost immediately following the Maastricht European Council, the Kohl government began its defense of the Treaty results at home. The dominant issue in the ratification debate was the loss of the German national currency, the D-mark, through the creation of an Economic and Monetary Union with a single European currency, the ECU, by 1999. This chapter first considers the constitutional changes relevant to the ratification procedure. An explanation of the main issues during the ratification debates in the Bundestag and Bundesrat follows. The influence of the "psychology of the mark" and the role of German civil servants are then analyzed. This analysis is made in context of the cases put before the Constitutional Court regarding the Treaty and its compatibility with the Basic Law. Finally this chapter assesses the parliamentary ratification of Maastricht in Germany, and the subsequent decision of the Constitutional Court in Karlsruhe, in terms of the three approaches used in this book.

THE RATIFICATION DEBATE OPENS

On 13 December, in a speech before the Bundestag, Chancellor Kohl energetically defended the decision on EMU by stating that the Maastricht Treaty illustrated "German handwriting on all decisive points."[1] Just two days before the Chancellor's speech, the results of the Maastricht European Council were presented to both the Foreign Affairs Committee and the *EG-Ausschuß* of the Bundestag and the EC Committee of the Bundesrat by State Minister Seiler-Albring. Her main task was to sell the Treaty for domestic ratification. A Liberal party politician in Kohl's CDU/CSU-FDP coalition government, Seiler-Albring, assisted throughout the ratification by a small number of civil servants in the *Auswärtiges Amt*, explained the important changes brought about by Maastricht. These included a reference in the Treaty text to the subsidiarity principle, the creation of a European citizenship, stronger powers for the European Parliament including a right of co-decision,[2] the establishment of the third pillar in home and justice affairs on Kohl's initiative and an evolutionary clause to allow for future steps in integration.

The federal government's task of selling the Treaty to a German parliament serving as "notary" was not an easy one. The need to obtain a 2/3 majority in the Bundestag meant courting the SPD-Opposition which expressed its discontent with the meager results acquired on behalf of the European Parliament.[3] The leading spokesperson for the SPD on European affairs, Heidemarie Wieczorek-Zeul, was herself a former member of the European Parliament. She switched to the Bundestag after two terms in Strasbourg to increase public awareness about the European policy of the

---

[1]"Parteien begrüßen im Bundestag die Ergebnisse von Maastricht," *Frankfurter Allgemeine Zeitung*, 14. Dezember 1991, 1. A detailed account of the Chancellor's remarks and the debate in the Bundestag is presented in Deutscher Bundestag, 12. Wahlperiode, 68. Sitzung. Bonn, Freitag, den 13. Dezember 1991, 5797–5833.

[2]During the last weeks prior to the Maastricht European Council, Kohl softened his negotiating stance on co-decision in light of British opposition. This led to accusations by the SPD that Kohl had caved in on political union. The Bonn government's presentation of its results on powers for the European Parliament is included in Deutscher Bundestag, "Bericht der Bundesregierung zum Stand der Arbeiten zur Stärkung des europäischen Parlaments in den Regierungskonferenzen zur Wirtschafts- und Währungsunion und zur politischen Union," Drucksache 12/2249, 12. März 1992, 1–5.

[3]Rainer Nahrendorf, "Parlament als Notar?," *Handelsblatt*, 13. Dezember 1991, 2.

federal government.[4] In spite of the SPD's vociferous objections to the Treaty results, there was strong support for European integration in the Bundestag. As Wieczorek-Zeul explained, Maastricht should not fail due to a German refusal to ratify the Treaty.[5]

The Kohl government also needed the support, by a 2/3 majority, of the Länder. A Social Democratic majority in the Bundesrat complicated the ratification process. However, it is important to view the differences over Maastricht as more of a struggle between the federal government and the Länder than between government and opposition. The Länder's use of Maastricht to obtain greater powers in European decision making involved high-stakes gamesmanship in which they tried to extract as much leverage as possible from the federal government in exchange for Treaty ratification. This made the Bundesrat the most formidable obstacle during the ratification process. The Bundesbank presented the least difficulties during the ratification debate. Yet its voice on the need to maintain strict convergence criteria in order to achieve EMU remained strong. Before considering the views of the Bundestag, Bundesrat and Bundesbank, it is necessary to mention the constitutional changes that were required.

CONSTITUTIONAL CHANGES

According to Article 59 (2) of the Basic Law, the Treaty on European Union required the consent or participation, in the form of a federal law, of the bodies competent for such federal legislation. The procedure for ratifying the Treaty in the Federal Republic related to two bills. The first was the bill on the ratification of the Treaty proper, creating the necessary conditions for Maastricht to come into force. The *Auswärtiges Amt* was the *federführend* ministry in charge of starting the process to ratify this bill. It was also responsible for any subsequent law endorsing the ratification of Maastricht. At the beginning of February, civil servants in the *Auswärtiges Amt* prepared the initial bill for presentation to the Kohl Cabinet. Throughout the ratification process, these civil servants supplied important information on the Treaty to the EC Committee in the Bundesrat and to the *EG-Ausschuß* as well as to a Special Committee on "European Union" (*Sonderausschuß "Europäische Union (Vertrag von Maastricht"*)) which was *federführend* for the ratification in the Bundestag and Bundesrat. In view of the fact that the Treaty contains

---

[4]Heidemarie Wieczorek-Zeul, "Europe's Self-Assertion—Four Criteria for a Progressive European Policy," in *The German Presidency and Beyond*, 63–64.

[5]———, "Der Vertrag von Maastricht im Deutschen Bundestag," *Europa-Archiv*, Folge 13–14 (1993): 405.

provisions which, to be applicable at the national level, required a change in the Constitution, the federal government tabled a second, parallel bill modifying the Basic Law. The federal ministry of the interior was the *federführend* ministry responsible for the amendment of two Articles: Article 28 BL, involving the right of nationals of other EC member states to stand and vote in German local as well as European elections and Article 88 BL on the transference of competencies to the European Central Bank.[6]

Since the bill relating to the Treaty on European Union required the consent of the Länder, their politicians insisted with considerable success on the introduction of a new *Europa-Artikel* (23 BL). According to Article 79 (2) BL, such constitutional changes have to be approved by a 2/3 majority of the Bundesrat and the Bundestag.[7] Meanwhile, a Constitutional Committee (*Verfassungskommission*), consisting of members of the Bundesrat and Bundestag under the chairmanship of Professor Rupert Stolz, prepared the constitutional reform. The amendments were approved on 26 June 1992.[8] In order to take Länder concerns into account, a compromise was achieved in the form of Article 23 BL. This amendment, and other constitutional changes, are mentioned in due course.

The Bundestag Ratification
The Bundestag debate on the results of the Maastricht European Council focused on five themes mentioned by Chancellor Kohl in his address to the German parliament: home and justice affairs; a federal structure for the Union; CFSP; greater powers for the European Parliament; and broader Community competencies.[9] Ingrid Matthaeus-Maier, the deputy parliamentary leader of the opposition Social Democrats, reproached Kohl for not having pushed German interests with enough energy. The results on political union were "simply pitiful." In her view, Kohl "gave way" on the matter of 18 extra German members as well as increased powers for the European Parliament and on social policy. Wolfgang Schäuble, the new parliamentary leader of the

---

[6]Colette Mazzucelli, "Germany at Maastricht: Diplomacy and Domestic Politics," in *Dimensions of German Unification*, eds. Bradley A. Shingleton, Marian J. Gibbon and Kathryn Mack (Boulder & Oxford: Westview, 1995), 66.

[7]Hans D. Jarass/Bodo Pieroth, *Grundgesetz für die Bundesrepublik Deutschland Kommentar* (München: C.H. Beck, 1992), 626–631.

[8]"Die Verfassungskommission sonnt sich in ersten Erfolgen," *Stuttgarter Zeitung*, 2. Juli 1992.

[9]Renate Hellwig, "Die Europa-Institutionen des Bundestags und seine großen Europa-Initiativen," in *Der Deutsche Bundestag und Europa* (Bonn: Aktuell, 1993), 46.

Christian Democrats (CDU), dismissed the SPD charge that Kohl had succumbed at Maastricht. He then asked if Germans should reject the results of the Maastricht European Council only because any one country could not succeed in its position 100% of the time.[10]

Early in the ratification process it was clear that all major political parties except the Party of Democratic Socialism (PDS) supported the Treaty despite a lack of democratic control over the Council of Ministers owing to a failure to transfer adequate powers to the European Parliament. Yet, mounting public concern over the loss of the D-mark, articulated in popular newspapers like *Bild* and reflected in public opinion polls, shifted the debate to EMU. At the popular level serious concerns were expressed about the stability of a single currency.[11] Individuals representing banking interests in Bonn argued that lasting damage could be caused to the Community's image at home if the popular impression were strengthened that Maastricht was designed to weaken German stability.[12]

By mid-March the chairman of the opposition SPD, Minister-President Björn Engholm, spoke out in favor of ratifying the Treaty. He denied that his party intended to use its majority in the Bundesrat to stall ratification.[13] Engholm also made several suggestions meant to improve provisions on EMU and political union. As he explained, the fact that the SPD denounced the "disequilibrium between EMU and political union" revealed that this disequilibrium was less of a "German problem than a democratic problem."[14] The SPD also insisted on the right to vote prior to the final transition from Stage Two to Stage Three of EMU. Moreover, the SPD wanted the structure of the Community to correspond to the democratic principles outlined in Article 20 BL by strengthening the powers of the European Parliament.

Improvements were also necessary in the area of social policy in order to achieve a citizen's Europe. The other issue that dominated the domestic agenda during the ratification debate, in terms of the political parties and public opinion, was asylum policy. Engholm explained how Article 16 BL, the most liberal asylum law in Europe, touched at the heart of the German people. This was in part because of German history and of popular awareness of the need to protect political refugees fleeing from dictatorial policies in their native lands.[15] Still German politicians did not have the luxury of debating

---

[10]Ibid., 47.

[11]Rita Beuter, "Germany and the Ratification of the Maastricht Treaty," in *The Ratification of the Maastricht Treaty*, 92–93.

[12]Interview, Wolfgang Neumann, German Association of Savings Banks, 30 April 1993.

[13]"Genscher Urges Germans to Back European Unity," *The Wall Street Journal Europe*, March 10, 1992, 8.

[14]Agence Europe, 11 mars 1992, 3.

[15]"Das Thema geht ans Herz," *Der Spiegel*, (49/1992): 32–35.

asylum policy. In a rapidly evolving socio-economic context, millions of refugees were entering Germany. This was true less for reasons of political exigency and more in the hope of finding steady work and to receive social benefits from the German state.

Engholm's remarks were made around the same time as a speech by Hans-Dietrich Genscher. He expressed alarm at German skepticism about the benefits of European integration. Genscher also feared a resurgence of nationalism in the Federal Republic. "As the motor for European unity we have gained the respect of the peoples of Europe. As European loiterers we would gamble it away," he said. "History does not repeat its offers. Only in Europe do we have a future."[16] Former economics minister Otto Graf Lambsdorff , the leader of the FDP, voiced his satisfaction that Kohl had emphasized that there would be no automaticity on the road to EMU. Lambsdorff was equally concerned about certain provisions of the Treaty, like the Article on European industrial policy. Despite his reservations about other aspects of Maastricht, Lambsdorff supported the CDU-CSU/FDP coalition policy that ruled out a renegotiation of the Treaty.[17]

On 17 May, Hans-Dietrich Genscher stepped down as foreign minister. Genscher was noted for his emphasis on an eastern policy by which a unified Germany would push strongly for enlargement negotiations to broaden the European Union after the ratification of Maastricht.[18] His successor, FDP colleague Klaus Kinkel, was a former justice minister with a solid background in the administrative civil service.[19] One of Kinkel's first actions was to visit Paris for talks with his counterpart Roland Dumas and Prime Minister Pierre Bérégovoy. Kinkel's goal was to affirm the priority of Franco-German relations in his country's European policy prior to the 59th Franco-German summit at La Rochelle on 21–22 May.[20] One result of these talks was the

---

[16]Philip Sherwell, "German Swing against the EC Alarms Bonn," *The Daily Telegraph*, March 10, 1992, 6.

[17]"Lambsdorff: Verbesserungen der Maastrichter Verträge erforderlich," *Handelsblatt*, 13. März 1992, 3.

[18]Daniel Vernet, "Les tâches de la diplomatie allemande," *Le Monde,* 2 mai 1992.

[19]Genscher's original choice of a successor as foreign minister was Irmgard Adam-Schwaetzer, Seiler-Albring's predecessor as Parliamentary State Minister for European affairs in the *Auswärtiges Amt.* However, Adam-Schwaetzer, who was at that time Minister of Construction and Urban Planning, did not receive the support of influential members within the Liberal party.

[20]"Le ministre allemand des affaires étrangères réaffirme la priorité des relations avec la France," *Le Monde* , 20 mai 1992, 4.

announcement of the plan for a Franco-German "Eurocorps," an army unit of 35,000–40,000 troops that would serve as the nucleus of a European army. The "Eurocorps" would equip the European Union with a tool for military actions. In case of conflict, its troops would be placed under NATO command.

Kinkel was barely in office a few weeks when the Danes rejected Maastricht on 2 June. Some German officials explained the Danish popular reaction as a citizen's rebellion against the French idea of a centralized Europe. The European Commission bureaucracy at the center reminded Danes of a feudal structure.[21] The German press reaction confirmed this interpretation. In an edition of *Der Spiegel*, its editor, Rudolf Augstein, wrote "We do not want France's Europe." Augstein made reference to the need to think about the lack of democracy in the Community. The Danish referendum illustrated that different views of democracy prevail in Germany and France.

Kohl reacted to the Danish referendum by urging his own countrymen to fight nationalism with unity in Europe. The Chancellor and the SPD were alarmed by rightist party gains in local and state elections.[22] The surge of attacks on foreign immigrants by neo-Nazis, known as Republicans, created a grave situation. The failure of the political establishment to control the influx of refugees, and the growing view that Kohl sold the D-mark for federalism Brussels style, gave the Republicans and their leader, Franz Schönhuber, renewed ambitions.[23] The Kohl government realized that it was essential to inform citizens about Europe and to address the "communication deficit" as one way of fighting the appeal made to the German youth by extremist political parties.[24]

After the Danish vote, Kinkel, and the rest of the Kohl government, were also anxious to calm the SPD's fears about Maastricht. The Social Democrats' demand that the Bundestag should vote on EMU in 1996, before any decision is made on whether it should start in 1997, remained a sensitive issue. This vote would not be legally binding; the government would merely "take it into account." "This is nothing like Britain's opt-out on EMU," said Heidemarie Wieczorek-Zeul. "We're all for the transfer of sovereignty, we just want a

---

[21] Interview, Prof. Dr. Martin Seidel, Federal Ministry of Economics, 2 March 1993.

[22] "Fight Nationalism With Swift Unity, Kohl Tells Europe," *International Herald Tribune*, June 8, 1992, 5.

[23] Ian Murray, "German Right Beats Drum against Rule by Eurocrats," *The Times*, June 15, 1992.

[24] Henri de Bresson, "Le chancelier Kohl passe à l'offensive pour défendre le traité de Maastricht," *Le Monde*, 17 juin 1992, 8.

democratic debate before it happens."[25]

Public opinion polls taken in Germany revealed much less support for the Community than the European Commission's Eurobarometer polls done twice yearly since 1973. National opinion surveys indicated three dominant viewpoints. First, the majority of Germans had doubts about the stability of a future European currency. Second, the German people wanted a Community open to the countries of central and eastern Europe. And third, in terms of the democratic deficit, an overwhelming majority wanted to retain national powers in Community decision making. Only 10 percent of the Germans wanted the European Parliament to have absolute influence in decisions in all areas of European policy making.[26] This popular sentiment, coupled with a statement by 62 German economists attacking the Treaty published in *Die Welt* and the *Frankfurter Allgemeine Zeitung*, was impossible for Kohl or his government to ignore.[27] In response, both finance minister Waigel and economics minister Möllemann confirmed the German government's insistence on the fulfillment of strict convergence criteria as a condition for entry into Stage Three of EMU.[28]

The final phase of the Bundestag ratification debate began during the third week in September. The slim margin of French approval for the Treaty made the German government more determined to conclude the ratification by the end of 1992.[29] Kohl consulted with Mitterrand in Paris two days after the French vote in an attempt to keep the momentum for the integration process going.[30] This task was complicated by Mitterrand's bout with prostrate cancer, Denmark's intentions to push for significant changes to the Treaty prior to a

---

[25]"We are not emused," *The Economist*, June 6, 1991, 32. The SPD's demands are stated in Deutscher Bundestag, 12. Wahlperiode, Antrag der Fraktion der SPD, Perspektiven der europäischen Integration, Drucksache 12/2813, 16.06.92, 1–3.

[26]Elisabeth Noelle-Neumann, "Die Deutschen beginnen sich zu fürchten," *Frankfurter Allgemeine Zeitung*, 23. Juni 1992, 11.

[27]"Economists Attack 'Soft' Criteria," *The Guardian*, June 12, 1992.

[28]"Waigel: Verwässerung der Kriterien wird Deutschland nicht zulassen," *Handelsblatt*, 12. Juni 1992, 1; Jürgen W. Möllemann, "Von Maastricht zum vereinten Europa," *Frankfurter Allgemeine Zeitung*, 15. Juli 1992.

[29]"Zustimmung zum Vertrag von Maastricht," *Bulletin*, 22. September 1992, 929.

[30]William Drozdiak, "Bonn and Paris in Urgent Talks but Silent on What Was Said," *International Herald Tribune*, September 23, 1992, 1 & 5.

second referendum, [31] and turmoil on the European currency markets. Both the English pound and the Italian lira were forced to drop out of the European Monetary System the week before. [32]

Chancellor Kohl spoke about the Maastricht ratification before a plenary session of the Bundestag on 25 September. In his references to the importance of a democratic and open Community close to citizens, Kohl emphasized the need to cut back the excessive way and frenzied pace of making European legislation. However, the Chancellor also honestly admitted that the Community's present crisis was not only the fault of the administration in Brussels but of national governments as well. In other words, the member states should learn from the Maastricht experience and take responsibility for their actions in the future by not pushing awkward issues toward Brussels. Kohl also passionately defended the EMS. In addition to an expression of support for the Bundesbank, the Chancellor affirmed his conviction that there was no need to change the parity relationship between the French franc and the German mark. [33]

Kohl's support of the Bundesbank's high interest rates did not help Germany's relations with Britain. Amidst speculation on the emergence of a two-speed Europe, with France, Germany and BENELUX comprising an "inner core," Kohl was prepared to work with Mitterrand and Major to get the Twelve back on track during a special European Council in Birmingham. [34]

On 8 October the Bundestag had its first reading of the Maastricht Treaty. The debate confirmed the favorable impression left by the debate on European affairs on 25 September. There was a wide majority in the Bundestag in favor of the Treaty. Only the PDS, former East German Communists who held 17 seats, opposed Maastricht. A broad majority wanted a statement made to counter public skepticism by clarifying the Treaty in some respects. During an eight-hour debate, parliamentarians from all parties expressed their concern about the loss already suffered by national parliaments in EC decision making,

---

[31]Tom Redburn, "Denmark to Push for Changes in European Treaty," *International Herald Tribune*, September 23, 1992, 1.

[32]The turbulence on the European financial markets took place on 16 September 1992. This was the same day that the Bosch Fellows were meeting with Chancellor Kohl. The Chancellor was called away from our discussion to speak on the telephone with Prime Minister John Major about the EMS crisis.

[33]Deutscher Bundestag, 12. Wahlperiode, 108. Sitzung, Bonn, Freitag, den 25. September 1992, 9219–9221.

[34]The Conclusions of the ECOFIN Council of 28 September 1992 reaffirmed the Community's goal to proceed toward EMU together. William Drozdiak, "5 'Inner Core' Nations in EC May Act Faster on Integration," *International Herald Tribune*, September 26–27, 1992, 1 & 5.

the lack of transparent decision making in the new structure of the Union and the lack of information available to the public.[35]

The PDS was the only party in the Bundestag that called for a referendum on the Treaty. Its chairman, Gregor Gysi, explained this opposition in terms of a fear that Maastricht would strengthen German predominance in Europe. In his view, nationalist parties, like the Republicans, wanted a dominant German role in Europe but were apprehensive nonetheless about further losses of German sovereignty to the Union's institutions. This apprehension could be used to play on popular sentiment which did not make it possible for the PDS to consent to Treaty ratification.[36]

Apart from the PDS, all parties rejected a renegotiation of Maastricht. Instead, improvements to allay the public's concern and to strengthen democratic control in the Union were called for. The Kohl government assured the Bundestag a say in the transition to Stage Three of EMU. Although Lambsdorff said a Bundestag vote must be binding for the government, Waigel and others said there could be no second ratification. There was a consensus among all political parties that the Bundestag should take the final decision on EMU. While Kinkel said that the decisions on Stage Three will be referred to the Bundestag for it to "deal with," Lambsdorff stated: "The words 'deal with' should be deleted. Either we have something to say or we have hardly anything to say. What should we "deal with?" Then we might as well take a coffee break." This statement was greeted by applause from FDP, CDU/CSU and SPD parliamentarians. Ingrid Matthäus-Maier, a member of the SPD, interrupted Lambsdorff to say: "Tell that to your government."[37] Lambsdorff pointed out that his FDP colleague, Kinkel, had stated in the Bundestag that he could not imagine a government agreeing to enter Stage Three if there was no parliamentary majority behind this decision.

---

[35]The Federal Press Office started its 20 million DM campaign to inform the public soon after. In Bonn tents were set up near the Rhine under which brochures were available about the European Union. Cuntz took me there one evening after work in the *Auswärtiges Amt*. The campaign was thoroughly prepared but started very late in the ratification process. This was done in part to save money. Interview, German Permanent Representation to the European Communities, 11 June 1993.

[36]Deutscher Bundestag, 12. Wahlperiode, 110. Sitzung, Bonn, Donnerstag, den 8. Oktober 1992, 9339–9340.

[37]The SPD's demand for a political decision by the Bundestag and the Bundesrat on entry into Stage Three of EMU is included in Deutscher Bundestag, 12. Wahlperiode, Entschließungsantrag der Fraktion der SPD, Drucksache 12/3311, 24.09.92, 2.

Heidemarie Wieczorek-Zeul then interjected: "That will also no longer be his government."[38]

Lambsdorff was also skeptical about a European currency and the EMU timetable, adding that subsidiarity is foreign to centralist countries like France and the United Kingdom. Kinkel explained that the Bonn government was making efforts regarding a binding appendix to the Treaty, in which EC responsibilities would be spelled out and Community decisions made clearer. He stated that the Community was better than any other institution to stop xenophobia and nationalism. Kinkel also explained that the Treaty opens the way for the CFSP and that joint action in defense must be added to joint action in foreign policy. Waigel said there would be no compromise regarding the stability requirements for EMU.[39] The DM would not be removed by EMU; it should live on as the "Euro-Mark." Kohl made a pledge to the new Länder that he would try to gain an extra 18 seats to represent them in the European Parliament after the European elections in June 1994. For its part, the Bundestag was contemplating the establishment of a strong Committee on the European Union (*Europaausschuß*), comprising prominent politicians, to replace its weaker committee on European affairs, the *EG-Ausschuß*.[40]

At its meeting on 14 October, the *EG-Ausschuß* supported the European Parliament's demands to reject any institutionalization of a Congress of Parliaments. Instead the *EG-Ausschuß* called for a strengthening of the EP's powers so that it could exercise effective parliamentary control. The *EG-Ausschuß* welcomed Parliament's intentions to strengthen cooperation with

---

[38]Deutscher Bundestag, 12. Wahlperiode, 110. Sitzung, Bonn, Donnerstag, den 8. Oktober 1992, 9337–9338.

[39]"Der Bundestag sagt trotz Bedenken ja zu Maastricht," *General- Anzeiger*, 9. Oktober 1992, 1.

[40]The Committee on European Affairs (*EG-Ausschuß*) was established in 1991. Some of its main tasks were to consider and debate further institutional developments in the European Community and to exercise national parliamentary control over European legislation. The implementation of the Maastricht Treaty on 1 November 1993 saw the creation of a Committee on the European Union (*Europaausschuß*). For the first time, it was possible to speak of a national parliamentary control of the German government negotiating European legislation in the Council of Ministers. A third *ad hoc* Committee on the European Union (Maastricht Treaty) was created for two months to avoid strife among the different committees responsible for policy issues discussed during the Maastricht ratification. Eberhard Schoof, *EG-Ausschuß* (Bonn: Deutscher Bundestag, 1993); Renate Hellwig, "Die Europa-Institutionen des Bundestages und seine großen Europa-Initiativen," 21–32.

national parliaments, outlined in the Cravinho Report,[41] but rejected any attempts to weaken or replace the EP's competencies in European legislation by national authorities.[42]

There were also differences of view among the political parties in the *EG-Ausschuß* about the SPD's demand for a vote on entry into Stage Three.[43] The CDU/CSU Fraktion was against a parliamentary reservation on this issue. Civil servants from the *Auswärtiges Amt*, in attendance during the session, were also cognizant of the fact that a parliamentary reservation went against Protocol 10 TEU on the irreversibility of the transition to Stage Three.[44]

Two days later, the special European Council in Birmingham took place. The heads of state and government discussed the subsidiarity principle. An attempt was made to ensure that the Community would only take action on those policies that could not be dealt with better at the national level. The European Council wanted to address the widespread public perception that the EC was undemocratic owing to excessive bureaucratic interference by European civil servants in national policy making. However, many officials, including Delors, feared that subsidiarity could weaken the Community at a critical stage in its development. In an address before the European Parliament just prior to Birmingham, President Delors said that the concept of subsidiarity, if not formulated carefully, "would lead to a paralysis of the institutions." It could revive the widespread use of national vetoes which stifled the EC twenty five years before in the wake of the Luxembourg Compromise. "The exercise of subsidiarity cannot be used to undermine the process of Community integration....Subsidiarity is a minefield. All kinds of ulterior motives are in place," Delors stated.[45]

The period from mid-October to the end of November included a series of meetings of the *Sonderausschuß "Europäische Union,"* the *ad hoc* Committee established to deal with the Maastricht ratification. At each meeting, different provisions of the Treaty were debated. The Chancellor, ministers or civil servants from five ministries, and the Bundesbank President were all present on different occasions depending on the provisions under discussion.

---

[41]This report was submitted to the European Parliament by a member of its Institutional Affairs Committee, João Cravinho.

[42]Interview, Renate Hellwig, *EG-Ausschuß*, 29 April 1993.

[43]The SPD's demand was made in its motion, dated 16 June 1992, on Perspectives in European Integration, Drucksache 12/2813, 2 which is cited in Note 25.

[44]Interview, *Auswärtiges Amt*, 29 January 1993.

[45]Charles Goldsmith and Martin Du Bois, "Delors Warns That Efforts to Rein in Reach of European Community Threaten Paralysis," *The Wall Street Journal Europe*, October 15, 1992.

On 2 December the Bundestag voted to ratify the Treaty on European Union by an overwhelming majority. The final result was 543 votes in favor of Maastricht, 17 votes against and 8 abstentions. There was almost the same outcome of 547 for, 16 against and 6 abstaining the resolution by the CDU/CSU, SPD and FDP on the draft law put forward by the government concerning the Treaty.[46]

The parliamentary debate that preceded the vote to ratify Maastricht illustrated once again the obvious concerns of all German political parties about the lack of progress on political union in view of the ambitious agenda for EMU. The first speaker for the SPD-Opposition, Heidemarie Wieczorek-Zeul, spoke of "the need for European integration as an anchor for Germany's political stability."[47] This was one of the main reasons that the SPD voted for the Treaty. Nonetheless, she described Maastricht as "very short on democracy."[48] On EMU, she reiterated the SPD's position, supported by the CSU, in favor of a parliamentary reserve regarding the entry into Stage Three. The difference between this position and that of members of the CDU was clear. The SPD, as well as the CSU, the FDP and the Greens, wanted a vote on Germany's entry into the final phase of EMU whereas for the CDU a simple "consideration" of the issue was sufficient.

In his speech before the Bundestag, Waigel clarified that prior to the government's decision on entry into Stage Three, a consenting vote on the part of the Bundestag and the Bundesrat would be necessary. Waigel emphasized that this was not meant to be a second ratification. The Bonn government's procedural proposal for the vote would be explained to Germany's Community partners by the German finance minister in order to foster a sense of clarity and trust on this issue among the Twelve.[49]

Kinkel stated that the Bundestag's vote would be "a clear signal to the other member states that we take German unification seriously, and that we want no return to the bad old days of nationalism, struggles for hegemony and

---

[46]The results of the votes on the Treaty and the CDU/CSU, SPD and FDP resolution are found in Deutscher Bundestag, Stenographischer Bericht, 12. Wahlperiode, 126. Sitzung, Bonn, Mittwoch, den 2. Dezember 1992, 10879–10884. The resolution is printed as Deutscher Bundestag, 12.Wahlperiode, Entschließungsantrag der Fraktionen der CDU/CSU, SPD und FDP zu dem Gesetzentwurf der Bundesregierung, Drucksache 12/3905, 02.12.92, 1–4.

[47]Ibid., 10813.

[48]Stephen Kinzer, "German Parliament Ratifies European Union Pact," *New York Times*, December 3, 1992.

[49]Deutscher Bundestag, Stenographischer Bericht, 12. Wahlperiode, 126. Sitzung, Bonn, Mittwoch, den 2. Dezember 1992, 10842.

balance of power politics." In a clear reference to Monnet's *Mémoires*, Kinkel explained that "people do not listen willingly to new ideas as long as they have the hope that things can remain the same." "But things do not remain the same and the Maastricht Treaty is the draft for the new situation, the correlate of German unity for the continuation of a policy of peace in Europe and in the world," Kinkel stated.[50]

During his address, Chancellor Kohl presented the Maastricht Treaty as a good and sound compromise made by the European Council a year earlier. Kohl also admitted that in certain respects, he wished the compromise had been struck quite differently. He was thankful though that the European Council achieved an outcome which laid the foundation for further developments in the integration process. In addition, Kohl mentioned that although the Germans could not achieve a breakthrough on strengthening the powers of the European Parliament, he believed that the present institutional state of affairs could not remain. A change was on the agenda of the 1996 Revision Conference. Moreover, the Chancellor asserted that "Europe *à la carte*, in which each partner chooses what he particularly likes about Europe, can be no more our goal than a Europe which has to move at the pace of the slowest ship in the convoy."[51]

Gerd Poppe, a former anti-Communist dissident in East Germany and member of the Alliance 90/Greens who voted against the Treaty, summed up the feelings of the small number of parliamentarians harboring anti-Maastricht sentiment: "We have awoken from our dream of Europe and have been given Maastricht."[52]

The Bundesrat Ratification

Just weeks after the Treaty on European Union was signed in Maastricht, on 7 February 1992, the Länder began to express dissatisfaction with the Treaty's content. Minister Wolfgang Clement, the head of the State Chancellery in North-Rhine Westphalia, spoke out in favor of changes to the Treaty text. Clement explained that the 16 Länder all agreed that a qualitative leap to EMU should only be risked on the basis of a stable political union. His criticisms were clearly directed at the agreed timetable for EMU. Other Treaty provisions which were questionable included the establishment of a "cohesion

---

[50]Rede des Bundesministers des Auswärtigen, Dr. Klaus Kinkel, bei der 2./3. Lesung des Vertrages über die Europäische Union und der damit verbundenen Gesetzentwürf im Deutschen Bundestag am 02. Dezember 1992, Mitteilung für die Presse Nr. 1192/92 (Bonn: Auswärtiges Amt, 1992), 3 & 11.

[51]Deutscher Bundestag, Stenographischer Bericht, 12. Wahlperiode, 126. Sitzung, Bonn, Mittwoch, den 2. Dezember 1992, 10823–10831.

[52]Ibid., 10822.

fund" for poorer Community member states, given the amount of money required to develop the new Länder and countries to the East, and the lack of control by the European Parliament over the Council of Ministers in the CFSP and home and justice affairs. Clement stated that the Länder saw "a link between the Treaty ratification and a substantial development of federal-state relations in European Community affairs including corresponding changes in the Basic Law."[53]

By mid-March German analysts and officials were confident that the ratification would remain on track. "There is a lot of noise and politics but, when it comes to the final vote, no political party wants to draw the wrath of Europe by blocking the treaties," explained Rüdiger Soltwedel, an economist at the Kiel Institute of World Economics. "There is an element of poker here and everyone wants to highlight their needs once more to get minor changes, but it is highly unlikely the treaties will be voted down," said another official in the *Auswärtiges Amt*.[54] A conference of the minister-presidents of the Länder on 12 March resulted in a decision of general support for the Treaty despite the fact that its provisions did not fully meet their expectations.

On 18 May Kohl and the minister-presidents agreed on an amendment to the Basic Law which would guarantee Länder rights in a united Europe. This accord was an important one to address Länder concerns about Maastricht.[55] As former Minister-President of Rhineland-Palatinate, Kohl understood the Länder position. He explained their interests to his European counterparts.

The approval of Article 23 BL by 59 of the 64 members of the Constitutional Committee in late June was a great success for the Länder. Under the new Article 23 BL, the basic principles of the Federal Constitution have to be preserved when transferring German sovereign rights to the EC.[56] Both the Bundestag and the Bundesrat have to give their consent (2/3 majority) if a transfer of sovereign rights has an impact on the Constitution. Thus, the federal government has to obtain the approval of the Bundesrat in areas where the Länder have exclusive competence. This is of particular importance for the new Länder where difficult economic and social conditions

---

[53]"NRW: Nachverhandlungen und Nachbesserungen," *Handelsblatt*, 25. Februar 1992, 3; "Unzufrieden mit den Ergebnissen von Maastricht," *Frankfurter Allgemeine Zeitung*, 13. März 1992, 15.

[54]Richard E. Smith, "Backing for Treaties Expected from States," *International Herald Tribune*, March 14, 1992.

[55]Agence Europe, 18 et 19 mai 1992, 3.

[56]"Seiters legt Maastricht-Artikel vor," *Frankfurter Allgemeine Zeitung*, 21. Juli 1992.

influence the level of support for European integration.[57] Essentially a distinction is made here between Community affairs, in which the Länder have a right to speak if their areas of national competence are involved (23 BL) and classical intergovernmental cooperation in which only the federal government may transfer sovereign powers to international institutions for reasons of collective security (24 BL).[58]

Furthermore, Article 23 (6) BL allows a Länder representative with ministerial rank to replace the representative of the federal government in Council negotiations if the issues discussed fall within the sole competence of the Länder, as stipulated in Article 146 TEU. This is true in culture, education and health policy.[59] The overall responsibility of the federation is not in question, however. It retains the sole right of representation in the Council on foreign policy.

On 21 July the Kohl government passed two bills The first, regarding the ratification of the Maastricht Treaty on the creation of a European Union, was then forwarded to the Bundesrat.[60] The second bill was on the constitutional changes brought about by the Maastricht ratification including Article 23 BL on federal-state relations in European Union affairs. Chancellor Kohl described the Maastricht ratification process as "the most important project of this legislative session." The Bavarian State Minister for European affairs, Thomas Goppel (CSU), argued that the compromise on the Länder participation in the making of Community legislation, as stated in Article 23 BL, should not be watered down. Goppel's task was to maintain contacts with members of the federal government during the ratification process. "Article 23 BL must pass in the Bundestag as it was passed in the Cabinet; only then can the Länder endorse the Maastricht Treaty," he explained.[61] Shortly after, the State Secretary for European affairs in Bavaria, Paul Wilhelm, wrote that the new Article 23 BL "will strengthen democracy and federalism in Germany and in Europe." As he explained, the need for a 2/3, and not merely a simple, majority in the Bundesrat and Bundestag to transfer sovereign competencies to the Union institutions is necessary to ensure the democratic nature of the integration process.

---

[57]Barbara Lippert, Dirk Günther and Stephen Woolcock, *The EC and the New German Länder: A Short-Lived Success Story?* (London: Anglo-German Foundation, 1993).

[58]Interview, Sabine Ehmke-Gendron, German Permanent Representation to the European Communities, 18 May 1992.

[59]Beuter, "Germany and the Ratification of the Maastricht Treaty, " 91.

[60]Agence Europe, 23 juillet 1992, 5.

[61]"Gesetzentwurf zu Maastricht vorgelegt Ratifizierungsverfahren eingeleitet," *Frankfurter Allgemeine Zeitung*, 22. Juli 1992, 4.

Wilhelm further clarified to the citizens in Bavaria why the European Community is good for the Federal Republic. Starting from the premise that the Maastricht Treaty allows a good deal of room to create a Union close to citizens via the subsidiarity principle, a Europe of Regions and greater democratic control at the national level, he also cited three good reasons for Europe. First, only through integration in Europe can many problems, such as environmental pollution, be solved. Second, only in Europe does Germany, an export-oriented economy, remain strong. And third only the Community offers the Federal Republic, the country geographically situated with the most neighbors in Europe, the opportunity to live in peace.[62]

The ratification entered its most decisive phase on 25 September with the first reading of the bill on changes to the Basic Law and the bill on the Treaty on European Union in the Bundesrat.[63] Two days before, the Kohl Cabinet had passed a draft of a near final version of Article 23 BL. During the Bundesrat debate the Minister-President of Bavaria, Edmund Stoiber, stated clearly that the entry into Stage Three should not be automatic; instead it would be dependent on the political will of national decision makers. If in 1996, 1997 or 1998, the Bundesrat and the Bundestag should decide by a majority vote that in their opinion the conditions for EMU were not fulfilled politically, then the enforcement of the Treaty could not take place.[64] In comparison to EMU, the Bundesrat deplored the fact that the progress on political union was too slim.

State Minister Seiler-Albring addressed the Länder during the debate. She recalled the constructive cooperation between the federal government and the Länder during the negotiations on political union, particularly with regard to the German memorandum on subsidiarity. Seiler-Albring also maintained that on the issue of the timetable for entry into Stage Three of EMU, a formal "parliamentary reservation" would not be in the interests of Germany or its European partners. She explained that, on an issue of such great importance for the German people, the federal government would seek to secure parliamentary approval of its course of action prior to any decision on Stage Three.[65]

---

[62]Paul Wilhelm, MdL, *Drei gute Gründe für Europa*, 76/07.12.1992 (Bonn: Euro Aktuell, 1992), 1–5.

[63]This was just a few days before the beginning of my tenure as a Bosch Fellow assisting Eckart Cuntz with the work on the Maastricht ratification in the *Auswärtiges Amt*.

[64]Bundesrat, Stenographischer Bericht, 646. Sitzung, Bonn, Freitag, den 25. September 1992, 426.

[65]Ibid., 436–438.

On 7 October the EC Committee of the Bundesrat[66] discussed the bill on the proposed Article 23 BL and made several suggestions for a plenary sitting of the Bundesrat with members of the federal government on 16 October. These suggestions included a stronger consideration of federal-state relations if projects in the area of competing legislation involve the Länder and the introduction of an assent requirement on the part of the Bundesrat for projects in the context of Article 235 of the EEC Treaty, [67] as well as the confirmation that the federal government would inform and involve the Länder in intergovernmental conferences and enlargement negotiations and the revalorization of the Länder offices in Brussels. This last measure was suggested in order to assign these offices the same diplomatic status as the German Permanent Representation (COREPER) in the eyes of the European Community institutions and the Belgian state.[68]

At the plenary session on 16 October, the federal government maintained its previous position concerning the Länder's rights. The federal government's remarks at the session, made by Parliamentary State Secretary Riedl of the ministry of economics, were criticized by the Bundesrat whose members thought that the federal government did not take Länder concerns sufficiently into account. One of the main Länder concerns was a right of assent on decisions taken unanimously by the Council of Ministers under Article 235

---

[66]"The Minister-Presidents of the Länder agreed to a "Special Committee Common Market and Free Trade Zone" in the Bundesrat which was established on 20 December 1957. In 1965 this committee was given its present name (*Ausschuß für Fragen der Europäischen Gemeinschaft*, or EC Committee) and became a permanent committee (*Ständiger Ausschuß*)." As cited in Wolfgang R. Stock, *The impact of the federal provisions in the Basic Law on the political discretion of the West German Government in the decision-making of the European Community*, D. Phil. thesis (Oxford: University College, 1990), 100.

[67]Article 235 EEC states "If action by the Community should prove necessary to attain, in the course of the operation of the common market, one of the objectives of the Community and this Treaty has not provided the necessary powers, the Council shall, acting unanimously on a proposal from the Commission and after consulting the European Parliament, take the appropriate measures." In the Treaty on European Union, this Article remained unchanged, but the name of the Treaty was amended to the Treaty establishing the European Community. As cited in *The New Treaty on European Union*, 402.

[68]Bundesrat, "Empfehlungen der Ausschüsse zum Entwurf eines Gesetzes über die Zusammenarbeit von Bund und Ländern in Angelegenheiten der europäischen Union," Drucksache 630/1/92, 08.10.92, Punkt 5 der 647. Sitzung des Bundesrates am 16. Oktober 1992, 1–16.

EEC. The federal government was of the opinion that only "fundamental" changes to the original Treaties, as amended through IGC diplomacy, required the assent of the Bundesrat and the Bundestag.[69] A particularly important point for the ministry of economics was that the Bundesrat should not have the last word on projects in areas of competing legislation involving the Länder, for example, decisions on industrial, structural or technology policy.

The federal ministry of economics (*Bundesministerium für Wirtschaft*) was the *federführend* ministry in charge of the bill on Article 23 BL due to its overall responsibility for federal-state relations.[70] In spite of this fact, it was obvious to Seiler-Albring and Cuntz during the session that the members of the Bundesrat repeatedly referred to State Minister Seiler-Albring as the representative of the federal government instead of State Secretary Erich Riedl. This indicated a confusion on the Länders' part as to the federal ministry in charge of the proceedings. This was just one example among many of the complexity of the process to ratify the Treaty.[71]

A few days later the *Verfassungskommission* finished its work on the changes to the Basic Law. The decisions taken in connection with EC affairs envisaged the amendment of Articles 50 and 52 BL relating to the participation of the Bundesrat in European Union affairs.[72] According to Article 52, the Bundesrat could establish a European Chamber whose decisions would count as the decisions of the Bundesrat. The ministers of the Länder would normally make up the European Chamber although this would depend on a given agenda and the ministers' availability. In contrast to the Bundesrat, it would be a more flexible instrument, able to meet at short notice and in secrecy.[73]

---

[69]Deutscher Bundestag, 12. Wahlperiode, "Gesetzentwurf der Bundesregierung, Entwurf eines Gesetzes zur Änderung des Grundgesetzes," Drucksache 12/3338, 02.10.92, Anlage 3, Gegenäußerung der Bundesregierung zur Stellungnahme des Bundesrates, 14.

[70]An account of earlier negotiations between the federal government and the Länder on the Länders' direct participation in EC matters written by the official in the economics ministry who led the negotiations for the federal government is Rudolf Morawitz, *Die Zusammenarbeit von Bund und Ländern bei Vorhaben der europäischen Gemeinschaft* (Bonn: Europa Union, 1981).

[71]This observation is based on my presence during the session with members of the delegation from the *Auswärtiges Amt*. Department EB7 in the ministry of economics is responsible for federal-state (Bund-Länder) relations on behalf of the federal government. Refer to Chapter III, Note 75.

[72]"Kommission beschließt die neuen Europa-Artikel," *Handelsblatt*, 19. Oktober 1992, 6.

[73]Beuter, "Germany and the Ratification of the Maastricht Treaty," 92.

By mid-November reports of tensions between the Bundesrat and the Bundestag over Article 23 BL appeared in the German press. The acting chairperson of the *Sonderausschuß "Europäische Union,"* Renate Hellwig (CDU), made critical remarks directed at the bill defining the future cooperation between the federal government and the Länder in European Union affairs. Hellwig feared that a constitutional quarrel would be pre-programmed if the Bundesrat was awarded the right to have its position taken decisively in consideration by the federal government during Council negotiations with significant consequences for existing Länder administrative procedures, even though the European legislation negotiated did not require Länder consent at the national level. If the new Article 23 BL should pass, without any further changes, the Länder would obtain, also in matters of exclusive federal competence, an excessive influence on European legislation. This would shift the division of competencies, as stated in the Basic Law, practically from the Bundestag to the Bundesrat and could mark the beginning of a disintegration process in Germany from a federation to a confederation, according to Hellwig.[74]

Goppel responded to Hellwig's criticisms by stating that the Länder should only have the last word in exclusive federal competencies if the European Community or the federal government interfered in the rights of the Länder as defined in the Basic Law. "As long as the Community and the federal government do not enact any administrative regulations and leave these to the Länder, respecting the subsidiarity principle, as the law states, then the Länder are not concerned," Goppel remarked. He also criticized Hellwig's comparison of the Bundesrat and the Bundestag as "inadmissible." "The Grundgesetz envisages the Bundesrat as a support for the federal government whereas the Bundestag is a means of parliamentary control," he explained. Goppel also insisted that in order to obtain the Länder consent to Maastricht, the federal government had to agree to give the Bundesrat the right of assent in negotiations to broaden the competencies of the European Union under Article 235 of the Treaty.[75]

In the weeks prior to the Bundesrat's vote, the Kohl government was preparing for a difficult European Council in Edinburgh on 11–12 December. The Danish dilemma was one of several trying issues on the agenda.[76] Other agenda items were all essential to German domestic interests: increasing the membership of the European Parliament from 81 to 99; locating the ECB in

---

[74]"Kontroverse um den neuen Europa-Artikel im Grundgesetz," *Frankfurter Allgemeine Zeitung,* 11. November 1992, 2.

[75]Ibid.

[76]Lionel Barber and Hilary Barnes, "Legalistic Acrobatics Rescue Denmark," *Financial Times,* December 14, 1992; Finn Laursen, "Denmark and the Ratification of the Maastricht Treaty," in *The Ratification of the Maastricht Treaty,* 71–73.

Frankfurt as part of a package deal on the sites of European institutions; and forging a compromise on budgetary questions in the context of the Delors II package. Shortly before Edinburgh, Kinkel expressed his concerns that the Kohl government had gone too far in obliging the Länder's demands for a right to speak in matters of European policy, particularly those with foreign policy dimensions, in exchange for the ratification of Maastricht. The Länders' view that European issues dealt with "internal" policy placed the foreign minister in an "unlucky" situation in which domestic and foreign policy are increasingly difficult to separate.[77]

On 18 December, the Bundesrat unanimously voted to ratify the Maastricht Treaty.[78] Minister-President Max Streibl of Bavaria was the first politician to speak. He emphasized many of the Länders' aspirations and concerns. In his view, it was necessary to counter public skepticism regarding the evolution of European integration. In this context, previous mistakes had to be taken in earnest: a lack of effective parliamentary control; complicated decision-making procedures unfathomable to citizens and policy-making results that were largely misunderstood. However, the Germans needed Europe to deal with pressing global problems, and Maastricht was a means to an end. However, the Treaty as such was but a half-way step; many more "Maastrichts" were yet to come.[79]

In the EMU context, Streibl emphasized that the Länder vote on entry into Stage Three would not accept a weakening of the strict criteria stated in the Treaty. In its suggestions to the Bundesrat plenary on 18 December, the EC Committee asked the federal government to send the Bundesrat a report on the evolution of economic convergence in the European Union beginning in 1994. It also advocated Frankfurt am Main as the seat of the future European Central Bank.[80]

Streibl accentuated the role of the Länder as engaged "promoters" of European unity instead of as the "brake" on the process. The anchoring of the

---

[77]Interview des Bundesministers des Auswärtigen, Dr. Klaus Kinkel, mit dem Süddeutschen Rundfunk, Mitteilung für die Presse Nr. 1190/92 (Bonn: Auswärtiges Amt, 1992), 1–5.

[78]My knowledge of the debate is based on my presence during the vote at the invitation of a friend, Annette Sierigk, who works for the Bavarian Representation for Federal and European Community Affairs to the Federal Government.

[79]Bundesrat, Stenographischer Bericht, 650. Sitzung, Bonn, Freitag, den 18. Dezember 1992, 638.

[80]Bundesrat, "Empfehlungen der Ausschüsse, Gesetz zum Vertrag vom 7. Februar 1992 über die Europäische Union," Drucksache 810/1/92, 11.12.92, 8–9.

subsidiarity principle in Article 3b TEU, the creation of a Committee of Regions[81] and the participation of the Länder in Council negotiations were steps that addressed their main concerns. He also thanked the federal government for its support as the Länder leaders took the initiative to speak with President Jacques Delors in May 1988 and to organize several conferences on a Europe of the Regions.[82]

The fact that the Länder were becoming more actively involved in European affairs was evident in the establishment of a permanent European Ministers' Conference of the 16 Länder on 1–2 October 1992 in Wildbad Kreuth, Bavaria.[83] Streibl concluded by stating that Article 23 BL was the instrument to check the threat to a federal construction of the German state. This came to pass due to the double discharge of the Länder competencies to the federal government and the provisions in Article 24 BL which the Länder had to accept, without any remedy, over a long period of time. The Länder sealed two great events on 18 December: yes to Europe and yes to a strengthening of federalism.[84]

As several of the other minister-presidents addressed the Bundesrat, Werner Kaufmann-Bühler, who directed Cuntz's work on the Treaty ratification, walked in. Kinkel arrived soon afterwards. He took the place of Seiler-Albring who had answered some previous questions on the situation in southeast Turkey for the federal government. Kinkel's speech on the Maastricht ratification and the changes to the Basic Law emphasized the successful results obtained on 11–12 December during the Edinburgh European Council. A solution for Denmark was found to allow the country a second referendum on the Maastricht Treaty without hindering progress for the rest of the Community notably on the negotiations about to open on enlargement to the EFTA states, Austria, Sweden and Finland. A willingness to find compromise on all sides, under the skillful chairmanship of Prime Minister Major, enabled difficult financial issues to be settled. These included a reform of the Common Agricultural Policy, an increase in structural funds and monies put aside for a cohesion fund to aid the poorer Community member states. The new Länder would receive 25 million DM from 1994–1999, and the relief measures available to help the new democracies in central and eastern Europe were also intensified.

---

[81]Christian Engel, "Regionen in der Europäischen Gemeinschaft: Eine integrationspolitische Rollensuche," *Integration* 14 (1/91): 9–20.

[82]Bundesrat, Stenographischer Bericht, 650. Sitzung, Bonn, Freitag, den 18. Dezember 1992, 639–640.

[83]Beuter, "Germany and the Ratification of the Maastricht Treaty," 96.

[84]Bundesrat, Stenographischer Bericht, 650. Sitzung, Bonn, Freitag, den 18. Dezember 1992, 639–640.

These results opened the way for solutions to other problems. An agreement on 18 extra seats for German parliamentarians representing the new Länder in the European Parliament was found. Seats for the European institutions were also chosen with the exception of the European Central Bank. On this point Kinkel stated that the Germans believed a decision in favor of Frankfurt would be reached at the next European Council. Although the results in Edinburgh were a common success for the Community member states, Kinkel once again pointed to the special role that Franco-German cooperation and friendship played in the process. [85] This cooperation was especially evident on the matter of stronger German representation in the European Parliament.

The German foreign minister stated that the new cooperation between the federal government and the Länder must bring about a conscious responsibility to work together constructively in the federal construction of Europe. Although Kinkel made no reference in his speech to a quotation from Monnet's *Mémoires*, his emphasis on "an edifice upon which to build further" was a clear indication of his belief in the evolving federal nature of the integration process.[86]

FROM MAASTRICHT TO KARLSRUHE: THE TREATY ON EUROPEAN UNION BEFORE THE CONSTITUTIONAL COURT
The Grounds for the Case

Despite a unanimous vote for Maastricht in the Bundesrat and an overwhelming majority that consented to the Treaty in the Bundestag, the German ratification law could not be signed by President Richard von Weizsäcker and deposited in Rome as specified in Article S TEU. On 21 December 1992 the Constitutional Court in Karlsruhe forwarded constitutional appeals to the federal government. The *Auswärtiges Amt*, which was in charge of the bill to ratify Maastricht, had until 15 January 1993 to remark on the appeals to the ratification of the Maastricht Treaty.[87] Of the 36 appeals registered before the Court between December 1992 and August 1993, 3 were the focus of attention during an oral hearing on 1–2 July 1993.

---

[85]Ibid., 649–650.

[86]Ibid. After asking me to find this book in the library at the *Auswärtiges Amt*, Cuntz then suggested a few lines, quoted from the *Mémoires*, for inclusion in a draft version of foreign minister Kinkel's speech to the Bundesrat.

[87]Ingo Winkelmann (Hg.) *Das Maastricht-Urteil des Bundes-verfassugsgericht vom 12. Oktober 1993* (Berlin: Duncker & Humblot, 1994), 22. Winkelmann is the civil servant in the Legal Department of the *Auswärtiges Amt* who dealt with the Maastricht ratification.

The first appeal was filed by a former *chef de cabinet* of Martin Bangemann at the European Commission, Manfred Brunner (FDP). The second was made by four members of the European Parliament in the Alliance 90/Green political group. The third came from a senior official in the federal ministry of justice, Hans A. Stöcker.[88] Brunner argued that the Treaty on European Union and the new Article 23 BL violate a number of basic principles of the Constitution. The suits filed by the four MEPs of the Alliance 90/Green group and Stöcker made similar claims. An additional argument of the MEPs was that these basic principles could not be changed according to the Constitution. In short, the claims were that the Treaty violated the Basic Law, national sovereignty and the democratic legitimacy of the popular will.[89]

Brunner's main argument was at the heart of the Court's deliberations. He reasoned that the Treaty on European Union transgressed Article 38 (1) BL. This Article stipulates that the Bundestag's members are elected in general, direct, free, equal and secret elections, that the parliament's members represent the entire people, and that they are answerable only to their conscience. Article 20 (2) BL stipulates that all state power originates from the people and that this power is executed by the people in elections and votes and through special organs of the legislative, executive and judicial branches of government. Brunner made the case that his right to participate in the execution of state power was substantially reduced to the extent that the Treaty transfers essential competencies from the Bundestag to organs of the Community and even empowers the Union, in Article F (3) TEU, to increase its own competencies.[90]

The Karlsruhe Decision
In its ruling of 12 October, the Constitutional Court focused some of its statements in a substantial way on democratic legitimacy. Headnotes 3 (a) and (b) and 4 of the decision are particularly relevant:[91]

---

[88]"Bundesverfassungsgericht verhandelt über Maastricht," *Frankfurter Allgemeine Zeitung*, 1. Juli 1993, 5; Peter Gumbel, "Maastricht Faces German Legal Test in Suit over Scope of Treaty's Powers," *The Wall Street Journal*, 15 June 1993.

[89]Beuter, "Germany and the Ratification of the Maastricht Treaty," 100.

[90]"Maastricht-Urteil," in *Entscheidungen des Bundesverfassungs- gerichts* 89. Band (Tübingen: J.C.B. Mohr, 1994), 155–156. Article F (3) TEU states: "The Union shall provide itself with the means necessary to attain its objectives and carry through its policies."

[91]As quoted from the Headnotes to the Judgement of the Federal Constitutional Court, Second Division, dated 12 October 1993 reprinted in *The Ratification of the Maastricht Treaty*, Annex X, 515.

3. (a) If a union of democratic states performs sovereign tasks through the exercise of sovereign authority it is first and foremost the citizens of the member states who must legitimize such action through a democratic process via their national parliaments. Thus democratic legitimation is achieved by referring the activities of European bodies to the parliaments of the member states; in addition as the nations of Europe grow closer together, democratic legitimation will increasingly be supplied, within the institutional structure of the European Union, by the European Parliament which is elected by the citizens of the member states.

3. (b) The pivotal factor is that the Union's democratic basis must be extended in line with the progress of integration and that living democracy is maintained in the member states during that process.

4. If, as at present, the citizens supply democratic legitimation via their national parliaments, then the expansion of the responsibilities and authority of the European Communities is limited by virtue of the democratic principle. The German Bundestag must be left with a substantial level of such tasks and authority.

The Karlsruhe decision clearly points to the need for stronger national democratic control over Community decision making. There is, as Uwe Thaysen notes, greater attention paid to democratic legitimacy than questions of national sovereignty. This points clearly to the differing conceptions of sovereignty between Germany and France, or Great Britain, alluded to earlier. The Court's decision fully supports the Bundestag's and the Bundesrat's demands for more involvement in the daily negotiations that define the integration process.[92] The Court's ruling also clarifies the procedures under which Germany would transfer to planned supranational institutions, like the ECB, some elements of decision making which at present are held nationally. For example, a shift of monetary powers from the Bundesbank to the ECB could be made only under conditions which conform to the democratic principles of the Basic Law, under which state power is held to emanate from the German people. More widely, the Bundestag will be under the obligation to ensure that European integration meets standards of legislative transparency and accountability which the German people legitimately require to be upheld.[93]

---

[92]Wieczorek-Zeul, "Der Vertrag von Maastricht im Deutschen Bundetag," 408.

[93]"Karlsruhe's sound ruling," *Financial Times*, October 13, 1993, 15.

The Karlsruhe ruling brought the German ratification and the Maastricht process to a close. Denmark had already voted on 18 May to accept the Maastricht Treaty in a second referendum. The final result, 56.8 percent of the votes for and 43.2 percent opposed to the Treaty, was motivated primarily by a fear of scenarios of Denmark after a "no" vote—soaring joblessness, diplomatic isolation and severed economic ties.[94] The British ratification came in the midst of the second currency crisis in the European Monetary System in early August 1993.[95]

The "Psychology of the Mark"

Prior to the Karlsruhe ruling, there were hearings on the case brought against the Treaty on European Union. The Treaty's Articles and protocols on EMU were central to the three suits heard before the Constitutional Court on 1–2 July. Since the adoption of a single currency implied a loss of national sovereignty, there was general agreement on the part of each petitioner whose appeal was presented during the two-day hearings that only the German people as sovereign could make such a historic decision. Brunner's legal representative, Karl Albrecht Schachtschneider, was inclined to think that the convergence criteria fixed in the Treaty were not the last word because the European Council would make a political decision on the final transition to EMU. This decision, made on the basis of the legal criteria in the Treaty, would provide the consent for Stage Three.[96]

Bundesbank President Schlesinger expressed the opinion, shared by the Kohl government, that monetary union could only be realized in parallel with political union. This argument stems in part from Germany's historical experience during the last century in which political union preceded monetary harmonization. The civil servant from the ministry of finance who defended the government's position on EMU was Gert Haller.[97] He explained that the convergence criteria were unconditionally desirable for the creation of EMU. Any changes to these criteria, allowed for in Protocol 6 TEU, could

---

[94]Colette Mazzucelli, "Maastricht: The Ratification Debate in Denmark," *Bulletin* 45 (Summer 1993): 28–31.

[95]Michael J. Baun, *An Imperfect Union* (Boulder: Westview Press, 1996), 118–122. Baun gives an overview of the 1993 EMS crisis which highlighted the divergencies among European economies.

[96]"In der Maastricht-Verhandlung wählt die Bundesregierung die Defensive," *Frankfurter Allgemeine Zeitung*, 3. Juli 1993, 2.

[97]At the time of the hearing, Haller was about to succeed Horst Köhler as State Secretary responsible for the newly created Division IX dealing with European and international financial issues in the ministry of finance.

only be made as a result of a unanimous vote.[98]

The Constitutional Court's judgment regarding EMU clarifies that the date for the entry into Stage Three needs to be considered more as an objective rather than a legally enforceable date. The convergence criteria could not be watered down by the Council without German consent. This implied considerable participation by the Bundestag which, in conjunction with the Bundesrat, must approve the transition to Stage Three. The Court's ruling confirms that EMU is neither automatic nor should it be subject to strict deadlines; instead it should adhere strictly to the established convergence criteria. The Karlsruhe ruling also states that a condition *sine qua non* for monetary union is price stability. If, in the event that this condition is not met, the "stability community" fails, the possibility of an "opt-out" is not excluded.[99]

Moreover, the Court's ruling sheds additional light on the notion of "the psychology of the mark" and the strength of its impact on German diplomacy during the IGCs and subsequent ratification debate. The "psychology of the mark" and its influence on the national consciousness are rooted in three facts relevant to Germany's history and geopolitical position in Europe. First, the German experience with runaway inflation in the aftermath of two world wars left its mark on the national psyche. Another such experience is to be avoided at all costs. Second, pride in the D-mark can be explained as a sense of accomplishment in the years after the total economic and political devastation of the country in 1945. One German civil servant put it in the following terms: "This is one thing we have done well." Third, Germany's geographical position in Europe and its potential dominance in the aftermath of unification place the country in a very sensitive situation vis-à-vis its partners in the Community. Public knowledge of this fact, coupled with a lack of any real popular understanding of the Treaty's provisions on EMU, contributed to the general belief that Maastricht could be a way "to tie Germany down." The fact that the country was in the throes of a national recession during the ratification debate further influenced public opinion against the Treaty.

---

[98]"In der Maastricht-Verhandlung wählt die Bundesregierung die Defensive," 2.

[99]Bundesverfassungsgericht, -BvR2134/92-, -BvR2159/92-, 72. The German text reads as follows: "Der Vertrag setzt langfristige Vorgaben, die das Stabilitätsziel zum Maßstab der Währungsunion machen, die durch institutionelle Vorkehrungen die Verwirklung dieses Ziels sicherzustellen suchen und letztlich—als ultima ratio—beim Scheitern der Stabilitätsgemeinschaft auch einer Lösung aus der Gemeinschaft nicht entgegenstehen." Also cited in Beuter, "Germany and the Ratification of the Maastricht Treaty," 103.

As one newspaper commentator observed, "Maastricht" is more than a Treaty. It has a symbolic meaning beyond the contents of the numerous Articles, protocols and declarations in the text. The Treaty's failure ran the risk of a return to the classical balance of power among European states upon which the integration process has superimposed itself. However, few people saw Maastricht as an alternative to a return to the history so marked by competing alliances and power politics. The "psychology of the mark" is a reflection of a national mentality struggling with the uncertainties of policy making in an emerging transnational polity. This state of mind is one of the biggest obstacles to further integration because of a lack of popular awareness of the economic or political need for European Union. One maxim remains true, however: the more uncertain the present and future appear, that much stronger the weight of history asserts itself.[100]

The Role of German Civil Servants

The appeals heard before the Constitutional Court on 1–2 July were complaints relating to infringement of the fundamental democratic principles of the Basic Law. Brunner's appeal was based on observations made during his tenure as *chef de cabinet* for Commissioner Bangemann. Brunner was disturbed by the fact that the Community's institutions gave themselves ever greater powers without democratic legitimation. In his complaint, he argued that Maastricht would enable government leaders to bypass their democratic parliaments. He had read about bureaucrats in the former Communist East Germany who knew that what they had been doing was wrong, but were too frightened to speak up. "My situation *was* comparable," Brunner explained. "I knew this centralized Europe would go wrong, and I thought that if I recognize this, then I cannot be as cowardly as the East Germans."[101]

Unlike Brunner, who was fired from his job in the Bangemann Cabinet in September 1992, Hans Stöcker kept his job in the federal ministry of justice. As a German civil servant, his first obligation is to the Constitution, not the people, and he cannot easily be dismissed. Stöcker was, however, moved in April 1993 to less interesting duties in the ministry. "They didn't say why, but it was quite clear," he said.[102]

Given the fact that this study illustrates the indispensable role of national civil servants during the Maastricht negotiations and German ratification process, it is also essential to highlight their contributions during the Karlsruhe hearings. In this context, civil servants in the Legal Department and the IGC

---

[100] Günther Nonnenmacher, "'Maastricht' ist mehr als ein Vertrag," *Frankfurter Allgemeine Zeitung,* 27. Juli 1993, 1.

[101] Gumbel, "Maastricht Faces German Legal Test in Suit over Scope of Treaty's Powers."

[102] Ibid.

on political union sub-department[103] of the *Auswärtiges Amt* played important roles. Three weeks before the hearings on 1–2 July, the Constitutional Court sent a list of 15 questions about Maastricht and its constitutional implications to Ingo Winkelmann in the *Auswärtiges Amt*. He prepared the answers which the government sent to the Court on 21 June.[104] Eckart Cuntz also supplied significant information on specific questions relating to financial resources in the proposed Union. This information had to be located by going through the numerous files that Cuntz and his documentation assistant, Roswitha Glänzer, had kept throughout the negotiations on political union.[105]

Three elements of the German ratification process made close working relations among federal and state civil servants, members of the Bundesrat and parliamentarians essential to its success. First, there were extreme time constraints and pressures. The government had about 6 months, from July to December 1992, to accomplish the ratification in order to keep with the established timetable fixed in the Maastricht Treaty. Second, the Länder's demands for increased influence in the integration process had to be met. And third, the ratification had to be achieved with the support of a large majority in the Bundesrat and Bundestag.[106]

Each of these elements defined the nature of their working relationship for federal civil servants, Bundesrat politicians and civil servants and Bundestag parliamentarians. The role of federal civil servants was always clearly defined as one of assisting the politicians by supplying information and, when necessary, input into the negotiation process to ratify the Treaty. Also clear, however, was that federal civil servants had more access to

---

[103] The IGC on political union sub-department, also known as 410–8, ceased to exist on 3 April 1993 when a European Division was created in the *Auswärtiges Amt*. "Veränderungen im Auswärtigen Amt," *Frankfurter Allgemeine Zeitung*, 23. März 1993. Eckart Cuntz left for a high-level post at the German Embassy in Tehran at that time. He returned to Germany briefly in July to be present during the Karlsruhe hearings.

[104] Winkelmann (Hg.), *Das Maastricht-Urteil des Bundes- verfassungsgericht vom 12. Oktober 1993,* 22; Interview, Dr. Ingo Winkelmann, *Auswärtiges Amt*, 16 June 1993.

[105] Since Cuntz was on his way back to Bonn from Tehran, Kaufmann-Bühler asked me to help Glänzer locate the information. This is how it was possible for me to assess the extent to which Cuntz had been responsible for organizing and communicating all the information on German positions during the political union negotiations among the different actors in Bonn, Brussels and other national capitals.

[106] Winkelmann, *Das Maastricht-Urteil des Bundesverfassungsgericht vom 12. Oktober 1993,* 19–20.

information on the negotiations, and a better detailed grasp of the Treaty's contents, than most Bundesrat leaders or Bundestag parliamentarians. This is evident by the number of civil servants whose articles on Maastricht are cited in this volume. German civil servants do not define their role as one of informing the people about Maastricht, however.[107] This is why the need to involve regional leaders and parliamentarians more in the integration process is a crucial one for democratic legitimacy in the proposed Union.

On the issue of democratic legitimacy, the Karlsruhe judgment elaborates less on the role of the European Parliament as a form of democratic control than on that of the national parliaments. Dr. Kaufmann-Bühler writes that the Karlsruhe decision, as it pertains to the European Parliament, strikes him as a "poor interpretation."[108] This is because the European institution receives only a supportive role. Kaufmann-Bühler's concern about a "danger of paralysis" in decision making underlines the need to strengthen the powers of the European Parliament as the principle of qualified majority voting is extended to different policy areas negotiated in the Council of Ministers.

As one of the key civil servants involved in the Maastricht process, Kaufmann-Bühler showed a respect for political authority and the democratic responsibility of politicians to explain to the people about developments in the integration process. He also displayed an understanding of the nature of his advisory role to political leaders and parliamentary state ministers. The same thing could be said of the other civil servants involved in the Maastricht process, most of whom were interviewed for this book. Kaufmann-Bühler also frankly admitted that the restricted way in which the Maastricht negotiations had been conducted, with only a few individuals really understanding the events taking place, was an "error" in judgment. This mistake needs to be corrected for the sake of the integration process as a whole.[109]

---

[107] Early in my work assisting Cuntz, he met with a group of Germans visiting the ministry. These people asked questions about Maastricht and its ratification. Their questions revealed, first and foremost, a concern for the national currency. More importantly, many of the young persons in the group asked no questions at all. This suggested to me that they did not know enough about the Treaty to question its contents. Although my work involved typing and mailing out several responses to German and French citizens regarding Maastricht, it was clear to me that most civil servants do not view this as their responsibility.

[108] Werner Kaufmann-Bühler, "Deutsche Europapolitik nach dem Karlsruher Urteil: Möglichkeiten und Hemmnisse," *Integration*, (1/94): 7.

[109] Interview, Dr. Werner Kaufmann-Bühler, *Auswärtiges Amt*, 29 December 1994.

INTERPRETING THE MAASTRICHT RATIFICATION IN GERMANY: THREE APPROACHES TO THE IGC PROCESS

Putnam's Two-Level Games

The analytical framework introduced in this study can help us to explain the way at the state level politico-administrative actors influenced the internal bargaining which took place during the German ratification of Maastricht. The fact that no popular referendum was involved to ratify the Treaty increased the influence of politico-administrative hybrids like Köhler and administrative civil servants like Kaufmann-Bühler and Cuntz, who provided Seiler-Albring with essential information, during internal bargaining with politicians in the Bundesrat and Bundestag. Elements of attitudinal structuring, distributive and intra-organizational bargaining were present to a greater extent than integrative bargaining as the federal government negotiated with the state governments and the Parliament to ratify the Treaty.

Putnam's approach is useful to explain the role of state institutions in the German ratification process. The two-level games approach can also be modified to assess the relevance of levels of negotiation by focusing on the different roles of Minister Waigel and State Secretary Köhler and Minister Genscher and Parliamentary State Minister Seiler-Albring. Their roles during the IGC negotiations shaped their subsequent participation as key players in the domestic ratification of Maastricht.

Domestic Institutions

During the Maastricht ratification both the Bundesrat and the Bundestag increased their participation in the European integration process as a result of the establishment of domestic institutions with competencies in European Union affairs. Likewise, the ministry of finance and the *Auswärtiges Amt*, created European Divisions to deal with the increased involvement of national civil servants in the integration process.

Under Article 52 BL, the Bundesrat may establish a European Chamber. Its decisions will count as decisions of the Bundesrat. In order to maintain the ability of the German negotiating line to achieve compromises in Brussels, meetings of the European Chamber will not be open to the public nor will its conclusions be published. In this way, the Bundesrat aims to react in as flexible a manner as the federal government during Council negotiations.[110] In addition to the creation of a European Chamber, there was the establishment on 1–2 October 1992 in Wildbad Kreuth, Bavaria of a permanent European

---

[110] Konrad Zumschlinge and Annette Sierigk, "Die Auswirkungen der Wiedervereinigung Deutschlands und der Integration Europas auf die Vertretungen der Deutschen Länder in Bonn, Berlin und Brüssel," *Die Verwaltung* (1994): 13.

Ministers' Conference of the Länder. This body meets four times a year to coordinate Länder positions during negotiations in Brussels. [111]

At the working level, an increase in the number of civil servants in Länder representations in Bonn who deal with European Union affairs is required. In addition, bureaucrats from ministries responsible for different policy areas in the Länder must participate in working groups with federal civil servants posted at the German Permanent Representation in Brussels. The question remains open as to whether the German Permanent Representation to the European Union is a representation of the federal government or the Federal Republic. In the second case, the right of Länder civil servants to work alongside their counterparts from the federal government will be asserted. [112]

According to Article 45 BL, a European Union Committee (*Europaausschuß*) has been established within the Bundestag. As a result of the Maastricht ratification, the original *EG-Ausschuß*, established on 12 June 1991, was replaced within three years of its birth by the *Europaausschuß*. The *EG-Ausschuß* became a necessity, in addition to the other specialized technical committees in the Bundestag, to consider the implementation of Community legislation at the domestic level. [113] In the Maastricht context, the task of the *Europaausschuß* is to make sure that the drafting of European legislation is made democratically accountable by sufficient input from the Bundestag. This input will also enable the Bundestag to make clear to the German people the necessity of European legislation. In this way, Germans may come to understand that what they perceive as legislation from "Brussels" actually is based on initiatives originating from German domestic ministries. [114]

The creation of *Europaabteilungen* in the ministry of finance and *Auswärtiges Amt* was also a direct result of the Maastricht ratification. At finance, Waigel aimed to make clear the ministry's competencies in international monetary affairs, a domain which took on additional significance in light of the EMU process. [115] At the *Auswärtiges Amt*, the creation of a

---

[111] Ibid., 14.

[112] Ibid., 17–18.

[113] Uwe Leonardy, "Bundestag und europäische Gemeinschaft: Notwendigkeit und Umfeld eines Europa-Ausschusses," *Zeitschrift für Parlamentsfragen* (4/89): 539.

[114] Hellwig, "Die Europa-Institutionen des Bundestages und seine großen Europa-Initiativen," 29.

[115] "Waigel richtet eine Europa-Abteilung ein," *Frankfurter Allgemeine Zeitung*, 7. Juli 1992.

European Division in April 1993 reflected changes introduced by the Maastricht Treaty. The Treaty's three pillars were mirrored in the structure of the European Division in which European Community affairs, CFSP and justice and home affairs issues were included. This was done at the initiative of the new State Secretary for European affairs, Jürgen Trumpf. There was also speculation that foreign minister Kinkel wanted to increase his domestic political profile and stature within his own party by creating the European Division.

Kinkel's position as foreign minister was a difficult one. His predecessor, Hans-Dietrich Genscher, had a virtual monopoly on foreign policy making for 18 years and enjoyed political influence as the leader of the Liberal party. During this time, Kinkel was a career bureaucrat known as an excellent deputy. He later became Minister of Justice. Among the political leaders involved in the Maastricht process, Kinkel, like Guigou, personified the idea of the bureaucratization of politicians owing to his administrative background. By the time he took over as foreign minister, Kohl, and close advisers in the Chancellery like Joachim Bitterlich, had already gained ground at the expense of the *Auswärtiges Amt*. The task Kinkel faced was dual: to make his mark as a political leader in the FDP party and to maintain, as much as possible, the influence of the *Auswärtiges Amt* in policy making. Thus, the creation of the European Division can be viewed as a political and an administrative necessity.

Negotiator's Strategies

The roles of the finance and foreign ministers during the Maastricht ratification illustrated that their participation in the process was key to domestic ratification. Once again this is indicative of the need to highlight levels below that of the chief of government in discussions of strategies in two-level games. On EMU, Waigel addressed the Bundestag and the Bundesrat. The Parliamentary State Secretary in the ministry of economics, Erich Riedl, also appeared in committee meetings during the ratification.

Kinkel played a very active role during the ratification, as did State Minister for European affairs Seiler-Albring. From the vantage point of the Bundestag, Genscher, and then Kinkel, were in dialogue with the Bundesrat and the Bundestag about the Maastricht negotiations. Seiler-Albring, however, was present throughout the negotiations and ratification process. Thus, she was a fixed point of reference with an innate feel for the domestic constraints in view of parliamentary ratification. The State Minister tailored the way in which she presented the Treaty in light of these constraints. This was not so much a strategy for Treaty ratification as a practical knowledge of what was necessary to achieve a domestic consensus concerning Maastricht. To do this, Seiler-Albring offered an element of continuity of information for members of both Houses as they dealt with the federal government.[116] For example, she pointed to the need for a Europe of the Regions to become a reality and ruled out the possibility of a renegotiation of the Treaty after the Danish "no" in the first referendum.[117]

Seiler-Albring's focus on Community affairs was necessary because the foreign minister could not be nearly as involved on a daily basis with negotiations in Brussels as she could owing to constraints of distance and time. This reinforces the idea that real influence on shaping the definition of IGC negotiating agendas occurs below the ministerial level: in other words, direction from the bottom up, not from the the the top down. This fact, coupled with the change at the level of foreign minister, emphasizes Seiler-Albring's role as State Minister during the ratification process.[118] Her main task was to assist Kinkel by using her detailed knowledge of the IGC negotiations to help him sell the Treaty to a domestic audience.

In terms of another aspect of the ministerial level of negotiation, and the implications for strategy formulation, one other point is relevant. As a result of Article 23 (6) BL, a representative of the Länder with ministerial rank can replace a member of the federal government in the Council if the issues under negotiation are within the sole competence of the Länder. This relates to education and vocational training, for example.[119]

A federal civil servant claims that in the education field effective policy making at the European level is difficult to achieve owing to the complex nature of the legal issues involved in federal-state relations at the domestic level. One Länder civil servant working on European issues at the Bavarian Representation to the Federal Government in Bonn admits that knowledge of what goes on during negotiations in Brussels is limited. However, the input of the Länder is essential, in his view, to preserve local rights in certain policy areas. He also explained that one of his colleagues is doing work on European issues in the European Division of the *Auswärtiges Amt*. This type of

---

[116] Hellwig, "Die Europa-Institutionen des Bundestages und seine großen Europa-Initiativen," 23.

[117] "Tout est possible, sauf une renégociation," *La Croix*, 23 septembre 1992, 3.

[118] Franz Peter Gallois, *Rechtsstellung und Aufgaben des Parlamentarischen Staatssekretärs*, Dissertation, Universität Mainz, 1983.

[119] Beuter, "Germany and the Ratification of the Maastricht Treaty," 91.

exchange maintains the close contacts between civil servants at the federal and Länder levels dealing with European integration.[120]

These contacts are particularly important because of the strained relations which often exist between the *Auswärtiges Amt* and the Länder despite the efforts made on both sides to maintain a dialogue at regular intervals throughout the IGC process. Indeed the Maastricht process highlighted the increased influence which state civil servants managed to obtain in European integration. Their weight throughout the IGC process made it necessary for federal civil servants, politico-administrative hybrids and politicians to communicate with them as a way to promote attitudinal structuring. This was often difficult as elements of distributive and intraorganizational bargaining were obvious throughout the Maastricht process.

Right from the start, the Länder aimed to increase their influence and power vis-à-vis the federal government during negotiations within the Council of Ministers in their specific areas of competence. It was clear that the Länder had the power to veto any potential treaty; thus politicians, politico-administrative hybrids and civil servants working for the federal government had to engage in intraorganizational bargaining by making sure that the Länders' interests in subsidiarity, increased institutional representation for the regions in Europe and greater voice in Council negotiations were taken into account. The Länder drove a hard bargain to achieve their goals with classic distributive bargaining techniques in which state politicians and civil servants sought to achieve as great a voice as possible in Brussels through the definition of Article 23 BL.

In the definition of Article 23 BL and the Bundestag's participation in the vote on the transition to the final stage of EMU, federal politicians, politico-administrative hybrids and civil servants tried to locate points of common interest where attitudes between the federal and state governments or the federal government and the Bundestag could be structured in the interest of European unity. Although the Treaty was ratified by both Houses, a structuring of attitudes was problematic at best because the Länder were determined to achieve a greater voice in Community affairs, and the Bundestag insisted on increased participation as well to make up for the fact that the European Parliament's powers were not substantially augmented. Such attitudes were sometimes colored by party affiliation, however. Renate Hellwig, a strong supporter of Chancellor Kohl within the CDU, openly criticized the Länders' insistence on greater voice in Council negotiations. She also stated that the Bundestag's general attitude was positive toward a shift in

---

[120] Interview, Michael Menthler, Bavarian Representation for Federal and European Community Affairs to the Federal Government, 13 October 1994.

legislative competencies to the European level. In this sense, parliamentarians across party lines were open to structuring attitudes as part of a continuous dialogue with federal representatives. Opportunities for integrative bargaining were more apparent between the federal government and Bundestag in that both sides consistently aimed to increase legislative influence and power in the European polity even if this meant a gradual shift of competencies from the national to the Community level.

The Länders' presence in Council negotiations injects a new dynamic into the integration process. Whether Article 23 BL, a political compromise between Kohl and the Länder to ratify Maastricht at the domestic level, can be made to work as a policy-making tool by administrative civil servants negotiating in working groups in Brussels is an entirely different question. [121] The implications of this question for strategy formulation during negotiations at all levels in the Council is an important one, however. Hellwig remains an outspoken opponent of Article 23 BL precisely because she believes it weakens the effective articulation of German interests during negotiations in the Council. [122]

Aberbach, Putnam and Rockman's Four Images of Civil Servants

In his remarks before the Bundestag on 13 December 1991, Chancellor Kohl thanked the civil servants who worked so hard to bring the Maastricht negotiations to a successful close. [123] Likewise, in her comments on the role of civil servants in the Maastricht process, Seiler-Albring emphasized the assistance these bureaucrats provide to politicians. In her view, their role in no way undermined the political goals of the government. [124] Instead the work of this small group of civil servants behind the scenes was the necessary glue that held the pieces of the puzzle involving European-domestic interactions together.

In comparison to the role of these civil servants at the working level, that of State Secretary Köhler more closely resembled the politico-administrative hybrid in the Aberbach, Putnam and Rockman mold. Early in the ratification process, Köhler summoned a briefing at the ministry of finance to voice his concern about the state of the European debate in Germany.

---

[121] Interview, Helge Engelhard, Federal Ministry of Education and Science, Department of European Community affairs, 8 December 1994.

[122] Renate Hellwig, Meeting with the Robert Bosch Foundation Fellows, 22 September 1994.

[123] Deutscher Bundestag, 12. Wahlperiode, 68. Sitzung, Bonn, Freitag, den 13. Dezember 1991, 5797.

[124] Interview, State Minister Ursula Seiler-Albring, *Auswärtiges Amt*, 16 April 1993.

I am concerned about the manner and the circumstances of the debate in Germany, because it makes it clear that German self-confidence has still not got very far," he said. "Who would dare to underestimate the meaning of the stability of the D-mark? It is the absolute essence of our political and economic meaning, of our self-confidence. The debate must not be reduced to the level of saying: 'They are endangering our D-mark and therefore they are traitors to the Fatherland.'[125]

Köhler's criticism was also directed at the Länder's desire for a substantial reinforcement of their control over the central government in return for ratification of the Maastricht Treaty.

They are mixing up their justified desire to preserve their own identities, with a fear that they face declining living standards, and with a misunderstanding of the nature of federalism.[126]

Köhler's frank outspokenness on such political issues distinguished his presence during the EMU conference[127] right until the end of the parliamentary ratification process. During this time he asked French officials on more than one occasion to assure the Germans of the independence of the *Banque de France*. This was particularly important given some French officials' doubt that German calls for closer political union had to be a prerequisite for a single currency. In their view, this notion went beyond the Treaty on European Union.[128]

Köhler's role as State Secretary placed him close to political power. Unlike Guigou, he could not rely on either the training or the network that an elite school like ENA could provide. Nor was Köhler a minister with a civil servant training; he was, instead, a civil servant who often had to take the place of his Minister during negotiations or public briefing sessions on EMU. Köhler's responsibilities were also limited to EMU issues even though his statements had political significance. Guigou's range of influence was much broader; as a Minister for European affairs, she also spoke out on issues of political union even though her technical background was primarily as a counselor to Mitterrand on economic and financial issues. Not surprisingly, Guigou's outstanding contributions were, like Köhler's, on EMU.

---

[125] Quentin Peel, "Bonn sees danger to unity in States' demands," *Financial Times*, 14 March 1992.

[126] Ibid.

[127] "Es gibt kein Zurück," *Der Spiegel*, 9. Dezember 1991, 126.

[128] Tom Buerkle, "France Rejects Call by Bonn on Monetary Union," *International Herald Tribune*, December 7, 1994, 17.

Köhler did not believe that monetary turbulence would prevent EMU and explained his views to the German business community and public. After his time as State Secretary, a position which he resigned in August 1993, Köhler became President of the German Association of Savings Banks. In this job, his main task is to prepare the German population for the transition to a single currency.[129] Like Guigou, his function during the 1996 process will be to inform the public about what is at stake for the future of the Union. However, there is one important difference. Guigou participates as a member of the Reflection Group to debate the 1996 conference agenda. Köhler's influence will be exerted from beyond, as opposed to within, closed doors. [130]

Moreover, during the Maastricht ratification, Jürgen Trumpf became State Secretary in the *Auswärtiges Amt* and was later named Secretary General of the Council of the European Union. In his role as Secretary General, Trumpf spoke out on political issues like the common foreign and security policy and the future of integration in the post-Maastricht era.[131] His public statements to international audiences marked Trumpf's emergence as a politico-administrative hybrid in Aberbach, Putnam and Rockman mold. This fact attests to a direct correlation between the evolution of the integration process and the emergence of Image IV hybrids in Europe.

The success of Köhler and Tumpf as politico-administrative hybrids has much to do with their astute awareness of German interests throughout the Maastricht process. As able negotiators and personable communicators, both men identify with the requirements of the German economic and political system while at the same time acknowledging the broader European interest. Each stressed the importance of federalism for Germany and for Europe, but neither man promoted German federalism as a means to check the integration process. Instead during internal bargaining, or mediation among domestic institutions, the accent was placed on the cooperative work of states and Community institutions. This cooperation would take place throughout the EMU process while bearing in mind that the path to the final stage would not be a simple one. Köhler's assessments in particular were consistently based on a realistic perception of the progress which could be achieved given the

---

[129] Interview, Wolfgang Neumann, Researcher, German Association of Savings Banks, 30 April 1993.

[130] "Köhler fordert von Bonn klare Worte," *Handelsblatt*, 28. März 1995, 35.

[131] Jürgen Trumpf, "The Future of the Maastricht Treaty and U.S.- E.U. Relations in the 1990s," Presentation for the Robert Bosch Foundation Spring Speaker Series on the Evolution of Europe in the 1990s, The University Club, May 4, 1995.

respective economic and political situations in the member states. Likewise this sense of political realism influenced Trumpf's public statements on the CFSP, an area where the preservation of national sovereignty was still dominant because of the domestic requirements in some of the member states.

Monnet's Approach

Throughout the Maastricht process German civil servants worked to implement goals that emphasized a federal approach. Their vision of the Union was not intergovernmental in nature with the Council as the most dominant institution. Instead there was a sense of cooperative relations among Council, Parliament and Commission with the Court of Justice playing an active role to promote the interests of a federal Union through law. In short, their emphasis was on developing the institutions of the Union and on the unity of structure in the Treaty with all areas of policy subject to Community decision making.

The civil servants most closely involved in the ratification process in the *Auswärtiges Amt* characterized their work as joint problem solvers in that their concern was to advance both German and European interests during the ratification. This was particularly important because the German ratification of Maastricht entered its decisive phase after the Danish "no" and during the British Presidency. This period of time was one of intense popular skepticism about European integration and increasing doubts about the relevance of the Community to German interests. The role of these civil servants did not correspond to that of the politico-administrative hybrid; their work was done in large part behind the scenes. However, as a network of individuals committed to advancing the integration process, these civil servants facilitated *engrenage*, a process key to Monnet's approach.

In regular Community business, *engrenage* is dependent on "the ability of the European Commission to engage economic elites and to help them recognize their self-interest in supporting greater unity." Usually these networks involve "outside producers and interest groups." In work on the European Coal and Steel Community, for example, the High Authority's consultation with representatives of "producers, workers and consumers helped to create new networks at the European level, affecting the policy process and the distinctive nature of integration."[132]

Throughout the Maastricht process, the Delors Commission maintained good relations with the Kohl government and the Länder. The Commission's Secretary General, David Williamson, made a point to speak on the IGCs at the Commission's Representation in Bonn. The Commission also received

---

[132] All quotes are taken from Kevin Featherstone, "Jean Monnet and the 'Democratic Deficit' in the European Union," *Journal of Common Market Studies* (June 1994): 155.

weekly reports on the progress of the national ratifications in the member states via its representations in national capitals. German civil servants helped to keep the Commission informed on the state of play in the German ratification. They also attended gatherings at the Commission's Representation in Bonn, like the one on 8 December during which Horst Köhler spoke on EMU as a way of maintaining a personal network of communication among national civil servants and Commission officials.

German politicians, politico-administrative hybrids and civil servants working on the Maastricht ratification realized that the Treaty was a practical means to an end: namely, to further the integration process. In the course of integration, these civil servants would continue to work on Union affairs, like the strategy for enlargement to the East, in tandem with the European Commission. However, depending on their generation and on their individual experiences with European Community affairs, the knowledge of Monnet and his approach was varied. Some individuals like Cuntz, Kaufmann-Bühler, Kuhn, Köhler and Trumpf were familiar with Monnet's approach to integration. Others like Seiler-Albring were less so.

Among the individuals involved in the IGC process, no one identified as closely with Monnet and his approach as Delors. For those Germans taking part throughout the Maastricht process, there was an awareness of the need to work with the Community institutions like the Commission, but two points must be underlined. First, the German institutional emphasis throughout the Maastricht process was on the European Parliament. Second, the German interest in a federal European Union, with supranational elements, is not in a Europe in which states will wither away. It is, quite to the contrary, a Union based on the interests of the member states. Therefore, the elements of Monnet's approach which emphasize integrative bargaining and *engrenage* are more useful to explain German participation in the Maastricht process than functionalist or neo-functionalist approaches to integration.

One of the results of the Maastricht process was that a personal network of German civil servants became intertwined with a European network in a way that may foster *engrenage*. When Trumpf was named State Secretary in the *Auswärtiges Amt*, Dietrich von Kyaw became German Permanent Representative in Brussels.[133] After Trumpf was appointed Secretary General of the Council, he subsequently chose Eckart Cuntz as his *chef de cabinet*. Günter Grosche took the position of Director of the Monetary Committee located inside the European Commission's complex. Another individual involved in the Maastricht process in the *Auswärtiges Amt*, Christoph Heusgens, was called to the minister's office to assist Klaus Kinkel. The

---

[133] "Ein Wechsel in Brüssel," *Handelsblatt*, 29–30. Januar 1993.

presence of a civil servant with significant experience in Community affairs continuously assisting the foreign minister is an indication of the importance of European integration for German foreign policy. Finally, another German civil servant who worked at the German Permanent Representation during the Maastricht process, Sabine Ehmke-Gendron, also moved into the Cabinet of Secretary General Trumpf to handle CFSP affairs. Trumpf, Cuntz, Ehmke-Gendron and Grosche are committed to the integration process as something more than inter-governmentalism. Each believes in a political system in which member states and European institutions work together to serve the European interest. And several of them will be in positions to mediate among competing national interests in search of points above the lowest common denominator to facilitate integrative bargaining at the European level precisely because they are aware of requirements within domestic systems.

Clearly one of the most difficult aspects to the Maastricht ratification in Germany involved the demands of the Länder. Their desire to bring the process closer to the people is one necessary component of civic education at the local level about the purposes of European integration. However, the integration process is already fraught with internal contradictions and tensions largely missed or misunderstood by the people. It is now more necessary than ever for Länder officials to spend part of their careers in Brussels or in a federal ministry learning about Community affairs. This means increased interactions at different levels of government, and among regional actors in different governments, will occur in order to make European policy. Future politico-administrative hybrids will follow in the footsteps of Köhler and Trumpf; they will undoubtedly be significant actors in internal bargaining and public communication as federal-state relations in the field of European policy making become more complicated and intertwined.

Maastricht revealed the Community at a vulnerable stage of development, a prime target for politicians looking to increase their own domestic power base at its expense. As Monnet realized, the key goal, facilitated by *engrenage*, is to work with the member states, not against them. The German ratification of Maastricht reveals that today, to an even greater extent than in Monnet's era, it remains an urgent necessity for member states to find points of agreement just above the lowest common denominator regarding clearly defined objectives. Only in this way can the integration process advance as the Union contemplates future enlargements in the decades ahead.

SUMMARY

The Maastricht ratification in the Federal Republic revealed that the German commitment to European integration must confront a tension between an elite understanding of the process and popular skepticism and discontent concerning the manner in which policy is made. The loss of the D-mark, which was the dominant theme throughout the ratification process, symbolized more than material concerns. This subject brought psychological issues to the fore as a majority of Germans wanted to preserve their symbol of accomplishment in the aftermath of the Second World War. A stable European currency was one of the major issues throughout the Maastricht negotiations and German ratification; thus, no analytical separation can be made which disrupts the sequence of events comprising the IGC process.

The analytical framework used in this study sheds light on several of the most important aspects of the Maastricht ratification in Germany. Two-level games show the importance of the domestic institutions, namely, the Chancellor's Office, *Auswärtiges Amt* and ministry of finance, Bundestag, Bundesrat and Bundesbank and the interactions among them during the IGC process. One key point to bear in mind is the impact of the Maastricht process on the structure of these institutions: either their adaptation to the integration process via the creation of European Divisions in the ministries or the strengthening of their competencies in European Union policy making via specialized Committees in the Bundestag and Bundesrat. These developments point to an increased national involvement in the making of Community legislation.

This evolution in the direction of greater interactions in policy making between the state and Community institutions is inextricably linked to the role of the actors which emerged as a result of the Maastricht process. As this chapter makes clear, the same German politicians and civil servants were involved throughout the IGC negotiations and treaty ratification. There were, however, individuals, defined as Image IV hybrids, who participated at a level between that of the political and administrative worlds. Although the main persons responsible to sell the Treaty on European Union to the Bundestag and Bundesrat were Kohl, Kinkel and Waigel, other individuals like Seiler-Albring and Köhler played essential political roles selling the Treaty to the German public. Seiler-Albring was to an even greater extent than Kinkel or Kohl involved in the internal bargaining processes to ratify the Treaty.

Since he was not a Parliamentary State Secretary, Köhler was not as directly involved in the internal bargaining with the Bundestag and Bundesrat as Seiler-Albring. However, he did speak out in public about the EMU process and voiced his concern about the demands of the Länder. His awareness of the domestic constraints under which the German delegation had to formulate its diplomacy during the IGCs guided his efforts to inform elites and citizens alike about the intricacies of EMU during the ratification process. For this task, Köhler was uniquely suited as one of about five or six individuals who really knew the substance of the IGC negotiations. Since he was the point man at the table during the EMU conference and for extended periods of time negotiated at the ministerial level, he knew the ins and outs of intraorganizational bargaining with domestic constituents as well as the traps of distributive bargaining with the Länder.

Köhler sought to use his knowledge of the negotiations and his personal relationships with others who negotiated for the different member states to promote attitudinal structuring, during the ratification debate in Germany. For example, while keeping the domestic requirements of the Bundesrat, Bundestag and Bundesbank in mind, he urged French officials to explain to their political leadership the need to make the *Banque de France* independent. He also publicly expressed his support and understanding for Italian efforts to reduce the state budget deficit. In so doing, Köhler was trying to address domestic concerns about EMU by keeping the political dialogue with other member states open concerning such issues as the convergence criteria and the independence of national central banks. Thus, on both the domestic and European levels, he was trying to facilitate attitudinal structuring.

The Karlsruhe decision on the compatibility of the Treaty on European Union with the Basic Law stresses the need for greater national democratic control over Community decision making. This fact clearly illustrates the significance of increased interactions between domestic and European institutions in an emerging transnational European polity. Despite these interactions, however, there will still be a need for politico-administrative hybrids who, by virtue of the detailed knowledge they possess as key actors in external negotiations, can facilitate internal and perhaps integrative bargaining among domestic institutions prior to and during the national ratifications that will occur as part of future IGC processes.

CHAPTER IX

Conclusion

> Nothing is ever really finished and it is a talent to know to stop at the point where too much attention upsets the balance.
>
> It is necessary to distinguish between what depends on will—objective, method and successive steps and what is linked to circumstances—the choice of the moment and the details to come to a conclusion.
>
> Jean Monnet, *Mémoires*

Using a framework of analysis which incorporates three approaches, this study assesses the extent of, and limits to, Franco-German cooperation during the Maastricht process. The Conclusion presents some final remarks about how the approaches used in tandem contribute to our understanding of both the role of the Franco-German couple in, and the nature of, the IGC process. Several modifications to the individual approaches are then suggested in light of the book's findings. Finally, the relevance of the Maastricht process to the future of European integration is assessed.

INTEGRATING LEVELS, IMAGES AND BARGAINS:
FRANCO-GERMAN RELATIONS IN THE MAASTRICHT CONTEXT
This volume explores the relationship between France and Germany during a period of transition on the Continent. Both countries had to adjust to the changing balance of power in Europe caused by German unification and the collapse of the Soviet empire. Their response to this new European context, in tandem with the Delors Commission, were negotiations to establish a European Union. The analytical framework introduced in this volume highlights the manner in which France and Germany acted together, or individually, to define the Maastricht process. With Great Britain content to retain the status quo, the two countries were the main state actors, along with the contributions of Commission President Delors, at the EMU table. On political union, the combined weight of France and Germany was decisive to the outcome of negotiations. In the midst of the national ratification processes, and after the Danish rejection of the Treaty, it was the French referendum results which determined the subsequent course of the Maastricht process. Finally, well after the deadline inscribed in the Treaty, the Karlsruhe decision

enabled the Treaty on European Union to come into force, thus bringing the German ratification and the IGC process to a close.

The analytical framework is useful to explain the connections among three interrelated aspects of the Maastricht process: (1) the structural and institutional differences at the unit level between the main states involved, France and Germany; (2) the contrast in the organization of key actors, politico-administrative hybrids and bureaucratic personnel, at the domestic and European levels during the two IGCs, EMU and political union; (3) the multifaceted nature of the internal bargaining and external negotiations within each IGC, and between their agendas, as well as the subsequent impact on the French and German ratification processes.

The analysis undertaken in this study indicates that differences in French and German domestic structures and institutions made it difficult for the two sides to understand each other. As a centralized state, France had more in common administratively and politically with Great Britain and Spain. The fact that France and Germany were able to agree at all on various issues during the IGC process attests to the strength of the "privileged partnership."

The crucial impact of France and Germany on the momentum of the Maastricht process, functioning as the "motor for Europe," is borne out by practical experience. When the two countries acted together, either to foster compromise solutions, like the date to start Stage Two of EMU on 1 January 1994, or to facilitate integrative bargaining, with Kohl accepting Mitterrand's proposal of 1999 as the latest date to create EMU, progress was registered in multilateral negotiations. When the two could not agree, negotiations stalled. This was the case during the political union conference until late October when Guigou indicated French acceptance for an increase in the scope of co-decision for the European Parliament. Her action in turn influenced progress on the EMU agenda owing to the linkage previously mentioned. Moreover, an implicit prerequisite of EMU, not spelled out in the Treaty, is that the initial core group of countries in Stage Three must include France and Germany as a matter of political necessity.[1] Other areas where France and Germany acted decisively to shape the final Treaty were on the CFSP dossier, including a defense dimension with a role for WEU, and the inclusion of Article 100c on visa policy within the Community sphere.

Even during the national ratification procedures, the Franco-German couple acted together to influence the overall acceptance of the Maastricht

---

[1] Elke Thiel, "The Shaping of a Framework for a Single Currency in the Course of the EMU Negotiations," Paper presented at the Fourth Biennial International Conference of the European Community Studies Association, Charleston, South Carolina, May 11–14, 1995, 15.

Treaty. When Denmark rejected the Treaty, Kohl and Mitterrand were determined to push ahead. Kohl even appeared on French television to allay French fears of German dominance in the Community. Each leader's awareness of the other's domestic situation was evident. This mutual awareness of the other partner's domestic situation could be seen at the ministerial and working levels as well in Paris and Bonn. Moreover, the solution found to the Danish dilemma, in the form of an "agreement" at Edinburgh, illustrated that the other Ten, taking note of the Franco-German accord, agreed to actions taken in the name of the Twelve. Thus, the European transnational polity produced a solution to a problem which originated in Danish domestic politics. The solution found at Level I to a problem with roots at Level II could not have been achieved by any one country acting alone. This is an indication of the increasing depth of the interactions between the two levels, European and domestic, and among the different levels of negotiation required to conclude the parallel IGC and national ratification processes.

Each of the above points raised in this volume reinforces the notion of France and Germany acting at the core of a changing Europe with other states trying to define their status as part of the core or adjust that status if it relegates them to the periphery.[2] This volume illustrates that the notion of the "core" is not only relevant among the different member states in the Union but also within their respective administrative structures. Specifically, the Maastricht process revealed the existence of tightly knit groups of national civil servants and politico-administrative hybrids who operate as both national and Community actors. Their work during the IGC process set them apart from other individuals working within their own national administrations.

Not surprisingly, the small number of civil servants and politico-administrative hybrids involved were among those individuals with the most invested in Maastricht. As some of them tried to defend the results of several years' work, they had to confront the reality that their communication could no longer take place in a politico-administrative vacuum. The IGC process had to be seen in its proper context: as part of a much larger continuous series of negotiations on the future of European integration. In this context, politico-administrative hybrids are judged as much on their ability to facilitate joint problem solving at different levels of negotiation as to articulate to ordinary citizens the nature of those issues which dominate the IGC process.

Whereas Köhler focused on the EMU agenda, Guigou actively participated in both IGCs. Both actors used their knowledge of domestic

---

[2] The "core-periphery" model is outlined in Baun, *An Imperfect Union*, 165–167.

constraints in internal bargaining and issues on the agendas of external negotiations to influence the IGC process in a decisive way. Although this study demonstrates the existence of both Image III civil servants and Image IV hybrids, the crucial difference between the two images is clear. Political actions taken by figures with predominantly administrative backgrounds like Guigou, Köhler and Delors are contrasted with the "behind the scenes" work of de Boissieu, Trumpf and Lamy. What this study also reveals, however, is the subsequent transformation of some of these Image III actors, like Trumpf, to Image IV hybrids as a direct result of the Maastricht process.

In this analytical framework the images of civil servants are situated between the other two approaches. During the prenegotiation, national civil servants were working steadily so that the two IGCs could open in mid-December 1990. Unlike their political masters, these officials, operating at a lower level of negotiation, were able to strike bargains without always searching for consensus. On EMU, their task was to limit and define the precise issues that remained to be negotiated. In the context of political union, their discussions were of a much more open-ended nature with the basic obstacle clear to all at the table: the inability of the political leadership to agree on a common definition of political union. This difficulty at the top contributed to an imbalance at all levels of negotiation. The untidy agenda on political union, stemming in large part from the desire of member states to advance their own interests, made integrative bargaining impossible. The lack of a thoroughly prepared text, like that of the European Commission's draft treaty on EMU, hindered the personal representatives' attempts at joint problem solving and limited the influence of the Delors Commission throughout the political union negotiations.

The analytical framework introduced here allows for a consideration of both the difficulties caused by the different preparations and goals of the two IGCs, and the impact of this complex European agenda on the French and German ratification processes. These differences can be seen from two distinct but interrelated vantage points. First, it is necessary to consider the impact of the two IGC agendas and subsequent national ratifications on interbureaucratic rivalry among domestic ministries. This was especially relevant to the German case. Second, these differences can be viewed through the eyes of the actors highlighted in this study, namely, politico-administrative hybrids and national civil servants.

Interbureaucratic rivalry complicated relations between France and Germany regarding issues on the EMU agenda. One of the more obvious differences of opinion between the French and German delegations during the EMU conference involved the role of the European Council. The French wanted the heads of state and government, assisted by the foreign ministers in the General Affairs Council, to determine the main guidelines of EMU policy making. The Germans were in favor of greater influence for the economics and finance ministers, assisted by the technical experts in the Monetary Committee, in EMU decision making. The solution between France and Germany on this issue was brokered at the official level between Trichet and Köhler and then agreed upon at the ministerial level.

Such bureaucratic differences were evident at the domestic level as well with the Elysée and the Quai d'Orsay asserting competence in monetary matters at the expense of the French ministry of economics and finance. In the German case, civil servants in both the *Auswärtiges Amt* and the ministry of economics expressed concern about the closed nature of the EMU process. This was problematic because of the link established between the two conferences and the need for bureaucratic personnel who could understand horizontal issues relating to both IGCs. The ministry of economics was in a particularly disadvantageous position. On EMU its influence was considerably less than that of Finance. During the political union negotiations, it had to follow the lead of the *Auswärtiges Amt*. The need to reconcile competing bureaucratic viewpoints regarding German positions during the two IGCs was more problematic for the political union negotiations. Fortunately, the negotiating skill and political acumen of Trumpf served German interests well during the conference. The German interest on EMU was defined by taking into account the viewpoints of representatives from three domestic ministries, the Chancellor's Office and the Bundesbank. The communication of the results of these internal discussions was direct from Grosche at the working level to Köhler and Waigel at the political level.

A broader vision of the entire Maastricht agenda was necessary to sell the Treaty during internal bargaining throughout the ratification processes. Here it is necessary to consider interbureaucratic rivalry through the eyes of the actors highlighted in this study. In the French case, Guigou's position as Minister for European affairs was unique. Her role throughout the IGC process was a pivotal one at the center of external negotiations, internal bargaining and public communication. The centralized nature of French IGC diplomacy was a tremendous advantage during the negotiations because it lessened the impact of interbureaucratic rivalry on the articulation of French positions. Yet, this diplomatic advantage did little to help sell the Treaty during the ratification process. Minister Guigou was perhaps the only other person besides President Mitterrand who knew enough about the IGC process to convince the French people to ratify Maastricht. Nonetheless, her broad knowledge of the Maastricht agenda did little to dispel the popular image of her as a technocrat.

In the German case, the individual who, like Guigou, had a broad vision of the Maastricht agenda was the State Minister for European affairs, Ursula Seiler-Albring. A FDP politician, Seiler-Albring had the advantage of being a constant reference point for the Länder and the Bundestag throughout the external negotiations and internal bargaining processes. However, the decentralized nature of the German polity accounted for the division of domestic competencies on EMU and political union. Although Seiler-Albring spoke to the public about EMU issues, the ministry of finance took the lead on this issue during the domestic ratification. Köhler's public role during the domestic ratification was necessary because of the broad scope of the two IGC agendas. The lack of coordination between the IGCs, a problem with roots in interbureaucratic rivalry, clearly impacted on the ratification debate. During this debate, Waigel was not always present and State Minister Seiler-Albring spoke on behalf of a ministry with competence in foreign affairs. Moreover, the *Auswärtiges Amt* was much more in favor of cooperation with France on EMU issues than the ministry of finance, which held a stricter line concerning German interests. An individual with enough experience of the EMU process was needed to allay business and popular fears about the proposed single European currency. Köhler's ability to play this public role distinguished him as a politico-administrative hybrid. As the EMU process approaches its final stage, other Image IV hybrids will most likely emerge to contribute to the public debate on German participation in economic and monetary union.

The framework used in this volume was developed to demonstrate the extent to which the IGC process, and the Franco-German role in the Maastricht experience, depart from a purely intergovernmentalist approach. Traditional theories of integration are not able to explain the *sui generis* nature of the IGC process or Franco-German cooperation within the process. As this study demonstrates, events which marked the Maastricht experience are interconnected with other developments which occurred prior to the IGC process. In the Maastricht context, no one traditional approach is adequate to explain a cumulative series of events.

Intergovernmentalism alone cannot explain the extent of Franco-German cooperation or the input of the Delors Commission during the EMU process. The findings of this book support the idea that *engrenage* reinforces "the notion of a shared culture, embedded in informal practices and formal procedures" by which the participants in the IGC process became locked into a collective process of decision making at all levels of negotiation.[3] On political union, agreement about the final goal among the Twelve and an adequate preparation of the conference agenda were clearly lacking. The intergovernmental approach was evident in the British negotiating position throughout the Maastricht process; however, it is necessary to use other approaches as well to interpret Franco-German contributions to both the SEA and Maastricht processes.

---

[3] Hayes-Renshaw and Wallace, "Executive power in the European Union," 564.

PUTNAM'S TWO-LEVEL GAMES

In an attempt to develop an analytical framework to explain the IGC process, it is also important to mention some of the deficiencies of the different approaches used in this study as revealed by the Maastricht experience. Two-level games allow for an explanation of the Maastricht process from the vantage point of the domestic requirements for parliamentary ratification of the two key member states at the table. As such, it takes into account important factors like domestic administrations and political parties, negotiators' strategies and preferences and coalitions among national civil servants. Its focus on national leaders who must serve as "gatekeepers" between the European and domestic levels is a useful way to capture the nature of some, but not all, of the interactions in the Europolity. In the French case, the dominant role of the President is underlined with the parliament and the central bank subordinate to his authority. In the German case, Kohl had to consider the constraints posed by the Länder, the Bundestag and the Bundesbank as he developed a strategy for the conferences.

The Maastricht process offers us an opportunity to refine Putnam's approach in light of experience. First, the emphasis on the "chief of government" needs to be modified to account for levels of negotiation featuring both political leaders and national civil servants. This is especially significant in light of the tensions that can exist among levels of negotiation below the chief of government and the ways this can influence strategy formulation during the actual IGC negotiations and then subsequently during the phase of national ratifications. The point to underline here is that the notion of strategy only makes sense if we consider the link between the ways in which it is used by states to negotiate a treaty and then sell it for domestic ratification. Strategy is thus relevant on two, and potentially more, levels with the same set of actors employing a chosen strategy in internal bargaining and external negotiations throughout the IGC process. This being said, however, it is equally important to observe that the notion of strategy does not warrant the emphasis in the case of Maastricht that Putnam's two-level games describes. Instead, a greater accent should be placed on the ways in which package deals are struck, which is often a matter of tactics and timing. Oftentimes, this is achieved at the last minute as a matter of necessity; the last hours of the Maastricht European Council illustrate this point quite well. Third, it is useful to assess Putnam's observations regarding "state autonomy" in light of French diplomacy throughout the Maastricht process. Two-level analysis implies that "the stronger the state is in terms of autonomy from domestic pressures, the weaker its relative bargaining position internationally."[4] In contrast to Putnam's assertions about state strength, the fact remains that Mitterrand's autonomy from domestic constraints, including his own civil servants, did not weaken his position during the IGC process. The observation here is that Putnam's approach does not pay sufficient attention to the advantages which highly centralized states can draw from IGC diplomacy in the absence of domestic constraints.[5]

Fourth, Putnam's approach makes no explicit mention of the use of a referendum at Level II to decide the fate of a treaty; Or how this might influence a state's negotiating behavior. Nor is there a discussion of options in light of a failed referendum. The conditions under which a treaty might be implemented in spite of a failed referendum, and, ratification process, are not adequately dealt with.[6] Interestingly, the case of Denmark would seem to refute Putnam's approach in that the member state that had formulated its IGC diplomacy the most carefully to take domestic constraints into account was the one which was forced involuntarily to reject the Treaty as a result of a failed national referendum. Finally, Lisa Martin suggests that for "the future of European integration and for the study of international cooperation more broadly, we should continue to consider the domestic factors that influence a state's ability to live up to its commitments."[7] The Maastricht process makes us aware of the need to focus on both European and domestic factors simultaneously and to consider the impact of links between them on IGC negotiations and national ratifications. Moreover, in our consideration of domestic factors, we must be willing to explore more than one level of power and influence in internal bargaining and external relations, as the impact of the Länder throughout the Maastricht process illustrates.

---

[4]Putnam, "Diplomacy and domestic politics," 449.

[5]In their edited volume, *Double-Edged Diplomacy*, Evans, Jacobson and Putnam argue that preserving autonomy over the entire course of a negotiation is a very difficult thing to do. In the same volume, Robert A. Pastor reasons in terms of the ability of "weak" states who have domestic constraints to advance their interests more than centralized systems. No analysis of the advantages derived from complete autonomy for a state like France is made. Evans, "Building an Integrative Approach" and Pastor, "The United States and Central America," in *Double- Edged Diplomacy*, eds. Evans, Jacobson and Putnam, 397–430 and 303–327.

[6]Mazzucelli, "Maastricht: The Ratification Debate in Denmark," 28–31.

[7]Lisa M. Martin, *The Influence of National Parliaments on European Integration*, Center for German and European Studies Working Paper 1.23 (Berkeley: University of California, 1994).

ABERBACH, PUTNAM AND ROCKMAN'S FOUR IMAGES OF CIVIL SERVANTS

The four images allow us to consider the ways in which politicians and civil servants work together at different levels of negotiation during the IGC process. This approach does not reveal an increasing bureaucratization of politicians as a result of the Maastricht process. It does explain, however, the emergence of Image IV politico-administrative hybrids as a direct result of the IGC experience.

Delors, in particular, showed his abilities as a joint problem solver, which raises the question of Image IV hybrids and how they relate to democratic government. As a non-elected official, Delors was quite influential in shaping the EMU agenda including the opt-out for Great Britain. On political union, he was also a facilitator of compromise on cohesion and social policy. Delors spoke out often on the need to give politics "a European dimension." Yet, unlike Guigou, he had no democratic base in the form of having to answer directly to a popularly elected head of state or government. The problem this poses for European construction in terms of popular perceptions of both the IGC and integration processes is a serious one. This is a priority which the Union must address if unity is to have any chance of success. This conclusion stands in contrast to that of Moravcsik who writes "...Ironically, the EC's 'democratic deficit' may be a fundamental source of its success."[8]

The four images also highlight the increased weight of national civil servants in the IGC and integration processes since the 1950s. Horst Köhler's actions as a politico-administrative hybrid energized the Maastricht process in an openly political way. This is significant because Image IV hybrids do not appear in national political systems to the same extent in Europe as they do in the United States. Suleiman argues, for example, that in the French system the emergence of politico-administrative hybrid actors is a recent phenomenon. Significantly, Köhler's work as an Image IV hybrid also indicated the limits to joint problem solving below the level of the European Council: only at the highest level of the heads of state and government could any final decisions on EMU be made.

Prior to negotiations at Apeldoorn, the German delegation did show some flexibility on the role of the EMI in Stage Two. This fact illustrates that the role of the personal representatives was to find solutions to common problems during the negotiations. Their goal could be described as searching for a way to establish EMU as a continuation of the integration dynamic which drives the internal market and thus facilitates *engrenage*, or joint actions on specific policies which promote the interlocking of states and Community institutions

---

[8]Moravcsik, "Preferences and Power in the European Community," 518.

in a continuous process of negotiation. There were times when both intergovernmentalism and neo-functionalism were in evidence during the EMU conference, but *engrenage* offers insights into Maastricht as a negotiating process that the others do not.

During the second IGC, joint problem solving was difficult at best owing to an inability among the member states to agree on a common definition of political union. The fact that the second and third pillars remain intergovernmental does not mean that the contrast between neo-functionalism and intergovernmentalism can explain everything about the negotiation. France and Germany agreed, and Great Britain conceded, to place Article 100c in the Community sphere. This suggests the possibility of further movement of policies currently subject to intergovernmentalism in the third pillar to the Community mode of decision making in the first pillar. This is not just because it is in the interest of German domestic politics to Europeanize these policies. It is also because the falling away of internal borders in the single market sets up a dynamic disequilibrium which must be addressed by further integrative measures. Integration is non-static, non-linear and open ended; it can lead to successive IGC processes to reform the Treaties. The personal representatives had their own states' interests in mind during the Maastricht process, but a good number of them, including Köhler and Guigou, were also aware of the interplay between Maastricht and the dynamics of integration.

The second pillar is more problematic in that CFSP is likely to remain intergovernmental in nature for years to come. Yet, this may not prevent greater pressure for the use of qualified majority voting in the Council on CFSP issues. A strengthening of the means to implement CFSP actions at the European level, by using the Council Secretariat to facilitate solutions in the European interest in dialogue with the European Commission and the Western European Union, has been discussed among European and national civil servants. The role of the Secretariat and its staff in the crafting of creative solutions to impasses during negotiations regarding Community policies is well-known. In the CFSP area, a similar role may not be possible to play; however, the Secretary General and his Cabinet members responsible for CFSP may exercise influence on policy making in the second pillar as politico-administrative hybrids. The prospect which the Maastricht process opens up is that Image IV hybrids will exercise more extensive influence in areas beyond the policy making in Community affairs, i.e., third pillar issues which, like EMU, strike at the heart of national sovereignty.

Finally, the role of the personal representatives as joint problem solvers does not consistently indicate the existence of Image IV hybrids. There were personal representatives, like de Boissieu and Trumpf, whose teamwork did a great deal to facilitate compromises and integrative bargaining at different levels. However, neither Trumpf nor de Boissieu spoke out in an openly political way about Maastricht leaving this task to their political masters.

At Maastricht it was Kohl who defined his conception of the national interest in a European Community framework and engaged himself thoroughly with Mitterrand in the process of integrative bargaining on EMU. His decision can be viewed as part of a larger effort by the heads of state and government to assert the existence of democratic, as opposed to technocratic, government in the name of integration and union. This does not address the issue of the need for more advances in parliamentary democracy at the European level, however, in order to check the predominance of the Council structure in the Community legislative process.

MONNET'S APPROACH

The relevance of this approach to the Maastricht process is in its emphasis on integrative bargaining as a sub-process of negotiations and on the process of *engrenage* as adapted to the IGC, as opposed to the regular Community, context.

This book illustrates that the EMU conference contained elements of distributive bargaining, or classic compromise tactics, as in the decision to delay the creation of the ECB until Stage Three by introducing a European Monetary Institute in Stage Two. Attitudinal structuring, or an emphasis on Community-building as opposed to a traditional reliance on balance of power politics, was also present in the attempts to formulate a decision-making procedure for the transition to Stage Three. And intraorganizational bargaining, as illustrated by Putnam's approach of dealing with national actors behind one's chair during negotiations, was evident in the nexus between internal bargaining and external negotiations.

The potential for integrative bargaining was also constantly present though in that the member states and the Commission were searching to line up the problems to be solved to achieve EMU on one side of the table and the negotiators on the other. The goal of the conference was, to use a phrase of Monnet's, "to search for a solution to a common problem," namely, how to achieve economic and monetary union in Europe.[9] That integrative bargaining on EMU reached its fullest expression in the European Council is not surprising—the final decision on such a significant step in European integration could only come from the highest political level of democratically elected leaders represented in a body that owes its origins to Monnet's last initiative some twenty years ago. In the Monnet tradition, an agreement was achieved at a point above the lowest common denominator on a policy which represented a risky leap into the unknown. Two seemingly irreconcilable

---

[9] Bini-Smaghi, Padoa-Schioppa and Papadia, *The Policy History of the Maastricht Treaty*, 42.

objectives, strict convergence criteria and a fixed timetable, were brought together to co-exist in a way that brings about a creative tension to infuse the entire process. In this sense, EMU is the concrete manifestation of integrative bargaining and the continuation of Monnet's "steps in time."

However, it is also necessary to underline the creation of a new institution, the European Central Bank, as part of a common solution to the problem of how to create EMU. The workings of the ECB have the potential to create a new psychological situation that transcends the old one and enables the Community to define integration in a completely different context. In its emphasis on the creation of a new institution, Monnet's approach is illustrative of a perspective in international relations known as "neoliberal institutionalism." This perspective does not assert that "states are always highly constrained by international institutions." Nor does it claim that "states ignore the effects of their actions on the wealth or power of other states." Neoliberal institutionalists, like Robert Keohane, do argue, however, that "state actions depend to a considerable degree on prevailing institutional arrangements, which affect: the flow of information and the opportunities to negotiate; the ability of governments to monitor others' compliance and to implement their own commitments; (and) prevailing expectations about the solidity of international agreements." [10]

Whether the creation of a European Central Bank will actually be able to redefine the context of integration in Europe in line with the tenets of neoliberal institutionalist thought, or whether internal strife on the bank's board of governors will reflect older suspicions and a return to classical balance of power politics, are questions for the future. The attempt to use Monnet's approach in the creation of EMU illustrates just how difficult it is to achieve integrative bargaining on complex issues, like a set date for entry into Stage Three, among states with such divergent national traditions. In this regard, the German delegation's insistence on a unanimous decision in order to decide on the passage to Stage Three was at variance with Chancellor Kohl's views and those of the other leaders in the European Council. This was because the Bundesbank was quicker than the Kohl government to believe that the goal of EMU was first and foremost the undermining of German power. Wilhelm Nölling, President of the National Bank of Hamburg, stated: "Let us have no illusions—in the actual discussions over the new monetary order in Europe, at stake are power, influence and the pursuit of national interests." [11]

Yet, there is little question that the Community's member states are trying to maximize joint gains. Whether the political will exists to make the tough

---

[10]Keohane, *International Institutions and State Power*, 2.

[11]Marsh, *Die Bundesbank*, 311–312.

choices at Level II which EMU will require a few years down the road is open to question. Agreement on a fixed date is a necessary point of departure. The use of integrative bargaining to achieve an accord on this point was decisive to the final outcome at Maastricht. The fulfillment of the required convergence criteria and securing the agreement of national parliaments to move on to the final stage are other matters. The issue of whether or not other member states, besides the Federal Republic of Germany, will agree to significant steps on the road to political union in exchange for a green light on the creation of the European Central Bank and a single currency is relevant in this context.

During the Maastricht process, *engrenage* was illustrated by the Commission's role on EMU as it aimed to educate national leaders and civil servants in the reality of their common interest. The negotiation and ratification of Maastricht involved an awareness by these same leaders and civil servants that integrative steps previously achieved, via the Single European Act, were "locked-in" and that the costs of opting out for France and Germany in particular were higher than those of continued involvement. The role of the European Commission in the Maastricht process cannot be likened to that in daily Community affairs; yet the input of Delors and his Cabinet influenced French and German elites close to Mitterrand and Kohl.

Delors' use of Monnet's approach was in the development of a strategy to enable the European Commission to play the role of a policy entrepreneur on EMU. Working alongside Mitterrand and Kohl, the Commission President placed EMU at the top of the Community agenda and kept it there until Maastricht was ratified. Yet, when Delors acted on his belief that "time is short" in 1990 and tried to confront the member states directly on issues of political union in 1991, he ran into trouble in the form of popular perceptions of change imposed from the "top down" during the national ratifications in 1992. This fact illustrates the need in IGC process to recognize the point just above the lowest common denominator to advance integration. Direct confrontations by the European Commission with member states, without a sense of the timing or balance in a negotiation, will not lead states to relinquish national sovereignty. This may only come about over time, after successive steps in the integration process, during which states perceive these steps to be in their interest. In this context, national publics, and particularly younger people, need to be more aware of the Union as a transnational polity and of the role of the European institutions in that polity. Although the Commission's role in the IGC process is misunderstood by popular opinion, the Maastricht experience reveals that it is uniquely placed to fulfill an important task as a strategist in the interest of European unity. This study reveals that the Commission must act to accomplish its tasks in tandem with the Council, not in place of the member states.[12]

LESSONS FROM EXPERIENCE: MAASTRICHT AND THE FUTURE OF EUROPEAN INTEGRATION

The increasing scope of interaction among member states at all levels of negotiation in the Council shows the limits to explaining the IGC process by contrasting neo-functionalism with intergovernmentalism.This is not only because the IGC process is inherently a political learning process for all participants, national and European. It is also because the EMU conference was an exercise in joint problem solving at different levels of negotiation. Both Kohl's decision on a fixed date for Stage Three and the German "yes" to Maastricht, in spite of limited progress on political union, indicate that domestic constraints on state action during negotiations and Treaty ratifications were not decisive. In this sense, Maastricht is not meant to empower the German state as much as to contribute to the German vision of a federal Europe.[13]

Two observations are noteworthy in this regard, however. First, the decision on the final transition to EMU will be made by the European Council. The authority of the heads of state and government to make this decision, as opposed to central bank governors and finance ministers, is clear. This is an assertion of state power over technical competence of a corporate nature demonstrated by the strong transnational links among financial experts in the Community. In this sense, it is very much in line with a French statist way of thinking. Second, in several important ways, Maastricht empowers the Länder more than it does the German federal government. Article 23 BL gives the Länder more input during negotiations in Brussels to make Community legislation. The impact of these new powers remains to be seen in practice, but this constitutional change implies movement in the direction of a Europe of the Regions in which local power continues to assert itself. This is a direct challenge to centralized authority predominant in a state like France.[14]

These contradictions suggest that the EMU negotiations must be understood as more than just the domestic political processes that shape bargaining positions by key member states. There was a European interest at

---

[12]Colette Mazzucelli, "The United States of Europe Revisited: Its Relevance to Integration in Practice," *International Affairs Review* (Summer 1995): 100–124.

[13]An evaluation of "state-centric arguments" is found in Gary Marks, Liesbet Hooghe and Kermit Blank, "European Integration and the State," Paper presented at the American Political Science Association Meeting, New York, September 1–4, 1994.

[14]Darrell Delamaide, *The New Superregions of Europe* (New York: Plume, 1995) discusses the economic and political significance of regional alliances across national borders.

stake in these negotiations, defended by the Delors Commission, which no one member state's domestic agenda could entirely dictate. Examples of this general interest include the decisions to establish a cohesion fund in the Treaty, which was not a goal of France, Germany or Great Britain, to set a timetable for Stage Three of EMU or to vote on the final transition by qualified majority in the Council. On cohesion, in particular, the influence of transnational interest groups, like the European Trade Union Confederation, on the IGC process could be discerned in conjunction with the national interests of the "Club Med" states. French and German interest groups, meeting in umbrella organizations at the European level, like the UNICE and the ETUC, did not view a state-to-state Treaty like Maastricht as a threat to their transnational alliances. On the contrary, their intent to use provisions on EMU, social policy and cohesion in the Treaty on European Union to their advantage in the aftermath of successful domestic ratifications is clear. These transnational interest groups are likely to be among the beneficiaries of Maastricht and any future Treaty reforms.[15]

The relevance of the Maastricht process to the future of European integration is in the lessons it taught politicians and civil servants about the need to open up the IGC process to the public and to make decision making on Community legislation more transparent and understandable to ordinary citizens. The Maastricht process also highlights the need for different levels of negotiation which differ from those necessary in the making of legislation in the European Community. An awareness of the points of access at each level of negotiation is significant for those persons or interest groups trying to gain input into future IGC processes.

It is clear that for France, more than for Germany, the preservation of national sovereignty will remain a priority throughout the next decade and into the next millennium. The French emphasis on sovereignty is not compatible with German aspirations for a federal Europe in which the institutions of the Union play significant roles. This tension between the Franco-German couple will undoubtedly be present during future IGC processes to redefine the institutional system of the Union. The Maastricht experience teaches us that France and Germany will find a way to establish joint positions, even if these are compromises at best. Moreover, French, German and European politico-administrative hybrids and civil servants will strive to maintain a working relationship between the two countries. Unlike their political masters, who operate in unstable electoral environments, these individuals emphasize continuity amidst the changes brought about by integration.

---

[15]The existence of these transnational groups and their links to domestic groups are mentioned briefly in Chapter III.

France and Germany will face a common challenge during future IGCs and enlargements of the Union. The Maastricht process illustrated that *engrenage* could not bridge the distance between elites and electorates. For the average French and German citizen the Union is a boring topic. The work of actors like Delors, Köhler and Guigou illustrates that part of the problem is that the EU makes laws; it does not capture the popular imagination by telling a good story about why there is an urgent need for its existence. In the absence of a threat from the East, the need for Union in Europe is not self-explanatory. In a sense, both France and Germany must re-evaluate how to sell their goals for Europe, both individual and joint, to national publics. This task will undoubtedly be complicated by a generation gap; older citizens may experience Europe less as a reality in their daily lives than younger students and workers, for example.

When Monnet was directly involved in the Schuman Conference in 1950, the influence of civil servants on IGC negotiations was not as heavy. The fact that Monnet himself had a dominant say for France during the Schuman Conference was illustrative of the elitist way in which foreign policy was made in an earlier era. The closed nature of the IGC process in 1991 illustrates that the European Commission was made a scapegoat for the failings of the process because most French and German citizens, regardless of their generation, were unaware of their governments' roles in the diplomacy of EMU and political union. This was due in large part to the minimal contact that ordinary civil servants have with public opinion. The task of Image IV hybrids is to bridge this gap between the elites and the public.

In sum, despite French insistence on the preservation of sovereignty, France and Germany will remain the "motor for Europe" driving the integration process. Future IGCs may not yield spectacular results, but both countries will find ways to compromise. The search for agreement may indeed be more difficult as the issues on future intergovernmental conference agendas, like CFSP, strike at the heart of state sovereignty. This study concludes that the Maastricht process will stand the test of time as a unique achievement in constitutional change. This is true in terms of the scope of Treaty reform undertaken in the two IGCs and the need, at a turning point in the history of integration, to convey to national publics the nature of the project to create a European Union.

Even with changes in French and German domestic politics, the European agenda for EMU and the prospect of enlargement will provide both countries with an impetus to cooperate. Specifically, they must work together bilaterally, and in tandem with the European Commission, to create a consensus within the framework of multilateral negotiations. Both partners must also be able and willing to define and locate points of agreement just above the lowest common denominator and to give just enough in substance to promote the development of the Union. The French know quite well that the

Federal Republic is their key economic partner, owing to the strength of the D-mark. Reason dictates that it is in both countries' joint interest to work closely together as the Union strives to accomplish two historic tasks: the creation of a single currency and the opening of its borders to the countries of central and eastern Europe in the early years of the twenty-first century.

The European Parliament's Decision-Making Procedures: Cooperation and Co-Decision Explained[1]

COOPERATION PROCEDURE (ARTICLE 189C)

1. Commission Proposal

2. Opinion of Parliament

3. Common position of Council by qualified majority vote

4. Communication of common position to European Parliament

5. Parliament

   a) approves within three months common position by qualified majority

   b) expresses no opinion within three months

   a) or b): Council adopts the act

   c) proposes amendments to common position by absolute majority within three months

   d) rejects common position by absolute majority of its members

   c) or d): Parliament forwards result to Council and Commission.

6. Commission reconsiders within one month its Proposal and submits re-examined Proposal and its opinion on Parliament's amendments which the Commission did not accept.

7. Council

   a) adopts within three months Commission's re-examined Proposal

   - by qualified majority

---

[1] Taken from *The New Treaty on European Union*, 28–30.

- by unanimity

(1) if Parliament rejected common position

(2) if Council wishes to adopt Parliament's amendments not accepted by the Commission or

(3) if Council wishes to amend the re-examined Proposal

    b) does not adopt the Proposal within three months; Proposal is deemed to have lapsed.

The period of three months may be prolonged by one month by common accord between Commission and Council.

CO-DECISION PROCEDURE (ARTICLE 189B)

1. Commission proposal[2]

2. Opinion of Parliament

3. Common position of the Council by qualified majority[3]

4. Parliament

 a) approves common position within three months

 b) expresses no opinion within three months

 a) or b): Council adopts the act

 c) indicates, by absolute majority, that it intends to reject common position; informs Council. Period of three months is prolonged by two months.

 d) proposes amendments to common position by absolute majority within three months. Forwarded to Council and Commission.

5. Commission and Council deliver opinion on Parliament's amendments.

6. Council

 -adopts Parliament's amendments within three months by qualified majority—or by unanimity where Commission's opinion is unfavorable; act adopted.

 -does not adopt the act. Conciliation Committee is convened, composed of equal number of Council and Parliament representatives. Agreement of Committee by qualified majority of Council members and majority of Parliament members.

7. Conciliation Committee

 a) approves joint text within six weeks. Parliament and Council must then adopt within six weeks or Proposal fails.

---

[2]Commission may alter its Proposal as long as Council has not adopted the act (Article 189a.2 EUT).

[3](except for two matters—culture and R&D, which are multi-annual framework programmes that require unanimity throughout).

b) does not agree. Proposal deemed to have not been adopted except if

- Council confirms its original common position within six weeks

- Parliament fails to veto by absolute majority of its members within six weeks of Council confirmation[4]

---

[4]Periods of three months and six weeks may be prolonged by two months or two weeks respectively by common agreement between Council and Parliament.

Bibliography

PRIMARY SOURCES
Government/Official Documents
Denmark
Danish Ministry of Foreign Affairs. *The White Paper on Denmark and the Maastricht Treaty.* Copenhagen: Ministry of Foreign Affairs, 1992.

European Communities/Union
Commission of the European Communities. *Intergovernmental Conferences: Contributions by the Commission.* Luxembourg: Office for Official Publications of the European Communities, 1991.
Committee of Governors of the Central Banks of the Member States of the European Economic Community. *Draft Statute of the European System of Central Banks and of the European Central Bank.* Basel, 27 November 1990.
Conclusions of the ECOFIN Council of 28 September 1992. Brussels: Council of the European Union, 1992.
Council of the European Union. *Draft Report of the Council on the Functioning of the Treaty on European Union.* 5082/95 Brussels: General Secretariat, 1995.
European Communities. *Treaties Establishing the European Communities.* Luxembourg: Office for Official Publications of the European Communities, 1987.
European Parliament. *Battling for the Union: Altiero Spinelli.* Luxembourg: Office for Official Publications of the European Communities, 1988.
General Secretariat. Council of the European Communities. *The Council of the European Community.* Luxembourg: Office for Official Publications of the European Communities, 1992.
Rat der Europäischen Gemeinschaften. Generalsekretariat. Mitteilung an die Presse 8400/91 (Presse 155). *Siebte Ministertagung der Regierungskonferenz über die Politischen Union.* Brüssel, den 30. September und 1. Oktober 1991.
Rat der Europäischen Gemeinschaften. Generalsekretariat. Mitteilung an die Presse 4863/91 (Presse 25). *Dritte Ministertagung der Regierungskonferenz über die Politischen Union.* Brüssel, den 4./5. März 1991.

The Delors Committee. *Report on Economic and Monetary Union in the European Community*. Luxembourg: Office for Official Publications of the European Communities, 1989.

France

Journal Officielle de la République Française. Débats Parlementaires. Assemblée Nationale, 27 novembre 1991.

Ministère des Affaires Etrangères. *La Politique Etrangère de la France*. Textes et Documents. Novembre-Decembre 1991. Paris: Ministère des Affaires Etrangères, 1991.

———. *La Politique Etrangère de la France*. Textes et Documents. Septembre-Octobre 1991. Paris: Ministère des Affaires Etrangères, 1991.

———. *La Politique Etrangère de la France*. Textes et Documents. Mai-Juin 1991. Paris: Ministère des Affaires Etrangères, 1991.

The French Constitution. London: Ambassade de France, 1986.

Who's Who in France, 1992–1993.

Germany

Bundesministerium für Wirtschaft. Pressestelle. Überlegungen zum gegenwärtigen Stand der Verhandlungen über die Europäische Wirtschafts- und Währungsunion. Bonn, den 22. Oktober 1991. Bonn: Bundesministerium für Wirtschaft, 1991.

Bundesrat. Stenographischer Bericht. 650. Sitzung. Bonn, Freitag, den 18. Dezember 1992. Bonn: Bundesrat, 1992.

———. Empfehlungen der Ausschüsse, Gesetz zum Vertrag vom 7. Februar 1992 über die Europäische Union. Drucksache 810/1/92. Bonn: Bundesrat, 1992.

———. Empfehlungen der Ausschüsse zum Entwurf eines Gesetzes über die Zusammenarbeit von Bund und Ländern in Angelegenheiten der Europäischen Union. Drucksache 630/1/92. Bonn: Bundesrat, 1992.

———. Stenographischer Bericht. 646. Sitzung. Bonn, Freitag, den 25. September 1992. Bonn: Bundesrat, 1992.

Deutscher Bundestag. 12. Wahlperiode. 68. Sitzung. Bonn, Freitag, den 13. Dezember 1991.

———. 12. Wahlperiode. Gesetzentwurf der Bundesregierung. Entwurf eines Gesetzes zur Änderung des Grundgesetzes. Drucksache 12/3338. Bonn: Deutscher Bundestag, 1992.

———. 12. Wahlperiode. 126. Sitzung. Bonn, Mittwoch, den 2. Dezember 1992.

———. 12. Wahlperiode. Entschließungsantrag der Fraktionen der CDU/CSU, SPD und FDP zu dem Gesetzentwurf der Bundesregierung. Drucksache 12/3905. Bonn: Deutscher Bundestag, 1992.

———. Beschlußempfehlung und Bericht des Sonderausschusses "Europäische Union (Vertrag von Maastricht)." Drucksache 12/3896. Bonn: Deutscher Bundestag, 1992.

———. Beschlußempfehlung und Bericht des Sonderausschusses "Europäische Union (Vertrag von Maastricht)." Drucksache 12/3895. Bonn: Deutscher Bundestag, 1992.

———. 12. Wahlperiode. 110. Sitzung. Bonn, Donnerstag, den 8. Oktober 1992.

———. 12. Wahlperiode. 108. Sitzung. Bonn, Freitag, den 25. September 1992.

———. 12. Wahlperiode. Entschließungsantrag der Fraktion der SPD. Drucksache 12/3311. Bonn: Deutscher Bundestag, 1992.

———. Antrag der Fraktion der SPD. Perspektiven der europäischen Integration. Drucksache 12/2813. Bonn: Deutscher Bundestag, 1992.

———. Bericht der Bundesregierung zum Stand der Arbeiten zur Stärkung des europäischen Parlaments in den Regierungskonferenzen zur Wirtschafts- und Währungsunion und zur politischen Union. Drucksache 12/2249. Bonn: Deutscher Bundestag, 1991.

———. 12. Wahlperiode. 68. Sitzung. Bonn, Freitag, den 13. Dezember 1991.

———. 12. Wahlperiode. Entschließungsantrag der Fraktionen der CDU/CSU und FDP zur Erklärung der Bundesregierung. Gipfeltreffen der Staats- und Regierungschefs der EG in Maastricht sowie der Staats- und Regierungschefs der NATO in Rom. Drucksache 12/1476. Bonn: Deutscher Bundestag, 1991.

———. 12. Wahlperiode. Antrag der Fraktion der SPD. Verhandlungen der Bundesregierung in den EG-Regierungskonferenzen zur politischen Union und zur Wirtschafts- und Währungsunion. Drucksache 12/1434. Bonn: Deutscher Bundestag, 1991.

———. 12. Wahlperiode. Antwort der Bundesregierung auf die kleine Anfrage der Fraktion der SPD. Drucksache 12/1068. Bonn: Deutscher Bundestag, 1991.

———. 12. Wahlperiode. Kleine Anfrage der Fraktion der SPD. Stand der Verhandlungen der EG-Regierungskonferenzen und Verhandlungsstrategie der Bundesregierung zur politischen Union und zur Europäischen Wirtschafts- und Währungsunion. Drucksache 12/833. Bonn: Deutscher Bundestag, 1991.

———. 12. Wahlperiode. 64. Sitzung. Bonn, Donnerstag, den 5. Dezember 1991.

———. 12. Wahlperiode. 64. Sitzung. Bonn, Mittwoch, den 30. Januar 1991.

———. 11.Wahlperiode. 233 Sitzung. Bonn, Dienstag, den 30. Oktober 1990.

Entscheidungen des Bundesverfassungsgerichts. (BverfGE) 89.Band. Tübingen: J.C.B. Mohr, 1994.

Genscher, Hans-Dietrich. "A European Currency Area and a European Bank." Memorandum to the General Affairs Council. Bonn: *Auswärtiges Amt*, 1988.

Handbuch der Bundesregierung. 12. WP, Mai 1993.

The Basic Law of the Federal Republic of Germany. Bonn: Press and Information
Office of the Federal Government, 1987.
Zustimmung zum Vertrag von Maastricht. *Bulletin.* 22. September 1992. Bonn:
Auswärtiges Amt, 1992.

Interviews

Bonn

1. Markus Berger, Assistant to Parliamentarian Alfred Dregger, Bundestag, 15 June
1993
2. Axel Bertuch-Samuels, Personal Assistant to State Secretary Horst Köhler, Federal
Ministry of Finance, 9 July 1993
3. Reimer von Borries, European Division, Federal Ministry of Economics, 14 June
1993
4. Klaus Botzet, European Legal Affairs Department, European Division, *Auswärtiges
Amt*, 11 November 1992
5. Dr. Eckart Cuntz, Intergovernmental Conference on Political Union Department,
Auswärtiges Amt, 29 January 1993
6. Rainer Eberle, European Division, *Auswärtiges Amt*, 16 April 1993
7. Prof. Dr. Johann Eekhoff, State Secretary, Economics Ministry, 18 June 1993
8. Christoph Eichhorn, Liaison Office to Federal Cabinet and Parliament, *Auswärtiges
Amt*, 16 October 1992
9. Helge Engelhard, Federal Ministry of Education and Science, Department of
European Community Affairs, 8 December 1994
10. Dr. Friederike von Estorff, International Monetary Division, Federal Ministry of
Economics, 17 February 1993
11. Michael Geier, Political Division, Franco-German Relations Department,
Auswärtiges Amt, 29 April 1993
12. Dr. Günter Grosche, European and International Monetary Division, Federal
Ministry of Finance, 26 April 1993
13. Dr. Gert Haller, State Secretary, Federal Ministry of Finance, 28 July 1993
14. Renate Hellwig, Chairman, *Europaausschuß*, Bundestag, 29 April 1993
15. Dr. Peter von Jagow, European Correspondent, *Auswärtiges Amt*, 29 June 1993
16. Wilhelm Kaiser, Head of Federal-State Relations Department, European Division,
Federal Ministry of Economics, 2 July 1993
17. Dr. Werner Kaufmann-Bühler, Head of European Institutional and Legal Affairs
Sub-Division, European Division, *Auswärtiges Amt*, 31 January 1993, 21 July
1993 and 29 December 1994
18. Dr. Jürgen Kühn, Head of European Division, Federal Ministry of Economics, 30
March 1993

19. Hanns Jürgen Küsters, Researcher, Institute for German Politics, 26 April 1993
20. Rose D. Lässing, *Auswärtiges Amt*, European Division, 21 April 1993
21. Friedrich Löhr, Political Department, Federal Chancellor's Office, 16 June 1993
22. Max Maldacker, Assistant to the German-French Coordinator, Dr. Gerhard Stoltenberg, *Auswärtiges Amt*, 28 June 1993
23. Joachim von Marschall, European Parliament Department, European Division, *Auswärtiges Amt*, 8 June 1993
24. Henning von Massow, European Division, Federal Ministry of Economics, 21 July 1993
25. Michael Menthler, Bavarian Representation for Federal and European Community Affairs to the Federal Government, 13 October 1994
26. Dr. Rudolf Morawitz, Head of European Law Division, Federal Ministry of Economics, 17 June 1993
27. Wolfgang Neumann, Researcher, German Association of Savings Banks, 30 April 1993
28. Prof. Dr. Gerhard Rambow, Head of European Division, Federal Ministry of Economics, 21 July 1993
29. Elfriede Regelsberger, Assistant to the Director, Institute for European Policy Studies, 1 July 1993
30. Joachim Reichert, New Federal States Planning Staff, Federal Ministry of Economics, 16 February 1993
31. Dr. Wilhelm Schönfelder, Head of European Foreign and Monetary Affairs Sub-Division, European Division, *Auswärtiges Amt*, 6 May 1993 and 27 December 1994
32. Charlotte Schwarzer, Civil and Trade Law Department, *Auswärtiges Amt*, 27 February 1992
33. Prof. Dr. Martin Seidel, European Division, Federal Ministry of Economics, 2 March 1993
34. Ursula Seiler-Albring, Minister of State for European Affairs, *Auswärtiges Amt*, 16 April 1993
35. Annette Sierigk, Assistant to the State Minister, Bavarian State Representation for Federal and European Community Affairs to the German Federal Government, 18 December 1992
36. Reinhardt Silberberg, Institutional Affairs Department, European Division, *Auswärtiges Amt*, 13 May 1993
37. Dr. Jürgen Trumpf, State Secretary, *Auswärtiges Amt*, 30 July 1993
38. Dr. Dietrich Vaubel, Head of European Constitutional Law Department, Federal Ministry of the Interior, 28 April 1993

39. Dr. Wolfgang Wessels, Director, Institute for European Policy Studies, 30 August 1991
40. Dr. Ingo Winkelmann, Legal Department, *Auswärtiges Amt*, 16 June 1993
41. Dr. Joachim Wuermerling, Counselor, Intergovernmental Conferences, Bavarian State Representation for Federal and European Community Affairs to the Federal Government, 18 February 1993

Brugge
42. Dr. Werner Ungerer, Rector, College of Europe, 7 July 1993

Brussels
43. Gustaaf M. Borchardt, Legal Adviser, Dutch Permanent Representation to the European Communities, 23 November 1992
44. Jöel de Bry, Secretariat General, Commission of the European Communities, 27 May 1992
45. Jean Cadet, Assistant to the Ambassador, French Permanent Representation to the European Communities, 15 July 1992
46. Poul Christophersen, Assistant to Secretary General Niels Ersbøll, Secretariat of the Council of Ministers, 27 May 1992
47. Giuseppe Ciavarini Azzi, Director, Institutional Affairs Division, Commission of the European Communities, 8 May 1992
48. Jim Cloos, Assistant to the Ambassador, Luxembourg Permanent Representation to the European Communities, 23 November 1992
49. Richard Corbett, Assistant to MEP David Martin, Institutional Affairs Committee, European Parliament Secretariat, 3 July 1992
50. Jean-Pierre Cot, Leader of the Socialist Group, European Parliament, 29 June 1992
51. Yves Doutriaux, Member of the Antici Group, French Permanent Representation to the European Communities, 22 June 1992
52. Sabine Ehmke-Gendron, German Permanent Representation to the European Communities, 18 May 1992
53. John Fitzmaurice, Head of Division, Relations with the European Parliament, Commission of the European Communities, 10 May 1992
54. Hans-Joachim Guenther, North Rhine-Westphalia Permanent Representation to the European Communities, 10 May 1992
55. Alexander Italianer, Commission of the European Communities, Directorate-General II—Economic and Financial Affairs, 25 May 1994
56. Peter Jabcke, German Permanent Representation to the European Communities, 10 July 1992 and 24 July 1992

57. Max Kohnstamm, Associate of Jean Monnet, Belmont Policy Center, 23 February 1993
58. Dietrich von Kyaw, Ambassador, German Permanent Representation to the European Communities, 11 June 1993
59. Jacqueline Lastenouse, Directorate General for Information Communication and Culture, Commission of the European Communities, 6 June 1992
60. Prof. Jean-Victor Louis, Director of Legal Services, National Bank of Belgium, 1 July 1992
61. Peter Ludlow, Director, Center for European Policy Studies, 15 May 1992
62. Theo Martens, German Permanent Representation to the European Communities, 10 July 1992
63. Roland Mauch, German Permanent Representation to the European Communities, 15 June 1992
64. Klaus-Peter Nanz, German Permanent Representation to the European Communities, 26 August 1992
65. Hartmut Offentle, Secretariat General, Commission of the European Communities, 17 June 1992
66. Raymond Rifflet, Special Counselor to President Jacques Delors, Commission of the European Communities, 26 May 1992
67. Jean de Ruyt, Belgian Diplomat, Ministry of Foreign Affairs, 14 May 1992
68. François Scheer, Ambassador, French Permanent Representation to the European Communities, 25 November 1992
69. Philippe de Schoutheete, Ambassador, Belgian Permanent Representation to the European Communities, 6 July 1992
70. Alain van Solinge, Secretariat General, Commission of the European Communities, 26 July 1992
71. Elmar Timpe, German Permanent Representation to the European Communities, 15 May 1992
72. Dr. Jürgen Trumpf, Ambassador, German Permanent Representation to the European Communities, 30 July 1992
73. Martin Westlake, Secretariat General, Commission of the European Communities, 10 July 1992
74. David Williamson, Secretary General, Commission of the European Communities, 11 June 1993

Florence
75. Egon Bahr, Visiting Professor, European University Institute, 24 October 1991
76. Pierre Hassner, Visiting Professor, European University Institute, 19 November 1991

77. Prof. Roger Morgan, Director, European Policy Unit, European University Institute, 29 October 1991

Ludwigsburg
78. Dr. Robert Picht, Director, Deutsch-Französisches Institut, 28 May 1993

Luxembourg
79. Dr. Thomas Grunert, Institutional and Political Affairs Division, Secretariat, European Parliament, 10 June 1993
80. Prof. Ghita Ionescu, President, IPSA Research Committee on European Unification, 2 June 1992

Paris
81. Daniel Barroy, Worms Company, Action Committee for Europe, 10 March 1993 and 7 July 1993
82. Thierry Bert, Technical Counselor, Elysée, 8 March 1993
83. Pierre de Boissieu, Director, Economic Affairs Division, Quai d'Orsay, 8 March 1993
84. Alfred Cahen, Belgian Ambassador to the Republic of France, Former Secretary General, Western European Union, 19 July 1993
85. René Foch, Associate of Jean Monnet, Action Committee for Europe, 28 June 1993
86. Dr. Jean Klein, Researcher, French Institute of International Relations, 21 June 1991
87. Dr. Christian Lequesne, Researcher, Center for the Study of International Relations, 21 May 1991
88. Ephraïm Marquer, Translation Department, Elysée, 6 July 1993
89. Dominique Moisi, Assistant to the Director, French Institute of International Relations, 12 May 1991
90. Philippe Moreau Defarges, Researcher, French Institute of International Relations, 12 May 1991
91. Walter Schütze, Director, Franco-German Committee, French Institute of International Relations, 12 May 1991
92. Pierre Vimont, Director, Cabinet of Minister for European Affairs Elisabeth Guigou, Quai d'Orsay, 8 March 1993

Rome
93. Dr. Gianni Bonvicini, Director, Istituto Affari Internazionali, 8 April 1993

Stuttgart
94. Berndt von Staden, Former State Secretary, *Auswärtiges Amt*, 5 December 1992

Washington, DC
95. Guy de Bassompierre, Belgian Diplomat, Embassy of Belgium, 15 March 1989
96. Sir William Nicoll, Fulbright Fellow, George Mason University, 2 May 1992
97. Jean de Ruyt, Belgian Diplomat, Embassy of Belgium, 10 October 1989
98. Ambassador J. Robert Schaetzel, President, The Jean Monnet Council, 11 January 1994

Information Obtained during Bosch Presentations and Work Sessions

99. Gérard Araud, Diplomatic Counselor, Ministry of Defense, Discussion with Fellows of the Robert Bosch Foundation, 9 March 1993
100. Jean-Claude Aurousseau, Prefect of the North Calais Region, Discussion with Fellows of the Robert Bosch Foundation, 15 March 1993
101. Dr. Martin Bangemann, Vice President, Commissioner for Industrial Affairs, Commission of the European Communities, Discussion with Fellows of the Robert Bosch Foundation, 18 March 1993
102. Robert Beecroft, Political Adviser, US Mission to NATO, Discussion with Fellows of the Robert Bosch Foundation, 19 March 1993
103. Pascal Bruckner, Philosopher, Discussion with Fellows of the Robert Bosch Foundation, 10 March 1993
104. Jacques Delors, President of the European Commission, Meeting with After-Maastricht Committee of the European Parliament, 22 May 1992
105. Hans-Dietrich Genscher, Former Foreign Minister, Federal Republic of Germany, Question and Answer Session with the Political Affairs Committee of the European Parliament, 22 January 1988
106. Nicole Gnesotto, Assistant to the Director, Institute for Security Studies, Western European Union, Discussion with Fellows of the Robert Bosch Foundation, 11 March 1993
107. Maurice Gourdault-Montagne, Assistant Director of Cabinet, Quai d'Orsay, Discussion with Fellows of the Robert Bosch Foundation, 12 March 1993
108. Dr. Henry A. Kissinger, Former Secretary of State, 1992 Arthur Burns Memorial Lecture, 28 October 1992
109. Dr. Egon A. Klepsch, President, European Parliament, Address to the Research Committee on European Unification, 2 June 1992
110. Horst Köhler, State Secretary, Federal Ministry of Finance, Speech at the Representation of the Commission of the European Communities in the Federal Republic of Germany, 8 December 1992
111. Dr. Helmut Kohl, Chancellor, Federal Republic of Germany, Discussion with Fellows of the Robert Bosch Foundation, 16 September 1992

112. Ruud Lubbers, Prime Minister, Kingdom of the Netherlands, Speech to Open the Academic Year at the European University Institute, 26 October 1991
113. Dr. Hans-Friedrich von Ploetz, Head of European Division, *Auswärtiges Amt*, Discussion with Fellows of the Robert Bosch Foundation, 19 March 1993
114. Dominique Schnapper, Director of Studies, School of Advanced Social Sciences, Discussion with Fellows of the Robert Bosch Foundation, 12 March 1993
115. David Spence, Head of Unit, Directorate-General for Audio-Visual, Information, Communication and Culture, Commission of the European Communities, Discussion with Fellows of the Robert Bosch Foundation, 17 March 1993
116. Bernard Stirn, Secretary General, Council of State, Discussion with Fellows of the Robert Bosch Foundation, 10 March 1993
117. Richard von Weizsäcker, President, Federal Republic of Germany, Discussion with Fellows of the Robert Bosch Foundation, 10 September 1992
118. Renate Hellwig, Chair, *Europaausschuß*, Bundestag, Discussion with Fellows of the Robert Bosch Foundation, 22 September 1994

Agence Europe
Agence Europe, 23 juillet 1992.
Agence Europe, 18 et 19 mai 1992.
Agence Europe, 11 mars 1992.
Agence Europe, 11 décembre 1991.
Agence Europe, 9 et 10 décembre 1991.
Agence Europe, 22 et 23 avril 1991.
Agence Europe, 12 janvier 1991.
Agence Europe, 9 septembre 1989.
Agence Europe, 7 septembre 1989.
Europe Documents. 5. Oktober 1991.

Unpublished Materials
"Address by Jacques Delors, President of the European Commission of the European Communities, at the Collège d'Europe." Bruges, Belgium, October 17, 1989 Brussels: Commission of the European Communities, 1989.
Auswärtiges Amt. Rede des Bundesministers des Auswärtigen, Dr. Klaus Kinkel, anläßlich des Abschiedsempfangs für Staatssekretär Dr. Lautenschlager auf dem Petersberg am 28. Januar 1993. Mitteilung für die Presse Nr. 1017/93. Bonn: *Auswärtiges Amt*, 1993.
———. Rede des Bundesministers des Auswärtigen, Dr. Klaus Kinkel, bei der 2./3. Lesung des Vertrages über die Europäische Union und der damit verbundenen

Gesetzentwürf im Deutschen Bundestag am 02. Dezember 1992. Mitteilung für die Presse Nr. 1192/92. Bonn: *Auswärtiges Amt*, 1992.

―――――. Interview des Bundesministers des Auswärtigen, Dr. Klaus Kinkel, mit dem Süddeutschen Rundfunk. Mitteilung für die Presse Nr. 1190/92. Bonn: *Auswärtiges Amt*, 1992.

―――――. Debattenbeitrag der Staatsministerin im Auswärtigen Amt, Ursula Seiler-Albring, in der Sitzung des Deutechen Bundesrats am 08. November 1991. Mitteilung für die Presse Nr. 1239/91. Bonn: *Auswärtiges Amt*, 1991.

―――――. Interview des Bundesministers des Auswärtigen, Hans-Dietrich Genscher, mit der niederländischen Zeitung Algemeen Dagblad (Ausgabe vom 16. Oktober 1991) zu Fragen der europäischen Integration. Mitteilung für die Presse Nr. 1221/91. Bonn: *Auswärtiges Amt*, 1991.

Déclaration de la Confédération Européenne des Syndicats. "Union Economique et Monétaire." Adoptée par le Comité Exécutif de la C.E.S. 19 et 20 avril 1990.

"J. Chaban-Delmas invité de France-Inter." Politique Intérieure, 19 septembre 1992 (mimeo): 1–20.

Lamy, Pascal. "The Brussels European Council of February 1988." Boston, 1 March 1988 (mimeo).

"Policy Statement by Helmut Kohl, Chancellor of the Federal Republic of Germany, in the German Bundestag on January 30, 1991." Statements and Speeches 14 New York: German Information Center, 1991.

"Policy Statement by Helmut Kohl, Federal Chancellor, to the Bundestag." 18 March 1987 In *European Political Cooperation*. Bonn: Press and Information Office, 1988.

Schönfelder, Wilhelm and Elke Thiel. "The Shaping of the Framework for a Single Currency in the Course of the EMU Negotiations." Presentation for the Robert Bosch Foundation Spring Speaker Series on the Evolution of Europe in the 1990s. The Cosmos Club, March 16, 1995.

Trumpf, Jürgen. "The Future of the Maastricht Treaty and U.S.-E.U. Relations in the 1990s." Presentation for the Robert Bosch Foundation Spring Speaker Series on the Evolution of Europe in the 1990s. The University Club, May 4, 1995.

UNICE Presse. "Déclaration des milieux d'affaires européennes: la 'Nouvelle Europe' entre en action." le 4 décembre 1990.

Wilhelm, Paul Dr., MdL. *Drei gute Gründe für Europa*. 76 / 07. 12. 1992 Bonn: Euro Aktuell, 1992.

SECONDARY SOURCES
Books

Aberbach, Joel D., Robert D. Putnam and Bert A. Rockman. *Bureaucrats and Politicians in Western Democracies.* Cambridge: Harvard University Press, 1981.

Allais, Maurice. *Erreurs et impasses de la construction européenne.* Paris: Juglar, 1992.

Allison, Graham T. *The Essence of Decision: Explaining the Cuban Missile Crisis.* Boston: Little, Brown, 1971.

Andrews, William G., and Stanley Hoffmann, eds. *The Impact of the Fifth Republic on France.* Albany: State University of New York Press, 1981.

Aron, Raymond. *Peace and War.* New York: Anchor Books, 1973.

Barrillon, R., J. M. Bérard, H. M. Bérard, G. Dupuis, A. Grangé Cabane, A.M. Le Bos Le Pourhiet et Y. Mény. *Dictionnaire de la constitution.* Paris: Cujas, 1986.

Barzini, Luigi. *The Europeans.* New York: Penguin, 1983.

Baun, Michael J. *An Imperfect Union.* Boulder: Westview, 1996.

Bialer, Seweryn. *The Domestic Context of Soviet Foreign Policy.* Boulder: Westview, 1981.

Bill, James A., and Robert L. Hardgrave, Jr. *Comparative Politics: The Quest for Theory.* Lanham, MD: University Press of America, 1981.

Bini-Smaghi, Lorenzo, Tommaso Padoa-Schioppa and Francesco Papadia. *The Policy History of the Maastricht Treaty: The Transition to the Final Stage of EMU.* Proceedings of the Conference held at La Coruna. Rome: Banca d'Italia, 1993.

Binnendijk, Hans, and Mary Locke, eds. *The Diplomatic Record 1991–1992.* Boulder: Westview, 1993.

Blondel, Jean, and Ferdinand Müller-Rommel, eds. *Governing Together.* New York: St. Martin's, 1993.

———. *Cabinets in Western Europe.* London: Macmillan, 1988.

Bodiguel, J.-L. & J.-L. Quermonne. *La haute fonction publique.* Paris: PUF, 1983.

Braudel, Fernand. *The Identity of France.* Volume 1: History & Environment. New York: Harper & Row, 1990.

Breslin, J. William, and Jeffrey Z. Rubin, eds. *Negotiation Theory and Practice.* Cambridge: The Program on Negotiation at Harvard Law School, 1991.

Brinkley, Douglas, and Clifford Hackett, eds. *Jean Monnet: The Path to European Unity.* New York: St. Martin's, 1991.

Buchan, David. *The Strange Superpower.* Aldershot: Dartmouth, 1993.

Bulmer, Simon, and William Paterson. *The Federal Republic of Germany and the European Community.* London: Allen & Unwin, 1987.

Bulmer, Simon, and Wolfgang Wessels. *The European Council.* New York: St. Martin's, 1987.

Bulmer, Simon. *The Domestic Structure of European Policy-Making in the Federal Republic of Germany.* New York: Garland, 1986.

Cafruny, Alan W., and Glenda G. Rosenthal, eds. *The State of the European Community.* Volume 2. Boulder and London: Lynne Rienner, 1993.

Campbell, Colin. *Managing the Presidency.* Pittsburgh: University of Pittsburgh Press, 1986.

——. *Governments Under Stress.* Toronto: University of Toronto Press, 1983.

Campbell, Colin, and Margaret Jane Wyszomirski, eds. *Executive Leadership in Anglo-American Systems.* Pittsburgh: University of Pittsburgh Press, 1991.

Campbell, Colin, and B. Guy Peters, eds. *Organizing Governance Governing Organizations.* Pittsburgh: University of Pittsburgh Press, 1988.

Campbell, Colin, and George J. Szablowski. *The Superbureaucrats: Structure and Behavior in Central Agencies.* Toronto: Macmillan, 1979.

Carmoy, Guy de. *Les politiques etrangères de la France 1944–1966.* Paris: La Table Ronde, 1967.

Cash, William. *Against a Federal Europe.* London: Duckworth, 1991.

Cecchini, Paolo. *The European Challenge 1992.* Aldershot: Wildwood House, 1988.

Cerny, Karl H., ed. *Germany at the Polls. The Bundestag Elections of the 1980s.* Durham: Duke University Press, 1989.

Cerny, Philip G. *The Changing Architecture of Politics.* London: Sage, 1990.

Cerny, Philip G., and Martin A. Schain, eds. *French Politics and Public Policy.* London: Frances Pinter Ltd., 1980.

Chodak, Szymon. *The New State.* Boulder and London: Lynne Rienner, 1989.

Claude Jr., Inis L. *Swords into Plowshares.* New York: Random House, 1984.

Clavel, Jean-Daniel. *De la négociation diplomatique multilaterale.* Bruxelles: Bruylant, 1991.

Cloos, J., G. Reinesch, D. Vignes et J. Weyland. *Le traité de Maastricht.* Bruxelles: Bruylant, 1994.

Cohen, Herb. *You Can Negotiate Anything.* Seacaucus, N.J.: Lyle Stuart, 1980.

Cohen, Samy. *La monarchie nucléaire.* Paris: Hachette, 1986.

——. *Les conseillers du président.* Paris: PUF, 1980.

Cohen-Tanugi, Laurent. *L'Europe en danger.* Paris: Fayard, 1992.

Cole, Alistair. *François Mitterrand: A Study in Political Leadership.* London and New York: Routledge, 1994.

Conradt, David P. *The German Polity.* New York: Longman, 1989

Corbett, Richard. *The Treaty of Maastricht.* Essex: Longman Group, 1993.

Cotta, Alain. *Pour l'Europe, contre Maastricht.* Paris: Fayard, 1992.

Craig, Gordon A. *The Germans.* New York: New American Library, 1982.

Crozier, Michel. *Etat modeste, Etat moderne.* Paris: Editions du Seuil, 1991.

——. *La Société bloquée*. Paris: Editions du Seuil, 1970.

——. *Le Phénomène bureaucratique*. Paris: Editions du Seuil, 1963.

Dahrendorf, Ralf. *Réflexions sur la Révolution en Europe 1989–1990*. Paris: Editions du Seuil, 1991.

Destler, I.M. *Presidents, Bureaucrats and Foreign Policy*. Princeton: Princeton University Press, 1972.

De Baecque, F., and J.-L. Quermonne. *Administration et politique sous la cinquième république*. Paris: FNSP, 1982.

De Bassompierre, Guy. *Changing the Guard in Brussels*. New York: CSIS and Praeger, 1988.

De Callieres, François. *On the Manner of Negotiating with Princes*. Notre Dame: University of Notre Dame Press, 1963.

De Gaulle, Charles. *Lettres, notes et carnets juillet 1966-avril 1969*. Paris: Plon, 1987.

——. *Mémoires d'espoir*. Paris: Plon, 1970.

Delamaide, Darrell. *The New Superregions of Europe*. New York: Plume, 1994.

Delors, Jacques. *Le nouveau concert européen*. Paris: Editions Odile Jacob, 1992.

De Porte, Anton W. *Europe Between the Superpowers*. New Haven: Yale University Press, 1979.

De Ruyt, Jean. *L'acte unique européen*. Bruxelles: Université Libre de Bruxelles, 1991.

Dinan, Desmond. *An Ever Closer Union?* Boulder: Lynne Rienner, 1994.

Dogan, Mattei, ed. *The Mandarins of Western Europe*. New York: Sage Publications, 1975.

Dogan, Mattei, and Richard Rose, eds. *European Politics*. London: Macmillan, 1971.

Doutriaux, Yves. *Le traité sur l'Union Européenne*. Paris: Armand Colin, 1992.

Downs, Anthony. *Inside Bureaucracy*. Boston: Little, Brown, 1967.

Drevet, Jean-François. *La France et l'europe des regions*. Paris: Syros-Alternatives, 1991.

Duchêne, François. *Jean Monnet: The First Statesman of Interdependence*. New York and London: W. W. Norton, 1994.

Duff, Andrew, John Pinder and Roy Pryce, eds. *Maastricht and Beyond*. London and New York: Routledge, 1994.

Duhamel, Alain. *De Gaulle-Mitterrand. La marque et la trace*. Paris: Flammarion, 1991.

Duhamel, Olivier. *Le pouvoir politique en France. Droit Constitutionnel, 1*. Paris: PUF, 1991.

Duhamel, Olivier, and Jérôme Jaffré, eds. *L'état de l'opinion*. Paris: Editions du Seuil, 1993.

——. *L'état de l'opinion*. Paris: Editions du Seuil, 1991.

Dyson, Kenneth. *Elusive Union.* London and New York: Longman Group Limited, 1994.

Echtler, Ulrich. *Einfluss und Macht in der Politik: Der beamtete Staatssekretär.* München: Wilhelm Goldmann Verlag, 1973.

Edwards, Geoffrey, and Elfriede Regelsberger, eds. *Europe's Global Links.* London: Pinter, 1990.

Edwards, Geoffrey, and David Spence, eds. *The European Commission.* Essex: Longman, 1994.

Engel, Christian, and Wolfgang Wessels, eds. *From Luxembourg to Maastricht: Institutional Change in the European Community after the Single European Act.* Bonn: Europa Union, 1992.

Eulau, Henry. *Micro-Macro Political Analysis.* Chicago: Aldine, 1969.

Evans, Peter B., Harold K. Jacobson, and Robert D. Putnam, eds. *Doubled-Edged Diplomacy.* Berkeley: University of California Press, 1993.

Featherstone, Kevin, and Roy H. Ginsberg. *The United States and the European Community in the 1990s.* New York: St. Martin's, 1993.

Fisher, Roger, and William Ury. *Getting to Yes: Negotiating Agreement Without Giving In.* New York: Penguin Books, 1981.

Follett, Mary Parker. *Creative Experience.* New York: Longmans, Green, 1924.

Fontaine, Pascal. *Jean Monnet. L'Inspirateur.* Paris: Jacques Grancher, 1988.

Fox, E. M., and L. Urwick, eds. *Dynamic Administration.* New York: Hippocrene, 1982.

Friedrich, Carl J. *Europe: An Emergent Nation?* New York: Harper & Row, 1970.

Friend, Julius W. *The Lynchpin: French-German Relations, 1950–1990.* New York: Praeger with CSIS, 1991.

Garaud, Marie-France, and Philippe Séguin. *De L'Europe en général et de la France en particulier.* Paris: Le Pré aux Clercs, 1992.

Genestar, Alain. *Les péchés du prince.* Paris: Grasset, 1992.

George, Stephen, ed. *Britain and the European Community.* Oxford: Clarendon Press, 1992.

Gerth H.H., and C. Wright Mills, trans. and eds. *From Max Weber: Essays in Sociology.* New York: Oxford, 1958.

Ginsberg, Roy H. *Foreign Policy Actions of the European Community.* Boulder: Lynne Rienner, 1989.

Goguel, François, and Alfred Grosser. *La Politique en France.* Paris: Armand Colin, 1984.

Grant, Charles. *Delors: Inside the House That Jacques Built.* London: Nicholas Brealey, 1994.

Gretschman, Klaus, ed. *Economic and Monetary Union.* Maastricht: European Institute of Public Administration, 1993.

Grosser, Alfred. *Affaires extérieures. La politique de la France 1944–1989.* Paris: Flammarion, 1989.

———. *L'Allemagne en occident.* Paris: Fayard, 1985.

———. *La République Fédérale d'Allemagne.* Paris: PUF, 1963.

———. *La IVe République et sa politique extérieure.* Paris: Armand Colin, 1961.

Grosser, Alfred, and Henri Ménudier. *La vie politique en allemagne fédérale.* Paris: Armand Colin, 1978.

Grundgesetz für die Bundesrepublik Deutschland. Kommentar von Jarass, Hans D., and Bodo Pieroth. München: Verlag C.H. Beck, 1992.

Guigou, Elisabeth. *Pour les européens.* Paris: Flammarion, 1994.

Gulick, Edward Vose. *Europe's Classical Balance of Power.* New York: W.W. Norton, 1967.

Haas, Ernst. *The Uniting of Europe: Political, Social and Economic Forces, 1950–1957.* London: Stevens & Sons, 1957.

Hackett, Clifford. *Cautious Revolution.* New York: Praeger, 1990.

Haftendorn, Helga, and Christian Tuschhoff, eds. *America and Europe in an Era of Change.* Boulder: Westview, 1993.

Halperin, Morton H. *Bureaucratic Politics and Foreign Policy.* Washington, D.C.: Brookings Institution, 1974.

Hanrieder, Wolfram F. *Germany, America, Europe.* New Haven: Yale University Press, 1989.

Harrison, Reginald. *Europe in Question.* London: Allen & Unwin, 1974.

Hayward, Jack, ed. *De Gaulle to Mitterrand. Presidential Power in France.* New York: NYU Press, 1993.

Heisenberg, Wolfgang. *German Unification in European Perspective.* London: Brassey's, 1991.

Hellwig, Renate (Hg.). *Der Deutsche Bundestag und Europa.* Bonn: Aktuell, 1993.

Henig, Stanley. *Power and Decision in Europe.* London: Europotentials, 1980.

Heymann-Doat, Arlette. *Les révisions constitutionnelles de la Ve République.* Paris: La documentation française. No. 705. 28 mai 1993.

Hoffmann, Stanley. *Decline or Renewal? France Since the 1930s.* New York: Viking, 1974.

———. *Contemporary Theory in International Relations.* Englewood Cliffs: Prentice Hall, 1963.

Hurwitz, Leon, and Christian Lequesne, eds. *The State of the European Community.* Volume 1. Boulder: Lynne Rienner, 1991.

Ikle, Fred C. *How Nations Negotiate.* New York: Harper & Row, 1964.

Jean Monnet, Proceedings of the Centenary Symposium Organized by the Commission of the European Communities, Brussels, 10 November 1988. Luxembourg: Office for Official Publications of the European Communities, 1989.

Johnston, Mary Troy. *The European Council.* Boulder, San Francisco and Oxford: Westview, 1994.

Joyaux, François, et Patrick Wajsman, eds. *Pour une nouvelle politique étrangère.* Paris: Hachette, 1986.

Kaufmann, Johan. *Conference Diplomacy: An Introductory Analysis.* Dordrecht: Martinus Nijhoff, 1988.

Kellerman, Barbara, and Jeffrey Z. Rubin, eds. *Leadership and Negotiation in the Middle East.* New York: Praeger, 1988.

Keohane, Nannerl. *Philosophy and the State in France.* Princeton: Princeton University Press, 1980.

Keohane, Robert O. and Stanley Hoffmann, eds. *The New European Community.* Boulder, San Francisco and Oxford: Westview, 1991.

Keohane, Robert O. *International Institutions and State Power.* Boulder and London: Westview, 1989.

Kiersch, Gerhard. *Les héritiers de Goethe et d'Auschwitz.* Paris: Flammarion, 1986.

Kirchner, E. J., and A. Tsagkari, eds. *The EC Council Presidency: The Dutch and Luxembourg Presidencies.* London: Association for Contemporary European Studies, 1993.

Kirchner, Emil Joseph. *Decision making in the European Community.* New York: St. Martin's, 1992.

Krause, Axel. *Inside the New Europe.* New York: Harper & Collins, 1991.

Lakos, Amos. *International Negotiations: A Bibliography.* Boulder: Westview, 1989.

Laufer, Heinz. *Der parlamentarische Staatssekretär.* München: C.H. Beck, 1969.

Laursen, Finn, and Sophie Vanhoonacker, eds. *The Ratification of the Maastricht Treaty: Issues, Debates and Future Implications.* Dordrecht: Martinus Nijhoff Publishers, 1994.

————. *The Intergovernmental Conference on Political Union.* Maastricht: EIPA, 1992.

Le Gloannec, Anne-Marie. *La Nation Orpheline.* Paris: Calmann-Levy, 1989.

Lequesne, Christian. *Paris-Bruxelles.* Paris: Presses de la Fondation Nationale des Sciences Politiques, 1993.

L'Equilibre Européen. Etudes rassemblées et publiées en hommage à Niels Ersbøll secrétaire général du conseil de l'union européenne (1980–1994) Bruxelles: Edition provisoire, 1995.

Les conférences intergouvernementales avant le conseil européen de Maastricht. Journée d'Etudes, 8 novembre 1991. Bruxelles: Institut d'Etudes Européennes, 1991.

Les conférences intergouvernementales au terme de la présidence luxembourgeoise. Journée d'études, 25 juin 1991. Bruxelles: Institut d'Etudes Européennes, 1991.

Lindberg, Leon. *The Political Dynamics of European Economic Integration.* Stanford: Stanford University Press, 1963.

Lindberg, Leon, and Stuart Scheingold. *Europe's Would-be Polity: Patterns of Change in the European Community.* Englewood Cliffs, N.J.: Prentice Hall, 1970.

Lodge, Juliet, ed. *The European Community and the Challenge of the Future.* New York: St. Martin's, 1989.

Ludlow, Peter, with Niels Ersbøll. *Preparing for 1996 and a Larger European Union: Principles and Priorities.* Brussels: CEPS, 1995.

Ludlow, Peter, Jørgen Mørtensen and Jacques Pelkmans, eds. *The Annual Review of European Community Affairs 1991.* Volume 2 London: Brassey's, 1992.

Ludlow, Peter, ed. *The Annual Review of European Community Affairs 1990.* Volume 1 London: Brassey's, 1990.

L'Union Politique. Etat d'avancement de la conférence intergouvernementale. Journée d'études, 27 avril 1991. Bruxelles: Institut d'Etudes Européennes, 1991.

Macridis, Roy C., ed. *Foreign Policy in World Politics.* Englewood Cliffs: Prentice Hall, 1989.

Majone, Giandomenico, Emile Noël and Peter Van den Bosche, eds. *Jean Monnet et l'Europe d'aujourd'hui.* Baden-Baden: Nomos, 1989.

Marsh, David. *Die Bundesbank.* München: C. Bertelsmann, 1992.

Mattingly, Garrett. *Renaissance Diplomacy.* New York: Dover, 1988.

Mayntz, Renate, and Fritz W. Scharpf. *Policy-Making in the German Federal Bureaucracy.* Amsterdam: Elsevier, 1975.

McCarthy, Patrick, ed. *France-Germany 1983–1993.* New York: Macmillan, 1993.

Ménudier, Henri. *L'Allemagne après 1945.* Paris: Armand Colin, 1972.

Menyesch, Dieter, and Bérénice Manac'h. *France-Allemagne Bibliographie 1963–1982.* München: K.G. Saur, 1984.

Merlini, Cesare, ed. *Economic Summits and Western Decision-Making.* London: Croom Helm, 1984.

Miall, Hugh. *Shaping a New European Order.* London: RIIA, 1994.

Miller, Stuart. *Painted in Blood. Understanding Europeans.* New York: Atheneum, 1987.

Minc, Alain. *La vengeance des nations.* Paris: Grasset, 1990.

Mitterrand, François. *Réflexions sur la politique extérieure de la France.* Paris: Fayard, 1986.

———. *Le coup d'etat permanent.* Paris: Librairie Plon, 1964.

Monnet, Jean. *Clefs pour l'action.* Paris: Association des Amis de Jean Monnet, 1988.

———. *Mémoires.* Paris: Fayard, 1976.

Morawitz, Rudolf. *Die Zusammenarbeit von Bund und Ländern bei Vorhaben der europäischen Gemeinschaft.* Bonn: Europa Union, 1981.

Morgan, Roger, and Caroline Bray, eds. *Partners and Rivals in Western Europe.* Aldershot: Gower, 1986.

Neumann, Wolfgang. *Auf dem Weg zu einer europäischen Wirtschafts- und Wahrungsunion.* Stuttgart: Deutscher Sparkassenverlag, 1991.

Nicolson, Harold. *Diplomacy.* Washington, D.C.: Institute for the Study of Diplomacy, 1989.

Nuttall, Simon. *European Political Cooperation.* Oxford: Clarendon Press, 1992.

O'Donnell, Rory, ed. *Economic and Monetary Union.* Studies in European Union No. 2 Dublin: Institute of European Affairs, 1991.

O'Keeffe, David, and Patrick M. Twomey, eds. *Legal Issues of the Maastricht Treaty.* London: John Wiley & Sons, 1994.

O'Nuallain, Colm, ed. *The Presidency of the European Council of Ministers.* London: Croom Helm, 1985.

Pentland, Charles. *International Theory and European Integration.* London: Faber, 1973.

Peters, B. Guy. *The Politics of Bureaucracy.* New York: Longmans, 1989.

Petitfils, Jean-Christian. *Le Gaullism.* Paris: PUF, 1977.

Pfister, Thierry. *La république des fonctionnaires.* Paris: Albin Michel, 1988.

Philippe, Annie and Daniel Hubscher. *Enquête à l'intérieur du parti socialiste.* Paris: Albin Michel, 1991.

Picht, Robert, and Wolfgang Wessels (Hrsg.). *Motor für Europa?* Bonn: Europa Union, 1990.

Picht, Robert, (Hg.). *Das Bündnis im Bündnis.* Berlin: Severin und Siedler, 1982.

Pinder, John. *European Community.* Oxford: Oxford, 1991.

Poidevin, Raymond, and Jacques Bariéty. *Les relations franco-allemandes, 1815–1975.* Paris: Armand Colin, 1977.

Pryce, Roy, ed. *The Dynamics of European Union.* London: Croom Helm, 1987.

Putnam, Robert D., and Nicholas Bayne. *Hanging Together.* Cambridge: Harvard University Press, 1987.

Quermonne, Jean-Louis. *L'appareil administratif de l'Etat.* Paris: Editions du Seuil, 1991.

Richardson, Jeremy, ed. *Policy Styles in Western Europe.* London: Allen & Unwin, 1982.

Rinsche, Günter, und Elmar Brok (Hrsg.). *Politik für Europa.* Herford: BusseSeewald, 1991.

Robin, Gabriel. *La diplomatie de Mitterrand.* Paris: Editions de la Bièvre, 1985.

Ross, George. *Jacques Delors and European Integration.* New York: Oxford, 1995.

Ross, George, Stanley Hoffmann and Sylvia Malzacher, eds. *The Mitterrand Experiment.* New York: Oxford, 1987.

Rourke, John T., Richard P. Hiskes and Cyrus Ernesto Zirakzadeh. *Direct Democracy and International Politics: Deciding International Issues Through Referendums.* Boulder & London: Lynne Rienner, 1992.

Rovan, Joseph. *France Allemagne deux nations, un avenir.* Paris: Julliard, 1988.

Rummel, Reinhardt, ed. *Toward Political Union.* Boulder, San Francisco and Oxford: Westview, 1992.

Rummel, Reinhardt, ed. with the assistance of Colette Mazzucelli. *The Evolution of an International Actor: Western Europe's New Assertiveness.* Boulder, San Francisco and Oxford: Westview, 1990.

Sasse, Christoph, Edouard Poullet, David Coombes and Gérard Deprez. *Decision Making in the European Community.* New York: Praeger, 1977.

Sbragia, Alberta M., ed. *Europolitics.* Washington: The Brookings Institution, 1992.

Schönfelder, Wilhelm, and Elke Thiel. *Ein Markt—eine Währung.* Baden-Baden: Nomos, 1994.

Schultz, George P. *Turmoil and Triumph.* New York: Charles Scribner's Sons, 1993.

Shingleton, A. Bradley, Marian J. Gibbon and Kathryn S. Mack, eds. *Dimensions of German Unification.* Boulder, San Francisco and Oxford: Westview, 1995.

Siégel, François. *L'Europe de Maastricht.* Paris: JClattès, 1992.

Simonian, Haig. *The Privileged Partnership.* Oxford: Clarendon, 1985.

Stein, Eric, Peter Hay and Michael Waelbroeck. *European Community Law and Institutions in Perspective.* Charlottesville, VA: Michie, 1976.

Stein, Janice Gross, ed. *Getting to the Table.* Baltimore and London: The Johns Hopkins University Press, 1989.

Steinkemper, Bärbel. *Klassiche und politische Burokraten in der Ministerialverwaltung der Bundesrepublik Deutschland.* Köln: Carl Heymanns, 1974.

Suleiman, Ezra. *Les élites en France.* Paris: Seuil, 1979.

———. *Les hauts fonctionnaires et la politique.* Paris: Seuil, 1976.

Szabo, Stephen F. *The Diplomacy of German Unification.* New York: St. Martin's, 1992.

Teltschik, Horst. *329 Tage.* Berlin: Siedler, 1991.

Thatcher, Margaret. *The Downing Street Years.* New York: HarperCollins, 1993.

The New Treaty on European Union. Volume 2: Legal and Political Analyses. Brussels: Belmont European Policy Centre, 1992.

Treverton, Gregory F., ed. *The Shape of the New Europe.* New York: Council on Foreign Relations, 1991.

Uri, Pierre. *Penser pour l'Action.* Paris: Editions Odile Jacob, 1991.

Walker, R.B.J. and Saul H. Mendlovitz. *Contending Sovereignties.* Boulder and London: Lynne Rienner, 1990.

Wallace, Helen. with Adam Ridley. *Europe: The Challenge of Diversity.* Chatham House Papers 29 London: The Royal Institute of International Affairs, 1985.

Wallace, Helen, William Wallace and Carole Webb, eds. *Policy-Making in the European Community.* London: John Wiley, 1983.

Wallace, William, ed. *The Dynamics of European Integration.* London: Pinter, 1990.

Wallace, William, and William E. Paterson, eds. *Foreign Policy-Making in Western Europe.* Great Britain: Saxon House, 1978.

Walton, Richard E., and Robert B. McKersie. *A Behavioral Theory of Labor Negotiations.* Ithaca: ILR, 1991.

Waltz, Kenneth N. *Man, the State and War.* New York: Columbia University Press, 1959.

Weidenfeld, Werner, and Wolfgang Wessels (Hrsg.). *Jahrbuch der europäischen Integration 1989/90.* Bonn: Institut für Europäische Politik, 1990.

Weisenfeld, Ernst. *Quelle Allemagne pour la France?* Paris: Armand Colin, 1989.

Werts, Jan. *The European Council.* Amsterdam: Elsevier, 1992.

Wessels, Wolfgang, & Elfriede Regelsberger, eds. *The Federal Republic of Germany and the European Community: The Presidency and Beyond.* Bonn: Europa Union, 1988.

Wilking, Susanne (Hrsg.). *Deutsche und italienische Europapolitik—Historische Grundlagen und aktuelle Fragen.* Bonn: Europa Union, 1991.

Williams, Abiodun, ed. *Many Voices.* Boulder: Westview, 1992.

Willis, F. Roy. *France, Germany and the New Europe, 1945–1967.* Stanford: Stanford University Press, 1968.

Winkelmann, Ingo (Hg.). *Das Maastricht-Urteil des Bundesverfassungs-gerichts vom 12. Oktober 1993.* Berlin: Duncker & Humblot, 1994.

Wright, Vincent. *The Government and Politics of France.* New York: Holmes & Meier, 1989.

Ysmal, Colette. *Les partis politiques sous la Ve république.* Paris: Montchrestien, 1989.

Zartman, I. William, and Maureen Berman. *The Practical Negotiator.* New Haven: Yale University Press, 1982.

Zartman, I. William. *The Politics of Trade Negotiations Between Africa and the European Economic Community.* Princeton: Princeton University Press, 1971.

Ziller, Gerhard. *Die bundesstaatliche Ordnung der Bundesrepublik Deutschland.* Bonn: Bouvier, 1990.

Ziller, Jacques. *Administrations comparées.* Paris: Editions Montchrestien, 1993.

Zorgbibe, Charles. *De Gaulle, Mitterrand et l'esprit de la Constitution.* Paris: Hachette, 1993.

Journal Articles

Andriessen, Frans. "In the Wake of the Brussels Summit." *European Affairs* 2 (Summer 1988): 14–26.

Asholt, Wolfgang, and Ingo Kolboom. "Frankreich und das vereinte Deutschland." *Europa-Archiv* 7 (1992): 179–186.

Bayne, Nicholas. "The Course of Summitry." *The World Today* 48 (1992): 27–30.

Brewin, Christopher, and Richard McAllister. "Annual Review of the Activities of the European Community in 1990." *Journal of Common Market Studies* XXIX (1991): 385–415.

Bulmer, Simon. "The European Council's First Decade: Between Interdependence and Domestic Politics." *Journal of Common Market Studies* 24 (1985): 89–104.

———. "Domestic Politics and European Community Policy-Making." *Journal of Common Market Studies* 21 (1983): 349–363.

Burley, Anne Marie. "The Once and Future German Question." *Foreign Affairs* 68 5 (Winter 1989–1990): 65–83.

Cohen, Elie. "Dirigisme, Politique Industrielle et Rhétorique Industrialiste." *Revue Française de Science Politique* 42 (avril 1992): 197–218.

Cohen, Samy. "Diplomatie: le syndrome de la présidence omnisciente." *Esprit* 164 (1990): 55–64.

Corbett, Richard. "The Intergovernmental Conference on Political Union." *Journal of Common Market Studies* XXX (September 1992): 271–298.

Cowles, Maria Green. "Setting the Agenda for a New Europe: The ERT and EC 1992," *Journal of Common Market Studies* 33 (December 1995): 501–526.

Dahl, Robert A. "A Democratic Dilemma: System Effectiveness versus Citizen Participation." *Political Science Quarterly* 109 (Spring 1994): 23–34.

Ehlermann, Claus-Dieter. "The Institutional Development of the EC under the Single European Act." *Aussenpolitik* (1990): 135–146.

Featherstone, Kevin. "Jean Monnet and the 'Democratic Deficit' in the European Union." *Journal of Common Market Studies* (June 1994): 149–170.

Feld, Werner J., and John K. Wildgren. "National Administrative Elites and European Integration: Saboteurs at Work?" *Journal of Common Market Studies* 13 (1975): 250–265.

Feldman, Lily Gardner. "Germany and the EC: Realism and Responsibility." *The Annals* 531 (January 1994): 25–43.

Flesch, Colette. "La diplomatie luxembourgeoise: Nécessité réalité et défi." *Studia diplomatica* XXXVI (1983): 145–162.

Freedman, Laurence. "Logic, Politics and Foreign Policy Processes." *International Affairs* 52 (1976): 434–449.

Fritsch-Bournazel, Renata. "Rapallo et son image en France." *Documents: Revue des Questions Allemandes* (2/82): 3–12.

Habert, Philippe. "Le choix de l'Europe et la décision de l'électeur." *Commentaire* 60 (1992–1993): 871–880.

Hayes-Renshaw, Fiona and Helen Wallace. "Executive power in the European Union: the functions and limits of the Council of Ministers." *Journal of European Public Policy* 2 (December 1995): 559–582.

Hayward, Elizabeth. "The European Policy of François Mitterrand." *Journal of Common Market Studies* 31 (June 1993): 269–282.

Hoffmann, Stanley. "The Case for Leadership." *Foreign Policy* 81 (Winter 1990–1991): 20–38.

———. "Reflections on the Nation-State in Western Europe Today." *Journal of Common Market Studies* 21 (September-December 1982): 21–37.

———. "An American Social Science: International Relations." *Daedalus* 106 3 (Summer 1977): 41–60.

———. "Obstinate or Obsolete: The Fate of the Nation-State and the Case of Western Europe." *Daedalus* 95 (1966): 862–917.

Imbert, Claude. "The End of French Exceptionalism." *Foreign Affairs* 68 4 (Fall 1989): 48–60.

Kaufmann-Bühler, Werner. "Deutsche Europapolitik nach dem Karlsruher Urteil: Möglichkeiten und Hemmnisse." *Integration* (1/94): 1–11.

Keohane, Robert O., and Joseph S. Nye, Jr. "Power and Interdependence Revisited." *International Organization* 41 (Autumn 1987): 725–753.

Kissinger, Henry A. "Domestic Structure and Foreign Policy." *Daedalus* 95 (Spring 1966): 503–529.

Laurent, Pierre-Henri. "Eureka, or the Technological Renaissance of Europe." *The Washington Quarterly* (Winter 1987): 55–65.

Leonardy, Uwe. "Bundestag und europäische Gemeinschaft: Notwendigkeit und Umfeld eines Europa-Ausschusses." *Zeitschrift für Parlamentsfragen* (4/89): 527–544.

Lequesne, Christian. "Europapolitik unter Mitterrand: Die französische Präsidentschaft als Etappenziel." *Integration* 4 (1989): 142–161.

Luchaire, François. "L'union européenne et la constitution: La décision du Conseil Constitutionnel." *(Première Partie) Revue de Droit Publique et de la Science Politique en France et à l'Etranger* 3 (1992): 589–616.

Mazzucelli, Colette. "The United States of Europe Revisited: Its Relevance to Integration in Practice." *International Affairs Review* 5 (Summer 1995): 100–124.

———. "Maastricht: The Ratification Debate in Germany." *Phoenix* 1 (Spring 1994): 70–72.

———. "Maastricht and the Younger Europeans: Signs of Generational Change." *International Affairs Review* 3 (Spring/Summer 1994): 66–86.

———. "Maastricht: The Ratification Debate in Denmark." *Bulletin* 45 (Summer 93): 28–31.

———. "Maastricht: The Ratification Debate in France." *Bulletin* 44 (Winter 92–93): 65–68.

Milner, Helen. "International Theories of Cooperation Among Nations: Strengths and Weaknesses" *World Politics* 44 (April 1992): 466–496.

Moravcsik, Andrew. "Preferences and Power in the European Community: A Liberal Intergovernmentalist Approach," *Journal of Common Market Studies* 31 (December 1993): 473–524.

———. "Negotiating the Single European Act: National Interests and Conventional Statecraft in the European Community." *International Organization* 45 (1991): 651–688.

Moreau Defarges, Philippe. "'...J'ai fait un rêve...' Le président François Mitterrand, artisan de l'union européenne." *Politique Etrangère* 2 1985 (Hiver 1985): 359–375.

Morillo, Francesco J. Fonseca, and Juan A. Martin Burgos. "La union europea: Genesis de Maastricht." *Revista de Instituciones Europeas* 19 (Mayo-Agosto 1992): 517–563.

Nanz, Klaus-Peter. "Der 3.Pfeiler der Europäische Union" *Integration* 3 (1992): 126–140.

Nye, Jr. Joseph S. "Neorealism and Neoliberalism," *World Politics* (1988): 230–255.

Pinder, John. "European Community and Nation-state: A Case for a Neo-federalism?" *International Affairs* 62 (Winter 1985–1986): 41–54.

Putnam, Robert D. "Diplomacy and Domestic Politics: The Logic of Two-Level Games." *International Organization* 42 (1988): 427–460.

———. "The Political Attitudes of Senior Civil Servants in Western Europe: A Preliminary Report." *British Journal of Political Science* 3 (1973): 257–290.

Rideau, Jöel. "La recherche de l'adéquation de la constitution française aux exigences de l'union européenne." *Revue des Affaires Européennes* 3 (1992): 7–52.

Ross, George. "Inside The Delors Cabinet." *Journal of Common Market Studies* (December 1994): 499–523.

Rourke, Francis E. "The 1993 John Gaus Lecture: Whose Bureaucracy Is This Anyway? Congress, the President and Public Administration." *Political Science and Politics* XXVI (1993): 690–697.

Sandholtz, Wayne. "Choosing Union: Monetary Politics and Maastricht." *International Organization* 47 (1993): 1–39.

Schlüter, Peter-Wilhelm. "Die Europäische Wirtschafts- und Währungsunion: Anmerkungen zur Regierungskonferenz." *Integration* (3/91): 106–114.

Slater, Martin. "Political Elites, Popular Indifference and Community Building." *Journal of Common Market Studies* XXI (1982): 69–93.

Smouts, Marie Claude. "French Foreign Policy: The Domestic Debate." *International Affairs* 53 1 (January 1977): 36–50.

Stavenhagen, Lutz G. "Durchbruch zur Politischen Union—Vor Dem Maastrichter Gipfel." *Integration* (4/91): 143–150.

Stern, Fritz. "Germany in a Semi-Gaullist Europe." *Foreign Affairs* 58 (Spring 1980): 867–886.

Steuer, Werner. "Maastricht und der Deutsche Bundestag." *Wirtschaftsdienst* 3 (1993): 138–142.

Sutton, Michael. "France and the Maastricht Design." *The World Today* (January 1993): 4–8.

———. "Who Beats the Nationalist Drum." *The World Today* (June 1991): 101–104.

Thiel, Elke. "From the Internal Market to an Economic and Monetary Union." *Aussenpolitik* (1989): 66–75.

Tiersky, Ronald. "France in the New Europe." *Foreign Affairs* 71 (Spring 1992): 131–146.

Tsakaloyannis, Panos. "The Acceleration of History and the Reopening of the Political Debate in the European Community." *Journal of European Integration* XIV (1991): 83–102.

Verba, Sidney. "The 1993 James Madison Award Lecture: The Voice of the People." *Political Science and Politics* XXVI (1993): 677–686.

Wallace, Helen. "Negotiations and Coalition Formation in the European Community." *Government and Opposition* 20 (1985): 453–472.

Wessels, Wolfgang. "Maastricht: Ergebnisse, Bewertungen, Langzeittrends." *Integration* 1 (1992): 2–16.

Weiler, Joseph H. H. "The European Community in Change: Exit, Voice and Loyalty." *Irish Studies in International Affairs* 3 (1990): 15–25.

Wieczorek-Zeul, Heidemarie. "Der Vertrag von Maastricht im Deutschen Bundestag." *Europa-Archiv* 13–14 (1993): 405–412.

Winham, Gilbert R. "Practitioners' Views of International Negotiation." *World Politics* 32 (1979): 111–135.

———. "Negotiation as a Management Process." *World Politics* 30 (1977): 87–114.

Ziller, Jacques. "Hauts fonctionnaires et politique en République Fédérale d'Allemagne." *Revue Internationale des Sciences Administratives* 1 (1981): 31–41.

Zumschlinge, Konrad, and Annette Sierigk. "Die Auswirkungen der Wiedervereinigung Deutschlands und der Integration Europas auf die Vertretungen der Deutschen Länder in Bonn, Berlin und Brüssel." *Die Verwaltung* (1994): 1–21.

Monographs

Kramer, Steven Philip. *France and the New Germany.* Washington, D.C.: American Institute for Contemporary German Studies, 1993.

Lippert, Barbara, Dirk Günther and Stephen Woolcock. *The EC and the New German Länder: A Short-Lived Success Story?* London: Anglo-German Foundation, 1993.

Martin, Lisa M. *The Influence of National Parliaments on European Integration.* Center for German and European Studies Working Paper 1.23. Berkeley: University of California, 1994.

Mazzucelli, Colette. *A Decision in Dublin, An Agenda in Rome: Convening Parallel Conferences on European Union.* Monnet Case Studies in European Affairs. New York: The Jean Monnet Council, 1995.

Schoof, Eberhard. *EG-Ausschuß.* Bonn: Deutscher Bundestag, 1993.

Newspaper Articles

"A German idea of Europe." *The Economist*, July 26, 1991.

"An der Leine." *Der Spiegel*, 10. Juni 1991.

Barber, Lionel, and Hilary Barnes. "Legalistic Acrobatics Rescue Denmark." *Financial Times*, December 14, 1992.

"Battle for Maastricht Heating up in Germany." *The Wall Street Journal Europe*, June 12, 1992.

Bréhier, Thierry. "M. Jacques Delors quitterait son poste en cas de victoire du 'non'." *Le Monde*, 2 septembre 1992.

Bobin, Frédéric, et Claire Tréan. "Un entretien avec Mme Elisabeth Guigou." *Le Monde*, 3 juin 1992.

Bobin, Frédéric, et Daniel Carton. "Les sénateurs souhaitent des garanties supplémentaires sur la citoyenneté européenne." *Le Monde*, 22 mai 1992.

Bollaert, Baudouin. "Les neuf 'mines' qui peuvent faire tout exploser." *Le Figaro*, 9 décembre 1991.

Bonilauri, Bernard. "Crozier: éloge de la Commission de Bruxelles." *Le Figaro*, 9 juin 1992.

Bresson, Gilles. "Maastricht: Chirac invente le oui à la carte." *Libération*, 4–5 juillet 1992.

———. "Quand Maastricht divise Jacques Chirac." *Libération*, 25 mai 1992.

Brock, George, and Michael Binyon. "Britain Accepts EC Goal of a United Policy on Defence." *The Times*, October 5, 1991.

Brock, George. "Dutch Challenged over Draft for Union Treaty." *The Times*, September 29, 1991.

———. "Federal Camp Wins First Round." *The Times*, September 26, 1991.

Brown, Colin, Sarah Helm and David Usborne. "Rifts with Europe Healing." *The Independent*, October 4, 1991.

Buchan, David, and David Marsh. "Currency Union Likely to Be a Tier-full Affair." *Financial Times*, December 10, 1991.

Buchan, David. "'Fast Forwards' Relish Their Victory in Battle over EMU Timetable." *Financial Times*, December 11, 1991.

———. "Lubbers Puts Faith in Social Policy Compromise." *Financial Times*, December 10, 1991.

———. "EC Divided over Future Plans for Defence." *Financial Times*, October 7, 1991.

———. "EC Presidency Seeks to End Political Union Row." *Financial Times*, June 4, 1991.

———. "Germany and Italy Draw up Plan on EC Power." *Financial Times*, April 11, 1991.

———. "EMU Train Stopped in Its Tracks." *Financial Times*, April 8, 1991.

———. "German Plan to Widen Powers of MEPs Upsets EC Partners." *Financial Times*, February 19, 1991.

Buerkle, Tom. "France Rejects Call by Bonn on Monetary Union." *International Herald Tribune*, December 7, 1994.

"Bundesverfassungsgericht verhandelt über Maastricht." *Frankfurter Allgemeine Zeitung*, 1. Juli 1993.

"CEE: dans l'ombre, les bâtisseurs." *L'Express*, 28 décembre 1990.

"C'est l'Europe qu'il faut maintenant plébisciter." *Libération*, 4 septembre 1992.

Cohen-Tanugi, Laurent. "Les leçons du syndrome danois." *Le Monde*, 11 juin 1992.

"Das Thema geht ans Herz." *Der Spiegel*, (49/1992): 32–35.

Dauvergne, Alain. "Les six acquis de Maastricht." *Le Point*, 14 décembre 1991.

Davidson, Ian. "French Clear Maastricht Treaty Hurdle." *Financial Times*, June 24, 1992.

——. "Vote Brings Ratification Nearer in France." *Financial Times*, June 18, 1992.

——. "French Gaullists Will Try to Block Maastricht Pact." *Financial Times*, February 19, 1992.

De Bresson, Henri. "Le chancelier Kohl passe à l'offensive pour défendre le traité de Maastricht." *Le Monde*, 17 juin 1992.

"Defenders of a 'franc fort'." *Financial Times*, January 6, 1994.

"Der Bundestag sagt trotz ja zu Maastricht." *General-Anzeiger*, 9. Oktober 1992.

"Die Drahtzieher." *Manager Magazin*, (5/92): 173–176.

"Die Niederlande auf der Suche nach ihrem Platz in Europa." *Neue Zürcher Zeitung*, 2. Juli 1991.

"Die Verfassungskommission sonnt sich in ersten Erfolgen." *Stuttgarter Zeitung*, 2. Juli 1992.

Docquiert, Jacques. "Paris prêt à accepter un renforcement des pouvoirs du Parlement Européen." *Les Echos*, 29 octobre 1991.

Drozdiak, William. "5 'Inner Core' Nations in EC May Act Faster on Integration." *International Herald Tribune*, September 26–27, 1992.

——. "Bonn and Paris in Urgent Talks but Silent on What Was Said." *International Herald Tribune*, September 23, 1992.

Dupin, Eric, and Pierre Giacometti. "Premier regard sur un paysage électoral mis sens dessus-dessous par le scrutin." *Libération*, 22 septembre 1992.

——. "57% du oui à sept semaines du référendum." *Libération*, 4 août 1992.

——. "La 'citoyenneté européenne' au coeur de la révision constitutionnelle." *Libération*, 11–12 avril 1992.

——. "Maastricht bouscule la constitution." *Libération*, 10 avril 1992.

"Economists Attack 'Soft' Criteria." *The Guardian*, June 12, 1992.

"Ein Wechsel in Brüssel." *Handelsblatt*, 29–30. Januar 1993.

"Es gibt kein Zurück." *Der Spiegel*, 9. Dezember 1991.

"Europe: Le Cactus Constitutionnel." *Libération*, 10 avril 1992.

"Europe Picks Money Chief." *New York Times*, October 5, 1993.

"European System Tying Currencies Faces a Rupture." *New York Times*, July 31, 1993.

Ferenczi, Thomas, et Jean-Pierre Langellier. "Un entretien avec Mme Guigou." *Le Monde*, 16 septembre 1992.

"Fight Nationalism with Swift Unity, Kohl Tells Europe." *International Herald Tribune*, June 8, 1992.

Fitchett, Joseph. "Halfway Home in Maastricht." *International Herald Tribune*, December 10, 1991.

"France's Road to Euro-Union." *Financial Times*, May 13, 1992.

"French Vote on EC Treaty Could Occur Next Month." *The Wall Street Journal*, June 24, 1992.

"Für eine europäische Industriepolitik." *Frankfurt Allgemeine Zeitung*, 9. Dezember 1991.

Gardner, David. "Cohesion Becomes Less of a Sticking Point." *Financial Times*, December 10, 1991.

Gedye, Robin. "'End of Beautiful Mark' Rouses Germans at Last." *The Daily Telegraph*, December 10, 1991.

"Genscher Urges Germans to Back European Unity." *The Wall Street Journal Europe*, March 10, 1992.

"Gesetzentwurf zu Maastricht vorgelegt, Ratifizierungsverfahren eingeleitet." *Frankfurter Allgemeine Zeitung*, 22. Juli 1992.

Goldsmith, Charles, and Martin Du Bois. "Delors Warns that Efforts to Rein in Reach of European Community Threaten Paralysis." *The Wall Street Journal Europe*, October 15, 1992.

Gow, David. "UK Offered Special EC Role." *The Guardian*, July 5, 1991.

Grosser, Alfred. "Traité difficile, 'oui' facile." *La Croix*, 10 juillet 1992.

Guigou, Jean-Louis. "La recomposition des territoires." *Libération*, 24 juillet 1992.

Gumbel, Peter. "Maastricht Faces German Legal Test in Suit over Scope of Treaty's Powers." *The Wall Street Journal*, 15 June 1993.

Haski, Pierre. "Le 'conseil d'ami' d'Helmut Kohl." *Libération*, 4 septembre 1992.

———. "Guigou: Ne plus faire l'Europe comme avant." *Libération*, 6 juin 1992.

———. "Visite de rattrapage de Mitterrand dans les Länder de l'Est." *Libération*, 18 septembre 1991.

Haski, Pierre, et Jean-Yves Lhomeau. "Le joker de François Mitterrand." *Libération*, 10 avril 1992.

Hauser, Erich. "Deutsche Ernüchterung und ein zerknirschter Kanzler." *Frankfurter Rundschau*, 7. Februar 1992.

"In der Maastricht Verhandlung wählt die Bundesregierung die Defensive." *Frankfurter Allgemeine Zeitung*, 3. Juli 1993.

James, Barry. "Behind Farm Crisis: French Fear the Loss of a 'Way of Life'." *International Herald Tribune*, November 27, 1992.

"Japan's Bureaucracy: No Sign It's Losing Any Power." *New York Times*, February 27, 1994.

Jenkins, Roy. "Who Will Lead Europe?" *Financial Times*, April 29, 1988.

Johnson, Boris. "Small Room That Could Shut the Door on Plans for Europe." *The Daily Telegraph*, December 12, 1991.

Johnson, Boris, and George Jones. "Kohl 'Wants to Start Train Now'." *The Daily Telegraph*, December 10, 1991.

"Karlsruhe's Sound Ruling." *Financial Times*, October 13, 1993.

Kinzer, Stephen. "German Parliament Ratifies European Union Pact." *New York Times*, December 3, 1992.

"Köhler fordert von Bonn klare Worte." *Handelsblatt*, 28. März 1995.

"Kommission beschließt die neuen Europa-Artikel." *Handelsblatt*, 19. Oktober 1992.

"Kontroverse um den neuen Europa-Artikel im Grundgesetz." *Frankfurter Allgemeine Zeitung*, 11. November 1992.

"Lambsdorff: Verbesserungen der Maastrichter Verträge erforderlich." *Handelsblatt*, 13. März 1992.

Lamy, Jean-Michel. "Mitterrand parie sur le duo franco-allemand pour conduire l'ambition européenne commune." *Les Echos*, 8 octobre 1991.

"L'avenir de l'Espagne dépend de son intégration à l'Europe." *Le Figaro*, 8 juin 1989.

Le Boucher, Eric. "Bonn: l'exploitation de la 'peur de l'Allemagne' dans la campagne irrite beaucoup...." *Le Monde*, 4 septembre 1992.

Lemaitre, Philippe. "M. Kohl et M. Mitterrand mettent la dernière main à la préparation du conseil." *Le Monde*, 15 novembre 1991.

————. "La France s'oppose à la Commission de Bruxelles sur le partage des pouvoirs dans une Communauté renforcée." *Le Monde*, 5 juin 1991.

————. "Les Douze divisés sur l'essentiel." *Le Quotidien*, 16 avril 1991.

————. "Les Douze restent divisés sur l'union politique européenne." *Le Monde*, 17 avril 1991.

————. "Le projet de la Commission sur l'union politique européenne diffère de celui de la France." *Le Monde*, 24 octobre 1990.

"Le ministre allemand des affaires étrangères réaffirm la priorité des relations avec la France." *Le Monde*, 20 mai 1992.

Lemoine, Patrick. "L'ENA entre deux sièges." *La Croix*, 7 juin 1993.

"Le sommet européen a confirmé les divergences sur l'union." *L'Echo*, 2 juillet 1991.

"L'union politique en discussion." *Libération*, 16 avril 1991.

"Major and Kohl risk isolation at Maastricht." *Financial Times*, December 9, 1991.

Marchais, Isabelle. "CEE: la marche vers l'union politique." *Le Figaro*, 16 avril 1991.

Marsh, David. "Germans Press for Central Bank in Frankfurt." *Financial Times*, December 10, 1991.

Marshall, Andrew. "Single Currency Comes a Step Closer." *The Independent*, December 10, 1991.

Merritt, Giles. "Making Brussels a Scapegoat for Failed European Leadership." *International Herald Tribune*, June 25, 1992.

Minc, Alain. "Not So Much a Crisis like a Catharsis." *The European*, June 11, 1992.

"Mind over Maastricht." *The Economist*, December 7, 1991.

Mital, Christine. "C'est l'homme le plus puissant de France." *Le Nouvel Observateur*, 19–25 mai 1994.

"Mitterrand pose sa question aux Français." *La Croix*, 3 juillet 1992.

"Mitterrand ne rénegociera pas Maastricht." *Libération*, 13 avril 1992.

Moinet, Jean-Philippe. "Pasqua: 'L'existence de la nation est en cause'." *Le Figaro*, 4 août 1992.

Möllemann, Jürgen W. "Von Maastricht zum vereinten Europa." *Frankfurter Allgemeine Zeitung*, 15. Juni 1992.

Murray, Ian. "German Right Beats Drum against Rule by Eurocrats." *The Times*, June 15, 1992.

Nahrendorf, Rainer. "Parlament als Notar?" *Handelsblatt*, 13. Dezember 1991.

Nelson, Mark M. "EC Officials Fail to Agree on Plan for Political Union." *The Wall Street Journal*, June 4, 1991.

Noelle-Neumann, Elisabeth "Die Deutschen beginnen sich zu fürchten." *Frankfurter Allgemeine Zeitung*, 23. Juni 1992.

Nonnenmacher, Günther. " 'Maastricht' ist mehr als ein Vertrag." *Frankfurter Allgemeine Zeitung*, 27. Juli 1993.

"NRW: Nachverhandlungen und Nachbesserungen." *Handelsblatt*, 25. Februar 1992.

Oakley, Robin. "Britain Sees Gaullist Trick on Defence." *The Times*, December 10, 1991.

Oakley, Robin, and George Brock. "Major Stands Firm on EMU Opt-out Clause." *The Times*, December 10, 1991.

"Oui Non." (supplément) *Libération*, 31 août 1992.

Palmer, John. "Paris Talks Raise Stakes in EC Drive for Union." *The Guardian*, October 7, 1991.

———. EC Ministers Seek Dutch Union Effort." *The Guardian*, October 1, 1991.

———. "Political Union Casts Long Shadow over Monetary Accord Progress." *The Guardian*, July 1, 1991.

"Paris-Bonn Deal 'key to European Unity'." *Financial Times*, May 11, 1988.

"Parteien begrüßen im Bundestag die Ergebnisse von Maastricht." *Frankfurter Allgemeine Zeitung*, 14. Dezember 1991.

Peel, Quentin. "Bonn Sees Danger to Unity in States' Demands." *Financial Times*, March 14, 1992.

———. "Bonn Warning on Political Union Treaty." *Financial Times*, October 18, 1991.

Quatremer, Jean. "Europe: Le Non Danois provoque un electrochoc." *Libération*, 4 juin 1992.

———. "La citoyenneté divise les Douze." *Libération*, 15 mai 1991.

Redburn, Tom. "Denmark to Push for Changes in European Treaty." *International Herald Tribune*, September 23, 1992.

———. "EC Agrees on a Single Currency." *International Herald Tribune*, December 10, 1991.

Reinhard, Philippe. "Référendum: l'effet d'annonce de Mitterrand." *Le Quotidien*, 4 juin 1992.

Riding, Alan. "Europeans Agree on a Pact Forging New Political Ties and Integrating Economies." *New York Times*, December 11, 1991.

Séguin, Philippe. "Dire non pour réveiller l'Europe." *Le Figaro*, 6 août 1992.

"Seiters legt Maastricht-Artikel vor." *Frankfurter Allgemeine Zeitung*, 21. Juli 1992.

Sherwell, Philip. "German Swing against the EC alarms Bonn." *The Daily Telegraph*, March 10, 1992.

Smith, Richard E. "Backing for Treaties Expected from States." *International Herald Tribune*, March 14, 1992.

Sormani, Pietro. "All' ambiziosa Olanda il timone della CEE." *Corriere della Sera*, 2 luglio 1991.

"SPD will Diskussion der Europa-Verträge." *Frankfurter Allgemeine Zeitung*, 9. September 1991.

Stephens, Philip. "Major Approaches Moment of Truth on British Concessions to Partners." *Financial Times*, December 10, 1991.

"Summit Sound-bites." *Financial Times*, December 10, 1991.

Sullivan, Scott. "Together or Not." *Newsweek*, September 14, 1992.

"The Deal is Done." *The Economist*, December 14, 1991.

"The History of the Maastricht Summit." *The Economist*, November 30, 1991.

"The Thinker Who Ran out of Ideas." *The Economist*, October 19, 1991.

Thenard, Jean-Michel. "Maastricht, le référendum renvoyé à l'automne." *Libération*, 25 juin 1992.

"Tout est possible, sauf une renégociation." *La Croix*, 23 septembre 1992.

Tréan, Claire. "Genèse d'un traité." *Le Monde*, 30 avril 1992.

———. "MM. Kohl et Mitterrand mettent en garde contre un échec à Maastricht." *Le Monde*, 18 octobre 1991.

"Unscharfe Konturen einer Europäischen Union." *Neue Zürcher Zeitung*, 22. April 1991.

"Unzufrieden mit den Ergebnissen von Maastricht." *Frankfurter Allgemeine Zeitung*, 13. März 1992.

Usborne, David. "Dutch EC Plans Rejected." *The Independent*, October 1, 1991.

"Veränderungen im Auswärtigen Amt." *Frankfurter Allgemeine Zeitung*, 23. März 1993.

"Vermittlungsausschuß für Rat und Europaparlament." *Handelsblatt*, February 19, 1991.

Vernet, Daniel. "L'Allemagne par-dessus tout." *Le Monde*, 23 mai 1992.

———. " Les tâches de la diplomatie allemande." *Le Monde*, 2 mai 1992.

"Waigel richtet eine Europa-Abteilung ein." *Frankfurter Allgemeine Zeitung*, 7. Juli 1992.

"Waigel: Verwässerung der Kriterien wird Deutschland nicht zulassen." *Handelsblatt*, 12. Juni 1992.

"Warnungen vor übereilter Währungsunion." *Frankfurter Allgemeine Zeitung*, 9. Dezember 1991.

Watson, Rory, and Nicholas Comfort. "Major Bites the Bullet to Set Maastricht Deal." *The European*, October 15, 1991.

"We Are Not Emused." *The Economist*, June 6, 1991.

Webster, Paul. "Maastricht Texts Bombard the French." *The Guardian*, August 19, 1992.

———. "French Leaders Seek Early Maastricht Poll." *The Guardian*, June 24, 1992.

Whitney, Craig. "Britain's Way: A Qualified Agreement." *New York Times*, December 11, 1991.

"Who Really Runs Japan? Stay Tuned." *New York Times*, December 24, 1993.

Wolberg-Stok, Andres. "Envoy Sees Oui Problem for Treaty." *Irish Press*, September 10, 1992.

Wolf, Julie. "Netherlands Retreats from Sweeping Plan on EC Political Union." *The Wall Street Journal*, October 1, 1991.

———. "Bonn and Rome unite to Set EC union agenda." *The Guardian*, April 11, 1991.

Zeldin, Theodore. "France's Murmuring Heart." *The Guardian*, September 17, 1992.

Unpublished Materials

De Schoutheete, Philippe. "Rapport sur l'union politique." Bruxelles: Université Libre de Bruxelles, 1992 (mimeo).

Dyson, Kenneth, Kevin Featherstone and George Michalopoulos. "Strapped to the Mast: EC Central Bankers Between Global Financial Markets and the Maastricht Treaty." European Consortium for Political Research Workshop: The Single Market and Global Economic Integration, Madrid, 17–22 April 1994.

———. "The Politics of EMU: The Maastricht Treaty and the Relevance of Bargaining Models." Paper for Delivery at the 1994 Annual Meeting of the American Political Science Association, New York, September 1–4, 1994.

Gallois, Franz Peter. *Rechtsstellung und Aufgaben des Parlamentarischen Staatssekretärs*. Dissertation, Universität Mainz, 1983.

George, Stephen. "The European Commission: Opportunities Seized, Problems Unresolved." Paper presented to the Fourth Biennial International Conference of the European Community Studies Association, Charleston, South Carolina, May 11–14, 1995.

Hayes-Renshaw, Fiona. *The Role of the Committee of Permanent Representatives in the Decision-Making Process of the European Community*. Ph.D. Thesis London: London School of Economics, 1990.

Heisenberg, Dorothee. "German Financial Hegemony or Simply Smaller Win-Sets? An Examination of the Bundesbank's Role in EMS and EMU Negotiations." Paper for Delivery at the 1994 Annual Meeting of the American Political Science Association, New York, September 1–4, 1994.

Lequesne, Christian. *L'appareil politico-administratif de la France et la Communauté Européenne Mai 1981-Mai 1991*. Thèse de Doctorat Paris: FNSP, 1992.

Marks, Gary, Liesbet Hooghe and Kermit Blank. "European Integration and the State." Paper presented at the American Political Science Association Meeting, New York, September 1–4, 1994.

Marquer, Ephräim. *L'Europe en poche. Quelques réflexions sur la méthode et le coût du remplacement des monnaies manuelles nationales par des pièces et billets en ECU*. Mémoire de fin d'études à l'Institut Supérieur du Commerce, Promotion 1992.

Mazzucelli, Colette. "Comparative Dimensions of Factionalism. The French Socialists and German Social Democrats: A Review of the Theses of Sartori, Beller and Belloni and Hine." Washington, DC: Georgetown University, 1989.

Pellegrom, Sandra. "National Civil Servants in EC Environment Policy: A New Elite and Its Role in European Integration." Paper presented at the workshop National Political Elites and European Integration, ECPR Joint Sessions of Workshops, Madrid, 17–22 April 1994 (mimeo).

Scheer, François. "Europe et Diplomatie." Conférence prononcée à l'occasion de la remise des diplômes aux étudiants de l'Institut d'études politiques de Strasbourg, samedi, 21 novembre 1992.

Staden, Berndt von. Seminar on European Integration. Washington, D.C.: Georgetown University, Spring 1990 (mimeo).

Stock, Wolfgang R. *The Impact of the Federal Provisions in the Basic Law on the Political Discretion of the West German Government in the Decision-making of the European Community*. D.Phil Thesis Oxford: University College, 1990.

Waever, Ole, Ulla Holm and Henrik Larsen. *The Struggle for "Europe": French and German Concepts of State, Nation and European Union* (mimeo). Florence: European University Institute, 1991.

Index

About the Author

Colette Mazzucelli, Ph.D. has been Civic Education Project (CEP) Lecturer and International Program Director at the Budapest Institute for Graduate International and Diplomatic Studies (BIGIS) since 1995. In addition, she is an instructor in negotiations training at the Hungarian Ministry of Foreign Affairs (*Külügyminisztérium*) and a guest lecturer in a seminar on European integration offered by Lord William Wallace at the Central European University (CEU). Professor Mazzucelli's previous publications include a volume on European security edited with Reinhardt Rummel, *The Evolution of an International Actor: Western Europe's New Assertiveness*, Westview, 1990. She is listed in *Who's Who in American Education* and *Dictionary of International Biography*.